# SAiNTS
## AND
# SINNERS

*The American Catholic Experience*

*Through Stories, Memoirs, Essays,*

*and Commentary*

# Edited by Greg Tobin

DOUBLEDAY

New York   London   Toronto   Sydney   Auckland

PUBLISHED BY DOUBLEDAY
a division of Random House, Inc.
1540 Broadway, New York, New York 10036

DOUBLEDAY and the portrayal of an anchor with a dolphin are trademarks of Doubleday,
a division of Random House, Inc.

Book design by Lynne Amft

Library of Congress Cataloging-in-Publication Data

Saints and sinners: the American Catholic experience through stories,
memoirs, essays, and commentary / edited by Greg Tobin. —1st ed.
p.      cm.
1. Catholics—United States—History—20th century.      2. Catholic
Church—United States—History—20th century.      3. Christianity
and culture—United States—History—20th century.      4. Catholics—United
States—Fiction.      I. Tobin, Greg.
BX1406.2.S25  1999
282′.73′ 0904—dc21      99-25167
CIP
ISBN 0-385-49331-2

October 1999

First Edition

1   3   5   7   9   10   8   6   4   2

# Contents

*This book is dedicated to the community
of the faithful.*

# Preface and Acknowledgments

As a writer and a reader, I have always been drawn to those writers who draw from the same or a similar well of experience to my own: the American Catholic experience. In recent years I have had cause to ask myself just what this experience means and how is it expressed in the literature of the post–World War II age. When I began digging into the literature by and about American Catholics—fiction and nonfiction, biography and theology, memoir and polemic—I quickly learned that the variety exceeds the sameness by a large measure.

The principles that governed this collection were few and, to be honest, a little loose. I wanted to focus on the past fifty or so years, since World War II, through the Second Vatican Council years, and into the 1990s. I wanted to represent the best prose works of this period. I wanted to learn and to share with intelligent readers what makes Catholic writers tick and what influences inform their writing. I wanted to make this selection American only, in order to draw from our national culture a sense of what it means to be Catholic *and* American, and what conflicts, if any, that represents.

Necessarily, these selections comprise a mere smattering of the material that has been written over a fertile, fifty-year period in our history. But for me, the pieces are like building blocks for an edifice that can, like a kid's play set, be constructed in almost any pattern one desires. I chose the organization you see before you; there could have been other ways to do it. I chose, and then rejected, a score or more extracts than appear here, and there could have been others—many others.

So, this is merely a tasting menu, as comprehensive as it can be within even these generous parameters.


This reader is the unexpected child of a conversation that was held in December 1996 between Alexander Hoyt and myself regarding an idea for another potential anthology. That book never came to be, but if it had not been for Alex's persistence and interest, this one never would have either.

Harold Rabinowitz of The Reference Works did the "heavy lifting" for this book: he and his staff performed the bulk of the searching, finding, photocopying, and scanning of the texts, as well as providing an overall editorial support, without which I could not have hoped to do my job.

Brian Thomsen, friend and colleague, became an unofficial consultant and coeditor of this book when I called on him in the later stages to help. His wisdom and experience in such ventures, as well as his visceral grasp of my vision of the book, pulled my fat from a threatening fire. Brian deserves a great deal of credit for both the selections and the insights contained herein.

Eric Major of Doubleday, the director of the religious publishing program, is the best in the business—and among the most patient. He saw great potential in the earliest proposal and decided to support our effort, putting the muscle of his redoubtable publishing house behind it. He led and responded encouragingly, yet firmly, else there would be no book at all.

A special thanks to the staff of the Walsh Library of Seton Hall University in South Orange, New Jersey, for their assistance in every phase of manuscript development.

My wife, Maureen, and boys, Patrick and Bryan, were tolerant and a bit curious about the whole thing, and they generously gave me the time and space to do the work necessary on what turned out to be a rather large endeavor. I thank them.

# Introduction: Saints and Sinners

The notion of an anthology of writings by Roman Catholics in America is the result of a convergence of surface-related circumstances, a series of personal coincidences.

I had been working for about three years on a novel about an American Catholic priest when I was approached by a friend to edit an anthology of American writing, but felt it was not the right project for me. I began instead to explore the life and writings of St. Patrick (in my "spare time"), with the thought of writing my first book of nonfiction. In fact, for most of my adulthood I had been desultory, at best, in religious observance (usually but not always in attendance at Sunday mass), but I have felt progressively more drawn than ever in my life to *spiritual* belief and practice. Meanwhile, I was elected to the school board of my sons' parochial school, and thus reentered the long historical stream of Catholic education. (I had attended St. Mary's parish elementary school in Independence, Missouri.) I was deeply moved at the ordination ceremony of a young man who had been very friendly with my family during his transitional deaconate at our parish in South Orange, New Jersey. In other words, I found myself becoming more Catholic, both overtly and internally Catholic.

It occurred to me one day that I would find it both educational and inspirational to read about others who took seriously the role of Catholic religion and spirituality in their lives and who wrote about it for a general, public audience (as opposed to a strictly sectarian readership that is served—often quite well—by Catholic publications). I am that audience. But I found no broadly representative work such as the one you have before you, no one book in which I might sample a wide range of thinking and style that is unified by a *Catholic* point of view—an *American* Catholic point of view.

Which leads us to a consideration of definitions—what is an American Catholic, anyway?—which further leads us down the slipperiest of paths toward contradiction and confusion. So, I have used the occasion of this book to attempt to bring definition to my own principles of faith and religious identity. You may consider it the purest form of indulgence.

In his masterful survey of the history of the Church in the United States, *American Catholic*, Charles R. Morris writes:

> Like no other generation in the history of the Church, active American Catholics are educated, literate, informed, and *interested* in their religion. And they are participants in it. Theological niceties aside, the message from Vatican II has been taken to heart: *they*, the people in the parishes, along with clergy and nuns and bishops and Pope, *are* the Church.[1]

Or, as Penelope Ryan has asked in her 1998 study *Practicing Catholic: The Search for a Livable Catholicism:*

> There are sixty million people in the country who describe themselves as Catholic; many of whom feel at odds with themselves about what the Church teaches, at odds with what they are hearing in homilies at Sunday Mass, and at odds with the proclamations coming from the Vatican . . . What makes a "good" Catholic, and what do I have to do and believe to be a practicing Catholic?[2]

These contemporary studies of Church life in the United States describe the history and practice of the Catholic faith in this country. They are helpful in setting a context: Catholicism is the largest single religious denomination in the United States, with about 60 million adherents, about 22 percent of the total population. Most immigrants are Catholic, given the large numbers of people coming here from predominantly Catholic countries. The Roman Catholic tradition of faith is thus firmly and deeply established within the United States, and has been since the earliest days of the European settlement of North America, through colonial times and the early republic.

It is clear, however, that not all Catholics are practicing or "good" Catholics. We are very diverse within our own faith tradition, with ethnic and language variations, political points of view, even disagreements on doctrinal matters. Some would dispute that those who disagree are really Catholic at all. Does he receive the sacraments? Are her children baptized in the faith? How can one not oppose abortion or the death penalty and call oneself Catholic? Can it be a self-defined condition or must certain minimum standards be met?

---

[1] Morris, Charles R., *American Catholic.* New York: Times Books, 1997. Page 430.

[2] Ryan, Penelope, Ph.D., *Practicing Catholic: The Search for a Livable Catholicism.* New York: Henry Holt and Company, 1998. Page xvii.

In brief, I will accept the very broadest definition—that includes non-communicant status—and cast the widest net to capture the fishes to be served up in this banquet of writings. We will not concern ourselves here with the issues of the practice of religion, rather, the issue of *being* Catholic—whether practicing, lapsed, questioning, or fervent. Again, we return to the question: what is an American Catholic—and specifically, what is an American Catholic writer?

Some brief autobiographical consideration may be appropriate here. I was born in St. Elizabeth's Hospital, Boston—coincidentally on the same saint's feast day—in 1954 and baptized in the Roman Catholic faith a few weeks later. Both parents were Irish Catholic. A great-aunt was a nun; a great-uncle, a priest. My family moved from Massachusetts to Missouri, where I grew up: in the city of Independence, right next door to Kansas City (hometown for my parents). After a brief and memorable (to me) sojourn in St. Francis Xavier parish, we became parishioners at St. Mary's, an old mission church from the earliest statehood days. There in the hundred-year-old church building, soon to be renovated, post–Vatican II, I made my First Communion, was confirmed, dreamed of becoming a priest; I attended the parochial school next door, from first through sixth grades. Gradually, as I focused on a new set of friends and activities in the public junior high school, I become a religiously disaffected teenager. In my late teens I was briefly active in another Christian denomination, but then, as an undergraduate at Grinnell College and Yale—as if struck by lightning—I became a nearly convinced agnostic, a would-be philosopher, and amateur bohemian (meaning, I dressed badly, drank and smoked too much, and cultivated pretensions of creativity). I remained a more or less convinced unbeliever for a dozen or so years until I awoke to the need for a source of strength and unconditional love in my life.

Married to a smart, spiritual woman (who had converted to Catholicism as a girl in her native Jamaica), the father of two healthy handfuls of pure boy, living in suburban New Jersey and commuting to New York City, employed in increasingly responsible jobs in the book-publishing business, writing paperback Western novels on the side to earn extra income: I rediscovered the faith of my boyhood, but not without doubts and deep ambiguities. With my family I began attending mass regularly on Sundays. My wife joined the parish choir and has remained a member for about a dozen years. We enrolled the boys in Our Lady of Sorrows elementary school and became active in the school and parish community, including Boy Scouts, school board, and pastoral council.

In other words, I began to "show up" for Mass and to put myself in the place where the faith community was (instead of staying away). By bringing my body, my mind and spirit were there to receive whatever message was promulgated. Thus, by a sort of osmosis, I reexposed myself to the faith of my more devout ancestors; it felt natural and right. I opened my mouth to respond to prayers and to sing hymns that soon became familiar again. I listened to the readings, put out my hand to exchange the sign of peace with others, attended spaghetti dinners and theological lectures and Christmas carol fests.

I am more curious than smug about my Catholic faith, appallingly ill-read in the subject until I undertook this project, a firm believer in spiritual progress rather than in the perfectibility of any human being, especially myself. I believe that the Church is a place for me to participate in a spiritual community of Christians bound by a faith to people around the world. My parish is the center of my Catholic spirituality, as it is intended to be. It is up to me, then, to participate in the life of the parish as one communicant among many. Each day I evaluate the quality of my faith, and each day I find myself wanting. Yet, I believe that in this process of questioning and praying and trying, I am granted immense gifts of grace and faith and forgiveness—more, perhaps, than I deserve.

In 1997 William F. Buckley Jr. published a memoir of his faith titled *Nearer, My God* (Doubleday). For nearly fifty years, Buckley has been an avatar of conservative Catholic intellectualism. He sees in the manifestation of Catholic Christianity a timelessness that supersedes sectarian and doctrinal divisions. In his words,

> But the Church is unique in that it is governed by a wisdom that has not changed in two thousand years. It tells us, in just about as many words, that we are not accidental biological accretions, we are creatures of a divine plan; that God who made us undertook to demonstrate his devotion to us as individual human beings by submitting to the pain and humiliation of the Cross. Nothing in that vision has ever changed, nothing at all, and this is for all Christians a mindshaking, for some a mind-altering certitude, with which Christians live, in our earnest if pitiable efforts to clear the way for a life that cannot be requited.[3]

On the opposite end of the political spectrum, activist and author Dorothy Day practiced a radical pacifist, even mystical Catholicism that influenced genera-

---

[3] Buckley, William F. Jr., *Nearer, My God: An Autobiography of Faith.* New York: Doubleday, 1997. Page xix.

tions of clergy and laypersons in the second half of the century. Although her active ministry and most of her writing was done in the years leading to the outbreak of World War II, I include her postwar work. In her biography she described the climate of her early years of political involvement:

> I do not remember any anti-religious articles in the *Call*. As a matter of fact there was a long article by Dante Barton, vice-chairman of the Committee on Industrial Relations, which was an interview with Father O'Rourke, a Jesuit preacher. Reading it over in the public library I was surprised to find many quotations from *Rerum Novarum* of Pope Leo XIII and a very fair exposition of the Church's social teachings. I paid no attention to it at the time. Catholics were a world apart, a people within a people, making little impression on the tremendous non-Catholic population of the country.
>
> There was no attack on religion because people were generally indifferent to religion. They were neither hot nor cold. They were the tepid, the materialistic, who hoped that by Sunday churchgoing they would be taking care of the afterlife, if there were an afterlife. Meanwhile they would get everything they could in this.[4]

Neither Day's nor Buckley's vision is shared by every American Catholic writer; they are notoriously independent in their thinking and expression. They are also as different as they can be within the broad spectrum of existence and experience within the American Church. This is what has made American Catholicism so rich and tumultuous in the years since World War II, which saw, as Charles Morris puts it, the Church triumphant. Now, with the end of a distinctly Catholic culture in the United States, the Church faces numerous issues that continue to divide believers and make it difficult for anyone seeking simple explanations.

The 1998 National Book Award for fiction was given to Alice McDermott for her novel *Charming Billy*. In the crescendo of critical and public attention that followed the award, Ms. McDermott noted in numerous interviews how her Irish Catholic roots have always fed and directed her writing, in a very overt way in her case. Not all the authors presented here are as straightforwardly connected to the same root system, but they spring from the same fertile, American earth.

Let us return to our quest for definition: American Catholic writers comprise a class or category as do Southern writers or New England writers or

---

[4] Day, Dorothy, *The Long Loneliness*. San Francisco: HarperCollins Publishers, 1952. Pages 62–63.

American Jewish writers. But why? That is, why bother to lump together any group of writers with the seeming arbitrary qualification of their faith (or lapse therefrom, in some cases)? Because, it seems to me, Catholicism is a distinct culture, or cluster of cultures, that molds and informs writers the same way that a landscape or economic class does.

I view "American Catholic" as a virtual or intellectual rather than geographic region. It is a state of mind that recognizes a hierarchy within the universe—whether accepting that hierarchy or rebelling against it. It is a state of mind that draws on common images and language to describe life. It is a place of belief in purpose and history (even more than religion): that is, we did not spring fully formed from the head of Zeus just yesterday. No, there is a vast tapestry of history to be acknowledged and, for some, to be rejected.

"American Catholic" is a tradition more than a school, a point of departure rather than a common meeting place.

Shortly after I was elected by my board colleagues to be president of our parochial school advisory board, the school principal said to me, "It will make you a better Catholic." I smiled at her indulgently; I would wait and see. Now, nearly two years later, having completed that term and this manuscript, I know that she was right: serving, experiencing, questioning, writing, believing, praying—all have increased my faith and made me a better person, and, yes, a better Catholic.

# SAiNTS

### AND

# SINNERS

# PART I

# POLITICS
## AND
# PROTEST

*The Catholic Conscience*

# Introduction

On a visit to the United States in 1995, the Pope asked, "Is there room for the mystery of God in American society?" Mystery has always been a valid category of the Catholic Church, and the pontiff may have been wondering if a society so determined to unearth every mystery, with a vigor born of the freedoms of inquiry and speech afforded Americans, could allow the sacred mysteries of the sacraments to go unchallenged by reason and undiluted by analysis. But the implication of the question—and in all likelihood Pope John Paul's intent—goes well beyond the philosophical to the political. For a society that professes to be governed by the will of an informed and sober electorate would, one would think, abhor a mystery of any kind, especially one that lies at the heart of issues that are part of the public discourse. Is there room, one may ask, for the mystery of the Catholic religion in the heart of those who would mold American society, namely its leaders and governors?

The question, so understood, seems no less powerful today than it did a century ago when Catholics looked on with a combination of pride and unease at Cardinal Gibbons hobnobbing with President Theodore Roosevelt. Is the very private relationship between the Church and its members, between priest and flock, one that could be brought into the arena of public discourse? Can a man, in short, be a devout practicing Catholic when he is in the marketplace of power and ideas that is American politics? The historical context of the question—the fact that the United States is a land founded on Protestant principles and that the flight from religious persecution that engendered the First Amendment of the Constitution made Americans wary of any centrally organized church, especially one based on foreign soil—tended to trivialize the question into one of influence: could a practicing Catholic be true to religious principles, which include fealty to the Church, while true to the Constitution which public officials are asked to take an oath to uphold? This was a trivialization because the Church had long understood the bifurcation of life into the sacred and the profane, and never viewed the supposed conflict with great seriousness. Thus, when the question was posed in just these terms to presidential candidate John F. Kennedy (after years of its being a nonissue during his tenure as a U.S. Congressman, when he should have been no less "torn" by supposed divided loyalties of church and state), he had little trouble fending off the questioners by saying he felt no pressure to yield to the dictates of a church hierarchy in executing his sworn duty as a representative of the people.

No, the real question, the last half century has shown, hasn't been "Can a public official who is Catholic act in accordance with his conscience in performing his duty?" but "Can a public official who is Catholic ignore the dictates of a conscience informed by his devotion to his religion and still be true to his principles?" That Catholics have wrestled with this more difficult and wrenching question only since the Second World War is part of the postwar legacy of American politics. Not that people weren't as concerned before the war as they were after, but the experience of an America bursting forth to prominence as a superpower made the entire enterprise of politics more serious and important. Every election became one that could determine the fate of the world—first the "free" world, but eventually the entire world—and this was the sort of event that could only be regarded as biblical in its import and proportions. When protest could eventually have the effect of reversing U.S. foreign policy or election to a governorship put one in line for possible ascendancy to the office of President, how could anyone allow deeply felt convictions to be set aside for the sake of the system?

The story of American Catholics and American politics of the past fifty years is the story of a community grappling with this tension with a newly discovered earnestness. The solutions and approaches have been highly individualized and this is very American; but they have also bespoken a unity that places them all within the confines of the Church, even when rejected by a church establishment and even when protesting that establishment's leadership. The readers of the selections in this section will be struck, it is hoped, by that unity, even as they travel down roads that on the surface seem so completely divergent.

•          •          •

The tradition that we now take for granted of Catholic protest and the affirmation of Catholic conscience—both of the left and, paradoxically, of the right—has its roots in the prewar career of Dorothy Day (1897–1980), a woman of extraordinary talents whom some observers regarded as "the most significant, interesting, and influential person in the history of American Catholicism." Born to a working-class Protestant household, Day became a radical socialist while a student at the University of Illinois, where she marched against the war and for the unions, being beaten and jailed on both accounts. She was a friend of Communists like John Reed; she interviewed Trotsky for a newspaper; and, after a series of casual affairs, had had an abortion.

Then in 1933, following the birth of a daughter from a common-law marriage, Day had a somewhat mystical experience that turned her to devout Catholicism and that coincided with a visit by the French intellectual Peter Maurin. With Maurin providing the vague but resolute direction, Day applied her considerable talents to the creation of a movement named after a publication she virtually single-handedly wrote and published, *The Catholic Worker.* America had never seen the likes of Dorothy Day—determined, personable, eloquent, idealistic, yet practical—and she soon established "hospitality houses" that fed the poor and preached pacifism across the country. What was so interesting about Day, which permeates her writings, as in the excerpt included here from *Loaves and Fishes,* is how she viewed the question of poverty as one of the most monumental religious import. Before Day, attending to the disadvantaged was, from a religious point of view, a matter of pity and compassion; after Day it became one of conscience and conviction. The movement went aground on her radical pacifism, which she professed even after Pearl Harbor, but the model she created endured well beyond the Catholic Worker movement.

As much as Day was defining a political activism that focused on the poor, other Catholics were defining a political activism focused on America's postwar battle against Communism. Perhaps most prominent of these was New York's Francis Cardinal Spellman, whose political clout was so great that at one time many thought he might be elected Pope. Spellman was the consummate politician, master of public relations and practitioner of the grand gesture; his Al Smith dinners were much covered events, as were his visits to U.S. troops in Korea. From a certain perspective, Spellman's career could be viewed as that of a very able and conscientious administrator of a trust on behalf of the Church—New York Catholics had never before been as privy to the corridors of power and the Vatican was enormously enriched by Spellman's contributions. But John Cooney's report on Spellman's behavior during a gravediggers' strike in 1949 reveals that Spellman was driven by deeply held convictions that equated the course of America's conflict with the forces of socialism and Communism with the course of Christianity and Christian civilization. Spellman had done more than find a venue for public pomp and institutional enrichment—he had found a confluence of purpose between the purposes of Americanism and the eschatology of the Church. Spellman may not have had the polish of a Fulton Sheen, but he was no less sincere, and the debacle of the Army-McCarthy hearings did not prevent Spellman from embracing Senator McCarthy at a public breakfast (albeit for New York City policemen) in 1954.

In the aftermath of Spellman's various involvements with labor disputes—always seen by Spellman in global terms and in light of the ongoing "struggle" between the forces of American capitalism and those of Russian

Communism—it may seem strange to claim him the precursor of a radical Catholic like Daniel Berrigan, jailed in 1970 for his antiwar activities in Danbury Federal Prison. Yet, insofar as they saw their faith as not simply granting them license for political action, but compelling them to take stands and become embroiled at the forefront, they are bound spiritually, however far apart we may consider them politically. Father Berrigan published his prison diary in 1974, following the completion of his parole. He saw his prison experience as a personal journey and not as an element of his political persona; making this clear in *Lights On in the House of the Dead* separated the Berrigans from other war protesters, for whom the pain of exile, imprisonment, and excoriation was a part of their activism. The Berrigans were practical—they, in fact, had little patience with the countercultural elements of the protest movement—and this made them particularly effective. They saw their protest as a ministry to America and not to their own congregation; with a view so broad that it could belong only to a poet, Daniel Berrigan looked upon his imprisonment as an annoyance that kept him from righting the wrongs of the world. New ground was being broken here, and in the selection there are intimations that Father Berrigan knew it, or at least hoped for it.

The result of the radicalism of the Berrigans—not their radical politics, but their radical religious activism—was a thoroughgoing Catholic political consciousness that awaited the inevitable agency of the right politician, the right theater, and the right climactic defining moment. This occurred in the mid-1980s in the person of New York governor Mario Cuomo, in the theater of the national debate over abortion, and the moment was the harsh confrontation between John Cardinal O'Connor and Cuomo over the governor's refusal to veto an abortion rights bill. The principles that guided Cuomo and the inner turmoil he felt are laid out in a remarkable speech delivered a year earlier in which the question of church and state and the unification and reconciliation of personal conviction and personal faith reached a depth of feeling and insight not previously known (or even suspected) of a public official. The few who heard the new chords being struck were both exhilarated and disturbed, and Gary Wills's analysis of the complexities of the Cuomo case points to the need for further study. Wills makes it clear that Mario Cuomo was not an anomaly; he simply refused to sidestep the fundamental questions even when it was politically expedient to do so. There are not likely to be many politicians who will wear their faith on their sleeves as clearly and as publicly as did Cuomo; his political fortunes may have been adversely affected by his forthrightness, and this will certainly not encourage others to follow in his footsteps. But the portrait and analysis presented by Wills is now part of the record, and the ongoing story of faith and politics, carried out in its most serious form in the Catholic consciousness, will resume, when it resumes, where Mario Cuomo left off.

The section ends with two selections that show how men and women of faith dealt with society's most difficult problems within the context of their faith and their devotion to the Church. In James Carroll's piece about a priest's life on a turbulent campus, faith and personal ministry are tested by the demands of loyalty and responsibility. Helen Prejean went even further and ministered to the most despicable in society and contrary to the popular opinion of her own Church. In both instances, the demands placed on the priest and penitent—and even the not-so-penitent—swept aside politically explosive qualms and allowed the core structure of the Church to be the single most operant and decisive context for these ministers. Confronting a parent at odds with a son's politics proves more difficult than risking arrest by the FBI, and preaching to a man convicted of a horrible murder is easier than attending to the spiritual needs of the victim's father. This is how it ought to be within the community of the Church, as long as the Church places a higher value on its service to the individual than on its effectiveness in the public arena. For it is within that service that the mystery of human contact, and ultimately the mystery of God, lies.

# Charity and Conscience

From: *Loaves and Fishes*

BY DOROTHY DAY

*A baby is always born with a loaf of bread under its arm*

This was the consoling remark my brother's Spanish mother-in-law used to make when a new baby was about to arrive. It is this philosophy which makes it possible for people to endure a life of poverty.

"Just give me a chance," I hear people say. "Just let me get my debts paid. Just let me get a few of the things I need and then I'll begin to think of poverty and its rewards. Meanwhile, I've had nothing but." But these people do not understand the difference between inflicted poverty and voluntary poverty; between being the victims and the champions of poverty. I prefer to call the one kind *destitution,* reserving the word *poverty* for what St. Francis called "Lady Poverty."

We know the misery being poor can cause. St. Francis was "the little poor man" and none was more joyful than he; yet Francis began with tears, in fear and trembling, hiding out in a cave from his irate father. He appropriated some of his father's goods (which he considered his rightful inheritance) in order to repair a church and rectory where he meant to live. It was only later that he came to love Lady Poverty. Perhaps kissing the leper was the great step that freed him not only from fastidiousness and a fear of disease but from attachment to worldly goods as well.

It is hard to advocate poverty when a visitor tells you how he and his family lived in a basement room and did sweatshop work at night to make ends meet, then how the landlord came in and abused them for not paying promptly his exorbitant rent.

It is hard to advocate poverty when the back yard at Chrystie Street still has the furniture piled to one side that was put out on the street in a recent eviction from a tenement next door.

How can we say to such people, "Be glad and rejoice, for your reward is very great in Heaven," especially when we are living comfortably in a warm house and sitting down to a good table, and are clothed warmly? I had occasion to visit the City Shelter last month, where homeless families are cared for. I sat there for a couple of hours contemplating poverty and destitution in a family. Two of the children were asleep in the parents' arms and four others were sprawling against them. Another young couple were also waiting, the mother pregnant. I did not want to appear to be spying, since all I was there for was the latest news on apartment-finding possibilities for homeless families. So I made myself known to the young man in charge. He apologized for having let me sit there; he'd thought, he explained, that I was "just one of the clients."

Sometimes, as in St. Francis's case, freedom from fastidiousness and detachment from worldly things, can be attained in only one step. We would like to think this is often so. And yet the older I get the more I see that life is made up of many steps, and they are very small ones, not giant strides. I have "kissed a leper" not once but twice—consciously—yet I cannot say I am much the better for it.

The first time was early one morning on the steps of Precious Blood Church. A woman with cancer of the face was begging (beggars are allowed only in slums), and when I gave her money—which was no sacrifice on my part but merely passing on alms someone had given me—she tried to kiss my hand. The only thing I could do was to kiss her dirty old face with the gaping hole in it where an eye and a nose had been. It sounds like a heroic deed, but it was not. We get used to ugliness so quickly. What we avert our eyes from today can be borne tomorrow when we have learned a little more about love. Nurses know this, and so do mothers.

The second time I was refusing a bed to a drunken prostitute with a huge, toothless, rouged mouth, a nightmare of a mouth. She had been raising a disturbance in the house. I kept remembering how St. Thérèse of Lisieux said that when you had to say no, when you had to refuse anyone anything, you could at least do it so that the person went away a bit happier. I had to deny this woman a bed, and when she asked me to kiss her I did, and it was a loathsome thing, the way she did it. It was scarcely a mark of normal human affection.

We suffer these things and they fade from memory. But daily, hourly, to give up our own possessions and especially to subordinate our own impulses and wishes to others—these are hard, hard things; and I don't think they ever get any easier.

You can strip yourself, you can be stripped, but still you will reach out like an octopus to seek your own comfort, your untroubled time, your ease, your refreshment. It may mean books or music—the gratification of the inner senses—or it may mean food and drink, coffee and cigarettes. The one kind of giving up is no easier than the other.

Occasionally—often after reading the life of such a saint as Benedict Joseph Labre—we start thinking about poverty, about going out alone, living with the destitute, sleeping on park benches or in the City Shelter, living in churches, sitting before the Blessed Sacrament as we see so many doing who come from the municipal lodging house or the Salvation Army around the corner. And when such thoughts come on warm spring days, when children are playing in the park and it is good to be out on the city streets, we know that we are only deceiving ourselves: for we are only dreaming of a form of luxury. What we want is the warm sun, and rest, and time to think and read, and freedom from the people who press in on us from early morning until late at night. No, it is not simple, this business of poverty.

Over and over again in the history of the Church the saints have emphasized voluntary poverty. Every religious community, begun in poverty and incredible hardship, but with a joyful acceptance of hardship by the rank-and-file priests, brothers, monks, or nuns who gave their youth and energy to good works, soon began to "thrive." Property was extended until holdings and buildings accumulated; and, although there is still individual poverty in the community, there is corporate wealth. It is hard to remain poor.

One way to keep poor is not to accept money which comes from defrauding the poor. Here is a story of St. Ignatius of Sardinia, a Capuchin recently canonized. Ignatius used to go out from his monastery with a sack to beg from the people of the town, but he would never go to a certain merchant who had built his fortune by defrauding the poor. Franchine, the rich man, fumed every time the saint passed his door. His concern, however, was not the loss of the opportunity to give alms but fear of public opinion. He complained at the friary, whereupon the Father Guardian ordered St. Ignatius to beg from the merchant the next time he went out.

"Very well," said Ignatius obediently. "If you wish it, Father, I will go, but I would not have the Capuchins dine on the blood of the poor."

The merchant received Ignatius with great flattery and gave him generous alms, asking him to come again in the future. But, as Ignatius was leaving the house with his sack on his shoulder, drops of blood began oozing from the sack. They trickled down on Franchine's doorstep and ran down through the street to the monastery. Everywhere Ignatius went a trail of blood followed him. When he arrived at the friary, he laid the sack at the Father Guardian's feet. "Here," Ignatius said, "is the blood of the poor."

This story appeared in the last column written by a great Catholic layman, a worker for social justice, F. P. Kenkel, editor of *Social Justice Review* in St. Louis (and always a friend of Peter Maurin's).

Mr. Kenkel's comment was that the universal crisis in the world today was created by love of money. "The Far East and the Near East [and he might have said all Latin America and Africa also] together constitute a great sack from which blood is oozing. The flow will not stop as long as our interests in these people are dominated largely by financial and economic considerations."

This and other facts seem to me to point more strongly than ever to the importance of voluntary poverty today. At least we can avoid being comfortable through the exploitation of others. And at least we can avoid physical wealth as the result of a war economy. There may be ever-improving standards of living in the United States, with every worker eventually owning his own home and driving his own car; but our whole modern economy is based on preparation for war, and this surely is one of the great arguments for poverty in our time. If the comfort one achieves results in the death of millions in the future, then that comfort shall be duly paid for. Indeed, to be literal, contributing to the war (misnamed "defense") effort is very difficult to avoid. If you work in a textile mill making cloth, or in a factory making dungarees or blankets, your work is still tied up with war. If you raise food or irrigate the land to raise food, you may be feeding troops or liberating others to serve as troops. If you ride a bus you are paying taxes. Whatever you buy is taxed, so that you are, in effect, helping to support the state's preparations for war exactly to the extent of your attachment to worldly things of whatever kind.

*       *       *

The act and spirit of giving are the best counter to the evil forces in the world today, and giving liberates the individual not only spiritually but materially. For, in a world enslaved through installment buying and mortgages, the only way to live in any true security is to live so close to the bottom that when you fall you do not have far to drop, you do not have much to lose.

And in a world of hates and fears, we can look to Peter Maurin's words for the liberation that love brings: "Voluntary poverty is the answer. We cannot see our brother in need without stripping ourselves. It is the only way we have of showing our love."

"Precarity," or precariousness, is an essential element in true voluntary poverty, a saintly French Canadian priest from Martinique has written us. "True poverty is rare," he writes. "Nowadays religious communities are good, I am sure, but they are mistaken about poverty. They accept, they admit, poverty on principle, but everything must be good and strong, buildings must be fire-proof. Precarity is everywhere rejected, and precarity is an essential element of poverty. This has been forgotten. Here in our monastery we have precarity in everything except the Church.

"These last days our refectory was near collapsing. We have put several supplementary beams in place and thus it will last maybe two or three years more. Some day it will fall on our heads and that will be funny. Precarity enables us better to help the poor. When a community is always building and enlarging and embellishing, which is good in itself, there is nothing left over for the poor. We have no right to do so as long as there are slums and breadlines anywhere."

People ask, How does property fit in? Does one have a right to private property? St. Thomas Aquinas said that a certain amount of goods is necessary to live a good life. Eric Gill said that property is "proper" to man. Recent Popes have written at length how justice rather than charity should be sought for the worker. Unions still fight for better wages and hours, though I have come more and more to feel that in itself is not the answer, in view of such factors as the steadily rising cost of living and dependence on war production.

Our experiences at the Catholic Worker have taught us much about the working of poverty, precarity, and destitution. We go from day to day on these principles. After thirty years we still have our poverty, but very little destitution. I am afraid, alas, our standards are higher than they used to be. This is partly due to the war. The young men who came back and resumed work with the Catholic Worker were used to having meat two or three times a day. In the thirties we had it only two or three times a week.

This note from *The Catholic Worker* in the mid-thirties will give you an idea of what our situation was then:

> The most extraordinary donation received during the course of the month—a crate of eggs, thirty dozen, shipped from Indiana by a Pullman conductor as a donation to the cause. God bless you, Mr. Greenen! The eggs we had been eating were all right scrambled, but they would not bear eating soft-boiled. They were rather sulphurous. Our friend, Mr. Minas, made them palatable by sprinkling red pepper over them plentifully, but we have not his oriental tastes. Fresh eggs! What a panegyric we could write on the subject! Soft-boiled for breakfast, with the morning paper and a symphony on the radio, preferably the first Brahms!
>
> A christening feast which took place in the Catholic Worker office was positively an egg orgy, to be alliterative. Dozens were consumed, with gusto, the guests coming from Brooklyn, the Bronx, and Manhattan, New Jersey and Long Island City, representing eight nationalities. Indeed if there had not been eggs there would have been no feast.
>
> Again, thank you, Mr. Greenen!

I can remember how, when we were first starting to publish our paper, in an effort to achieve a little of the destitution of our neighbors we gave away our furniture and sat on boxes. But as fast as we gave things away people brought more. We gave blankets to needy families, and when we started our first house of hospitality people gathered together all the blankets we needed. We gave away food, and more food came in: exotic food, some of it—a haunch of venison from the Canadian Northwest, a can of oysters from Maryland, a container of honey from Illinois. Even now it comes in. We've even had salmon from Seattle, flown across the continent. No one working at the Catholic Worker gets a salary, so our readers feel called upon to give, and to help us keep the work going. We experience a poverty of another kind, a poverty of reputation. It is often said, with some scorn, "Why don't they get jobs and help the poor that way? Why are they begging and living off others?"

All I can say to such critics is that it would complicate things to give a salary to Charles or Ed or Arthur for working fourteen hours a day in the kitchen, clothes room, and office; to pay Deane or Jean or Dianne for running the women's house, for writing articles and answering letters all day and helping with the sick and the poor; and then have them all turn the money right back to support the work. Or, if we wanted to make our situation even more complicated, they might all go out and get jobs, and bring the money home to pay for their board and room and the salaries of others to run the house. It is simpler just to be poor. It is simpler to beg. The thing is not to hold on to anything.

The tragedy is, however, that we do, we all do hold on. We hold on to our books, radios, our tools such as typewriters, our clothes; and instead of rejoicing when they are taken from us, we lament. We protest when people take our time or our privacy. We are holding on to these "goods," also.

Attempting to live in the spirit of poverty certainly does not relieve us of the headaches of practical problems. Feeding hundreds of people every day is no easy task, and just how to pay for the supply of food we need is an exercise in faith and hope.

The location of the house makes a difference, for one thing. In some cities the houses of hospitality get a great deal of food from restaurants and even hospitals. In New York City it is against the law to pick up such leftovers, however. This regulation goes pretty far, I sometimes think. A friend of ours, an airline hostess, marched in indignantly one day. "Our flight was canceled and here were a hundred chicken pies going to waste and when I asked for them for the Catholic Worker, they said no, it was against the law to give them away. They were all thrown out—to be fed to the pigs over in New Jersey! I guess the farmers must have the garbage can concession."

In the New York house we buy a great deal of coffee, sugar, milk, tea, and oleo. Our butcher is a friend who gives us meat at a very cheap price. We get free fish from the market—the tails and heads from swordfish after the steaks have been cut off. Every Friday we have chowder or baked fish. Sometimes there is enough for two days, Saturday as well as Friday. Occasionally, someone hands us sacks of rice, and then we have boiled rice for breakfast, which we serve like a cereal with sugar and skim milk.

But our problem is not just one of food. For the rents we must have cash. This comes to more than a thousand dollars a month, not to speak of taxes on the Staten Island farm, which are now fifteen hundred a year and going up all the time. Gas and electricity for a dozen apartments, as well as the house of hospitality, are especially heavy in winter.

In spring and fall we send out an appeal. We must give an accounting of this to the city: how much it costs to send out an appeal; how much comes in; how it is spent. Since no salaries are paid, and we in turn pay no city, state, or federal tax, our accounting is quite simple. How I rack my brains in March and October to talk about our needs so that our readers will be moved to help us! Sometimes, without embroidering it, I tell a true story of destitution, like that of Marie, who had been spending the nights with her husband on the fire escape of any old abandoned slum building until her approaching confinement made her come to us. Sometimes I talk about the soup line. But most often I retell Biblical stories, which are imbued with a grace that touches the heart and turns the eyes to God—the story of the importunate widow, of the friend who came to borrow an extra loaf for his guest, of Elias fed under the juniper tree, of Daniel fed in the lions' den.

Do we get much help from Catholic charities? We are often asked this question. I can say only that it is not the Church or the state to which we turn when we ask for help in these appeals. Cardinal Spellman did not ask us to undertake this work, nor did the Mayor of New York. It just happened. It is the living from day to day, taking no thought for the morrow, seeing Christ in all who come to us, trying literally to follow the Gospel, that resulted in this work.

"Give to him that asketh of thee, and from him that would borrow of thee turn not away. . . . Love your enemies; do good to those who hate you, pray for those who persecute and caluminate you."

We do not ask church or state for help, but we ask individuals, those who have subscribed to *The Catholic Worker* and so are evidently interested in what we are doing, presumably willing and able to help. Many a priest and bishop sends help year after year. Somehow the dollars that come in cover current bills, help us to catch up with payments on back debts, and make it possible for us to keep on going. There is never anything left over, and we always have a few debts to keep us worrying, to make us more like the very poor we are trying to help. The wolf is not at the door, but he is trotting along beside us. We make friends with him, too, as St. Francis did. We pray for the help we need, and it comes.

Once we overdrew our account by $200. On the way home from the printers, where we had been putting the paper to bed, we stopped in Chinatown at the little Church of the Transfiguration and said a prayer to St. Joseph. When we got to the office a woman was waiting to visit with us. We served her tea and toast and presently she went on her way, leaving us a check for the exact amount of the overdraft. We had not mentioned our need.

What we pray for we receive, but of course many times when we ask help from our fellows we are refused. This is hard to take but we go on asking. Once, when an old journalist who had been staying with us was dying after a stroke, I asked a mutual acquaintance if he could give us money for sheets and find a bathrobe for the old man. He was the sick man's friend, but he told us, "He is no responsibility of mine."

But such experiences are balanced by heartening contrasts. On another occasion I told Michael Grace (I might as well mention his name) about a family which was in need; and he took care of that family for over a year, until the man of the house could have a painful but not too serious operation and so regain his strength to work again. I like to recall this because it did away with much of my class-war attitude.

St. John the Baptist, when asked what was to be done, said, "He that hath two coats let him give to him who hath none." And we must ask for greater things than immediate necessities. I believe that we should ask the rich to help the poor, as Vinoba Bhave does in India, but this is hard to do; we can only make it easier by practice. "Let your abundance supply their want," St. Paul says.

Easiest of all is to have so little, to have given away so much, that there is nothing left to give. But is this ever true? This point of view leads to endless discussions; but the principle remains the same. We *are* our brother's keeper. Whatever we have beyond our own needs belongs to the poor. If we sow sparingly we will reap sparingly. And it is sad but true that we must give far more than bread, than shelter.

If you are the weaker one in substance, in mental or physical health, then you must receive, too, with humility and a sense of brotherhood. I always admired that simplicity of Alyosha in *The Brothers Karamazov* which led him to accept quite simply the support he needed from the benefactors who took him in.

If we do give in this way, then the increase comes. There will be enough. Somehow we will survive; "The pot of meal shall not waste, nor the cruze of oil be diminished," for all our giving away the last bit of substance we have.

At the same time we must often be settling down happily to the cornmeal cakes, the last bit of food in the house, before the miracle of the increase comes about. Any large family knows these things—that somehow everything works out. It works out naturally and it works out religiously.

# Cardinal Spellman and the Gravediggers' Strike

From: *The American Pope: The Life and Times of Francis Cardinal Spellman*

BY JOHN COONEY

The March 1949 day was raw, and the cold chilled the men pacing slowly in front of the heavy metal gates at the entrance to Calvary Cemetery in the borough of Queens. Others stood in knots around trash cans bright with fire. They were gravediggers, members of United Cemetery Workers Local 293, who had been on strike since mid-January. Suddenly, a large bus rumbled up to the gate. The first person to alight was Cardinal Spellman, his clerical collar peeking above denim overalls, who stood by the front door, impatiently waving his right hand and saying, "Come on! Come on!" Dozens of youths in Windbreakers and khaki pants tumbled into the icy air. They were from St. Joseph's Seminary, at Dunwoodie, Yonkers, and Spellman defiantly led them past the strikers into the cemetery. The Cardinal was using seminarians as scabs.

Spellman's step wasn't undertaken lightly, but he saw the need for dramatic action. Labor was a constant headache for him because the archdiocese was an employer on a monumental scale. Each year, Spellman paid out some $30 million in wages just to the building-trade unions that constructed his many projects. The archdiocese spent millions more on salaries for priests, teachers, hospital workers, groundskeepers, maids, and hosts of other tradespeople. The Cardinal had always been opposed to unions, but, against his better judgment, he had accepted the collective bargaining of the cemetery workers three years earlier when they had joined their local, an affiliate of the Food, Tobacco, Agricultural and Allied Workers Union of America.

Now, when the Church was actually struck, the Cardinal was convinced the whole union business had gotten out of hand. Just a year earlier, he had been embarrassed when the Association of Catholic Trade Unionists had organized a strike for clerical help on Wall Street; John Coleman and others had complained bitterly about Catholics' acting like Communists. Spellman had privately agreed with Coleman, but publicly he remained neutral. The ACTU was an anti-Communist union sanctioned by the Church as an alternative to Communism. Besides, that hadn't been his strike, and this one was. Thus, Spellman decided to break the gravediggers' union as an example to other archdiocesan workers who might be contemplating a union.

Spellman's tactics aroused more hostility toward him among his priests than any of his other actions to date. Some pleaded with him to stay out of the issue; but they were ignored or punished for their advice. Once Spellman's mind was made up, there was little dissuading him.

The Cardinal was encouraged by Monsignor George C. Ehardt, his director of cemeteries. A stocky, balding cynic who always had a cigar jutting from the corner of his mouth, Ehardt was as dogmatic as Spellman. When the workers' contract expired on December 31, Spellman had told him to hold the line on wages. Ehardt had taken that as a mandate to insult the gravediggers as well. When the negotiating team sat down with Ehardt and his assistant, a quiet priest named Henry Cauley, the monsignor placed a crucifix in the middle of the bargaining table. The first union contract had been signed in 1946. Now, three years later, the gravediggers petitioned for more than the $59 a week they earned and a five-day, forty-hour week, instead of their six-day, forty-eight-hour week. The meeting concluded when the men made their demands. It was during the second meeting that Ehardt made the archdiocese's first, and final, offer. Again Cauley was at his side, looking uncomfortable. "The most we can do is a dollar a week," Ehardt said. "Take it or leave it." He added pointedly, "The Cardinal's behind me."

The gravediggers were dumbfounded. At first, they thought the monsignor was joking, but they swiftly realized he was not. Sam Cimaglia, one of the negotiators, began arguing. He believed he had a strong case, since he had read a lot of labor literature, including papal encyclicals, on the rights of workers. "The Pope says that a worker with a family of four should get about sixty-eight dollars a week," he began.

"Where'd you read that?" Ehardt interrupted.

Cimaglia told him in *The Sign,* a publication of the Passionist Fathers.

"The Passionists," Ehardt retorted. "Why do you listen to those guys? They're a bunch of bandits."

Cimaglia and his men were all devout Catholics. Many of them went to mass every morning. Never having heard a priest refer to other priests in such a fashion, they were shocked. "You're a man of God," Cimaglia said. "You can't believe that."

Ehardt answered him cynically: "You read the Bible?"

Cimaglia nodded yes.

"Don't you know then that there is no God?" Ehardt asked.

During the exchange Father Cauley blushed crimson. He kicked Ehardt under the table, trying to get him to shut up. "Only a fool would say there is no God," he said, his voice cracking.

Ehardt didn't heed him. "You guys are so religious, why don't you be like God?" he said. "He worked six days a week."

Stonewalled and dismayed, the workers took the only recourse they believed was available. "Put away your rosary beads and go out," Cimaglia recalled Edward Ruggieri, their leader, saying. The sour experience made them realize an aspect of working for the archdiocese that they hadn't previously accepted. "They are just bosses," Ruggieri stated.

Spellman reacted as if he had been betrayed. Like other churchmen, the Cardinal expressed a certain paternalism for people who worked for him. People should be honored to work for the Church, the sentiment went, and be willing to accept less pay for the privilege. In this case, Spellman was angry because the strikers had challenged not only that notion but also his authority. To Spellman, the insolence he perceived was the direct result of the activities of labor priests who encouraged workers to challenge authority.

The man behind the Catholic labor movement in New York was John Patrick Monaghan, the feisty priest with a rich Irish brogue who had been a Spellman contemporary at the North American College. Monaghan represented a different side of the priesthood than Spellman. Instead of choosing a political career, Monaghan became a professor of literature at Fordham and a labor organizer—and a thorn in the Cardinal's side. The two were always at loggerheads, a clash of idealism and pragmatism. Monaghan championed the poor and the working class, saying they had to tear from the hands of capitalists what was rightfully theirs. Spellman saw the labor movement as dangerous.

In seeking someone to help him deal with the gravediggers, Spellman didn't call on the labor experts among his priests. Rather, he turned to Godfrey Schmidt, a conservative lawyer and professor at Fordham, to work with him to prevent unions from gaining members at all Church institutions, including schools and hospitals. "What are these labor priests writing and talking about?" Schmidt recalled Spellman asking him when he sat down with the Cardinal. "They act as though they know how to run the companies, but they don't know anything."

Labor priests in the archdiocese had tried to temper Spellman's intention to steamroller the union. Father John Byrne, who knew the gut issues involved, criticized the handling of the dispute and warned the Cardinal to stay away from it. It was simply a matter of more money and shorter hours, issues the labor movement was pressing across the nation. For his trouble, Byrne was removed from his faculty position at the cathedral seminary and banished to live with Father Ford, the outcast at Corpus Christi. He wasn't alone. Priests who had nothing directly to do with the strike found their careers singed by the heat of Spellman's wrath. Father George Kelly, for instance, had written a column in the Catholic press shortly before the strike, espousing the virtues of organized labor. Suddenly, Kelly found that as far as the Powerhouse was concerned, he was persona non grata, a status that remained unchanged for years.

The gravediggers found themselves in a similar position. Their savings quickly evaporated; the help they expected from other unions never materialized, and the lesson they learned was bitter. At first, representatives of labor organizations approached them, including teamsters and stevedores, but they quickly disappeared. The only financial assistance the cemetery workers received was a $5,000 check from the transport workers, and even that was awkward. Mike Quill demanded that the gravediggers keep his union's gift quiet. "We were up against the Powerhouse," Cimaglia related. "Everybody was afraid to touch us." Dorothy Day was one of the few who publicly supported the union. She and some of her staff from *The Catholic Worker* passed out leaflets in front of the Cardinal's residence and were arrested. The police forbade the gravediggers to picket Spellman's house.

Spellman met with Schmidt and Ehardt to determine their best course of action. The result showed how out of touch with reality they were. Schmidt issued a public statement in which he proposed that the dispute should be submitted to "an impartial board of three distinguished moral theologians."

Their next step was much more serious and calculated to lose all sympathy for the union: they accused the local leadership of being Communists. In light of the times, the charge was particularly vicious. A dozen men were on trial, at the federal courthouse at New York's Foley Square, on Communist-conspiracy charges, and their story was headlined almost daily. Paul Robeson's passport had been invalidated; Herb Philbrick was giving sensational press accounts of his years as a Red that would be turned into the book and television series *I Led Three Lives.*

The gravediggers were shocked by the charge and were dismayed when many people apparently believed the Cardinal. Spellman, however, also lost support by the move. Some people who had sympathized with him, thinking him concerned about the families of the mounting numbers of unburied, now thought he acted maliciously. The liberal journal *Commonweal,* for instance, criticized his handling of the strike. "I'll never forgive *Commonweal,*" Spellman said. "Not in this world or the next."

The novelist Ernest Hemingway was so offended that he wrote Spellman a blistering letter.

"My Dear Cardinal, In every picture that I see of you there is more mealy mouthed arrogance, fatness and over-confidence," Hemingway wrote. "As a strike breaker against Catholic workers, as an attacker of Mrs. Roosevelt I feel strongly that you are overextending yourself." The writer contended that Spellman "lied about the Spanish Republic" and noted that in Europe it was rumored Spellman would be "the next and first American Pope," adding "do not keep pressing so hard. You will never be Pope as long as I'm alive."

More meaningful criticism came from the Association of Catholic Trade Unionists, which denied the strike was Communist-inspired. ACTU President John Manning condemned the charge as a red herring and a "vicious attempt to smash the union."

Six weeks into the strike, Spellman sent telegrams to all the union members, with the exception of the five-man negotiating team. He wanted to meet personally with the men, apparently believing that his position within the Church would awe them into submission. Thus, on a snowy day in February, the men gathered at Cathedral High School. The Cardinal met them at the door and was extremely cordial. Dressed in his scarlet robes, he greeted each man as he entered. Each worker awkwardly genuflected and kissed his ring, while Spellman asked if he was married and had children. The strikers were ill at ease, but the men had made a pact that they wouldn't stay there unless the Cardinal let the negotiating team into the gathering. The five negotiators were anxiously waiting outside. When Spellman took his place before the microphone, he didn't get a chance to speak. A big striker with a voice like a bullhorn, Frank Malkowski, immediately asked the Cardinal to admit the negotiators: "Your Eminence, why are our five committee members not here?"

"They are not wanted," Spellman replied.

To a man, the three hundred twenty-five cemetery workers stood up and started leaving the hall. The Cardinal was startled, and, for one of the few times in his life, he lost his composure in public. He started running after the men, stumbling over his floor-length silk garments and yelling, "Wait! Wait!"

"If I talk to the committee will you stay?" the breathless Spellman asked.

The men agreed. The Cardinal went to the front door, met the negotiators, and took them to another room, where he started off tough. "I can't deal with you," he said. "You're Communists."

The men angrily denied the charge. Most of them felt guilty about the strike: they were torn between their family duties and their Church. The Communism charge made them feel worse. Their parent union, the Food, Tobacco, Agricultural and Allied Workers Union of America, doubtless had Communists in it; any number of large unions did. Their local, however, had never had any. The men themselves were bitterly anti-Communist. Some had even gotten into fistfights with Communists who had criticized the Cardinal. Moreover, the men suspected that Spellman was simply using the issue as a cudgel to get his own way. When some adverse publicity erupted over his making the charge, the Cardinal retreated. Instead of saying the men were Communists, he softened the indictment, saying they used "Communist tactics."

Now, outside the cathedral school, Cimaglia told Spellman that raising the Communist charge was "pretty hypocritical," adding: "You signed two contracts with us in the past. If we took a dollar-a-week raise, you wouldn't think we were Communists."

The Cardinal quickly backed down. He obviously wanted the meeting with the men, so he removed the last obstacle from its being held. "I can see you are not Communists," he abruptly told them.

Ironically, Communists had used an intermediary to approach the union, offering support. If they agreed to align themselves with Communists, the cemetery workers were promised a massive rally at Madison Square Garden as well as strike pay of $65 or $70 a week. The Communists wanted to make a cause out of the Church's exploiting labor. The union leaders had rejected the offer out of hand, but they had kept the encounter to themselves. One reason Spellman was so anxious to meet with the cemetery workers was that he had asked the F.B.I. to monitor the union. He apparently wanted to get something on the record indicating the men were Communists.

Shortly after the negotiators walked into the meeting room, however, Spellman lost control over the proceedings. The men asked him questions, and he couldn't steer the discussion in the direction he wanted it to go. At one point, Spellman was asked why he had finally decided to meet with them after so many weeks. He replied, "Because I love you and your families!"

The questioner looked nonplussed at the Cardinal and shook his head. "God save us from love like that," he said.

Spellman never regained his composure. He returned to his office and told Schmidt that the men had referred to him as "a little runt" and worse. "He told me that they reviled him and called him all kinds of names," Schmidt recalled. "They were a coarse, vulgar group." (The men deny making such remarks.)

"Don't take it to heart," Schmidt told Spellman.

Spellman was next approached by a committee of strikers' wives. They believed that if the Cardinal sat down with them, they could clear up the mess. The women were alarmed at the way the strike had turned out and they believed Spellman had a gross misunderstanding of what kinds of men their husbands were and what they were doing. The Cardinal agreed to see them, and when the meeting was held, the women were in awe. Spellman heightened the effect by sitting on the throne in the reception room in his residence. He was dressed in ermine and scarlet and the sun streamed through a window behind him. "He looked so holy," Mary Czak later told her husband, Siggy, a member of the strike committee.

For the occasion, Spellman was a grave Jehovah. "The men have put their union above their Church," he declared.

"No!" Mrs. Czak replied. "The men are not fighting the Church but they are fighting you as an employer."

The Cardinal focused on the men's disobedience. They refused to bury the dead, and this, he declared, went against the Church's teachings on the corporeal works of mercy. The meeting was fruitless, ending with the following statement by the women: "Because of our Catholic faith, we are deeply aggrieved by the reckless and misguided charge of Communism hurled at our loved ones. . . ."

The women were dejected. They had asked for a decent wage for their husbands, and Spellman had acted as if they wanted the Vatican treasury. Mrs. Czak told the press: "The archbishop promised us nothing. He wants the men to go back to work as individuals, not as union men, and he would not allow members of the strikers committee to go back to work because they were ringleaders. . . . The archbishop was adamant. He promised nothing except that the strikers could return with a small increase, but not as union men. He wants no part of the union. We got no place to go."

Publicly, Spellman expressed nothing but solicitude. "I feel as badly for them as if it were my own mother in the same circumstances," he said. But he added abruptly, "They had nothing to offer me, and I had nothing to offer them."

Thus, when Spellman led the seminarians into the graveyard, there was a great deal of bitterness on both sides. He wanted to see how everything went the first day. The second day, he called in the press; reporters and photographers swarmed over the cemetery, and Spellman always found time for an interview. The strike, he contended, had reached "crisis" proportions. He said he was considering formal burial squads at parishes around the archdiocese. "I could have put an unlimited number of volunteers to work," he claimed, surveying the seminarians as they dug graves. "But this won't be necessary. My boys will return to Calvary daily until the job is finished and everything is normal."

The strikebreaking was extremely controversial; its merits were debated in rectories and by the public. Though many priests condemned Spellman behind his back, few besides John Byrne had the nerve to tell Spellman he was wrong. Seminarians were also distraught: some left the seminary as a result of the experience; most of them took the tips they had received from families of the aggrieved and surreptitiously gave them to the strikers. "Very few seminarians wouldn't go because they were frightened about what would happen if they refused," explained Monsignor Myles Burke, who taught at Dunwoodie at the time.

The Cardinal gained the support of columnists Dorothy Kilgallen and Westbrook Pegler. Pegler found that the use of seminarians as scabs was "a sweet example to other employers" who had to deal with "Communists or fellow travelers . . . usually grim and hateful strangers to the boss and most of the help." The strikers felt the brunt of such antagonism, and they began to back down. While the Cardinal urged on his seminarians, the cemetery workers passed two resolutions: One condemned the anti-union stance of the archdiocese. The other, however, was an anti-Communist oath. Moreover, the local voted to break with the Food, Tobacco, Agricultural and Allied Workers Union of America, as a sign of their good faith. That the men felt compelled to prove their anti-Communism was a sign of how easily a smear campaign worked. Ironically, their union meetings had always had the trappings of Holy Name Society gatherings rather than Communist cells. Such sessions opened with members reciting the Lord's Prayer, a Hail Mary, and the Workers Prayer of the Association of Catholic Trade Unionists, which began: "Lord Jesus, Carpenter of Nazareth, You were a worker as I am. . . ."

Nonetheless, the gravediggers met at their meeting hall, the Anoroc Democratic Club in Queens, and declared they weren't Reds. Ed Ruggieri, chairman of the negotiating committee, asked them to repeat the following: "We here as Catholic gentlemen declare that we are opposed to Communism and all it means in all walks of life. Be it recorded, however, that Communism is not the basic issue here."

When Spellman heard of the anti-Communist actions that the union had taken, he wasn't inclined toward forgiveness. He knew that hadn't been the issue. "They're getting repentant kind of late," he said.

In the end, the men couldn't hold out. Their bills mounted, and some of them had sick children and no heat in the house. As the Powerhouse directed, the strikers voted to link with the AFL Building Service Employees Union, which Spellman considered safe. Negotiations were handled by David Sullivan, the international's vice president, who was considered one of Spellman's people. An independent mediator was brought in. Two days later, the strike was settled. The men received a wage increase of 8.33 percent. The issue of shorter hours went to mediation, where it was left unresolved. The reason the Powerhouse liked the new union was evident. Sullivan blamed the strike on irresponsible union leadership. Moreover, he told the Cardinal that no such strike would occur under his leadership.

The Cardinal made a show of sending each of the strikers $65 from his personal funds as a sign that all was forgiven. Privately, the union negotiators were harassed in an effort to get them fired. The only loose end for Spellman was trying to generate some sort of public blessing for his stand, preferably from the holder of the highest public office in the nation. He sent the embarrassed seminarians to Washington to tour the capital as a reward for their assistance. The Cardinal audaciously asked Truman to meet with the young men while they were in town. "I would not expect the President to go through the ordeal of shaking hands with each one, but if a five-minute audience could be arranged, I am sure the honor and privilege would remain with them as an unforgettable memory," Spellman wrote to Matthew Connelly, the President's secretary. The effort was worth making, but it didn't work. There was nothing in it for Truman. The President wasn't about to attempt to pull Spellman's chestnuts out of the fire by offending the labor vote. Truman answered that he would meet with Spellman—alone and in private.

Spellman, however, had the last word: "Thus is brought to a close one of the most difficult, grievous, heartbreaking issues that has ever come within my time as archbishop of New York, and it will be my daily prayer that if ever again the working men of this archdiocese must make their choice between following their faith or faithless leadership, they will, of their own free and immediate choice, choose—God!"

# Lights On in the House of the Dead

From: *Lights On in the House of the Dead*

BY DANIEL BERRIGAN

✛

LETTER TO J.C.

I said to myself the other night, sleepless as a night frog, bug-eyed between stars (real, unseen) and waters (real, unseeable), why, I will write Him a letter. Possibly a long one, possibly a short. I do not know. I do not know how it will come off, whether He will favor it in this place where I am caught in a net and nailed down with some seven hundred others for an indefinite time. I do not know if it may come off, I am appalled and reduced all the day long, usually sleepless at night, guarded and kept like an animal, in a pit where Caesar calls the game. But I must try to think. I said so to another prisoner, whom I steal away to talk to in the hospital, usually with a cup of coffee in my hand for him and me. He is a young war resister, sensitive and intelligent. On occasion, with supreme rightness and good sense, he has flipped his lid in this place. Coming back, he is sane, calm, and of good judgment. And he said to me: OK. You must try.

It is, after all, fifty years since You fashioned me through my father and mother and brothers and school and the Jesuits and books and photos and university and cities around the world—tramping, flying, reading, arguing, and yes praying, everywhere on this globe. You have not been a stranger to me, I have been no strange to men and women. I have been literally everywhere—usually, I hope, on your errands. The things I have seen, the faces I have looked into! I have skulked underground for months, before I was flushed by the bird watchers, a most exotic survival, and brought here, and caged—for the duration. And here, with Philip and the others I have not ceased to cry out to You—quite the contrary; I have had daily to exorcise from my bones the constricting horror of the lockup, the seamy underside of creation, the little plot of earth hardly bigger than a mass grave, with its tattered vegetation and dripping webs—a limbo of the heart if ever there was one.

No stranger, Brother. Philip and I have held our scalded hearts in our hands, for You to see. We have stood at the improvised table in the chaplain's office, summoned "up front" over the loudspeakers—those faceless iron throats that call men to meals, to lockup, to justice within justice. They might as easily summon them to the furnaces. Eucharist!

The seven hundred are locked out, in principle. We stand there in perpetual exhaustion, looking down at the bread and wine, raising our eyes to the barred window and beyond, the tatterdemalion November flowers, the shuffle of passing men; the words stick in our mouth like a fistful of sand. Remember, Lord . . . Shall the Lord remember? Or has He not forgotten us forever—the prisoners, the walking dead, the inhabitants of some cold moon, the wraiths of All Saints' Eve? Remember, Lord. Remember even us . . .

Fomenter of dread and fear, wielder of a sword wilder and more bloodletting than Jehovah's, troublemaker, tenderest of sons, brother of malefactors, of no-goods, junkies, beggars, grifters, counterfeiters, liars, society's offal: remember we pray to You—us, the scum, refuse of the world, those who play a foul game badly and are caught at it; the itchy-fingered, the lovers of dirty money, traders in drugs, the halfhearted, the repeaters, those tattooed on the arm: "born to lose," and truthfully so.

Far world, far from the company of lovers and saints and hermits and virgins, and heroes and peacemakers, and guitarists and singers and children (far from children our arms ache for . . .).

Remember us. Out of the depths; for we are brought very low . . .

•        •        •

They do not know what to say to us, they do not know what to expect of us. Their reactions generally are of two kinds: the young, who have no "connections," for whom the church is dead as a doornail (it is, almost; here, its last legs), and the oldsters, who expect fully that we in discarded army mufti and disposable missals will "show up" for the wretched Sunday service (which we do). The first sleep in; the second make do. Which group is right, or whether we are right in joining, for a half hour on Sunday A.M., the second, we do not know. I am not recording this in order to justify the option we take. We take it nonetheless, even when sitting or standing there or walking up to take the host, or consenting to read the Gospel (thereupon to hear it ground into hamburg) makes a stone grow in the pit of the stomach . . .

It is terrible to be powerless. It is doubly terrible to witness powerlessly the mutilation of the word, the death of a living, beautiful, and truthful word, by the slovenly retailers of religion whose vestment might in truth be a butcher's apron.

Out of the depths. Monday Tuesday Wednesday Thursday Friday depths.

Saturday you are free to wander the yard, to talk or read, to roll the stone out of the depths. Sunday, out of the depths; a "religious" hell for a secular. You may sleep in, you may rise early for a bad sermon, a stale Eucharist. The choices are not large. Mauriac spoke of them; you do not come to this God as to a great one of this world holding court in a pentagon; the flag, the cross. No, you assemble, broken men, to break bread. At the edge of the world, where you scarcely are tolerated, where you barely can claim space, air; you gather, when all is said. To do what he did; with the same results, predictably.

I used to walk to the filthy macadam yard at St. Peter's, Jersey City—how many years ago? Trying to put together enough reason, enough energy, to go on for another single day. In 1947: ten years later I was walking off my private devils on the Brooklyn pavement; bedeviled by insomnia, seeing no rhyme or reason in policing and drilling kids, the day only starting after school or on weekends when we would go, a few students and I, into Manhattan's East Side to work at some storefront, to gather some neighborhood youngsters, at Walt Janer's mission center . . . Or when I could read and study until 2 A.M. sleepless as a bat, toss until four and rise and steal out to say Mass alone.

I was back from Europe, I thought good days were ahead; I landed back where I most dreaded—high school drilling, cafeteria policing, the childish games that were supposed to prove one was with it. The headmaster, who played a poker-faced politics of loyalty and no opposition allowed, one day slipped and gave away his hand: "What did you do to land here?" he asked me. Alas, I had no crime to confess to, even for my own relief . . .

And tried nonetheless, with all the grace of an oil-slicked gull, to take You at Your word.

The old priest who guards the office where we say Mass here (he cannot bear looking in our faces) burst out one day: but why are they all leaving the priesthood, and you are not leaving . . . He would have been much more able to bear with the reversal of those happenings; if most were not leaving and we, manifest pot stirrers and poltergeists, were gracefully or otherwise bowing out . . .

We have tried to take You at Your word.

·          ·          ·

It has been for as long as I can remember, crisis upon crisis.

How much of it was by Your will and intent for me? How much was my own wrong turns, my self-will and deception? I must, in such a place, at such a time, leave the answer to You, which is to say, to Mercy.

Beyond doubt the tongs of generation set a pinch of brimstone into my bones.

What a father we had! I was landlocked at Newark Airport (Dante's third

circle of hell) sometime in February of 1970, thinking of him in that foul and
dreary place, as I wandered outdoors among loading ramps, barrels, incessant
noise and traffic, the greasy rain staining the earth to foulness. I thought of
him, and of that night . . .

I had hurried home in response to an urgent call: he is sinking. Come. Jerry
drove me over, we rehashed the last weeks; the intransigence of those old
bones, the dour humors, the skill which never deserted him, even at ninety-
one, to keep his family on edge, to deride, show contempt, order about, ignore.
He was losing as he had lived, gracelessly. For some three weeks he had
launched into a new tactic, since the last fall had broken his hip. He would neither eat nor take therapy nor in any way show a will to live. The doctors said
his limb had healed without fault; there was nothing to impede his walking
again, his old frame was sound and strong.

He willed to die: whether out of spite of us, or what else, none of us will
ever know.

In a letter to You (as You see) he has taken over, as he always and invariably took over upon any scene that included his family. Pertinacious, self-cen-
tered, generally joyless, recounting the past interminably, quick-witted, acid,
fierce to seize upon weakness, knowing his strength and determined never to
lose out, an old-school tyrant—something to give the angels pause where they
hovered!

We will never see his like again. No one will: least of all ourselves. There
is but one father granted a man. The son will carry his father to his own grave;
whatever else he can become, he is that man's son, born of his seed, parrying
his shadow.

The struggle through that night! He took the oxygen like a desperate,
spent runner nearing the tape, shaking the bed; the bed shook like a vessel in
storm: What a man he was, the old nurse said in wonder, lifting his great hand
to take his pulse, just see those bones!

We were alone, in that solitude death encloses in its wings—

I paced the room, I sat and read, I rose to look at you, to adjust the covers, the oxygen, to pray. I held your hand. I had never in all our lives held your
hand. As you grew older, you used to embrace us when we returned home, but
the embrace was always yours, not mine. I submitted to it, I could not give you
my love, you had never known how to seek it—

I held your hand and repeated prayers of your childhood and mine. Our
Father, Hail Mary . . . O my God I am heartily sorry . . . and miraculously, your
struggle quieted, the quivering of your frame; you were listening, you were
praying with me.

In prison tonight, my father, I remember. Do you know, one year after
your death, in another sodden November—do you know I am here? and why?

And do you approve at last, and would you tell me so, with an altogether new gentleness?

Could there be a father who awaits us, his six sons; who is all you never were, generous, kind of heart and speech—a father you never were to us—and yet yourself, purified by fire, longing for that love we so longed to give and to receive?

He worshiped, bit in mouth; another task, an uphill climb on Sundays. We entered into that rhythm as children do, ignorant of any other conduct, the Sunday rhythm of Mass and communion, a better dinner than usual. Peaceful by mandate; Pa was in the house, at table, in the yard. I cannot remember your ever showing that Sunday would flow over upon us, that we had rights as God did, that we counted for something, as He counted so heavily . . .

We buried him in his shroud and a plain box. For a few dollars, with a notice in the paper that contributions could be sent to a peace group. Peace to your ashes, who had known so little peace! There was no "viewing," none of the expensive cosmetic daubing over the fact and primary presence of death. In the A.M., Mass; in the P.M., open house with a buffet for friends, who greeted us, ate and drank, spread through the house, came and went. Mom in midst, calm and dignity the crown of those mad hatter's fifty-three years, in which she had borne so much with such grace, attaining that inner light which is both sanity and healing.

We lowered his body ourselves, his sons, on the slope of a hill south of the city, within sight of the farmland where he had been born, ninety years before.

Requiescat. It is a wholesome thought to pray for the dead. From my prison I pray him deliverance from his; so that, father and sons, we may meet as free men in eternity—all debts paid, old rancors dissolved in that Love, that Light.

I have never found You an easy Master.

Undoubtedly, said a friend, you have a cave of dark pessimism at your heart. What I wonder at, is that you function so well, in spite of all . . .

So be it. And yet there are moments even in prison when the dark caul lifts from one's eyes, and in knowing You, Your presence, Your love, one may breathe more deeply the air of another land.

I wanted You to be Lord of the imagination; to help me imagine ways of living in the world which would be both true to the values I loved and and an endlessly rich and spontaneous variation upon them . . .

# The Campaign for Governor

From: *Diaries of Mario M. Cuomo*

BY  MARIO  M.  CUOMO

*Speech delivered at Sunday service, St. John the Divine*
*New York City, November, 27, 1983*

As a Catholic, I am particularly honored to be invited here to this magnificent seat of the Protestant Episcopal Church of New York, one of the true architectural jewels of Christendom and one of the great houses of commitment, service and, therefore, worship.

I know that in ritual and theology my church and your church are close. They always have been. Two centuries ago, in fact, Benjamin Franklin described the differences this way: the Roman Church, he said, claims to be "infallible," while the Episcopal thinks of itself as "never in the wrong." Since Vatican II, we've grown even closer. The Archbishop of Canterbury has traveled to Rome to kneel at the tomb of Peter, and the Bishop of Rome has prayed in the mother church of the Episcopal faith. Each has spoken about the respective responsibility of their churches in the schism that divided us some four centuries ago.

Closer indeed. Recently, I spoke with a good friend who is a bishop in my Church. I mentioned the invitation I had to speak here today and asked him about the differences that still divide us. The Bishop thought a moment, then said, "If I'm not mistaken, the Episcopalians still don't have a second collection on Sundays."

. . .

But I haven't come here to talk about the ecumenical progress between Catholics and Episcopalians. You've asked me to speak this morning on "The

Stewardship of Political Power." Or, as Dean Morton[1] has written, on the "sacred dimension" that infuses and surrounds every human activity, even politics. This isn't an easy thing for me to do. I'm not a theologian. My grasp of the Bible is probably not much better than that of any ordinary lay person. And while I have a learned and accomplished biblical scholar and homilist on my staff—Rabbi Israel Mowshowitz—he parts theological company with me at the end of what we Christians call the Old Testament.

If, then, I'm to talk honestly and meaningfully about the idea of "stewardship" or "the sacred," it can't be from the perspective of a scholar or an exegete. It must be from my own experience—from the perspective of a person who struggles to be a believer, a person raised in the pre-Vatican II American Church, an immigrant Church of ethnic loyalties and theological certainties that were rarely questioned.

Ours was a Catholicism closer to the peasant roots of its practitioners than to the high intellectual traditions of Catholic theology and philosophy. We perceived the world then as a sort of cosmic basic training course, filled by God with obstacles and traps to weed out the recruits unfit for eventual service in the Heavenly Host. At this, God had been exceedingly successful: the obstacles were everywhere. Our fate on earth was to be "the poor banished children of Eve, mourning and weeping in this vale of tears," until by some combination of luck and grace and good works, we escaped final damnation.

I don't mean to belittle the Church of that time. Indeed, it was not the Church so much as it was we churchgoers. Our faith reflected the collective experience of people who through most of their history had little chance to concern themselves with helping the poor or healing the world's wounds. They *were* the poor. Their poverty and their endless—sometimes losing—struggle to feed themselves and hold their families together had varied little across the centuries.

But what I now understand is that, in those days, in our preoccupation with evil and temptation, we often put guilt before responsibility and we obscured a central part of Christian truth: that God did not intend this world only as a test of our purity but, rather, as an expression of his love. That we are meant to live actively, intensely, totally in this world and, in so doing, to make it better for all whom we can touch, no matter how remotely.

Many of us in the Church had to learn that lesson. The great Jesuit scientist and theologian Teilhard de Chardin was the first to teach us. He reoriented

---

[1]The very Reverend Parks Morton, dean of the Cathedral Church of St. John the Divine. St. John the Divine is the mother church of the Episcopal Diocese of New York.

our theology and rewrote its language. His wonderful book *The Divine Milieu,* dedicated to "those who love this world," made negativism a sin.

What an extraordinary reaffirmation of Christian optimism. What a wonderful consolation to those of us who didn't want to think of the world as God's cruel challenge. Teilhard de Chardin glorified the world and everything in it. He said the whole universe—even the pain and imperfection we see—is sacred, every part of it touched and transformed by the Incarnation. Faith, he said, is not a call to escape the world but to embrace it. Creation isn't an elaborate testing ground but an invitation to join in the work of restoration and completion.

All together these exciting new articulations of the world's beauty helped an entire generation of Catholics to realize that salvation consisted of something more than simply escaping the pains of hell. We were challenged to have the faith that Paul speaks of in today's epistle, a faith that "knows what hour it is, how it is full time . . . to wake from sleep."

So for people like me, struggling to believe, my Catholic faith and the understanding it gives me of stewardship aren't a part of my politics. Rather, my politics is, as far as I can make it happen, an extension of this faith and the understanding. There is a paradox here, of course, one I must face daily and one every American who belongs to a religious faith must also face. In fact, it would be impossible to stand here as a Catholic governor—as one elected by Moslems and Sikhs and deists and animists and agnostics and atheists—and talk about politics and Christian stewardship without addressing this paradox.

The paradox was most recently raised in a letter I received on the executive order I issued banning discrimination against homosexuals in state government. The writer attacked what I had written. He took a stand on the executive order that most of us here today would disagree with. Yet the question he raises of religious belief and governmental action is a valid one. And, in one form or another, all of us who mix our faith and our politics—certainly those of us concerned about the stewardship of power—must be ready to answer it. In part, the letter says the following: "Governor Cuomo, you call yourself a Christian yet how can you claim to be a Christian when you go out of your way to proclaim the right of people to be what is an abomination in the sight of God?"

The answer, I think, drives to the very heart of the question of where private morality ends and public policy begins—how I involve myself in the political life of a world broad enough to include people who don't believe all the things I believe about God and conduct. Am I obliged to seek to legislate my particular morality—in all of its exquisite detail—and if I fail, am I then required to surrender stewardship rather than risk hypocrisy?

The answer, I think, is reflected in the one foundation on which all of us as citizens must try to balance our political and religious commitments—the Constitution. Those who founded this nation knew that you *could* form a government that embodied the particular beliefs and moral taboos of one religion. They knew that choice was available to them. Indeed, at that time there was hardly a government in the world that operated otherwise. Catholic countries reflected Catholic values and did their best to stamp out or contain Protestantism. Protestant countries upheld their own values. Their laws forbade the Mass, and in some places, like the Dutch settlement at Nieuw Amsterdam, the law said that any Catholic priest discovered within its walls was to be hanged, drawn and quartered. And everywhere, as they'd been for centuries, the Jews were persecuted and forced to work and live under whole sets of legal disabilities. That was the world our Constitution was written in.

To secure religious peace, the Constitution demanded toleration. It said no group, not even a majority, has the right to force its religious views on any part of the community. It said that where matters of private morality are involved—belief or actions that don't impinge on other people or deprive them of their rights—the state has no right to intervene.

This neutrality didn't forbid Christians or Jews or Moslems to be involved in politics. Just the opposite; by destroying the basis for religious tests, by destroying the basis for making people's beliefs and private lives a matter of government's concern, it *secured* that involvement, ensured it, encouraged it. Our Constitution provides that there are areas the state has no business intruding in, freedoms that are basic and inalienable. In creating this common political ground, it created a place where we could all stand—Episcopalians, Catholics, Jews, atheists—a place where we could tolerate each other's differences and respect each other's freedom.

Yet our Constitution isn't simply an invitation to selfishness, for in it is also embodied a central truth of the Judeo-Christian tradition—that is, a sense of the common good. It says, as the Gospel says, that freedom isn't license; that liberty creates responsibility; that if we have been given freedom, it is to encourage us to pursue that common good.

And if the Constitution restricts the powers of the state in order to save us from the temptation to judge and to persecute others, it doesn't thereby deny the necessity of the shared commitments—to help one another—shared commitments that are the basis for justice and mercy and human dignity and therefore the basis, the most fundamental basis, of any religion that believes in a loving God.

There is, I think, a clear concept of stewardship in the Constitution. And the government it sets up is meant to embody that stewardship.

I think my religion encourages me to be involved in government because it is very much a part of the world God so loves. And I think that if I am given the burdens and the opportunities of stewardship, my principal obligation is to use government not to impose a universal oath of religious allegiance, or a form of ritual, or even a life style, but to move us toward the shared commitments that are basic to all forms of compassionate belief.

Until recently, most Americans accepted this proposition. It was accepted that government was created among us—by us—"to promote the general welfare," to protect our water and soil and air from contamination, to secure decent care for those who can't care for themselves—the sick, the indigent, the homeless, the people in wheelchairs—to help people find the dignity of work. Until recently, our history had been largely one of expanding that concept of stewardship, reaching out to include those once excluded—women, Blacks and other minorities.

But this belief in benevolent stewardship—in the commitment of each to the welfare of all, especially to the least among us—is today increasingly attacked and ridiculed and denied. There is a powerful move toward a new ethic for government, one that says, "God helps those whom God has helped, and if God has left you out, who are we to presume on his will by trying to help you?"

In a country as religious as our, where over 90 percent of the people express a belief in God and a majority profess attachment to a formal religious faith, it is hard to understand how this denial of the compassionate heart of all the world's great faiths could succeed.

Yet it is succeeding. More money for bombs, less for babies. More help for the rich, more poor than ever.

And the success of this Darwinian view presents us with a choice: either we swim with the tide and accept the notion that the best way to help the unfortunate is to help the fortunate and then hope that personal charity will induce them voluntarily to take care of the rest of us, or we resist. We resist by affirming as our moral and political foundation the idea that we *are* our brother's keeper, all of us, as a people, as a *government;* that our responsibility to our brothers and our sisters is greater than any one of us and that it doesn't end when they are out of the individual reach of our hand or our charity or our love.

This is not a comfortable disposition, believing that as we express ourselves through our government, we have an obligation to love. It can haunt us. It can nag at us in moments of happiness and personal success, disturbing our sleep and giving us that sense of guilt and unworthiness that the modern age is so eager to deny. And it can accuse us—from the faces of the starving and the dispossessed and the wounded, faces that stare back at us from the front page of our newspapers, images from across the world that blink momentarily on our television screens.

I was homeless, it says, and you gave me theories of supply and demand.

I was imprisoned and silenced for justice's sake, and you washed the hands of my torturers.

I asked for bread, and you built the world's most sophisticated nuclear arsenal.

Yet, as people who claim Christ's name—who dare to call ourselves Christians—what choice do we really have but to hear that voice and to answer its challenge?

* * *

Teilhard de Chardin in just a few magnificent sentences captured everything I've tried to say here about this challenge of stewardship. Talking about our obligations to involve ourselves in the things of this world, he wrote: "We must try everything for Christ. . . . Jerusalem, lift up your head. Look at the immense crowds of those who build and those who seek. All over the world, men are toiling—in laboratories, in studios, in deserts, in factories—in the vast social crucible. The ferment that is taking place by their instrumentality in art and science and thought is happening for your sake. Open, then, your arms and your heart, like Christ your Lord, and welcome the waters, the flood and the sap of humanity. Accept it, this sap—for without its baptism, you will wither, without desire, like a flower out of water; and tend it, since, without your sun, it will disperse itself wildly in sterile shoots."

And Jesus, answering the question of a lawyer in language to be understood by all, said that the law and the prophets, their wisdom and vision and insight, their teaching about religious obligation and stewardship, were all contained in two commandments: "You shall love the Lord your God with all your heart, and with all your soul, and with all your mind. You shall love your neighbor as yourself."

That is the law, as simply as it can be expressed—for both the stewards and those in their charge, for both the governed and those who govern them, for all who look to Christ's mercy, wherever they might find themselves.

Thank you.

# The Case of Mario Cuomo

From: *Under God: Religion and American Politics*

BY GARRY WILLS

Catholics, 28 percent of the population, and Jews, only 2 percent, have had a powerful influence on America's Protestant majority. Both groups have a highly developed tradition, strongly inculcated, that was brought to America. Each resisted for a long time the dilution of its community by intermarriage. American Protestantism, individualist and improvisational, diffuses its impact in sectarian rivalries. It lives by revivals, starting over from scratch. The strength of Catholicism and Judaism lies, by contrast, in their continuity.

Of these two groups, Catholics have the stronger structure of authority, prompting Lenny Bruce to call Catholicism the only *the* church. This church influences American politics in two ways, on separate tracks. It addresses outsiders, "men [*sic*] of goodwill," with well-formulated arguments from a long natural-law tradition, while delivering doctrinal fiats to its own members, who are expected to act from them in the public arena. Thus arguments are used against contraception in public debate, while those arguments *and* church tradition are held to bind Catholics.

This double approach has been taken even when the strict teaching authority of the church (its magisterium) is not involved. Thus Catholic bishops argued in the public realm, mainly through lay people, for the Hollywood Production Code, as a matter of civil decency, and, at the same time, they enlisted Catholics in the Legion of Decency, condemning movies with moral authority.

In the same way, the Catholic bishops in America say that abortion is not a religious issue when addressing the public at large. In that forum, they rely on natural law, common sense, and probabilist arguments (even if the fetus is only *probably* human, one should not kill what *might* be alive). But Catholics are told they must hold to the church's position out of loyalty to their ecclesiastical rulers. The two tracks were clearly marked in 1990 when the hierarchy paid millions of dollars to a public-relations firm to make its public case, while bishops in New York State said that the Catholic governor of New York, Mario Cuomo, was endangering his soul and could not speak in diocesan institutions because he did not support a legal ban on abortion.

In earlier presidential campaigns, Edward Kennedy's in 1980 and Geraldine Ferraro's as the running mate for Walter Mondale in 1984, Catholics were particularly punitive to their own on the abortion issue. Kennedy's position, for instance, did not differ from Jimmy Carter's during the Democratic primaries of 1980; nor, obviously, did Geraldine Ferraro's differ from Walter Mondale's in 1984. But Catholics picketed and appealed to their bishops against Kennedy and Ferraro while largely ignoring the stands of Carter and Mondale. Partly, of course, this was just a matter of striking where one could have the most impact. But the situation that made that impact possible was the double standard by which Catholics are reachable—not only by the arguments made to all political candidates but by a special bond that is supposed to limit Catholics in what they can do while claiming membership in good standing with their fellow believers.

Mario Cuomo was not new to these pressures when, in 1990, Bishop Austin Vaughan publicly opined that he might be on his way to hell. Cardinal John O'Connor, Vaughan's superior in the archdiocese of New York, had entertained and not rejected a public call for excommunicating Cuomo in 1984, at the time when pressures were being brought to bear on Congresswoman Ferraro. Cuomo was watching O'Connor on television when this occurred. So was his fourteen-year-old son Christopher, who asked if his father was about to be dischurched. Mario Cuomo is a very sincere Catholic, an intensely devoted family man, proud, competitive, and thin-skinned. His wife said, after watching him react to this public challenge: "Boy, did he [the cardinal] pick on the wrong person." Three months later, at a widely publicized event at the University of Notre Dame, Cuomo delivered his answer to the cardinal, a speech he crafted very carefully. His biographer calls this "a brilliantly argued answer." When, four years later, the Catholic former governor of Arizona ran for president, he was able to answer questions about abortion by subscribing to "the Cuomo position." Bruce Babbitt told reporters: "Geraldine [Ferraro] got into trouble on the issue because she didn't have her facts straight. Mario got it right." Cuomo had cleared the way for other Catholics.

Some compared Cuomo's Notre Dame speech with John Kennedy's 1960 address to Protestant ministers in Houston. But in some ways Cuomo was in a tighter bind. Kennedy was addressing non-Catholics, who might be opposed to him but would observe certain restraints of our pluralist code. He had the

Catholic community rallying behind him, even if he went farther than some bishops would have preferred. He granted the existence of the two different claims on Catholic loyalty but said that, if the private exertion of authority conflicted with the public appeal to natural reason, he would resign before putting the purely Catholic appeal above public arguments from the common good. The clearinghouse, in any case, was his conscience. The only hold the church had on him was his own free acceptance of church authority. That was enough for most critics in 1960.

More was demanded of Cuomo in 1984, though he did not really deliver more. The surface difference lay in his exposed position as a Catholic arguing not only with other Catholics but with his ecclesiastical superiors. Columnist Mary McGrory wrote at the time: "Cuomo is the first Catholic politician to pick a fight with a prelate. Not so long ago, such an initiative on the part of a Catholic politician would have been nothing less than suicide."

It was a close call, even so. Cuomo's speech, kept under careful embargo and worked on to the last minute, was rushed ahead for Father Theodore Hesburgh, the Notre Dame president, to read before he would risk introducing the governor. Then the president played a characteristically careful game by welcoming Cuomo to the campus in the name of free exchange yet rushing a criticism of the speech out through a specially syndicated column given national release. Some conservatives on the Notre Dame campus grilled Cuomo at the press conference before his talk. He had arrived late, after a harrowing flight through storms in his small governor's airplane. (Jokes about divine disfavor were bounced about the cabin.) Orange juice jostled onto the one corrected copy of his speech made its pages stick as he delivered his talk, prying at the edges of the next page as he read the one just uncaked from its fellows. In moving from the press conference to the site of the speech, he was bumped by picketers, one of whom called him a murderer. It was a severe test of the combative man's equanimity.

Yet he was irenic in the tone of his address. He stood his ground; but he made no advance on the Kennedy position of 1960. He, too, admitted there are separate claims on his conscience. As a Catholic, he accepts "church doctrine" on abortion (i.e., that it is impermissible). Yet, as a public official, he accepts the political sense of the community, as articulated in the law. If the law allows abortion, and he is elected to uphold the law, he is not himself committing abortions—this preserves his conscience on the matter; but he is also not overriding the majority vote of the authorized legislators—not, that is, forcing his conscience on others, who do not have his reason for submission to his church. If he fills a double role, it is because the church itself distinguishes between its two "tracks."

Why was that position, satisfactory in 1960, felt to be inadequate in 1984?

Some objected that, for one who recognizes the evil of abortion, Cuomo was doing very little to persuade others of that view—as he would do, say, if slavery were the issue. He might, like Lincoln in 1860, have to administer a political entity with slavery legally in place; but he could speak out against slavery, express a hope to see its abolition, lobby and argue and maneuver toward that—none of which Cuomo was doing for the abolition of abortion.

But, more important, a vast change had occurred in Catholic attitudes towards authority, especially on sexual matters, since John Kennedy spoke in Houston. The Second Vatican Council redefined the church in public ways as a "people of God" rather than a government of prelates, and, at the same time, Pope John XXIII set up a commission of that people (clerical and lay) to reconsider the traditional position on birth control. When the commission reported *against* the old ban on artificial means of contraception, the persuasive track was clearly moving apart from the authoritative track, even within the church's own councils. The commission was made up of responsible Catholics, all raised under the old norms, all professing belief in the natural-law premises on which the old teaching was supposedly based. Paul VI, after he succeeded to the Papacy in 1963, expanded the commission, adding bishops and theologians (who should have made it a more predictable body). Yet a majority of the commission—three to one in the case of the bishops involved, four to one of the theologians—rejected the "natural law" argument against contraception.

It was at this point that Pope Paul VI, after much soul-searching, took a momentous step: He overruled the commission with his 1968 encyclical *Humanae Vitae,* saying this was a question to be settled "by Ourself" *(per Nosmetipsos).* It is important to see just why this action mattered so much. It was a resort to *sheer* church authority where persuasion had failed—and this in an area not of direct revelation but of natural reason. Contraception is never mentioned in Scripture. Church authorities had differed on the subject in the past. This was not a matter that belonged to "the deposit of faith" as preserved in ancient creeds or the purely theological conclusions of doctrine-shaping councils. Those matters—the nature of the Incarnation, the Trinity, saving grace, and so on—are intimately involved with the Christian revelation. By the logic of the church's two forms of address in American politics, those matters should be the principal concern of authoritative pronouncement, for Catholics to observe as part of their recognition of church authority. Matters of natural ethics are better suited to the "track" of open discourse with all people concerned about morality. For the pope to use church authority (though not infallible "defining" authority) to maintain church discipline on an ethical issue, while confessing that he could not *convince* Catholics, undermined the very powers invoked.

It is quite wrong to say the laity "rebelled" against a clerical ban on contraception contained in Pope Paul VI's encyclical *Humanae Vitae*. Fertility studies had shown widespread use of contraceptives by Catholics as early as the fifties, and in 1963, five years before the pope's encyclical, 50 percent of Catholics told pollsters that contraceptives were not immoral. Even in the Depression of the 1930s, Catholic birthrates had indicated a turn to contraceptives (though observant Catholics may still have been confessing that as a sin).

What changed in 1968 was not the observance of the ban but the attitude toward authority expressed in it: Priests and seminarians, no more convinced than other Catholics by the papal arguments, were forced to teach what they did not believe. They had to accept external compliance as a condition of ordination, maintaining a system of mutual pretense with their bishops—all to satisfy Roman edicts on seminary training and the discipline of the confessional.

This system bred a skepticism about church authority that manifests itself in ways going far beyond the issue of contraception itself. Some seminarians refused to dissemble as the price of being ordained. Others went through the motions in a way that destroyed respect for the process. The need for outer compliance is one of the many things that has destroyed morale in the priesthood, leading to unprecedented defections and low levels of recruiting. It also helped destroy the credibility of the nun's life as a submission to church discipline, draining away the teaching pool at Catholic schools. The sudden unpredicted falloff of Catholic regard for and use of the confessional was affected by the rules priests were supposed to impose and uphold there. Either they observed these rules or they refused to—in either case, the moral authority of this intimate tribunal was damaged.

The Papacy had tried to use doctrinal authority for an essentially ascetical purpose—the rhetoric of Roman prelates held that contraception was a yielding to modern hedonism and sensuality. This argument has great force for people whose celibate vocation calls for resistance to even normal sexual solicitings. It is out of place in married and secular life. The ban on contraception was part of a whole constellation of rulings that show clerical preoccupation with sexual matters—the maintenance of a celibate and all-male priesthood; the policing of reproductive processes (not only as regards contraception and abortion but in bans on sterilization and artificial insemination); the nonlegitimacy of any sexual pleasure not "open to" reproduction (not only masturbation, indulgence in pornography, fornication, and adultery, but even intercourse in marriage that is interrupted, blocked by contraception, or conducted after deliberate sterilization); and the censorship of explicitly depicted sex.

Most Catholics have concluded that their clerical leaders are unhinged on the subject of sex. Thus a stand taken to defy the world's permissiveness has backfired and *introduced* a whole new sexual ethic among Catholics. Until the

1960s, Catholics were measurably more ascetical in their sexual attitudes than other Americans. Since then, they have become more tolerant than the national average—accepting premarital sex, for instance, in twice the numbers reported for Protestants. This tolerance has undermined teachings that even liberal priests once thought unchangeable (e.g., the bans on divorce and homosexuality). And on abortion, Catholics are no longer very different from most of their fellow Americans, either in belief or practice. Cuomo was able to use this datum in his Notre Dame speech, noting that the bishops were calling for a law that would forbid abortion not only for those non-Catholics who find nothing wrong with it, but for Catholics as well. Where their own teaching has failed with their own people, they would resort to state coercion, just as they tried to use papal coercion to forbid contraception.

As Cuomo said in his Notre Dame speech:

> Despite the teaching in our homes and schools and pulpits, despite the sermons and pleadings of parents and priests and prelates, despite all the effort at defining our opposition to the sin of abortion, collectively we Catholics apparently believe—and perhaps act—little differently from those who don't share our commitment.
>
> Are we asking government to make criminal what we believe to be sinful because we ourselves can't stop committing the sin?

Yet Cuomo reasserted his sincere belief that abortion *is* sin. He still accepted "church doctrine" as his own personal discipline, even on a matter not directly revealed. He spoke of the *church's* teaching as if "the people of God" were not the church but only the teaching authorities *in* that church. He spoke like John Kennedy, though the contraception dispute had changed Catholic attitudes toward "church teaching" on sexual matters.

In fact, as a ploy against the bishops, he stressed the *similarity* of the ban on contraception and that on abortion, and reminded the bishops that they have given up their effort to change the law for everyone on the sale and use of contraceptives:

> On divorce and birth control, without changing its moral teaching, the Church [by which he means leaders of the church] abides by the civil law as it now stands, thereby accepting—without making much of a point of it—that in our pluralistic society we are not required to insist that all our religious values be the law of the land.

Cuomo was not challenging the "church doctrine" on contraception or divorce, just pointing out that the application of one's beliefs to political debate—what he called the job of prudentially "translating Catholic teachings into public policy"—varies according to circumstance.

Cuomo's position was bound to be unsatisfactory. By accepting a "church teaching" valid for him as a Catholic, he makes some wonder why he does not show enthusiasm for that teaching in public debate. He merely *receives* it passively in his own case—despite the fact that this particular teaching indicates that murder is being committed. (Abortion is like genocide to those who think human persons are being killed—not something one can witness *without* moral protest.)

On the other hand, for those who question the credibility of clerical decrees on ethics, Cuomo's docility is the frustrating aspect of his speech. Why should he accept "doctrine" in this case (or in that contraception, the parallel he invokes)? After all, popes have no special expertise for telling when life begins. *They* are not "applying" the Bible or some theological truth. If they have a good case to make, it must be one that convinces even Catholics in the *public* discourse that failed on contraception. If they have a better case on abortion, they must *make* it, and Cuomo should lend these arguments his eloquence. But he does not argue the matter; he merely accepts (privately) and sets aside (in public) the datum that a fetus is a human life from conception. This is very different from his eloquence and enthusiasm in opposing the death penalty, on which he has strong personal convictions.

What this means, of course, is that Cuomo claims to believe the church's teaching on abortion, but *acts* as if he does not. Pro-choice critics are infuriated by his belief; pro-life believers are just as indignant at his actions (or lack of them). Since most of the public is not simply classifiable as pro-life or pro-choice, this may be a shrewd political position; but it damages Cuomo in his claim to be a Catholic intellectual who reaches his conclusions from a well-trained conscience and not as a matter of political expediency.

If popes have no sure answer to the question When does life begin, neither does modern science. It depends on what one means by human life. Christian theologians have long said what *they* mean by that term—they mean the soul that is saved by Jesus' redemption; but that gets one no nearer an answer to the question of when that soul comes into existence. In fact, it was precisely because of St. Augustine's theology of the soul that he confessed repeatedly, in his period of episcopal teaching, that he did not know when or how the soul was joined to the body.

St. Augustine's theological concerns made him ask most urgently not when *life* begins but when *guilt* does. He was certain of two revealed truths: that the sacrifice of Jesus redeems the baptized soul, and that original sin made that redemption necessary. But when and how does the soul join the human race in its communal experience of historical guilt? If God creates each soul directly, can He be blamed for producing defective goods (the soul flawed by original sin)? If the soul is one with Adam, does that mean it descends from his soul as well as his body? But *how?* Aristotle said animal souls were carried in male semen, but in the Christian scheme, this would mean souls are somehow lost when semen does not impregnate. Did God create a kind of bank *(thesaurus)* of soul stuff, from which He could draw in supplying later bodies? If so, then the soul stuff in that treasure house must have sinned in solidarity with the two embodied human souls (Adam and Eve). Baffled by these difficulties, Augustine kept flirting with the suspect view of Origen that the individual soul had sinned before being consigned to the death-prone bodies derived from Adam. In agonies of ingenuity, Augustine even made up his own heretical-sounding hypothesis—that the soul of an unbaptized child might return to God while the body goes out of existence forever ("I have not heard of this opinion or read it elsewhere"). After listing the only four hypotheses he could support, Augustine was careful not to favor or exclude any of them (even one approximating Origen's) because

> I have not been able to discover in the accepted books of Scripture anything at all certain on the origin of the soul. . . . And when a thing obscure in itself defeats our capacity, and nothing else in Scripture comes to our help, it is not safe for humans to presume they can pronounce on it.

When St. Thomas Aquinas addressed the problem of the fetus's humanity, he followed Aristotle in thinking there are successive animations (ensoulments) of a fetus—a vital soul *(anima)* when the embryo grows like a plant in the woman's body (the umbilicus is the "root" planted in the woman's body), an animal soul when the fetus initiates its own moves, a rational soul when it reflects on what it does. Evidence of rationality occurs only after birth, so Aquinas was not sure when God infuses the immortal soul. But it is clearly not in the early stages of vital and animal ensoulment—that is why St. Thomas opposed the doctrine of the Virgin Mary's "immaculate conception." Her sinless soul would not have been infused at conception.

The evidence of church belief derivable from its baptismal practices shows a similar lack of certitude about when there is a soul to baptize. St. Thomas was against baptizing the fetus while it is still in the womb, where "it cannot be subject to the operation of the ministers of the church, or it is not known to men" (or, presumably, capable of knowing response). There was a wide variety of beliefs and practice on baptizing aborted fetuses, and baptism after birth was sometimes delayed to wait for clear signs of rationality.

Church authorities have more recently argued that the rational soul is infused at the moment of conception. They were influenced in part by the doctrine of the Immaculate Conception. This is the hodgepodge of considerations Mario Cuomo is bowing to when he accepts without question the "doctrine of the church" on abortion. He does not advance arguments of his own to repeat, enforce, or explain that doctrine. He simply deposits it in his own little *thesaurus* of faith, not to be expended outside his home.

There are elements in this theological history that are suggestive. St. Augustine thought of the beginning of life as the entry into the *social* nexus with history called original sin. You become an individual by becoming Adam's child, one of the people destined to inhabit the City of God or the Earthly City. St. Thomas's stress on the lack of interaction with other humans in the enwombed fetus points in the same direction. St. Augustine argued in *The Trinity* that persons exist only in interaction with other persons, even in the triune divinity. Modern theorists treat the human as coming to expression when it acquires a historically specific language system—including the gestures and body language Augustine observed in his baby son Adeodatus and described with such empathy in book one of the *Confessions.*

To say this is not to declare the fetus outside the human community. We humanize each other by our willingness to *include* others within that basic fellowship—the sick, the deformed, the retarded, the old. We have not become fully human unless we recognize their humanity. It is a mark of the humane to extend its own obligations—even to a kindness toward animals. The theologian Cuomo likes to cite, Teilhard de Chardin, thought that all of evolution was working toward a general "personalization" of the universe.

A stress on human community would contrast not only with the biological-mechanical approach that some Catholics think of as "natural law," but with the extreme pro-choice position that says a woman can do anything with the body she "owns." This view of private property as giving the owner laissez-faire rights is at odds with leftist positions on property as entailing social responsibility—as something held within a community, part of a nexus of mutual commitments.

William Buckley, in his early defenses of an absolutely private right in property, used to say that he could, with perfect morality, build a great palace on a mountaintop and blow it up. If it was his, he could do anything he wanted with it. That was Ronald Reagan's attitude toward the Panama Canal in the 1970s: "We bought it, we paid for it, it's ours." We can keep it, do what we want with it—blow it up, presumably, if that is how we mean to dispose of the thing we bought absolutely.

John Locke treated the self as a "first property" *(proprium),* but even he said it was given in trust by God—which means one cannot reject the gift unilaterally by suicide. When society condemns suicide, it says that even the right to one's body is not absolute. Disposal of that item affects others—parents, spouses, friends, children, the political community—for whom a person, so long as he or she remains responsible, must have regard. Even the apparently lone person must not be encouraged to give up hopes or claims on the community, as if his or her loss were to be considered of no wider concern. Among other things, this would foster a callousness of society toward its members.

Those who treat the fetus simply as property sometimes take a proprietary air toward the very *discussion* of abortion. They say only a woman can decide not only in the specific case of her own action but on the general values to be upheld. Logically, this should mean that only women who are or have been pregnant can form the moral discourse on this topic. In their own way, such feminists re-create the separate "woman's sphere" that Tocqueville described in nineteenth-century America. Both forms of this separatism are at odds with the citizen values of republicanism, wherein everyone in the community is invited to ponder together all moral issues. We do not say, in a republic, that only the military can decide on the role of the military in public life, that only the academy can frame educational issues, that only believers can frame religious issues, and so forth. Cuomo seems to be taking an enlightened stand when he apologizes, as a man, for speaking on abortion, but it is a nonrepublican position.

Yet, *because* the community has its claims, the fetus should have no more absolute a right to life than the woman has an absolute right to her "property." Pro-life champions who treat (and act for) the fetus as a full person, with all the rights of one, have their own form of possessive individualism: The putative baby's rights are equal to the mother's, sealed off within it, to be played off against the mother's—hardly a communal arrangement. This, if logically pursued, would mean the state must give full protection to the fetus, even against the mother, by sheltering it from damaging "aggressions" like maternal smoking, drinking, drug use, and poor health practices. It would mean mothers must be forced to deliver fetuses whose humanity they and their most trusted associates doubt or firmly deny. Anti-abortion activists take the enforcement of this right into their own hands when, in the name of the fetus, they mount assaults on the fetus's mother in her attempt to reach an abortion clinic.

If the pregnant woman has social responsibility, it is asymmetrical to give the fetus all of the formed person's human rights and no responsibilities. The woman is called on to be self-sacrificing in certain social circumstances—for example, to protect her family or country. The fetus, if given human rights, does not (cannot) balance those with responsibilities. The mother can deny herself for the fetus's sake. The fetus cannot reciprocate. If we could imagine for a moment, *per impossibile,* the fetus as having any moral claims against it as a responsible person, it would have to recognize that *its* right to itself is no more absolute than the mother's, that it would have to sacrifice itself for others, for the common good, for the country.

Trying to pit the rights of the fetus against those of its own mother and her helpers raises problems not only of enforceability—Cuomo says it would be like trying to enforce Prohibition—but of communal morality. Where there is disagreement on whether an object has entered the language-system of recognized mutual responsibilities, and that language-system of debate and exhortation is not so evil as to justify overthrow—as the slave system or the Nazi regime was—then attempts to coerce rather than persuade violate the humane concerns of the community. That is why pro-life comparisons of abortion to slavery or the Holocaust are misguided.

It is true that some religious extremists *do* think modern society is basically evil and corrupt—Godless in its government, pagan in its sensuality, morally unresponsive to divine signals. For them, overthrowing the communal arrangements is desirable, though few would use force. But their focus on abortion as merely one symptom of the pervasive evil should have no influence on those who, however uncertain themselves on the abortion issue, do not doubt the good faith of those debating it. It also shows bad faith for the religious extremists to try to use a corrupt government to suppress one practice. They are resorting to tactics meant to undermine the regime itself and not the single practice.

This is not an argument for the disposability of a human life. But, precisely because we do not know—any more than the pope does, or science, or St. Augustine—when the person begins, to treat the questionable human as having *more than* normal human immunities and exemptions is morally absurd. It is especially dubious to assume a full contractual partnership between the "individuum" in the womb and that part of the human community, the mother, that is its mode of passage into partnership with others.

If Cuomo were to take a communal approach to abortion, little in his practical recommendations would have to change (counseling, adoption, support of mothers and their babies, better social services after birth)—though some things would be different because "church doctrine" would not be deferred to: Better education on contraception would be a Cuomo cause, and wider distribution of free condoms. The real difference would be a consonance between his practice and his profession. That would free him to use argument and rhetoric with a passion and consistency that he has stored in the deposit box with that "church doctrine" he claims to be preserving.

There is nothing in the approach I have recommended that conflicts with Catholic faith, so far as I am aware. It may even be more consonant with Augustine's theology of the person—a theology that made it impossible for him to find a single demarcation point for the joining of the human community. It certainly does conflict with the discipline the pope and bishops would like to impose on the subject of abortion. But this is the same discipline they have tried to impose on the subject of contraception, and most Catholics, clerical and lay, now recognize that discipline as an elaborate sham. The church "line" on abortion is also obsolete. It is a useful fiction for the bishops. For Mario Cuomo, it is more like a political dodge. I know it is unrealistic to expect a Catholic politician to defy the bishops, but I am not considering the man's career, just his argument. Those who think, with Bruce Babbitt, that "Mario got it right" are probably too sanguine.

# A Priest Forever

### From: *An American Requiem*

### BY JAMES CARROLL

⊕

The war would be at the center of my life as a priest, even if I was always on the margin of the movement to end it. After ordination—it was 1969—I was assigned to the campus ministry at Boston University. At first, after all those years in the seminary, I was intimidated and mystified by the freedom and rampant joy—by Jansenist standards, true hedonism—of the students I encountered. BU was one of the capitals of the student antiwar movement. For a moment in history, *they* were the teachers. In fact, BU students gave form to instincts and impulses I already had myself. Being with them freed me.

The Catholic Student Center, also known as Newman House, became controversial. I permitted a group to open a health food restaurant in our basement, and when they asked me to suggest a name, I offered "Hedgeschool," for the Irish resistance. To my surprise, Hedgeschool became a left-wing organizing center. The sheep of my flock were not the timid Catholics, the puritans and patriots, I'd been sent there to serve. They were radicals, Jews, feminists, gays, SDS kids, draft dodgers, resisters, misfits, and wackos. Not sheep at all.

I became a draft counselor, helping kids avoid induction. With colleagues who were already in the Berrigan network, I became part of the underground—the self-styled East Coast Conspiracy to Save Lives—helping to get conscripts and deserters to Canada before FBI agents could find them. My brother Brian, operating out of the Philadelphia field office meanwhile, was on the fugitive squad, tracking draft dodgers.

The greatest fugitive of all, beginning in April 1970, when he disappeared rather than turn himself in to serve time for the Catonsville action, was Father

Daniel Berrigan, S.J. He played cat and mouse with the FBI, traveling incognito up and down the East Coast with the help of hundreds. J. Edgar Hoover was enraged as Berrigan, popping up at rallies and giving interviews, made fools of the Bureau. That I was moved by the Jesuit's courageous witness to deepen my involvement in antiwar activity was hardly unique. Thousands of us were recruited. "We are summoned to act in unison with our friends," he wrote, and I heard the words as addressed to me, "to join in conspiracy, in jeopardy, in illegal nonviolent actions, to hotten up the scene wherever we are."

We tried to hotten up the scene at BU. Several professors, including some Jewish professors who were less likely to draw FBI notice, were part of the underground network hiding Berrigan, and he often seemed close at hand. We held celebrations and rallies, always evoking his name and always hoping he would show up. We helped stage sit-ins to block military recruitment. On Good Friday we picketed the Brighton residence of Cardinal Humberto Medeiros, asking him to denounce the war. "Another Crucifixion in Indochina," read the sign I carried. As his priests and nuns, we asked to see His Eminence. When he admitted us, he said sadly how tormented he was about the war. But his torment, compared to that of the Vietnamese, seemed beside the point. I was not rebelling against authority. I was in search of it.

Daniel Berrigan became my authority. In relation to him I'd found a voice, and I used it against the war as forthrightly as I could, while he was underground and then when he was in prison. One day I received a phone call from a producer at *The Dick Cavett Show*. "Frankly," she said, "it's Father Berrigan we're interested in interviewing, but he's not available." She laughed, and I didn't. "We're told you could speak for him."

"Me? I don't even know Dan Berrigan."

"Look," the producer said impatiently, "Mr. Cavett is trying to get your guy's point of view on the air. They've approved you. Don't say no."

With a sinking feeling I though, Christ, they know about Dad. They want me because of Dad, the sensation it will cause. But then, exactly because I'd thought of him, I realized I had to do it. In the early afternoon of the day of my appearance on the Cavett show, the street outside the Catholic Student Center was blocked with demonstrators trying to keep a Marine recruiter from entering the nearby BU placement office. Invited, even goaded by the university president, John Silber, Boston police swooped onto campus and savagely attacked the students: "Ho, Ho, Ho Chi Minh my ass!" Cops invaded Newman House, threatening my secretary and shoving me aside to get at the fleeing kids. By midafternoon I was hoarse from screaming at police, taking badge numbers, stalking the sergeants and captains. "If you're with them, Father, fuck you!"

I was still trembling with anger and frustration by the time I arrived for the early evening taping at the ABC studios in New York. The producer greeted me and showed me to the green room, where Cavett's other guests were wait-ing. They were the comics Jack Klugman and Henny ("Take my wife—please") Youngman, the singer John Sebastian, and, looking very sexy, the actress Elizabeth Ashley, soon to appear on Broadway as Maggie in *Cat on a Hot Tin Roof.* When I entered the small soundproof room, no one looked at me. The other guests continued their hushed chatting with their handlers and agents. There was nothing to note in my appearance. I was wearing, as usual, black chi-nos, a black turtleneck, and a dark J. Press tweed sportcoat that I'd bought at an Episcopal church rummage sale.

I began to wonder where Dick Cavett was, and, sure enough, just before showtime the producer put her head in the room to say Dick was ill. My heart sank when she asked Jack Klugman if he would sit in as host. The goofy Klugman? What about Cavett's impulse to put in a word for Berrigan? What about the solemn agenda that had brought me here? Klugman hurried out.

More than an hour later, after all the other guests had done their self-pro-moting shticks, the producer came for me. I had just poured yet another cup of coffee. I carried it along, as if I were an old hand at this. When I stepped out into the backstage area, the unmuffled sound of the show's band jolted me, and just as the announcer was speaking my name—"Father James Carroll, an anti-war priest"—I spilled the coffee all over the crotch of my pants. Numbness gave way to a feeling of nausea, and even as I heard the dutiful applause of the studio audience, I frantically wiped at my pants. Only at the last second did I determine that the coffee stain was invisible. Thank God for black.

John Sebastian and Henny Youngman greeted me warmly, as if we hadn't ignored one another in the green room. Then Elizabeth Ashley kissed me full on the lips, a wet kiss that drew hoots from the audience. Take that, Father. I was to be their straight man. Very straight.

When I'd taken my place on the couch, nearest Klugman, who was at Cavett's desk, the comic's opening line to me, aimed at my turtleneck, was, "Where's your dog collar?" The audience gasped pleasurably at the gibe, then waited for my reply. Oh, this could be fun.

"I'm sorry?" I stalled, trying to think of something to say.

"Your dog collar, Father. You know, woof-woof." *Ba-boom* went the drum-mer. More laughter. Get with it, Jimmy.

I stared at him. The audience grew silent. The hapless Klugman was a Boston cop, his nightstick at my throat. I said, "Is it priests in general you want to insult, or only me?"

Klugman made a hammy face at the audience, but the scattered applause was for me.

I smiled as broadly as I could, still aware of my wet pants. I reached across to put a friendly hand on Klugman's arm. "We aren't dogs anymore, Jack. But we still bite." More applause, an advantage to be pressed. "Now can we talk for a minute about something serious?"

"Oh, now, Father, if we—"

I cut him off. "That's why I came here. I want to tell these folks about a police riot I just left. Not three hours ago, I was roughed up by cops myself."

The clean statement, the start of a narrative that had to be completed, stopped him. He glanced at the audience, saw their interest, and so sat back and let me talk. Which I then did. Beginning with a description of the clash at BU, including a swipe at Silber's outrageous encouragement of police brutality, and moving on to state my appreciation and concern for Daniel Berrigan, I spoke uninterruped for what seemed like a long time. I called on everyone present and everyone watching to do what they could to oppose the war. Then I stopped.

There was a moment of awkward silence. Klugman was nonplused. He looked toward Henny Youngman, who for once had nothing to say. Then some members of the audience began to applaud. The floor manager waved at Klugman from behind the camera. He stammered, "I guess we'll take a break." During the commercial, no one on the set spoke to me. Klugman huddled with the producer. After the break, in an unheard-of-departure, the band played an entire number and the show ended.

I learned from my mother the next day that my parents had not seen the show, but that she had heard about it from friends. "What did you hear?" I asked.

"That your hair is too long, and you wore sandals."

"My hair is fine," I said. "What did Dad say?"

"I didn't tell him, and I'm not going to. He doesn't need to know that you've deliberately embarrassed him."

"Embarrassing Dad had nothing to do with it."

"Don't be ridiculous. They only asked you onto their program because of him."

"That's not true, Mom." To my horror, I heard the whine in my voice. How I'd feared at first that it *was* true. "They didn't even know about Dad. He never came up."

"Then why did they ask you?"

My question too. "I don't know, Mom. I've been writing things. I've given speeches."

"Come on, Jim. You really think a national TV show asked you because of *you?*"

"I guess I do, Mom."

She said nothing for a long time, then broke the silence with her sternest voice. "Just don't you embarrass your father. And don't embarrass Brian."

"Wait a minute, Mom. Wait a minute. What if they're embarrassing me?"
There was no answer. I heard the click when she hung up.


Later that year, "Philip Berrigan and seven others," as the press always
referred to them, were charged with plotting to blow up steam pipes under the
Pentagon and to kidnap Henry Kissinger, the architect of Nixon's air-war esca-
lations. Phil was in prison in Lewisburg, Pennsylvania. He had trusted another
inmate, who had study-release privileges, to smuggle letters to and from Sister
Elizabeth McAlister, a radical nun at New York's Marymount College, where
I'd met her. The inmate was an FBI plant. In fact, the McAlister letters did contain reports of conversations about antiwar strategies, including a proposed
"Citizens Arrest" of Henry Kissinger. The letters also provided the FBI with
the crucial clue to Dan Berrigan's hiding place on Block Island, where he was
finally arrested. The FBI vendetta against the Berrigans continued with indictments and the trial of the so-called Harrisburg 8.

The by now broad Berrigan network, which was centered on but not limited to Catholics, used the trial as another mobilizing event. I helped organize
support. At one point my campus ministry colleague, a former nun named
Anne Walsh, was subpoenaed to testify about Phil's activities, which she
refused to do. She was charged with contempt of court, and I traveled to
Harrisburg to testify as a character witness for her. I wore the Roman collar
when I took the stand.

At an outdoor rally in Harrisburg one night, I gave a speech and read my
poems. It may have seemed to others that I was successfully reinventing myself
on the model of Daniel Berrigan, a priest-poet at last. But the truth was,
inwardly I was terribly frightened all the time. That night, after my appearance,
while I stood on the edge of the crowd listening to another speaker, a derelict
approached me. Repelled by his stink, I sidled away, but he followed. His
shabby beard and matted hair and soiled clothing made him seem half mad. I
moved again, but he stayed with me, drawing close enough to whisper, "If you
don't tell your friends about me, I won't tell mine about you." He flashed a shit-
eating grin. Brian. Before I could answer, my FBI-agent brother melted back
into the crowd.

Jesus told his disciples, "You will have trouble," and when I did, I tried to
take it as a mark of the faith to which I was clinging. I was raised to be obedient, polite, and good. Yet I had become someone I did not recognize—defiant, angry, and irreverent. There were good reasons for the changes, of course,
but I did not like myself that way. I got in trouble with John Silber for
denouncing him on the Cavett show. I got in trouble with the cardinal when
parents complained that I was advising their sexually active college-age chil-

dren to use birth control. The cardinal heard rumors that I was concelebrating a weekly midnight Eucharist with an Episcopal priest, that we'd merged our congregations. It was true. The cardinal received objections about sit-ins organized at Newman House. Ultimately, he heard hysterical reports that my colleague—a nun! a woman!—had said the Mass in my absence. It was true, all true.

Once I even got in trouble with my new allies, the peace movement heavies who had shielded Dan Berrigan and were now shielding each other. They had heard reports that I had an FBI agent for a brother, and they labeled me as one not to be trusted. I was an informant, a provocateur. When I learned of this, I confronted the man most responsible—a "friend"—and demonstrated that there was no secret about my brother, or my father for that matter. I had written of both in poems and articles. I had wrecked myself at home, yet now I was accused of having maintained that first loyalty. I felt betrayed and angry beyond anything that man could understand. The rumors about me stopped.

But maybe FBI agents themselves had heard the rumors, because one day a pair made a visit to my office. I could have told them all we had in common, but I said nothing. Then I realized: they knew. They asked me about certain fugitives, a couple of whom I had known. I said nothing. Finally, exasperated by my refusal to answer their questions, one of the agents, a Jesuit-trained Irish Catholic who had no category for priest and nun resisters, blurted the question, "What kind of creatures are they, Father?"

"We're human beings," I answered.

To my knowledge, my father never learned of my Air Force arrest. It took place, Oedipally enough, at a protest at the main gate of Hanscom Air Force Base, outside Boston. Hanscom, a high-tech research center associated with MIT, was the development site of a program code-named Igloo White. It was a system of tiny electronic sensors that, when salted onto the fields and paddies of Vietnam, would pick up any movement and trigger air strikes by B-52s. Igloo White was an integral part of the Nixon-Kissinger escalation of the air war. The bombers would come when the triggering movement was of an infiltrating North Vietnamese soldier—or of a water buffalo or a rice-harvesting peasant. As a weapon that did not distinguish between combatant and civilian, Igloo White seemed the perfect emblem of the war's evil. I had no qualm about joining in the pointed protest against it. I remember the faces of the air policemen standing by as local police picked me up from the road after I, like my twenty or thirty comrades, went limp and refused to move. The APs were acne-ridden kids like those who'd saluted me as I drove my old man's car through the gate at Bolling. At the bus to which I was carried, and onto which

I still refused to climb, a man in civilian clothes leaned over me, clipboard in hand. He warned me that if I did not cooperate, I could get hurt.

"You're with the OSI, right?" I said.

He was shocked that I knew of it.

I told him that my father was its first director. He stared hard at me, then said, "Your name is Carroll."

I nodded. Oddly, I felt a rush of pride that a decade and a half after my father had left OSI, the agent knew his name. And at last I didn't care if he told on me.

On March 8, 1971, something completely unexpected occurred—an event that drew even tighter the web in which Brian and I had become entangled. Unnamed members of the Catholic left, retaliating for FBI harassment, broke into the FBI resident agency in Media, Pennsylvania. They called themselves the Citizens' Commission to Investigate the FBI, and set about at once to publish the various documents they stole from the office. Never before had FBI files been revealed without authorization. The image of a rogue agency manipulating, infiltrating, and interfering not only with militant groups but with mainstream, even innocuous organizations like the phone company and the Boy Scouts was given substance by memos and reports that described such tactics in detail. For the first time in its history, the FBI was made to seem to the public at large simultaneously sinister and ridiculous.

I was part of the Boston effort to exploit the Media sources. I helped organize a "citizens' tribunal" that indicted J. Edgar Hoover himself. We convened in Boston's Faneuil Hall, and various activists, drawing on Media documents and other sources, "testified" to FBI abuses. Behind these "witnesses" were massive oil paintings and busts displaying the heroes of the Revolution. Faneuil Hall, famous as America's "Cradle of Liberty," was built by a merchant whose stock-in-trade was human beings, the slave trader Peter Faneuil.

Among the witnesses testifying that day was a Pentagon official, one of McNamara's whiz kids, whose insider description of the illegal conduct of the war was particularly riveting. This was his first public act of dissent, and I remember feeling sorry for him, he seemed so nervous. Like everyone, I was edified by his willingness to risk his career by joining us. His name meant nothing, although by June, only weeks later, everyone in America would know him, Daniel Ellsberg, as the person who leaked the Pentagon Papers. At the tribunal's conclusion, a dozen of us trekked over to the JFK Building, across Government Center, to the FBI field office on an upper floor, to deliver our verdict on J. Edgar Hoover. Guilty!

Sometime later, after Hoover died, Brian gave me a T-shirt bearing Hoover's picture above the words "J. Edgar Hoover is coming back, and is he pissed!" He was sure pissed that month. He suspended the head of the Media office without pay and launched a nationwide manhunt with his best agents to find those responsible for what in Bureau argot was immediately dubbed MED-BURG. A few Catholic pacifists had done what no gangster (not Roger Touhy) and no KGB operative (not Colonel Abel) had ever done before, and, by God, the director wanted them!

My father, meanwhile, was the chairman of a gala Washington dinner at which an association of former FBI agents was to honor Hoover. I received a phone call from Dad, the first I'd had directly from him since before I was ordained. He stunned me by asking if I would come to Washington and attend the dinner, so that I could offer the benediction. "Everyone knows my son is a priest," he said. "The director himself mentioned it."

"I thought I'd embarrassed you, Dad."

"Your mother tells me I shouldn't be asking you to do this. But it would mean a lot to me. It would mean a lot to Mr. Hoover. They still think of you as a former employee."

It was so easy to imagine what my friends would say: Do it. Turn it into an action. Throw blood on the table in front of him. Denounce Hoover to his face!

I heard the plaintive not in my father's voice. He was asking for far more than a few pious words from me at the beginning of a meal. He was trying to redeem my entire priesthood, to wrench it back within the sacred margins. He was also trying to redeem our relationship. If I did this, everything would be good between us again. How could I possibly explain that if I dutifully said yes, there was no way I could follow through with it, standing before a ballroom full of FBI men in black tie, blessing them, affirming what they believed, praying for what they did. And as for Hoover, he was as close to a personal enemy as I had. I would never throw blood, but if I went to the banquet, it could only be to denounce him.

Which I would never do to you, Dad, I wanted to say, and, This refusal is my act of love. Instead, I said only, "I can't, Dad."

He did not press. He hung up, and it was clear to me that he would not ask for anything from me again. I told no one in the movement of the chance I'd passed up. I was a traitor after all.

# Prayer for the Dead

### From: *Dead Man Walking*

#### BY HELEN PREJEAN

Lloyd LeBlanc, the father of young, murdered David. With him, I end this narrative.

In the years immediately after Pat Sonnier's Pardon Board hearing, my encounters with Lloyd were friendly but tentative. We talked on the telephone, wrote notes. I paid a few visits. My first visits to his home in St. Martinville had been especially difficult for Eula, Lloyd's wife. The thought of someone coming into her house who had befriended her son's murderers was at first too much for her. When I would come, she would leave the house. It's better now.

One day two years ago in a telephone conversation, Lloyd said that he goes to pray every Friday from 4:00 to 5:00 A.M. in a small "perpetual adoration" chapel in St. Martinville, and I asked if I might join him. He said he would like that very much. I know I want to do this, even if it's four o'clock in the morning. Words of Rainer Maria Rilke come:

> *Work of the eyes is done, now*
> *go and do heart-work.*

I drive into Baton Rouge the night before to shorten the distance of the drive, and Louie comes to sleep over at Mama's house so we can save time in the morning. Good brother that he is, he says I should not make the trip alone. We have figured that if we leave Baton Rouge at 2:45 we can reach St. Martinville by 4:00. Louie fills the thermos with coffee.

Riding in the dark across Acadian Louisiana reminds me of when I was eight years old and I would get up with Mama during Lent to go to early-morning Mass. I remember the still, cold air, the feeling of mystery that is always there in the dark when you are awake and the rest of the world is asleep.

In his note Lloyd has told me how he prays for "everyone, especially the poor and suffering." He prays for "the repose of the soul" of David and for his wife, Eula. He prays in thanksgiving for his daughter, Vickie, and her four healthy children. It is the grandchildren—little Ryan, Derek, Megan, and Jacob—who have brought Eula back to life—but it has taken a long, long time. For a year after David's murder, Lloyd had frequently taken her to visit David's grave. Unless he took her there, he once told me, "she couldn't carry on, she couldn't pick up the day, she couldn't live." For three years his wife had cried, and he said the house was like a tomb and he found himself working long hours out of the house "to keep my sanity."

Once, during one of my visits, he took me to his office—he is a construction worker—and showed me the grandfather clock he was making after his day's work was done. "It's good to keep busy," he says.

Lloyd LeBlanc prays for Loretta Bourque and her family. The Bourques had been more anxious than he to witness the execution of Patrick Sonnier. The day before the Pardon Board was to hear Pat's appeal, members of the Bourque family had visited Lloyd to urge him to attend the hearing and press for the death sentence. A few months earlier, trying to evade witnessing the execution, Lloyd had asked his brother to take his place, but the brother had a heart attack and couldn't.

There, at the Pardon Board hearing, Lloyd LeBlanc had done what was asked of him. Speaking for both families, he asked that the law of execution be carried out. But after the execution he was troubled and sought out his parish priest and went to confession.

Now, Lloyd LeBlanc prays for the Sonniers—for Pat and for Eddie and for Gladys, their mother. "What grief for this mother's heart," he once said to me in a letter. Yes, for the Sonniers, too, he prays. He knows I visit Eddie, and in his letters he sometimes includes a ten-dollar bill with the note: "For your prison ministry to God's children." And shortly before Gladys Sonnier's death in January 1991, Lloyd LeBlanc went to see her to comfort her.

Louie and I drive Interstate 10 West, then turn off at Breaux Bridge for the last twenty miles. We go through Parks, the last place David and Loretta were seen alive, and drive into the parking lot of the very old wooden church of St. Martin of Tours. Light shines in a steady slant from the tall stained-glass window of the chapel. Red, green, and yellow speckle the grass. All around is darkness. Nearby, large hundred-year-old oak trees spread their branches.

I tap the door of the chapel and a young woman with long dark hair lets us in with a quiet smile. She has a blanket around her. Her hour of vigil has been from three to four o'clock. We find out that she has eight children. Her husband preceded her in prayer earlier in the night. Louie and I are glad to get out of the cold. The fall weather is setting in.

Inside the chapel I see a sign hand-printed in black letters on white paper, a quotation from the Gospel of John: "Because you have seen me, you believe. Blessed are those who do not see and yet believe." The round wafer of bread consecrated at Mass is elevated in a gold vessel with clear glass at the center so the host can be seen. Gold rays, emanating outward, draw the eye to the center. Two pews along the back wall. Two kneelers, four red sanctuary candles on the floor. On the wall a crucifix and a picture of Mary, the mother of Jesus.

At five minutes to four Lloyd drives up. "You made it," he says, "I'm glad you're safe, you know those highways," and I introduce him to Louie. The chapel is warm and close and filled with silence and the smell of beeswax. Lloyd and I kneel on the prie-dieux. He takes his rosary out of his pocket. Louie, in the pew behind us, already has his rosary in his hands.

We "tell" the beads, as the old French people used to say. *One at a time— Hail Mary, Holy Mary, Hail Mary, the mysteries of Christ and our own, life and joy, suffering and death—we round the beads one by one, a circle and round we go, dying and behold we live, the soul stretched taut, the soul which says: No more, I can take no more. Hail Mary, Holy Mary, breathed in and breathed out, linking what eyes cannot see but what the heart knows and doubts and knows again.*

Holding a rosary is a physical, tangible act—you touch and hold the small, smooth beads awhile and then let go. "Do not cling to me," Jesus had said to Mary Magdalene. The great secret: *To hold on, let go. Nothing is solid. Everything moves. Except love—hold on to love. Do what love requires.*

We pray the sorrowful mysteries. Jesus agonizing before he is led to execution. Jesus afraid. Jesus sweating blood. Were there beads of sweat on David's brow when he realized the mortal danger? Was it when the kidnappers turned the car down a road that he knew ended in a cane field? Was it when he was told to lie face down on the ground? His mother had bought him a new blue velour shirt that he was wearing that night. Standing by the kitchen sink, he wrapped his arms around himself and patted the new shirt and said, "Mama, this is going to keep me warm at the game tonight."

And Loretta . . . her last evening of life at a football game . . . She had seen friends there, laughed and talked and cheered her team, safe in the globe of stadium light, unaware of the dark road soon to be hers.

Lloyd LeBlanc has told me that he would have been content with imprisonment for Patrick Sonnier. He went to the execution, he says, not for revenge, but hoping for an apology. Patrick Sonnier had not disappointed him. Before sitting in the electric chair he had said, "Mr. LeBlanc, I want to ask your forgiveness for what me and Eddie done," and Lloyd LeBlanc had nodded his head, signaling a forgiveness he had already given. He says that when he arrived with sheriff's deputies there in the cane field to identify his son, he had knelt by his boy—"laying down there with his two little eyes sticking out like bullets"—and prayed the Our Father. And when he came to the words: "Forgive us our trespasses as we forgive those who trespass against us," he had not halted or equivocated, and he said, "Whoever did this, I forgive them." But he acknowledges that it's a struggle to overcome the feelings of bitterness and revenge that well up, especially as he remembers David's birthday year by year and loses him all over again: David at twenty, David at twenty-five, David getting married, David standing at the back door with his little ones clustered around his knees, grown-up David, a man like himself, whom he will never know. Forgiveness is never going to be easy. Each day it must be prayed for and struggled for and won.

## Postscript

Since the publication of this book in 1993 the states of Kansas (1994) and New York (1995) have reinstated the death penalty and Congress has enacted the Violent Crime Control and Law Enforcement Act (1994), which expands federal crimes punishable by death to about 60 offenses.

# PART II

# WiTNESS

## AND

# DISSENT

*American, Catholic, and Intellectual*

✛

# Introduction

W hether in the university or in public discourse, in the arts and in the realm of politics, Catholics have taken an active role in postwar American intellectual life. Catholic writers—faithful and lapsed, conservative or liberal, clerical and lay—have expressed themselves in a culture that has often been hostile to their faith tradition, which creates a natural tension against which they work to persuade their audiences. They employ rhetoric, religion, literary prose, sociological statistics, and faith to make an argument or describe a state of being. Sometimes their Catholicism is a polemical weapon, at other times a point of retreat and comfort.

The Rev. John Courtenay Murray, a philosopher and respected professor at the Woodstock, Maryland, Jesuit seminary, became famous in the 1950s and '60s for his efforts to reconcile Roman Catholic theology and American democracy. In contrast, some members of the American hierarchy, such as Francis Cardinal Spellman of New York, staunchly discouraged any debate on any issues of doctrine or conformity with Rome. Before the Vietnam era, intellectuals caused mere ripples on the otherwise placid surface of American Catholicism; their writings were received and appreciated by a relatively small number of people, with the exception perhaps of Fulton J. Sheen, who became a popular television evangelizer and vivid presence on the public scene.

After the Hollywood images of Crosby, Tracy, O'Brien, and Fitzgerald, the authentic image of "the Catholic priest" via the media was undoubtedly Archbishop Sheen who (with his invisible angel assistants) was every bit as much of a pioneer of early television as Milton Berle and Howdy Doody. Sheen's "sermons" for the public showed his mastery at explaining to lay Catholics and other viewers the mysteries of the faith, including as in this excerpt a reconciliation that was available between modern psychology and the Catholic faith.

Although it is not my intention to install President John F. Kennedy among the pantheon of postwar Catholic intellectuals, he is remembered for his eloquence, his quick wit, his Pulitzer prize for the book *Profiles in Courage,* and, among other speeches, his remarks to the Greater Houston Ministerial

Association on September 12, 1960, as the presidential campaign was gaining momentum and galvanizing the voting public. He was, no doubt, a clever practitioner of conventional politics, and a very smart man. And that crucial moment, as he spoke on the subject of the Catholic religion and the American presidency, will long be remembered when we debate the principle of separation of church and state.

Kennedy took pains to affirm that, despite accusations and the belief of some, he had never sworn allegiance to the Pope, he could not be excommunicated for any presidential act contrary to Church teaching, and he was acutely cognizant of the issue and would always err on the side of secular, constitutional concerns if—unlikely as it was—the issue should ever arise in a substantial way. He told the ministers the following:

> I am not the Catholic candidate for president, I am the Democratic party's candidate for president who happens to also be a Catholic. I do not speak for my Church on public matters, and the Church does not speak for me.
>
> . . . If my Church attempted to influence me in a way that was improper or which affected adversely my responsibility as a public servant, sworn to uphold the Constitution, then I would reply to them that this was an improper action on their part, that it was one to which I could not subscribe, that I was opposed to it and that it would be an unfortunate breach, and interference with the American political system. I am confident there would be no such interference.

Questions from the ministers followed the candidate's remarks. One asked whether the Vatican might be asked to issue a statement to authorize Kennedy's position as that of all American Catholics. Another asked directly whether the candidate had the Vatican's approval for what he had said in his speech. Doctrinal issue were broached, including the tradition of Roman Catholic clergy in the United States "instructing" their faithful on political issues. Kennedy skillfully deflected the Protestant ministers' concerns and stated that in the spirit of the American tradition of religious freedom he welcomed their questions as "reasonable."

He stated, in conclusion: "My only objection would be if somebody said, 'Regardless of how much evidence he's given . . . I still wouldn't vote for him because he's a member of that Church.' Kennedy won the general election by a razor-thin margin that has been challenged by some historians, and he became the first Roman Catholic President of the United States.

Even with a Catholic in the White House, and later with the memory of his martyrdom, intellectuals—both conservative and liberal—found themselves swimming against the mainstream culture. This is true at least partly because they were engaging in an internal family squabble about freedom of thought and expression; in the general, predominantly non-Catholic culture, these debates were arcane and precious at best (for those who paid any attention). Some personalities, however, burst into public awareness.

William F. Buckley Jr., the patrician-in-boxing-gloves who spans the entire period covered in this anthology, spearheaded the ultraconservative movement in secular politics with his devastatingly sharp arguments, and he "grew up" in the warmest of anti-Communist hothouses in the late forties and early fifties. He was not afraid to engage in partisan politics as a candidate himself for public office. He lost. (His brother James won a single term as a Republican-Conservative U.S. senator from New York.)

Father Andrew M. Greeley, a sociologist by trade, emerged as a prolific, polemical author, essayist, and teacher, and a bestselling writer of fiction with a distinctly liberal bent. He foresaw the disenchantment that would blanket American Catholics even after the reforms of the Second Vatican Council. He wrote about the crisis in vocations—the dwindling population of priests and religious that has drained the Church of leadership. Meanwhile, he penned a number of popular novels, including *The Cardinal Sins,* which told the story of a corrupt archbishop of a major U.S. city—and which was modeled on the controversial career of Chicago's John Cardinal Cody.

The spirit of triumphalism and the establishment of a vibrant Catholic culture in America, as vividly described by Charles R. Morris in his landmark 1997 study *American Catholic,* only highlighted the chasm between conservative intellectuals (clergy *and* laymen) and liberals (again clerical and lay). As Catholic immigrant and ethnic groups solidified their participation in the secular, materialist American Dream—through service in the military, hard work in business, focus on parochial education and parish life, cultural achievements, and deep-seated faith—there was a private rather than public accounting of difference with other Americans from other faith traditions. At the same time, cultural differences within the Catholic population became more pronounced. Among communities of Irish, Italian, Polish, and Hispanic descent, to name some of the major groups (see Part III of this anthology), there was little common ground but for their Catholicism and their American citizenship.

Furthermore, the traditions of secrecy, hierarchy, and authority within the Roman Catholic Church have met with resistance from within its own ranks in the United States. In the past fifty years Catholic universities have become more and more secular; regular attendance at church has waned despite a boon in the total Catholic population. It is evident that not all of the crucibles that a Catholic must face in today's society are matters of faith. Witness the trials faced by Joseph Cardinal Bernardin of Chicago; it was his faith, bolstered by his intellect and his powers of communication, however, that gave him the strength to endure false accusations of sexual misconduct and later, terminal cancer.

The actual concept of American Catholicism and perhaps more important how American Catholics see themselves will be the subjects of debate well into the next century, as will the explosion of non-mutually exclusive traits—ethnic background, religious practice, languages, theological shades of difference— that make up the amalgam of today's Church community in America.

Intellectuals of every stripe must, as always, make their own way in the world, and must work as hard as ever to educate and to persuade, now and in the future.

# The Philosophy of Anxiety

From: *Peace of Soul*

BY FULTON J. SHEEN

One of the favorite psychological descriptions of modern man is to say that he has an anxiety complex. Psychology is more right than it suspects, but for a more profound reason than it knows. There is no doubt that anxiety has been increased and complicated by our metropolitan and industrialized civilization. An increasing number of persons are afflicted with neuroses, complexes, fears, irritabilities, and ulcers; they are, perhaps, not so much "run down" as "wound up"; not so much set on fire by the sparks of daily life as they are burning up from internal combustion. Few of them have the felicity of the good Negro woman who said, "When I works, I works hard; when I sits, I sits loose; and when I thinks, I goes to sleep."

But modern anxiety is different from the anxiety of previous and more normal ages in two ways. In other days men were anxious about their souls, but modern anxiety is principally concerned with the body; the major worries of today are economic security, health, the complexion, wealth, social prestige, and sex. To read modern advertisements, one would think that the greatest calamity that could befall a human being would be to have dishpan hands or a cough in the T-zone. This overemphasis on corporal security is not healthy; it has begotten a generation that is much more concerned about having life belts to wear on a sea journey than about the cabin it will occupy and enjoy. The second characteristic of modern anxiety is that it is not a fear of objective, natural dangers, such as lightning, beasts, famine; it is subjective, a vague fear of what one believes would be dangerous if it happened. That is why it is so difficult to deal with people who have today's types of anxieties; it does no good to tell them that there is no outside danger, because the danger that they fear is inside of them and therefore is abnormally real to them. Their condition is aggravated by a sense of helplessness to do anything about the danger. They constantly sense a disproportion between their own forces and those marshaled by what they believe to be the enemy. These people become like fish caught in nets and birds trapped in a snare, increasing their own entanglements and anxieties by the fierceness of their disorderly exertions to overcome them.

Modern psychologists have done an admirable service in studying anxieties, revealing a phase of human nature which has been to some extent closed to us.[1] But the cause of anxiety is deeper than the psychological. Anxiety may take on new forms in our disordered civilization, but anxiety itself has always been rooted in the nature of man. There has never been an age, there has never been a human being in the history of the world without an anxiety complex; in other times, it was studied on *all* the levels of life. The Old Testament, for example, has one book which is concerned solely with the problem of anxiety—the Book of Job. The Sermon on the Mount is a warning against the wrong kind of anxieties. St. Augustine's writings center around what he called the restless soul. Pascal wrote about human misery. A modern philosopher, Kierkegaard, bases his philosophy on dread, or *Angst,* and Heidegger has told us *Dasein ist Sorge,* "Self-existence is worry."

It is important to inquire into the basic reason and ground of anxiety, according to man's present historical condition, of which the psychological is only one superficial manifestation. The philosophy of anxiety looks to the fact that man is a fallen being composed of body and soul. Standing midway between the animal and the angel, living in a finite world and aspiring toward the infinite, moving in time and seeking the eternal, he is pulled at one moment toward the pleasures of the body and at another moment to the joys of the spirit. He is in a constant state of suspension between matter and spirit and may be likened to a mountain climber who aspires to the great peak above and yet, looking back from his present position, fears falling to the abyss below. This state of indeterminancy and tension between what he ought to be and what he actually is, this pull between his capacity for enjoyment and its tawdry realization, this consciousness of distance between his yearning for abiding love without satiety and his particular loves with their intermittent sense of "fed-up-ness," this wavering between sacrificing lesser values to attain higher ideals or else abdicating the higher ideals entirely, this pull of the old Adam and the beautiful attraction of the new Adam, this necessity of choice which offers him two roads, one leading to God and the other away from Him—all this makes man anxious about his destiny beyond the stars and fearful of his fall to the depths beneath.

In every human being, there is a double law of gravitation, one pulling him to the earth, where he has his time of trial, and the other pulling him to God, where he has his happiness. The anxiety underlying all modern man's anxieties arises from his trying to be himself without God or from his trying to get beyond himself without God. The example of the mountain climber is not exact, for such a man has no helper on the upper peak to which he aspires. Man, however, has a helper—God on the upper peak of eternity reaches out His Omnipotent Hand to lift him up, even before man raises his voice in plea. It is evident that, even though we escaped all the anxieties of modern economic life, even though we avoided all the tensions which psychology finds in the unconsciousness and consciousness, we should still have that great basic fundamental anxiety born of our creatureliness. Anxiety stems fundamentally from irregulated desires, from the creature wanting something that is unnecessary for him or contrary to his nature or positively harmful to his soul. Anxiety increases in direct ratio and proportion as man departs from God. Every man in the world has an anxiety complex because he has the capacity to be either saint or sinner.

Let it be not believed that man has an anxiety complex "because he still has traces of his animal origin"; indeed, animals left to themselves never have anxieties. They have natural fears, which are good, but they have no subjective anxieties. Birds do not develop a psychosis about whether they should take a winter trip to California or Florida. An animal never becomes less than it is; but a man can do just that, because a man is a composite of both spirit and matter.

When we see a monkey acting foolishly, we do not say to the monkey, "Do not act like a nut"; but when we see a man acting foolishly, we do say, "Do not act like a monkey." Because a man is spirit, as well as matter, he can descend to the level of beasts (though not so completely as to destroy the image of God in his soul). It is this possibility that makes the pec liar tragedy of man. Cows have no psychoses, and pigs have no ne roses, and chickens are not frustrated (unless these frustrations are artificially produced by man); neither would man be frustrated or have an anxiety complex if he were an animal made *only for this world*. It takes eternity to make a man despair. "Man is both strong and weak, both free and bound, both blind and farseeing. He stands at the juncture of nature and spirit; and is involved in both freedom and necessity. It is always partly an effort to obscure his blindness by overestimating the degree of his sight and to obscure his insecurity by stretching his power beyond its limits."[2]

Dread arises because man becomes aware, however dimly, of his contingency and finiteness. He is not the absolute, though he wants it; he is not even all that he is or all that he could be. This tension between possibility and fact, this oscillation between wanting to be with God and wanting to be God is a deeper side of his anxiety. Alfred Adler has always emphasized that back of neuroses is the striving of man to become like God, a striving as impotent as the goal is impossible. The root of every psychological tension is basically metaphysical.

Despair and anxiety are possible because there is a rational soul. They presuppose the capacity of self-reflection. Only a being capable of contemplating itself can dread annihilation in face of the infinite, can despair either of itself or of its destiny. Despair, Kierkegaard tells us, is two-fold. It is a desperate desire either to be oneself or to be not oneself; man wants either to make himself into an absolute, unconditioned being, independent, self-subsistent; or else he wants desperately to get rid of his being, with its limitations, its contingency, and its finiteness. Both these attitudes manifest the eternal revolt of the finite against the infinite: *Non serviam.* By such a revolt, man exposes himself to the awareness of his nothingness and his solitude. Instead of finding a support in the knowledge that he, though contingent, is held in existence by a loving God, he now seeks reliance within himself and, necessarily failing to find it, becomes the victim of dread. For dread is related to an unknown, overwhelming, all-powerful something—which may strike one knows not when or where. Dread is everywhere and nowhere, all around us, terrible and indefinite, threatening man with an annihilation which he cannot imagine or even conceive. Such fear is man's alone. Because an animal has no soul capable of knowing perfect love, because it has to render no account of its stewardship beyond the corridors of the grave, because it is not like a pendulum swinging between eternity and time, it is devoid of those eternal relationships which man possesses; therefore it can have only a sick body, never a sick soul. Thus a psychology which denies the human soul is constantly contradicting itself. It calls man an animal and then proceeds to describe a human anxiety which is never found in any animal devoid of a rational soul.

Since the basic cause of man's anxiety is the possibility of being either a saint or a sinner, it follows that there are only two alternatives for him. Man can either mount upward to the peak of eternity or else slip backward to the chasms of despair and frustration. Yet there are many who think there is yet another alternative, namely, that of indifference. They think that, just as bears hibernate for a season in a state of suspended animation, so they, too, can sleep through life without choosing to live for God or against Him. But hibernation is no escape; winter ends, and one is then forced to make a decision—indeed, the very choice of indifference itself is a decision. White fences do not remain white fences by having nothing done to them; they soon become black fences. Since there is a tendency in us that pulls us back to the animal, the mere fact that we do not resist it operates to our own destruction. Just as life is the sum of the forces that resist death, so, too, man's will must be the sum of the forces that resist frustration. A man who has taken poison into his system can ignore the antidote, or he can throw it out of the window; it makes no difference which he does, for death is already on the march. St. Paul warns us, "How shall we escape if we neglect . . ." (Heb. 2:3). By the mere fact that we do not go forward, we go backward. There are no plains in the spiritual life; we are either going uphill or coming down. Furthermore the pose of indifference is only intellectual. The will *must* choose. And even though an "indifferent" soul does not positively reject the infinite, the infinite rejects it. The talents that are unused are taken away, and the Scriptures tell us that, "But because thou art lukewarm, and neither cold nor hot, I will begin to vomit thee out of my mouth" (Apoc. 3:16).

Returning to the supreme alternatives, man can choose between an earthly love to the exclusion of Divine Love, or he can choose a Divine Love which includes a healthy, sacramental, earthly love. Either he can make the soul subject to the body, or he can make the body subject to the soul. Consider first those who resolve their anxiety in favor of Godlessness. They invariably end by substituting one of the false gods for the true God of Love.

This god can be the ego, or self. This happens in atheism when there is a denial of dependence on the true God, or when there is an affirmation of one's own wish and pleasure as the absolute law, or when freedom is interpreted as the right to do what one pleases. When such a false god is adored, religion is rejected as a rationalization or an escape, or even as a fear to affirm one's own self as supreme.

Atheists commit the sin of *pride,* by which a man pretends to be that which he is not, namely, a god. Pride is inordinate self-love, an exaltation of the conditional and relative self into an absolute. It tries to gratify the thirst for the infinite by giving to one's own finitude a pretension to divinity. In some, pride blinds the self to its weakness and becomes "hot" pride; in others, it recognizes its own weakness and overcomes it by a self-exaltation which becomes "cold" pride: Pride kills docility and makes a man incapable of ever being helped by God. The limited knowledge of the puny mind pretends to be final and absolute. In the face of other intellects it resorts to two techniques, either the technique of omniscience, by which it seeks to convince others how much it knows, or the technique of nescience, which tries to convince others how little they know. When such pride is unconscious, it becomes almost incurable, for it identifies truth with *its* truth. Pride is an admission of weakness; it secretly fears all competition and dreads all rivals. It is rarely cured when the person himself is vertical—*i.e.,* healthy and prosperous—but it can be cured when the patient is horizontal—sick and disillusioned. That is why catastrophes are necessary in an era of pride to bring men back again to God and the salvation of their souls.

The false god of the atheist can be *another* person, cherished, not as a bearer of human values, but as an object to be devoured and used for one's own pleasure. In such a case, the vocabulary of religion is invoked to solicit the object, such as "adore," "angel," "worship," "god," and "goddess." From it is born the sin of *lust,* or the adoration of another person's vitality as the end and goal of life. Lust is not the inevitable result of the flesh, any more than a cataract is directly caused by eyesight; it is due, rather, to the rebellion of the flesh against the spirit and of the person against God. As St. Augustine says,

> If any man say that flesh is the cause of the viciousness of the soul, he is ignorant of man's nature. This corruption, which is so burdensome to the soul, is the punishment for the first sin, and not its cause. The corruptible flesh made not the soul to sin, but the sinning soul made the flesh corruptible; from which corruption, although there arise some incitements to sin, and some vicious desires, yet are not all sins of an evil life to be laid to the flesh, otherwise, we shall make the devil, who has no flesh, sinless.[3]

Flesh in revolt (or lust) is related to pride. The conquest of the one desired may serve the individual's need of excessive self-exaltation; but consummated lust leads to despair (or the opposite of self-exaltation) by the inner tension or sadness resulting from an uneasy conscience. It is this effect which divorces it from a purely biological phenomenon, for in no creature except man is there any act which involves such an interactivity of matter and spirit, body and soul. It need hardly be noted that lust is not sex in the ordinary sense of the term but, rather, its deorientation—a sign that man has become excentric, isolated from God, and enamored of the physically good to such an excess that he is like the serpent which devours its own tail and eventually destroys itself.

The unbeliever's god can be things by which he seeks to remedy his own sense of nothingness. Some men seek this compensation in wealth, which gives them the false sense of power. External luxury is pursued to conceal the nakedness of their own souls. Such worship of wealth leads to tyranny and injustice toward others, and thus is born the sin of *avarice.*

Avarice is the material expression of one's own insufficiency and a challenge to the sublime truth that "our sufficiency is from God." Filling up its own lack at the storehouse of the earthly, the soul hopes to find at least a temporary escape from Divinity itself. All intense interest in luxury is a mark of inner poverty. The less grace there is in the soul, the more ornament must be on the body. It was only after Adam and Eve fell that they perceived themselves to be naked; when their souls were rich with original justice, their bodies were so suffused with its reflection that they felt no need for clothes. But once the Divine-internal was lost, they sought a compensation in the material, the external. Excessive dediction to temporal security is one of the ways a society's loss of eternal security manifests itself. The quest for wealth and luxury can be infinite, and for the moment it satisfies the godless souls. A man can reach a point of marginal utility in the accumulation of ice-cream cones, but not in the accumulation of credits, for there is an infinity to these ambitions. Thus does man seek to become God in gratifying limitless desires for riches, when he impoverishes himself from within. "Life wants to secure itself against the void that is raging within. The risk of eternal void is to be met by the premium of temporal insurance . . . social security, old age pensions, etc. It springs no less from metaphysical despair than from material misery."[4]

Pride, lust, avarice; the devil, the flesh and the world; the pride of life, the concupiscence of the flesh, and the concupiscence of the eyes—these constitute the new unholy trinity by which man is wooed away from the Holy Trinity and from the discovery of the goal of life. It was these three things Our Lord described in the parable of those who offered excuses for not coming to the banquet; one refused because he had bought a farm, another because he had purchased a yoke of oxen, and the third because he had taken unto himself a woman. Love of self, love of person, and love of property are not in themselves wrong, but they do become wrong when they are made ends in themselves, are torn up from their true purpose, which is to lead us to God. Because there are some who abuse love of self and love of person and love of property, the Church has encouraged the three vows of obedience, chastity, and poverty to make reparation for those who make gods out of their opinions, their flesh, and their money. Anxiety and frustration invariably follow when the desires of the heart are centered on anything less than God, for all pleasures of earth, pursued as final ends, turn out to be the exact opposite of what was expected. The expectation is joyous, the realization is disgust. Out of this disappointment are born those lesser anxieties which modern psychology knows so well; but the root of them all is the meaninglessness of life due to the abandonment of Perfect Life, Truth, and Love, which is God.

The alternative to such anxieties consists in letting oneself go, not by a surrender of the spirit to the world, the flesh, and the Devil, but by an act of proper abandonment, in which the body is disciplined and made subject to the spirit and the whole personality is directed to God. Here the basic anxiety of life is transcended in three ways, each of which brings a peace of soul that only the God-loving enjoy: (1) by controlling desires; (2) by transferring anxiety from body to soul; (3) by surrender to the Will of God.

1. By controlling desires. Anxieties and frustrations are due to uncontrolled desires. When a soul does not get what it wants, it falls into sadness and

distress. In other generations men's desires were less numerous or else were controlled; today even luxuries are considered necessities. Disappointment increases in direct ratio and proportion to our failure to obtain the things we believe essential to our enjoyment. One of the greatest deceptions of today is the belief that leisure and money are the two essentials of happiness. The sad fact of life is that there are no more frustrated people on the face of the earth than those who have nothing to do and those who have too much money for their own good. Work never killed anybody, but worry has. It is assumed by many reformers that the principal and major cause of unhappiness is economic insecurity, but this theory forgets that there are economic problems only because men have not solved the problems of their own souls. Economic disorder is a symptom of spiritual disorder.

To conquer anxiety does not mean eliminating our desires, but, rather arranging them in a hierarchy, as Our Lord reminded us when He said that life is more than the raiment. This pyramid of values places things at the bottom—and things include everything material in the universe, from a star that inspires a poet to wheat used for the baker's bread. Above things comes man, and at the peak of the pyramid is God. A religious man orders his life by the pattern of the pyramid. He overcomes anxiety by making all material things subject to the human, by discipling the body until it is subject to the spirit, and by submitting the whole personality to God. "For all are yours; and you are Christ's; and Christ is God's" (I Cor. 3:22, 23). Once the soul recognizes that it is made for God, it abandons the bourgeois idea that every person is to be judged by what he has. There follows, not only a renunciation of evil, but even a voluntary surrender of some things that are lawful, in order that the spirit be freer to love God. When the sacrifices of Our Lord become the inspiration of a life, the its burdens are borne with more than resignation—they are accepted as providential calls to greater intimacy with Him.

But quite apart from Christian motivations—even viewed from a purely natural point of view, it is wise for man to renounce some desires, simply because the soul cannot find satisfaction in fulfilling them. The desire for wealth is one of these. There are two kinds of wealth: *natural* wealth, which takes the form of the necessary food, clothing, and shelter to sustain the life of the individual or family; *artificial* wealth, which is money, credit, stocks, and bonds. It is possible for a man to satisfy his desires for natural wealth, because his stomach soon reaches a point where it can consume no more food. But there is no limit to the desire for artificial wealth. A man who has a million is never satisfied with that million. There is a certain false infinity about artificial wealth because a man can always want more and more of it. Because natural wealth imposes its own limitations, farming and gardening are among the most satisfying experiences of human life.

If we desire possessions, we never have enough of them. We become frustrated. There is a psychological difference between "frustration" and "renunciation." Frustration occurs only when man feels himself a passive victim of extrinsic forces, against which he is powerless; renunciation springs from man's own free decision. Parents recognize this difference: a child who has got hold of something he is not allowed to have is told by his parent, "Give it to me, or else I shall have to take it away from you." Often the child will renounce the thing rather than be compelled. The words addressed to the child have left him this way to safeguard his dignity and independence: he does what he must do in any case, but he does it with at least the semblance of freedom. And this freedom makes all the difference. If man can convince himself that he does not truly need this or that (although he may desire it), to abandon his striving will not frustrate him. It is only if he is forced to renunciation that he feels frustrated.

Uncontrolled desires grow like weeds and stifle the spirit. Material possessions bring a relative pleasure for a time, but sooner or later a malaise is experienced; a sense of emptiness, a feeling that something is wrong comes over the soul. This is God's way of saying that the soul is hungry and that He alone can satisfy it. It is to such modern, frustrated, starved, and anxious souls that the Saviour extends the invitation, "Come to me, all you that labour, and are burdened, and I will refresh you" (Matt. 11:28).

2. The second way man can transcend unhealthy anxiety is by transferring his concern from the body to the soul—by being wisely anxious. For there are two kinds of anxieties, one about time, the other about eternity. Most souls are anxious about the very things they should not be anxious about. Our Divine Lord mentioned at least nine things about which we should not worry: about having our body killed; about what we shall say in days of persecution when we are called on the carpet before commissars; about whether we should build another barn (or another skyscraper); about family disputes because we accept the faith about mother-in-law troubles; about our meals, our drinks, our fashions, our complexion (Luke 12). He did tell us that we should be very anxious about one thing and one thing only— our souls (Matt. 16:24–28).

Our Lord does not mean that worldly activities are unnecessary. He only said that if we were anxious about our souls the lesser anxieties would dissolve: "Seek ye *first* [not *only*] the kingdom of God and His justice, and all these things shall be added unto you" (Luke 12:31). It used to be that the true Christian was set apart from others by the intensity of his healthy anxiety about his soul. (Now he is differentiated by the mere fact that he believes he has a soul to save.) Anxiety is present in all love. And every human being must love or go crazy, because no man is sufficient for himself. Direct love toward God, and peace comes over the soul: turn it from God, and the heart becomes a broken fountain where tears fall, "from the sighful branches of mind." The nobler the heart that breaks, in its refusal to be anxious about God's love, the meaner it becomes in its lovelessness and ungodliness. But there is hope: the greater the frustration, the more complex the anxiety of the godless heart, the more capable it is of being metamorphosed to a saint.

There is hope for everyone. The things he has done pass away; the doer remains, responsible for his future acts. He can begin to cultivate healthy anxiety now. If the modern souls did but know it, the things they have been most anxious about are only trashy substitutes for Him Who alone can calm their spirits. Charlatans advise man to forget eternity and to satisfy his bodily desires—but what man would want to be a contented cow? The Lord's way to be happy is to concentrate on the narrow gate: "Enter ye in at the narrow gate; for wide is the gate, and broad is the way that leadeth to destruction, and many there are who go in threat. How narrow is the gate, and strait is the way that leadeth to life, and few there are that find it" (Matt. 7:13–14).

3. The third way to transcend anxieties is by increasing our trust in God. Love is reciprocal; it is received in proportion as it is given. We generally trust only those who trust us; that is why there is a special Providence for those who trust in God. Contrast two children, one child in a happy family, well provided with food, clothing, and education, the other a homeless orphan of the streets. The first child lives in an area of love; the second is outside of that area and enjoys none of its privileges. Many souls deliberately choose to exclude themselves from the area of the Heavenly Father's Love where they might live as His children. They trust only in their own resourcefulness, their own bank account, their own devices. This is particularly true of many families, who consider the rearing of children solely an economic problem, never once invoking the Heavenly Father's Love: they are like a son who in time of need never called on his wealthy father for assistance. The result is they lose many of the blessings reserved for those who throw themselves into the loving arms of God. This law applies to nations as well as individuals: "Because thou hast had confidence in the king of Syria, and not in the Lord thy God, therefore, hath the army of the king of Syria escaped out of thy hand" (II Par. 16:7). Many favors and blessings are hanging from heaven to relieve our temporal anxieties if we would only cut them down with the sword of our trust in God. Relief from all wrong anxiety comes, not from giving ourselves to God by halves, but by an all-encompassing love, wherein we go back, not to the past in fear or to the future in anxiety, but lie quietly in His Hand, having no will but His. Then the former shadows of life are seen as "The shade of His Hand outstretched caressingly."[5]

Everyone has anxiety. A complex according to the usage of contemporary psychology is a group of memories and desires of which we are not conscious but which nevertheless affect our personality. An anxiety complex would be a system of unhappy memories submerged in the unconscious and producing many kinds of symptoms. Everyone has anxiety; fortunately, everyone does not have an anxiety complex. The difference between peace of soul and discontent comes from the *kind* of anxiety we have; the broadest division of all is between anxiety over the things of time and the values of eternity. Of the first, Our Lord said, "Be not anxious, for your Heavenly Father knoweth you have need of these things" (Matt. 6:8). The second kind of anxiety is normal because it is bound up with human freedom and is a result of our creatureliness. This anxiety is a restlessness with anything short of the perfect happiness which is God.

Ultimately, anxiety, or dread, is related to man's finiteness and to his vague awareness of an infinite being in comparison with which he is almost nothing. Man, it has been said, may falsely try to overcome his finiteness either by denying his creatureliness (which is pride) or by escaping into an idolatry of sensuality. Then his anxiety still remains in the form of dread—which is not the same as fear. For fear is a response to a human danger and, as St. Thomas says, is always mixed with a certain degree of hope. But dread knows no hope; it expresses itself in purposeless ways, for it has no obvious cause and comes from man's half-conscious sense of the precariousness of his being. In this way dread is related to the idea of death, the great unknown, the one inescapable thing of which man has no experiential knowledge. When this dread is properly resolved by recognizing our dependency on God, it becomes the pathway to peace of soul. But no one in the world, even then, escapes the fact of anxiety or outgrows a feeling of the tension between the finite and the infinite. Such normal anxiety may be covered over, but it will break out somewhere and somehow. Alfred Adler had a glimpse of this truth when he said that neurotics are animated by an unruly ambition to be "like God." The various tensions which psychology studies are very often the reflections of the deeper metaphysical tension, inherent in every human being, between his contingent and limited being and the Infinite and Absolute Being. This tension would not be felt unless man were free and had the responsibility of choosing between self-frustration and self-perfection through the use of creatures as a means to God.

Peace of soul comes to those who have the right kind of anxiety about attaining perfect happiness, which is God. A soul has anxiety because its final and eternal state is not yet decided; it is still and always at the crossroads of life. This fundamental anxiety cannot be cured by a surrender to passions and instincts; the basic cause of our anxiety is a restlessness within time which comes because we are made for eternity. If there were anywhere on earth a resting place other than God, we may be very sure that the human soul in its long history would have found it before this. As St. Augustine has said, "Our hearts were made for Thee. They are restless until they rest in Thee, O God."

---

I. Anxiety is a phenomenon of both consciousness and unconsciousness. An "unconscious" anxiety may mean two things. Either it may mean that the objective seat of the anxiety is unknown to consciousness, in which case the consciously experienced emotional state is related, *e.g.*, by way of a "secondary rationalization," to some fictitious object in a manner which appears unfounded and nonsensical to the individual but which nevertheless imposes itself with a compulsory force, as in phobias. Or it may mean that the emotional state itself is relegated into and kept in the unconscious, so that it becomes manifest, not as anxiety, but as some other "symptom." Anxiety is also conscious and when experienced is a subject of psychological study, in children and adults, in normal and in abnormal people.

2. Reinhold Niebuhr, *The Nature and Destiny of Man*, p. 181, Charles Scribner's Sons, 1941.

3. *De Civitate Dei*, Book XIV, Chap. 3.

4. Franz Werfel, *Between Heaven and Earth*, p. 71, Hutchinson & Company, Ltd., London, 1947.

5. Francis Thompson, "The Hound of Heaven."

# Conquistador, Tourist, and Indian

## From: *"A Letter to Pablo Antonio Cuadra Concerning Giants"*

### BY THOMAS MERTON

Let me consider the question of the world's future, if it has one. The leaders of the opposed ideologies are persuaded that it has. The masters of Russia think that the self-destruction of our commercial culture will usher in the golden age of peace and love. Our leaders think that if we and they can somehow shoot the rapids of the cold war, waged with the chemically pure threat of nuclear weapons, we will both emerge into a future of happiness, the nature and the possibility of which still remain to be explained.

For my part, I believe in the very serious possibility that both powers may wake up one morning, so to speak, to find that they have burned and blasted each other off the map during the night, and nothing will remain but the spasmodic exercise of automatic weapons still in the throes of what has casually been called "post-mortem retaliation."

In this new situation it is conceivable that Indonesia, Latin America, Southern Africa, and Australia may find themselves heirs to the opportunities and objectives that the U.S.S.R. and the U.S.A. shrugged off with such careless abandon.

The largest, richest, and best-developed single land mass south of the Equator is South America. The vast majority of its population is Indian, or of mixed Indian blood. The white minority in South Africa would quite probably disappear. A relic of European stock might survive in Australia and New Zealand. Let us also hopefully assume the partial survival of India and of some Moslem populations in central and northern Africa.

If this should happen it will be an event fraught with a rather extraordinary spiritual significance. It will mean that the more cerebral and mechanistic

cultures, which have tended to live more and more by abstractions and to iso-
late themselves more and more from the natural world by rationalization, will
be succeeded by the sections of the human race which they oppressed and
exploited without the slightest appreciation for, or understanding for, their
human reality.

Characteristic of these races is a totally different outlook on life, a spiritual
outlook which is not abstract but concrete, not pragmatic but hieratic, intuitive
and affective rather than rationalistic and aggressive. The deepest springs of
vitality in these races have been sealed up by the Conqueror and Colonizer,
where they have not actually been poisoned by him. But if this stone is
removed from the spring perhaps its waters will purify themselves by new life
and regain their creative, fructifying power.

Let me be quite succinct: the greatest sin of the European-Russian-
American complex which we call the West (and this sin has spread its own way
to China), is not only greed and cruelty, not only moral dishonesty and infidelity to truth, but above all *its unmitigated arrogance toward the rest of the human
race.* Western civilization is now in full decline into barbarism (a barbarism that
springs *from within itself*) because it has been guilty of a twofold disloyalty: to
God and to Man. To a Christian who believes in the mystery of the
Incarnation, and who by that belief means something more than a pious theory without real humanistic implications, this is not two disloyalties but one.
Since the Word was made Flesh, God is in man. God is in *all men.* All men are
to be seen and treated as Christ. Failure to do this, the Lord tells us, involves
condemnation for disloyalty to the most fundamental of revealed truths. "I
was thirsty and you gave me not to drink. I was hungry and you gave me not
to eat. . . ." This could be extended in every possible sense: and it is meant to
be so extended, all over the entire area of human needs, not only for bread, for
work, for liberty, for health, but also for truth, for belief, for love, for acceptance, for fellowship and understanding.

One of the great tragedies of the Christian West was the almost complete
destruction of the Indian cultures of America by European and Christian con-
querors. In the north the Indian was wiped out by Puritans who appealed to
the Old Testament example of the conquest of Canaan, and felt themselves
exercising a divine mandate to exterminate the godless savage. In South
America the appeal was more sophisticated. In the name of Aristotle and the
natural law, as well as of scholastic theology, savagery and treachery in war
against the Indian were considered fully justified for several reasons. First, it
was just to wipe out a civilization that violated the natural law by its idolatrous
worship. Second, it was just to subjugate in warfare an inferior people, destined
by its very nature for slavery (Aristotle). Third, it was legitimate to exploit and
oppress men who were not fully human, were not really rational animals, and

did not really have souls. These ideas were righteously held, with full subjective sincerity, by men who believed themselves to be in possession not only of the full light of divinely revealed truth, but of a social structure that embodied all that was good, noble, and Christian. In imposing their opinions and customs, even in the most violent and unscrupulous ways, they felt that they were acting as the approved agents of the divine will. They could not recognize that *the races they had conquered were essentially equal to themselves and in some ways superior.* Such is the warmaker's thought process in every age, not excluding our own.

It was certainly right that Christian Europe should bring Christ to the Indians of Mexico and the Andes, as well as to the Hindus and the Chinese: but where they failed was in their inability to *encounter Christ* already potentially present in the Indians, the Hindus, and the Chinese.

Christians have too often forgotten the fact that Christianity found its way into Greek and Roman civilization partly by its spontaneous and creative adaptation of the pre-Christian natural values it found in that civilization. The martyrs rejected all the grossness, the cynicism and falsity of the cult of the state gods which was simply a cult of secular power, but Clement of Alexandria, Justin, and Origen believed that Herakleitos and Socrates had been precursors of Christ. They thought that while God had manifested himself to the Jews through the Law and the Prophets he had also spoken to the Gentiles through their philosophers. Christianity made its way in the world of the first century not by imposing Jewish cultural and social standards on the rest of the world, but by abandoning them, getting free of them so as to be "all things to all men." This was the great drama and the supreme lesson of the Apostolic Age. By the end of the Middle Ages that lesson had been *forgotten.* The preachers of the Gospel to newly discovered continents became preachers and disseminators of European culture and power. They did not enter into dialogue with ancient civilizations: they imposed their own monologue and in preaching Christ they also preached themselves. The very ardor of their self-sacrifice and of their humility enabled them to do this with a clean conscience. But they had omitted to listen to the voice of Christ in the unfamiliar accents of the Indian, as Clement had listened for it in the pre-Socratics.

Whatever India may have had to say to the West, she was forced to remain silent. Whatever China had to say, though some of the first missionaries heard it and understood it, the message was generally ignored as irrelevant. Did anyone pay attention to the voices of the Maya and the Inca, who had deep things to say? By and large their witness was merely suppressed. No one considered that the children of the Sun might, after all, hold in their hearts a spiritual secret. On the contrary, abstract discussions were engaged in to determine whether, in terms of academic philosophy, the Indian was to be considered a rational animal. One shudders at the voice of cerebral Western arrogance even then eviscerated by the rationalism that is ours today, judging the living spiritual mystery of primitive man and condemning it to exclusion from the category on which love, friendship, respect, and communion were made to depend.

God speaks, and God is to be heard, not only on Sinai, not only in my own heart, but in the *voice of the stranger*. That is why the peoples of the Orient, and all primitive peoples in general, make so much of the mystery of hospitality.

God must be allowed the right to speak unpredictably. The Holy Spirit, the very voice of Divine Liberty, must always be like the wind in "blowing where he pleases" (John 3:8). In the mystery of the Old Testament there was already a tension between the Law and the Prophets. In the New Testament the Spirit himself is Law, and he is everywhere. He certainly inspires and protects the visible Church, but if we cannot see him unexpectedly in the stranger and the alien, we will not understand him even in the Church. We must find him in our enemy, or we may lose him even in our friend. We must find him in the pagan or we will lose him in our own selves, substituting for his living presence an empty abstraction. How can we reveal to others what we cannot discover in them ourselves? We must, then, see the truth in the stranger, and the truth we see must be a newly living truth, not just a projection of a dead conventional idea of our own—a projection of our own self upon the stranger.

There is more than one way of morally liquidating the "stranger" and the "alien." It is sufficient to destroy, in some way, that in him which is different and disconcerting. By pressure, persuasion, or force one can impose on him one's own ideas and attitudes toward life. One can indoctrinate him, brainwash him. He is no longer different. He has been reduced to conformity with one's own outlook. The Communist, who does nothing if not thoroughly, believes in the thorough liquidation of differences, and the reduction of everyone else to a carbon copy of himself. The Capitalist is somewhat more quixotic: the stranger becomes part of his own screen of fantasies, part of the collective dream life which is manufactured for him on Madison Avenue and in Hollywood. For all practical purposes, the stranger no longer exists. He is not even seen. He is replaced by a fantastic image. What is seen and approved, in a vague, superficial way, is the stereotype that has been created by the travel agency.

This accounts for the spurious cosmopolitanism of the naïve tourist and traveling businessman, who wanders everywhere with his camera, his exposure meter, his spectacles, his sunglasses, his binoculars, and though gazing around him in all directions never sees what is there. He is not capable of doing so. He is too docile to his instructors, to those who have told him everything beforehand. He believes the advertisements of the travel agent at whose suggestion he bought the ticket that landed him wherever he may be. He has been told what he was going to see, and he thinks he is seeing it. Under no circumstances does it occur to him to become interested in what is actually there. Still less to enter into a fully human rapport with the human beings who are before him. It just does not occur to him that they might have a life, a spirit, a thought, a culture of their own which has its own peculiar individual character.

He does not know why he is traveling in the first place: indeed he is traveling at somebody else's suggestion. Even at home he is alien from himself. He is doubly alienated when he is out of his own atmosphere. He cannot possibly realize that the stranger has something very valuable, something irreplaceable to give him: something that can never be bought with money, never estimated by publicists, never exploited by political agitators: the spiritual understanding of a friend who belongs to a different culture. The tourist lacks nothing except brothers. For him these do not exist.

The tourist never meets anyone, never encounters anyone, never finds the brother in the stranger. This is his tragedy.

If only North Americans had realized, after a hundred and fifty years, that Latin Americans really existed. That they were really people. That they spoke a different language. That they had a culture. That they had more than something to sell! Money has totally corrupted the brotherhood that should have united all the peoples of America. It has destroyed the sense of relationship, the spiritual community that had already begun to flourish in the years of Bolivar. But no! Most North Americans still don't know, and don't care, that Brazil speaks a language other than Spanish, that all Latin Americans do not live for the siesta, that all do not spend their days and nights playing the guitar and making love. They have never awakened to the fact that Latin America is by and large culturally superior to the United States, not only on the level of the wealthy minority which has absorbed more of the sophistication of Europe, but also among the desperately poor indigenous cultures, some of which are rooted in a past that has never yet been surpassed on this continent.

So the tourist drinks tequila, and thinks it is no good, and waits for the fiesta he has been told to wait for. How should he realize that the Indian who walks down the street with half a house on his head and a hole in his pants, is Christ? All the tourist thinks is that it is odd for so many Indians to be called Jesus.

So much for the modern scene. I am no prophet, no one is, for now we have learned to get along without prophets. But I would say that if Russia and North America are to destroy one another, which they seem quite anxious to do, it would be a great pity if the survivors in the "Third World" attempted to reproduce their collective alienation, horror, and insanity, and thus build up another corrupt world to be destroyed by another war. To the whole third world I would say there is one lesson to be learned from the present situation, one lesson of the greatest urgency: be unlike the two great destroyers. Mark

what they do, and act differently. Mark their official pronouncements, their ideologies, and without difficulty you will find them hollow. Mark their behavior:
their bluster, their violence, their blandishments, their hypocrisy: by their fruits
you shall know them. In all their boastfulness they have become the victims of
their own terror, which is nothing but the emptiness of their own hearts. They
claim to be humanists, they claim to know and love man. They have come to
liberate man, they say. But they do not know what man is. They are themselves
less human than their fathers were, less articulate, less sensitive, less profound,
less capable of genuine concern. They are turning into giant insects. Their
societies are becoming anthills, without purpose, without meaning, without
spirit and joy.

What is wrong with their humanism? It is a humanism of termites,
because without God man becomes an insect, a worm in the wood, and even
if he can fly, so what? There are flying ants. Even if man flies all over the universe, he is still nothing but a flying ant until he recovers a human center and
a human spirit in the depth of his own being.

# Religion at Yale

From: *God and Man at Yale*

BY WILLIAM F. BUCKLEY JR.

*I call on all members of the faculty, as members of a thinking body, freely to recognize the tremendous validity and power of the teachings of Christ in our life-and-death struggle against the forces of selfish materialism. If we lose that struggle, judging from present events abroad, scholarship as well as religion will disappear.*

—PRESIDENT CHARLES SEYMOR
INAUGURAL ADDRESS, OCTOBER 16, 1937

In evaluating the role of Christianity and religion at Yale, I have not in mind the ideal that the University should be composed of a company of scholars exclusively or even primarily concerned with spreading the Word of the Lord. I do not feel that Yale should treat her students as potential candidates for divinity school. It has been said that there are those who "want to make a damned seminary" out of Yale. There may be some who do, but I do not count myself among these.

But we can, without going that far, raise the question whether Yale fortifies or shatters the average student's respect for Christianity. There are, of course, some students who will emerge stronger Christians from any institution and others who will reject religion wherever they are sent. But if the atmosphere of a college is overwhelmingly secular, if the influential members of the faculty tend to discourage religious inclinations, or to persuade the student that Christianity is nothing more than "ghost-fear," or "twentieth-century witchcraft," university policy quite properly becomes a matter of concern to those parents and alumni who deem active Christian faith a powerful force for good and for personal happiness.

I think of Yale, then, as a nondenominational educational institution not exclusively interested in the propagation of Christianity. The question must then arise whether or not the weight of academic activity at Yale tends to reinforce or to subvert Christianity, or to do neither the one nor the other. It is clear that insight into this problem cannot be had from counting the number of faculty members who believe as opposed to those that do not believe. Some instructors deal with subject matter that has little, if any, academic bearing upon religion. Some have more influence than others. Some teach classes that as a matter of course attract a large number of students, while others seldom address more than a half dozen or so.

The handiest arguments of those who vaunt the pro-religious atmosphere at Yale is that the University has a large religion department, a great number of strong and influential men whose beliefs are strongly pro-Christian on its faculty, and a powerful and pervasive "religious tradition."

To a greater or lesser extent, these statements are true. And yet, it remains that Yale, corporately speaking, is neither pro-Christian, nor even, I believe, neutral toward religion.

To begin with, it is impossible to gauge the Christian purpose of a college by counting the number of courses offered in religion. It is, of course, of interest that such courses are offered, because this serves as an official indication, at least, that the University recognizes religion as an important field of learning, worthy of the student's academic endeavor. But it is important to remember that a student may major in Christianity and not be pro-Christian, just as he can major in Far Eastern Studies and be anti-oriental.

Also relevant is the number of students who are influenced by the religious department of a university or avail themselves of the college's religious facilities. Professor Clarence P. Shedd, of Yale, speaking on the radio program "Yale Interprets the News" on August 15, 1948, insisted upon the dramatic upswing in postwar religious interest, but added: "I talked with a chaplain in a large state university only last week who asserted that all the religious influences in his university were not significantly influencing more than ten percent of the undergraduates. My own figure for the large university situation nationally has been fifteen percent."

The degree to which a college is pro-Christian depends then, not so much on the number of religion courses it offers or even the number of students electing such courses, but on the orientation and direction given to the students by the instructors in these courses, and, most especially, in other courses that deal or should deal with religious values.

At Yale, the religion course which consistently attracts the greatest number of students is entitled the Historical and Literary Aspects of the Old

Testament. Mr. Lovett, the widely admired University Chaplain,* teaches this course; but he does not proselytize the Christian faith or, indeed, *teach* religion at all. Even the title of the course does not call for understanding of, or even sympathy with, Christianity. Mr. Lovett, to be sure, has both; but he apparently feels that it would be presumptuous to speak on behalf of Christianity in a course so dispassionately designated. Strictly speaking he is right, though the cause of Christianity suffers to a certain degree from a treatment which focuses upon the Bible as a "monument over the grave of Christianity." It must be acknowledged that Mr. Lovett's personal interest in religion can be, and frequently has been, quietly contagious. Through the years, many students, impressed by his faith and goodness, have sought out religion on their own. And some of these have ended up at divinity schools.

My point is that a Bible course no more bespeaks an influence on behalf of Christianity than a course on *Das Kapital* would necessarily indicate an influence on behalf of Marxism. Attendance at Dr. Lovett's classes is deceptive in itself, because far from signifying an interest in "religion" it indicates, on the part of many undergraduates, nothing more than a fruitful search for a "gut." It is notorious that far less is expected of a student in this course than in most others in the University, as, it seems, is the case in many other colleges:

> All that glitters in the catalogues is not mentally respectable gold, and courses in religion, as any experienced observer knows, are often "snaps" or "crips." . . . Put purely on the basis of grades, seldom is it as difficult to get an A in religion as it is in philosophy or biology or economics. Yet God is a God of judgment as well as of mercy.

We move to the next largest course in the Religion Department, the Philosophy of Religion taught by Professor T. M. Greene. While Mr. Greene is a Christian by a great many definitions (he replies ambiguously when asked if he believes in the divinity of Christ), his course is largely a completely

---

*"No aspect of my administration [President Seymour has written] has brought deeper satisfaction than the devoted and fruitful service of Mr. Lovett in the maintenance of religious values on our campus. Not merely as pastor of the church and as Woolsey Professor of Biblical Literature, but in his personal contacts and with his genius for stimulating cooperative effort, he has unobtrusively and effectively brought religious interest into the center of college life" (*Report of the President of Yale University to the Alumni*, 1949–1950, p. 32). Mr. Seymour here pays tribute to Mr. Lovett in two distinct senses. The first acknowledges his devoted service and personal interest, and I cannot see two points of view about this; the other applauds his religious influence and the results it has had on the Yale campus. This *is*, as I hope to point out, another thing entirely.

nondogmatic examination of the philosophies of religion. Mr. Greene is unflinching in his respect for Christian ethics, but it is, after all, assumed that most people are. Therefore, while some students are moved by Mr. Greene's approach to his problem and by his patent respect for Christianity, there is a widespread opinion that what he teaches is ethics, not religion.*

Much the same can be said of Professor Schroeder's (he is the chairman of the Religion Department) courses on Problems of Religious Thought and the Development of Religious Thought in Western Civilization. Mr. Schroeder, an ordained minister, is emphatically an influence toward the good, but not necessarily through the instrument of his religion. While respecting Christianity and what it represents, Mr. Schroeder does not seek to persuade his students to believe in Christ, largely because he has not, as I understand it, been completely able to persuade himself.†

Next in line is Mr. Goodenough, the renowned scholar of Judaism, who teaches Types of Religious Experience, and Judaism and Jesus. Mr. Goodenough was once a Congregationalist minister, and surprisingly, a number of persons who are, on the face of it, intimately acquainted with the University, have remarked that he "is considered a good Congregationalist."

And yet, I know of at least one occasion on which Mr. Goodenough has classified himself, before his students, as "80 percent atheist and 20 percent agnostic." No wonder that the preponderant influence of a scholar of his persuasion is to drive his students *away* from religion, the subject he "teaches."

There are three or four other instructors in the Religion Department, most notably Mr. Latourette, a staunchly pro-Christian minister who teaches mostly at the Divinity School, but maintains contact with undergraduates by offering a course on the history of Christianity. Unfortunately, the enrollment in this

---

*I make no apology for defining "religion" in the Christian sense, and eschewing the nebulous, personalized definitions given to that term by so many latter-day psychologists, sociologists, *et al.* Here and elsewhere, along with Webster, I mean by religion a belief in a Supreme Being, "arousing reverence, love, gratitude, the will to obey and serve, and the like." Other definitions, perhaps more topical and specifically relating to Christianity, are the World Council of Churches' "a belief in Jesus Christ as God and Savior," and the Federal Council of Churches' "Jesus Christ as Divine Lord and Savior." In February, 1951, Dr. Reinhold Niebuhr, a prominent Protestant spokesman, addressed the Yale University Christian Association, and was unequivocal: "Christian faith stands or falls on the proposition that a character named Jesus, in a particular place at a particular time in history, is more than a man in history, but is a revelation of the mystery of self and of the ultimate mystery of existence."

†It is important to bear in mind that what is relevant to this survey is the teacher's attitude *as it is understood by his students,* even if this be, at times, at variance with personal convictions that the teacher keeps to himself.

course is very small. Mr. Walton (of the Philosophy Department), a Roman Catholic, teaches a course on scholastic philosophy which is even more lightly subscribed.

Even if we assume, then, that a vigorous Religion Department indicates the prevalence of religion on the campus, we find that at Yale there does not even exist within the Religion Department itself a remarkably pro-religious bias. It is staffed by able scholars, many of whom several universities would be glad to add to their teaching staff. Academically, in other words, it is everything one could wish. But to the student who seeks intellectual and inspirational support for his faith, it is necessarily a keen disappointment.

Let us not forget that even if the courses offered by the Religion Department did lead to a more active faith in Christianity, it would still remain true that less than 10 percent of the student body elect courses in the Department.* We must remember, too, that Yale sets up a number of "required studies" for the students of the liberal arts. Unless he can earn an exemption for this or that exceptional reason, he must take a full-year course in each of the following fields: (1) English, Latin, or Greek, (2) Modern Language, (3) Formal Thinking (Mathematics, Logic, or Linguistics), (4) Laboratory Science, (5) Classical Languages, Literature, and Civilization, (6) Modern Literature, the Fine Arts, and Music, (7) Anthropology, Economics, Geography, Political Science, Psychology, Sociology, (8) History, Philosophy, Religion, and (9) Natural or Physical Science.

It is to be noted that the group which includes religion allows the option of a course in history or philosophy. Statistics reveal that the overwhelming majority of students avail themselves of these alternatives. Thus, the University insists that the student take a course in a laboratory science, in a modern language, and in classical civilization, but accepts history and philosophy as alternatives to religion. In so doing, it denies equal status with, say, French or Spanish grammar and pronunciation, to the teaching that has played the most vital role in our civilization and can play the most vital role in our lives.† . . .

Much has been written about a "revival" of religion that has swept the

---

*The figures are for the academic year 1950–51, which list 472 persons as enrolled in the Department. These figures are themselves deceptive since many students take more than one course and are thus counted twice, or three times.

†There has been serious discussion, at least in undergraduate Yale, of the advisability of a requirement in the field of religion. One student submitted a concrete set of proposals to the Aurelian Honor Society, which voted them down by a narrow margin in the fall of 1949. President Seymour was at least not shocked when the proposal was informally made to him that such a requirement should be instituted if there are to be any requirements at all. But he cited financial difficulties and a number of additional technical obstacles.

country since the war's end. Much of this, the analysts insist, has centered about the college campus. Professor Merrimon Cuninggim has written a book called *The College Seeks Religion,* and on the local scene, Professor Clarence P. Shedd of Yale has broadcast under the title "Religious Activities in Increase in the Colleges." We may, indeed, be riding the crest of a wave. The state of religion often tends to be cast about, at the mercy of the times; and the times today, as perhaps never before, conduce to a return to the God that has been so emphatically renounced by the world's troublemakers. I have read that the period of skepticism that followed the Revolutionary War in this country saw a Yale at which, for several years, fewer than 10 percent of the student body (at that time about a hundred) professed religion openly; but it was only a matter of time before Timothy Dwight "preached . . . and all infidelity skulked and hid its head."

Perhaps we are witnessing a grass roots movement back to religion. But this is highly debatable. After devoting several hundred pages to the encouraging indications of a revival of religious interest in the colleges, Professor Cuninggim concludes sadly, *"Secularism is too widespread for one to be able glibly to conclude that colleges are more Christian in atmosphere than in 1900."*

More explicitly, in a later section, Professor Cuninggim exposes the "religious front" of so many colleges, among which I would number Yale:

> If we center our attention solely upon the collegiate interest in religion and the religious programs of instruction, worship, and activity, we may hopefully conclude that the campus atmosphere is religious in quality and that students breathe clean air. But when we broaden our consideration to include all institutional interests and all aspects of college life, then we must perforce admit that the tone of higher education is secular *and the total impact upon the majority of students is, if not anti-, at least nonreligious* [italics added].

If we are, indeed, witnessing a religious revival, it would seem to be only against the rigid resistance of probably the most influential, and certainly the best publicized, policy-makers in education. The two most widely circularized attempts to analyze the plight of education at the half-century point are revealing. The first of these was sponsored by Harvard; after exhaustive consultations, an expenditure of $60,000, and three years' work, the project appeared in 1945 and under the title *General Education in a Free Society.*

In this exhaustive work, religion is mentioned only a few times, and then merely to note the historic association of Christianity with democracy and humanism. The importance which the educators who drafted this document attached to religion is symbolized by their acknowledgement of the educational value of Harvard's glee club and orchestra, while saying "nothing of the chapel or of Brooks House, long a center of religious and social service." The Report is explicit when it states:

> We are not at all unmindful of the importance of religious belief in the completely good life. But, given the American scene with its varieties of faith and even of unfaith, we did not feel justified in proposing religious instruction as a part of the curriculum.

President Lowry of the College of Wooster, in his critique, points out at least one of the fallacies in this statement when he says:

> By the same token, politics might be excluded because there are Democrats and Republicans; physics, because there are divergent views about cosmic rays; or athletics because some like Harvard and some like Yale. On this theory, any matter lively enough to call forth more than one deeply or widely held point of view is a doubtful item in the curriculum.

The report emphatically discards religion as a potential source of the desired "unifying purpose and idea" of education: "Whatever one's views, religion is not now for most colleges a practicable [or desirable, the report urges throughout] source of intellectual unity."

Some comfort is yet to be derived from the report's stipulation of goals: The student should learn *"to think effectively, to communicate thought, to make relevant judgments, to discriminate among values"* (italics in the original).

President Lowry acutely points out that

> . . . the document is asking for leading ideas and a quality in the human life that religion, time out of mind, has notably fostered. Therefore, the Christian can hardly be blamed if he sees his own faith, not alien to, but actually the forming and completing agent of the kind of education Harvard describes. . . .

The second influential document to which I refer is the Report of the [U.S.] President's Commission on Higher Education, *Higher Education for American Democracy.** While this report is primarily a highly controversial package of political and economic ideas looking to increasing educational benefits, more student subsidies, and tripled college enrollments in the next ten years, the doc-

---

*Published after vast research and seventeen months of study, in March 1947.

ument, by indirection, deals a body blow to religion, whose relevance it does not so much as acknowledge. Pages are spent in a discussion of democratic ideals, and much is made of our cultural heritage. The report, where education is concerned, is one more victory for the secularists. President Lowry comments that

> [This is] no particular surprise. . . . The Commission was not opening the Senate or laying a cornerstone and was therefore under no obligation to unite in prayer. It passes on, apparently as a rumor, the fact that "religion is held to be a major force in creating the system of human values on which democracy is predicated." It is concerned almost dangerously with the production of citizens who can realize certain social goals—dangerous in spite of all the Report's talk about the free citizen, his self-discipline and appreciation of a wide range of values, because the ethical standards the citizen will have, if he follows the implication of the Report, will be the same utilitarian and relative standards that have put mankind in the mess it is now in. The Commission is composed of high-minded men who, obviously, want more than that. But not even in a minority report or in an appendix have they dared say more than that. Again, we should feel no particular surprise. We have become accustomed to writing nobly of American ideals without either the historical accuracy or the common candor of recognizing that these ideals grew largely out of a mind and conscience that believed in God and in some eternal standards. *Almost our subtlest form of self-deception is our amiable habit of talking about our "cultural heritage" with the main inheritance left out* [italics added].

On the sixth of October 1950, A. Whitney Griswold was confirmed as sixteenth president of Yale University in the simple and impressive ritual that has marked presidential inaugurations for 250 years. According to custom, the new president delivers an inaugural address, an oration of some interest since it is customarily interpreted as a fundamental pronouncement of his educational policy.

The incessantly cited Christian "symbols" of Yale were forthright and unambiguous; all was in keeping with the Connecticut Charter of 1701 which conferred upon the president and the Fellows of Yale "liberty to erect a collegiate school wherein youth may be instructed in the arts and sciences and who through the blessings of almighty God may be fitted for public employment both for church and civil state." Indeed, of the four men who raised their voices on that afternoon, three were clergymen, one of them the presiding bishop of the Episcopal Church of America. Hymns were sung, and a footnote on the program extended an invitation to tea to the members of the "congregation."

The traditions and the atmosphere had no apparent effect on President Griswold's thinking as revealed in his address. He did not cite or pay tribute to the contribution to the good life which for so many generations was regarded as the distinctive attribute of Christian education. He did not mention religion.

It was more than a mere omission, for the president summoned to the attention of his audience three "vital forces" at Yale which are supported by "powerful traditions." *Christianity was not among those he cited,* which makes Mr. Griswold, even considering him exclusively as a historian, guilty of astonishing lapses regarding the relative importance of Yale's traditions.

Failure to mention religion in an educational address can signify preoccupation with other things. Failure to mention religion in a speech of such outstanding importance as an inaugural address is sheer dereliction. Failure to mention religion in an inaugural address at which other cultural inheritances are mentioned is unexplainable.

> ... the statements of college presidents which omit the subject [of religion] might signify merely the incompleteness of their treatment. But one would hardly suppose that such obviously important statements as inaugural addresses would be intentionally incomplete. [Griswold address]

Too much significance can, of course, be attributed to an inaugural address. President Seymour had made a clarion call for a return to Christian values in 1937, but that did not exorcise the extreme secularism that characterized Yale at least during the last four years of his administration:

> Yale was dedicated to the upraising of spiritual leaders [President Seymour had said]. We betray our trust if we fail to explore the various ways in which the youth who come to us may learn to appreciate spiritual values, whether by the example of our own lives or through the cogency of our philosophical arguments. The simple and direct way is through the maintenance and upbuilding of the Christian religion as a vital part of university life. [Griswold address]

For, after all, it is the policies of the university president that count: "No observer of the college scene can take undiluted delight in the mere fact that lots of colleges go through the motions. The motions must be meaningful or they are worse than meaningless." [Griswold address]

President Seymour's devotion to Christianity and his scholarly appreciation of religious values are on the record for all to see. What I call a failure to Christianize Yale was not due to any lack of sympathy or understanding of religion on his part. It was due, rather, to the shibboleths of "academic freedom" that have so decisively hamstrung so many educators in the past fifty years. More of this later. Of Mr. Griswold, it was said by the editors of the *Yale Alumni Magazine* on the occasion of his election to the presidency, ". . . here's to Whitney Griswold. The Lord, in whom he devoutly believes, bless him and this University." Rumor has it that he too is a religious man. It will, in any case, matter little what he said or did not say at his inauguration if he wages an earnest campaign to improve the lot of religion on the campus.

There can be no judgment of President Griswold's policies and no prediction as to his intentions at this early date. We can do no better at this time than to invoke the same prayer of his friends on the alumni magazine: may the Lord, in whom he devoutly believes, bless him and his University—the University which was founded by churchmen, whose trustees for two hundred years were exclusively ministers of the gospel, whose corporation meetings are even today opened by prayer, whose every symbol commits it to furthering God's fight.

# The Persistence of Community

## From: *The Persistence of Religion*

### BY ANDREW M. GREELEY

✛

O ne of the most striking events of the past decade has been the emergence of small group communities in the midst of Western urban industrial society. Some social scientists have told us that community was dead, that man lived an isolated anomic life as part of a mass society or a "lonely crowd." Some theologians have "celebrated" the glories of the freedom and the privacy that came to man in this lonely crowd. If he no longer belonged to anything, it was argued, he was now the master of his own fate; he made his own decisions quite independent of the social pressures of the tribe and the clan.

But while the obsequies of community were being celebrated in one part of the university campus, in another part of the campus astrology groups were being organized. Sensitivity training and marathon encounter sessions were beginning. Communes were being formed, covens of witches appeared, and before one knew it there was the extraordinary phenomenon of the Jesus people, those primitive Christians, breaking into the drug-infested counterculture and bearing witness to the saving grace of Jesus. The old religious and tribal communities may have been dead but new religio-tribal communities were being born.

Some observers interpreted these communities as evidence of a "resurgence" of religion with either joy or sorrow, depending on their frame of reference. However, in the context of the present issue of *Concilium*, it is argued that the new communitarian movement, to the extent that it is religious, represents a persistence of religion, although obviously a persistence in a new form, a form that is not altogether without dangers.

Four different questions will be posed in this paper, firstly, how can we explain the communitarian movement; secondly, whether it is a religious movement; thirdly, the dangers of such a movement; and fourthly, how traditional churches should respond to the communitarian movement.

Before we answer these questions, however, we must first have a definition of community.

> By community I mean something that goes far beyond mere local community. The word, as we find it in much nineteenth- and twentieth-century thought, encompasses all forms of relationship which are characterized by a high degree of personal intimacy, emotional depth, moral commitment, social cohesion and continuity in time. Community is founded on man conceived in his wholeness rather than in one or another of the roles, taken separately, that he may hold in a social order. It draws its psychological strength from levels of motivation deeper than those of mere volition or interest, and it achieves its fulfillment in a submergence of individual will that is not possible in unions of mere convenience of rational assent. Community is a fusion of feeling and thought, of tradition and commitment, of membership and volition. It may be found in, or be given symbolic expression by, locality, religion, nation, race, occupation or crusade. Its archetype, both historically and symbolically, is the family, and in almost every type of genuine community the nomenclature of family is prominent. Fundamental to the strength of the bond of community is the real or imagined antithesis formed in the same social setting by the noncommunal relations of competition or conflict, utility or contractual assent. These, by their relative impersonality and anonymity, highlight the close personal ties of community.[1]

The Nisbet definition is certainly accurate for community as the term has been used in the past. However, today, there is frequently a new dimension added to the category "community," a dimension which is almost always present in the communitarian movement and is generally present, too, when a young clergyman says that he thinks the role of the priest is to "create community." That new dimension is one of interpersonal intimacy. It is not merely required that one associate with one's "own kind of people," it is also necessary that the association be intimate; that is to say, that the relationship be characterized by so powerful and so systematic a trust that most of the masks and the defense mechanisms which make everyday life relationships tolerable if impersonal are dropped and we relate to one another with the

---

[1] Robert Nisbet, *The Sociological Tradition* (New York, 1966), pp. 47–8.

totality of our selfhoods. Even in those communes which are not given over to complete sexual freedom, the intimacy which is supposed to exist between husband and wife is still held up at least implicitly as a model for all other human relationships.

## I. Why the Quest for Community?

The distinguished anthropologist Clifford Geertz has argued that fundamental and primordial groups seem to be one of the "givens" of human society.

> By a primordial attachment is meant one that stems from the "givens"—or more precisely, as culture is inevitably involved in such matters, the "assumed" givens—of social existence: immediate contiguity and kin connection mainly, but beyond them, the givenness that stems from being born into a particular religious community speaking a particular language, or even a dialect of language, and following particular social patterns. These congruities of blood, speech, custom, and so on, are seen to have an ineffable, and at time overpowering, coerciveness in and of themselves. One is bound to one's kinsman, one's neighbor, one's fellow believer, *ipso facto,* as a result not merely of one's personal affection, practical necessity, common interest, or incurred obligation, but at least in great part by the virtue of some unaccountable absolute import attributed to the very tie itself. The general strength of such primordial bonds, and the types of them that are important, differ from person to person, from society to society, and from time to time. But for virtually every person, in every society, at almost all times, some attachments seem to flow more from a sense of natural—some would say spiritual—affinity than from social interaction.[2]

The most popular theoretical explanation for the "resurgence" of community is that under the pressure of urbanization and industrialization the old communities have collapsed. The mass society, the lonely crowd emerged during the 1950s and the 1960s, as everyone from Ortega y Gasset to Harvey Cox predicted; but men found that the loneliness and the isolation of the impersonal mass society was intolerable. They turned to radical political movements, psychological encounter groups, new religious forms (such as astrology and the Jesus people), and counterculture communes in order to recapture the

---

[2] Clifford Geertz, "The Integrative Revolution," in *Old Societies and New States,* ed. Clifford Geertz (Glencoe, Ill., 1963).

intimacy that had been lost on the pilgrimage from *Gemeinschaft* to *Gesellschaft*. It is precisely the most lonely and the most alienated, according to such an argument, who will flock to the communitarian movement.

There is perhaps something to be said for such an explanation, but it also seems to be rather naïve, both in its romanticization of the old community and in its description of contemporary society. One very much doubts, for example, that there was much in the way of interpersonal intimacy in the old peasant village. Strong social support there was, and also strong social control, but intimacy of the sort that the new communitarians seek was practically unknown. The peasant village was not an open, honest and trusting place; it was closed, suspicious and rigid. Most of the enthusiasts for the new communes would have found the old villages intolerable.

There is an extensive sociological literature which offers convincing evidence that *Gemeinschaft* has survived and prospered in the midst of a *Gesellschaft* society. Informal friendship groups permeate factories, residential neighborhoods, the military establishment, the marketplace, and even the political order. The extended family is not nearly so extinct as many observers would like to believe. For example, more than half the American population lives within fifteen minutes of the parent of one of the spouses. The majority of Americans are more likely to visit each week with their brothers and sisters than they are with anyone else.

Far from there being less intimacy in urban industrial society than there ever has been in the past, there is probably more. One could make a very persuasive case that more intimacy is both possible and expected between husband and wife than in any previous time in history. The psychological breakthroughs of Freudian therapy and existential personalism make trust and openness among friends more likely now than ever before. There may be much more impersonality in human relationships today than in the past, but there is also more intimacy. The reason these two assertions are not contradictory is that the sheer number of human relationships has increased dramatically.

Thus, the "alienation" explanation for the new communities, while it may have some merit, also misses many important phenomena in modern society. There are a number of other explanations which must be combined with the alienation theory before we begin to understand the new communes.

1. The sheer fact that men and women have more time to devote to things other than just staying alive is extremely important in explaining the quest for intimacy. You don't have time to worry about whether you love or are loved or whether you "belong" to anything when you do not know where your next meal will come from. It is precisely in the newly affluent upper middle class that the quest for intimate communities is the most powerful. I am not sug-

gesting that affluence causes the quest, rather that an increase in affluence makes it possible for more people than ever before to seek something besides the bread that is necessary to sustain physical life.

2. Modern psychology, with its strong emphasis on personal relationships and self-fulfillment, has provided men and women with a vocabulary that enables them to make their needs for intimacy explicit. The contemporary world of human relationships is not harsher than the world of the past, but I would argue that our expectations of what those relationships ought to be like has changed notably. Marriage, of course, is a classic example of this. The maintenance of the family property, continuation of the family line, effective working of the family farm, and the satisfaction of minimum sexual needs was enough for husband and wife relationships in a peasant society. One does not want to be so naïve as to say that there was never any depth of love between spouses; there was indeed in many cases. The point is that the ecstasies of romantic love were not expected, and the marriage relationship could survive without them—as in many cases, no doubt, it had to. In the contemporary world, the marriage relationship is expected to provide the fundamental life satisfaction as a relationship quite independent of any other social or cultural role. One lives for one's spouse in a way that would not have been intelligible in years gone by. Men and women may very well be much more skilled in the arts of interpersonal intimacy than they were in the past, but if they have acquired both greater skills and greater opportunities for intimacy, so, too, have they acquired much greater expectations. Here is the problem not only for marriage but for all human relationships. It is not that the interpersonal ambience has deteriorated since the past; on the contrary, it has got much better. Our expectations for psychological satisfaction from human relationships have increased, and increased much more rapidly than the quality of human relationships. It is not that we are getting less out of relationships, it is rather that we expect much more.

3. Finally, in past times, men did not have options about the community to which they belonged. One was part of the group into which one was born. Only by leaving the group physically—a most extraordinary thing to do—did one exercise a choice, and that was a choice that gave no assurance that one could ever become part of another community. The immigrant was a marginal man and was likely to remain marginal for all his life. However, there is in the world today a number of options about one's primordial group. One can *choose* where one is going to belong. While from the point of view of freedom this increase of options represents an improvement, it also poses a new obligation on the human person, particularly the young human person. If one is able to choose, it is difficult to escape the responsibility of choice, and now the issue of where one chooses to belong becomes an explicit and occasionally terrify-

ing question. Affiliation is now a matter of choice and, hence, a burden and a responsibility. One does not necessarily inherit one's primary belonging as did one's predecessors. Hence, the search for something to belong to becomes more important, and for those who lack security in their own personal worth, also more agonized.

Choice, affluence, and a revolution of rising expectations—these factors explain why many of those who drift into the new communities are not especially alienated or lonely. We are not dealing, in fact, with an attempt to recover interpersonal intimacy that existed in some mythological past. On the contrary, the new communitarian movement, however it may refer romantically to past stages in human history, represents an attempt to create something entirely new: a culture based on openness, trust and explicit affection. It is as something fundamentally new in the human condition that it must be evaluated; and to the extent that it is religious, it should be understood not as a resurgence of religion but rather as a development of a quite new religious form.[3]

## II. Are They Religious?

There is considerable debate among those who are studying the new communities as to whether they are religious or secular and whether they will survive. Not a few of the debaters have vested interests in contending that the new communities are neither religious nor likely to survive. It is certainly true that most of the communities collapse after a rather brief life. It is also true that many of them are not explicitly religious (particularly the psychological encounter groups and the political communes). Finally, it is true that most of those who join communes do so only for brief periods of time and do not intend to, or at least do not in fact, commit the rest of their lives to such behavior.

One reply to those who deny either the religiousness or the permanence

---

[3] I am not suggesting that there was no search for intimacy and trust in past religious forms. Surely, many of the founding groups of the great religious orders were seeking—though not with such an explicit vocabulary—the same thing the new communitarians seek. The men whom Vincent, Francis, Ignatius, Benedict and Dominic gathered around them were at least for a time intimate communities. However, as soon as canon law intervened, these communities adopted an organized structure, and they lost their primitive communal forms. The rhetoric, the vocabulary and the ideology of the contemporary communitarian would strongly resist such "institutionalization." The new communitarians will argue that the Jesuits were much better off when they were a handful of men around Ignatius, and the Franciscans were much better off before Brother Elias "institutionalized" them. But the important point is not that the new community will strongly resist institutionalization; it is that the old communities would not have understood the problem in the terms that are taken for granted today.

of the new groups is to assert that at least some of them are quite explicitly religious and that others, particularly the rural farm communes, have taken on a religious coloring—complete with sacramentals, rituals, purification rites, and frequently strong astrological views of reality.

While something can be said for this response, my own inclination would be to take a broader view with the observation that whatever happens to a particular group and however brief the involvement of many people may be and however explicitly religious or unreligious the communities may be, the important phenomenon is rather the widespread quest for intimacy, a quest of which communitarian movements themselves may only be the tip of the iceberg. It is virtually impossible to share the kind of trust and intimacy which contemporary personalism thinks is the highest goal of human life unless one shares fundamental values and worldview with those among whom one seeks intimacy. The quest for intimacy, I would assert, is always religious, and probably, in the long run, always sacred.

Extremely powerful psychological forces are released when one takes and permits oneself to be taken in an intimate relationship. In themselves, these forces are neutral; they can be positive or negative, constructive or destructive, but they are primordial human drives that are normally contained within systematic defense mechanisms. The openness, defenselessness and psychological nakedness involved in the quest for intimacy reveals, or at least purports to reveal, the most basic selfhood of the person. Under such circumstances, great powers of both love and hatred can be released. Whether love or hate will predominate depends to a considerable extent on whether the people involved share the same primal convictions about the nature of reality. Much of the disillusionment, disappointment and tragedy that are so frequent in the commune movement results from the fact that either common worldviews are not shared or that, if they are, convictions about them are so weak that they cannot overcome the fear, the anguish and, at times, the terror that intimacy creates.

One seeks intimacy, then, with one's own kind of people because in the final analysis it is only with one's own kind of people—that is to say people with whom one shares the most profound and powerful convictions—that intimacy is possible. The commune movements call forth a religious response almost inevitably because they touch that which is most fundamental and basic in man: the core of his selfhood. The group member necessarily deals with his own primal conceptions about the nature of the Real.

The quest for community, I would suggest, represents at first implicitly and then explicitly—frequently in a quite painful fashion—the quest for a common faith to share. This faith may be an explicitly religious transcendental faith or it may simply be a view of the Ultimate without a transcendental referent. From a social science viewpoint, it matters little. In both cases, man's search for intimacy involves him willy-nilly in a search for the Ultimate.

In this frame of reference, then, the question of whether the new communitarian groups are a permanent or a transitory phenomenon becomes less important. I doubt very much that any social science observer of the contemporary world doubts that the quest for interpersonal intimacy will persist. So long as men and women are seeking to reconstruct their own particular segment of the world along personalistic lines, the religious question will remain an extremely important one. If, as I have argued previously, the quest for intimacy represents not a return to the past but a beginning of a rather new phenomenon in human history, then it would follow that we are also witnessing the beginning of a new development in man's religious behavior; an increasing number of men and women will be seeking for a religious perspective powerful enough to overcome the fears and tame the wild passions that are released by the search for intimacy. If these assumptions are correct, then it may very well be that religion is not merely persisting but is entering a whole new era, an era in which religious faith (or basic worldview, to use more neutral words) becomes the explicit basis for the creation of very new and much more intense kinds of personal relationships.

## III. What Are the Dangers?

In a previous article for *Concilium,* I pointed out a number of the dangers of the new religious phenomenon. There are some special dangers in the communitarian component: (a) a man who seeks intimacy—at least who seeks it honestly—makes himself extremely vulnerable. He opens himself up to others, and in that act he becomes very weak in his psychological position vis-à-vis others. The man seeking intimacy says, in effect, "Here I am, trusting and defenseless before you." Only the most naïve would think that this man is not running a risk of being badly hurt. Trust is admirable, but there are also a considerable number of people whom one really ought not to trust.

When one gives oneself over in intimate relationships to a group, one is at the mercy of tremendous group pressures. It is well known that some people can be personally "destroyed" in the tough and brutal interaction of a marathon encounter group. Those who best survive such sessions are not the most honest but those with the toughest skin. Those most likely to be hurt are not necessarily the most aggressive but often those who are most gentle and vulnerable. A disturbed but vigorous person, understanding the mechanics of group dynamics, can wreak havoc on others in an intimate group setting, and a group which contains a number of such people will almost certainly create an extraordinarily dangerous situation.

In intimate groups there is a tendency for everyone to fall back on those defenses against intimacy one learns in one's earliest years. Thus, intimate communities often represent simply a collective regression to childhood behavior patterns, in which all one's partners in the group become surrogate parental or sibling figures. Under such circumstances, all the group's energy is expended in a usually fruitless attempt to straighten out the kinks of interpersonal relationships, and the attempt will never be successful precisely because it suits the purposes of many if not all of the members of the group to keep it fixated on interpersonal problems. Thereby, it need not face any of its responsibilities to the world beyond itself. The phenomenon of collective regression is really a form of psychiatric gnosticism.

Frequently the defense mechanisms that arise in such groups to protect its members from intimacy become more elaborate and more vicious than those that are practised in ordinary human relationships. In the name of a libertarian ideology and using the rhetoric of psychological personalism, narrow, oppressive and rigid tyrannies come into being. The tragedy of the so-called "Manson family", which was involved in several murders in California, is but a bizarre extreme phenomenon that occurs not infrequently in other communal groups. The strong members dominate the weak, in the name of freedom and openness, indeed, but in fact with an oppression that is all the more dangerous because it masquerades as freedom.

In summary, intimate communities are only for those who are personally mature and psychologically sophisticated. Unfortunately, many of those who are attracted to such communities possess neither quality. Those who do possess them have no particular need to join dubious communitarian efforts. Mankind may have invented a vocabulary for *talking about* personal intimacy and increased its expectations of experiencing such intimacy, but the development of those skills which are required for *living in* community seems to have lagged behind. The search for personal intimacy is not likely to cease, despite the grave injury many people suffer in such a search. Those who embark on the search for community should be aware that it may turn out to be a very dangerous and unpleasant voyage.

## IV. What Does It All Mean for the Churches?

It is fashionable in some religious circles to see the communitarian movement as a judgment on the churches. It is argued that young people who are flocking to the communes are searching for something the Church should offer but hasn't. They reject the Church because the Church is not living up to its own professed communitarian principles.

A point must be conceded in this argument: there can be no doubt that Jesus did demand a high level of trust and openness in those who enter the kingdom of his Father, although it must also be asserted that trust was a consequence of the grateful acceptance of God's gracious love and not a cause of it. If in the long history of Christianity more of us had believed in the Good News of Jesus and loved one another in the confidence of our faith, there would be much more intimacy in the human race than there is at the present. But it does not follow that we can achieve instant intimacy or convert the world into one gigantic commune overnight simply by an act of will. The attempts of some clergymen to become like hippies and of others to form communes in which intimacy is achieved instantaneously demonstrate theological, psychological and sociological naïveté. The growth of the human personality is gradual and organic; it cannot be speeded up by high-pressure techniques. Similarly, the Holy Spirit works where he will, and our enthusiasm and energy can no more constrain him to blow whither we will than can our rigid organizational structures. The enthusiasm of some clergy for "creating community" is simplistic when it is not dangerous. If the Church has failed in the past to respect human dignity and integrity because of the rigidity of its formal structures, it can all too easily continue to fail today by misguided attempts to force highly stylized forms of intimacy on everyone, whether they are ready for it or not.

But if the churches must be wary of a false intimacy that is imposed on the instant, they should not be blinded to the importance of the personalist quest as a sign of the times. The fundamental theme of this issue of *Concilium* is that religion persists and that what may look like simplistic evolution is in fact a periodicity of alternating factors. This periodicity is not merely circular. The rhythm between church and sect is inherent in the Christian tradition. Men will alternately develop sects that are highly exclusive and then develop churches which are inclusive. The communitarian movement, both inside and outside the Church, is essentially an exercise in sect formation. But while the new sects have something in common with the enthusiastic sects of the past, with both the Montanists and the Franciscans, for example, they still represent a critically new development in the human religious pilgrimage. New sects may run the risk of gnosticism, oppression, manipulation, suffering and disillusionment; but they also represent a conscious, explicit and psychologically sophisticated attempt to love one another even as Jesus loved us. They are not a resurgence of religion; they are rather a persistence of religion, but a persistence of religion in a new, interesting and potentially productive form. Theologians would be well advised to reflect on the meaning of this quest for community, to inquire what light the Christian symbol system might be able to shed upon it. Churchmen, working out of the richness of the Christian theological and communitarian heritage, should not be afraid to assume a position of leadership in the communitarian quest. Christianity certainly cannot take exception to a movement which in its best manifestations seeks to bind men together in faith and in love.

# The Two Cultures of American Catholicism

From: *Tomorrow's Catholics/Yesterday's Church*

BY EUGENE KENNEDY

## Thomas Merton Died for Our Sins

*I am the way, the truth, and the life...*
— JOHN 14:6

*Artistic growth is, more that it is anything else,*
*a refining of the sense of truthfulness.*
*The stupid believe that to be truthful is easy;*
*only the artist, the great artist, knows how difficult it is.*
— WILLA CATHER, THE SONG OF THE LARK

As previously noted, the two cultures of American Catholicism may be distinguished in terms of the voices to which they listen. There is presently considerable overlap in this regard, another function of Catholic education's reclamation of the humanistic tradition of which the church was once the unexcelled champion. The American Catholic as philistine, the self-assured censor and skeptical derider of all that was new, is not now an appropriate stereotype. If Culture One no longer excludes any but the most pietistic of artists, Culture Two Catholics not only accept but identify with the struggles of all true artists, sensing the essentially religious nature of their labors, recognizing that they expend the same spiritual energies that they themselves do pursuing the mystery of daily life.

In the once terrible beauty of Culture One, the church seemed a glistening cloud-beribboned castle whose monarchs felt that they not only monopolized but had a right to monitor, judge, and control all religious experience. The institution claimed the exclusive world rights to holiness, grudgingly allowing that intense spiritual lives could be led outside its walls but only in extreme circumstances or according to instructive providential designs. Such non-Catholic religious persons were thereby invisibly tied to the official church, which arrogated jurisdiction over them to itself, conferring on them an honorary, and therefore controllable, Catholic identity through such notions as "anonymous" Christianity and "baptism of desire."

Currently, Culture Two Catholics understand that the official supervision and licensing of the spiritual life are as antithetical to its nature as to the nature of art itself. Ecclesiastical administrators cannot exercise control over what is, at heart, utterly human and mysterious. His papal sponsor may have nagged Michelangelo, lying flat on his scaffolding contemplating divine truths, but he could not enter into or shape his creative work or his spiritual vision. The Christian life is, in fact, a work of art, its dynamics exactly those familiar to every honest artist—the awesome dying and being born again that are the inner strength and spiritual source of authority for any true creation. The authority of genuine art is, therefore, nonmanipulative and essentially simple; art speaks for itself. Great art, like a great life, addresses us in a unique voice; that is why we turn and give our attention to both of these, willingly obedient to their internal authority. They are versions of the quest for the grail, for that essentially spiritual mythic search, the pilgrimage, as in the myth of the Knights of King Arthur, always begun at the forest wall where no trail had yet been cut, in itself both poses the mystical question and answers it at the same time.

A holy life is a creative achievement that delivers the concentrated truth of an individual existence. Like the artist, the good person is aware of all that is "grave and constant," joyous and tragic, in the human landscape, and is committed to a transformation of the inner self, a passage through suffering and death to resurrection and a fuller experience of being alive. In the work of art and in holy lives we sense our own experience lived more intensely, lived, we might say, with authority. We respond willingly to good lives and good art, effortlessly acknowledging this authority. Again, this is not blind obedience to the will of another but a positive response to the evidence of our senses that nourishes and moves the imagination. Deep calls out to deep, health to health, and what the saint and the artist tell us of human experience deepens our understanding of our own. This critical exchange is healthy, for we emerge from it more alive than we were before it took place; every engagement with real holiness or genuine art is a resurrection.

The institutional church is true to its own organizational nature; it is only being itself when it attempts to control what is fundamentally beyond control—the natural, healthy instincts of good persons. One might say that the notion of perfection held by the organizational church has been a case of mistaken identity. Its administrators misidentified obsessive orderliness as holiness, consequently ruling out the moderate, common, and eminently tolerable disorder of imperfection that is the condition of any well-lived and healthy life. Health was ruled out on a technicality because it did not fit easily into any canonical category. But no one can write rules for healthy people. That is the burden of St. Paul's extraordinary reflections on the nature of love in First Corinthians. Love and health share the same simplicity of appearance, the same lack of manipulative intent. For centuries, however, healthy people were made to feel guilty because they could not lead unhealthy lives perfectly, while many neurotic people were rewarded because they could. The thought of all the generous, earnest efforts on the part of good people to subdue what was humanly healthy about themselves in order to fit the institutional model of sanctity retains a terrible power to break the heart.

Such good persons—seminarians and men and women candidates for the religious life—thought that their superiors knew what they were doing and submitted to their wishes, often with disastrous consequences for themselves. Those who survived these regimes, which forced a Cartesian dualism into their spiritual lives, did so because of their basic health. Similarly, married people made heroic efforts to comply with institutional expectations about their own conduct, frequently at a tragically high price to themselves and their families. Indeed, the darker aspects of the culture so dominated by the imperial institution became the theme of great exile Catholic artists. No writer more clearly explored the lonely, conflicted, and unsentimentalized world of the priesthood during that early century high point of clerical culture than J. F. Powers. It took such artists to examine and exorcise the demons of estrangement, loneliness, and heartbreak that entered so many people through this split spiritual vision of the human person. It is, therefore, not surprising that many people have now pulled back from automatically accepting the authority of those institutional churchmen who insist on the hierarchical ordering not only of the church but of the spiritual life as well. What healthy people sense about such self-appointed supervisors is their distance from the realities of human experience.

The institution's claim that the crown of holiness was granted to those who observed with exhausting exactitude myriad regulations led to demonic and debilitating ascetic competitions, many of which had a pathological underside, in which the tension arose from a basic, if unacknowledged, conflict between the individual and the organization. Individuals who kept the rules heroically, going beyond the institution's demands, won freedom, as we will see presently, from its supervisory power and, in many cases, such as those of the great medieval women saints, became a threat to it. For the moment, however, we may observe that goodness and health are not easily categorized and certainly cannot be subjected to domination by others without suffering serious loss or distortion. Culture Two Catholics have recaptured a basic Christian understanding of personality by embracing health as the most trustworthy sign of the spirit. This represents a return to the spiritual life as art rather than as law, and to metaphor rather than concrete discourse as religion's native language. This is the territory of the artist and the saint, human, ever mysterious and ambivalent, chartable only one step at a time. One thinks of St. John of the Cross's remark about the summit of perfection, "There is no way here." That matches exactly the instruction given the Arthurian knights as they departed on their quests; each was, as mentioned, to "enter the forest at its darkest part." There was, and is, no spiritual grail to be found at the end of a path hacked out by another. On any pilgrimage powerful enough to change us, we are on our own.

A holy life, like a poem, a painting, or a piece of sculpture, is, as its linguistic roots attest, something whole. The root of the word holy is *kailo,* which in old English became *hal,* or whole, as in *halsum,* or wholesome. Is it accidental that in French we come upon it as the sturdy support of the feminine name *Hel*oise? Or that *health, holy,* and *hallow* bloom from this same stem of language? Holiness is not to be associated with the denial of existence, the refusal to see or hear or eat, but with its affirmation and the good use of the senses. So Jesus says, in John, "I have come that they may have life, and life to the full." In a classic evocation of holiness, St. Irenaeus says that "the glory of God is a man fully alive."

The quest for holiness and the struggle for true art are intimately related efforts. Both seek to render human experience whole and intelligible. Holiness perceived fundamentally as a gradual extirpation of the earthy components of personality, a steady effort to purify the self of every claim of the body, represented an estrangement from the traditional understanding of holiness implicit in the church's central teaching of the Incarnation, in which God does not reject but "takes on the body of a man," accepting all human aches and joys, save sin, at the same time.

Institutional church leaders appear never to have observed the bright and revealing irony of their post-mortem appreciation of the body and sanctity. During life's arduous passage toward holiness the body was to be despised, maltreated in the name of spiritual perfection. At the moment of death the corpse, the flesh safe now from its familiar shudders, became sacred, an appraisal reinforced, peculiarly enough, if after death's visitation the body remained lifelike in appearance. Such a body was feasted on by its venerators, and relics of hair and bone, even articles of clothing or objects touched to the corpse, were thought to have curative powers, and, inserted as minute fragments into miniature, monstrance-like vessels, became important not only to the cult of the deceased but to the unabashed commercial enterprises that grew from them. Culture One, at its zenith, had an enormous inventory of blessed remains under its jurisdiction. Like seeds cast into the wind, these relics were found everywhere in the culture—at the shrines of the saints, in glinting reliquaries on thousands of mantelpieces, pinned on the swaddling clothes of infants and the bed linen of the dying. The institution was able to revere in death the body that it barely tolerated in life.

Culture Two Catholics have sensed the incongruity of notions of sanctity that celebrated the body only after rigor mortis had set in. This was, in effect, an institutional act of sacrilege against the teachings of Jesus and, indeed, against the most obvious meaning of his having "taken on the body of a man." The church, its profoundly human inclinations revived by the fresh waters of Vatican II theology, has renewed its incarnational self-understanding. In the conciliar documents, the church defines itself not as an institution but as mystery, a people of God, a mystery, then, of active human relationships that do not need death to validate their simple goodness. Culture Two Catholics no longer romanticize the ideal of sanctity split off from the pursuit of a full and honorable life in the compelling, mysterious unity of soul and body. The great battle of existence cannot pit these elements against each other; the struggle is to become whole, even imperfectly, rather than to endure a false division of the self. This striving for integrity resembles that of the artist and the effort is not only lighted from within by its own distinctive authority. So, too, it is intrinsically generative, shorn of meaning unless it gives and nourishes life. Sanctity, in the healthiest intuition of Culture Two, cannot be life denying or deliberately barren.

Many sincere Culture One Catholics still give strong evidence of their indoctrination during the golden age in which religion was partitioned off from life in general, so that it fell, in what seemed an almost natural way, under the aegis and control of the administrative church. Religion was not permitted far beyond this closely guarded area; Sunday was the day for faith, the interval in which to contemplate the supernatural plane that floated just beyond the reach of earthlings. Anything wholly "natural," such as a spontaneous response of love, could only be made worthy, that is "supernaturalized," through a mental transformation that invested the act with grace. Otherwise, despite the authority such responses bore because of their generosity or nobility, they were merely "natural," pagan distant cousins to institutionally validated examples of holiness. Culture One actively rejected the integration of faith into the other activities of life.

That careful distinction between the personal, spiritual life and the public, professional life allowed the development of the famous Catholic political and business consciences. Men felt that, if they fulfilled their institutional religious obligations, they were free to become friendly on their own terms with the mammon of iniquity during the rest of the week. Papal encyclicals on labor were not warmly welcomed by many Catholic businessmen, who felt that the church should mind its own spiritual preserves and stay out of theirs. If soul and body and spirit and flesh were divisible, so were these universes of concern. One of my most vivid encounters with that mentality occurred when I visited an old politician in a federal prison and he spent most of the time speaking of his pilgrimages to religious shrines and of his continuing habit of sleeping on his side to leave room for his guardian angel. In short, how to be a good Catholic while serving time for mail fraud and embezzlement.

This is the landscape poet T. S. Eliot once described as the "Waste Land," which, as Joseph Campbell has observed, is "a world in which . . . force and not love, indoctrination, not education, authority, not experience, prevail in the ordering of lives, and where the myths and rites enforced and received are consequently unrelated to the actual inward realizations, needs, and potentialities of those upon whom they are impressed."*

"And we are here," as Matthew Arnold wrote of the same forsaken place, "as on a darkling plain / Swept with confused alarms of struggle and flight / Where ignorant armies clash by night."† The intuitively spiritual—mystics, artists, and healthy ordinary people—stand together, as they have throughout history, as the true counterculturists, who feel deep within themselves the falseness of the apparent triumphs of their times. This occurs whenever appearances are valued more than reality and are propped up by a combination of power and deceptive language. Such strategies betray the healthy and healing quest for truth—for authoritative truth, we might say—the search for the grail that is the calling of all creative and generative people. Throughout history, such persons have stood apart from the insistent, power-imbued culture, whether of church or state, to reject its hypocrisy, and, at that darkened mass of forest, to find their own path.

Indeed, the condition described by Eliot in his famous 1922 poem ("I Tiresias, though blind, throbbing between two lives . . .") was that, not only of our time, but of the world, as Campbell observes, "torn between honor and love . . . that was to be cured of its irresolution" through the experience described in the legend of the Holy Grail.‡ And, as rendered by Wolfram von Eschenbach, this story of Parzival is a tale of devastated Christianity—that is, a waste land of corrupted authority—"symbolically attributed to the awesome wounding of young Grail King Anfortas . . . This calamity was symbolic . . . of the dissociation within Christendom of spirit from nature: the denial of nature

---

*The Masks of God: Creative Mythology,* New York, Viking Press, 1968, p. 388.

†"Dover Beach," stanza 4.

‡Joseph Campbell, *Myths to Live By,* New York, Bantam edition, 1973, p. 166.

as corrupt, the imposition of what was supposed to be authority *super*naturally endowed, and the actual demolishment of both nature and truth in consequence."* But, in order to grasp the dynamics of this legend, so clearly the same ones experienced by all who seek spiritual truth today, let Joseph Campbell tell us the rest of this story:

> The mystical law governing the adventure required that the hero to achieve it should have no knowledge of its task or rules, but accomplish all spontaneously on the impulse of his nature. . . . And the task then expected of him, when the maimed king on his litter would be carried into the stately hall, would be simply to ask what ailed him. The wound would immediately heal, the waste land would become green. . . . However, on the occasion of his first arrival and reception, Parzival, though moved to compassion, politely held his peace, for he had been taught . . . that a knight does not ask questions. Thus he allowed concern for his social image to inhibit the impulse of his nature—which, of course, was exactly what everyone else in the world was doing in that period and was the cause of all that was wrong.†

As a result, as those familiar with the story know, the young misguided knight was exiled from the Grail realm and only as he persisted, out of compassion for the wounded king, was he ultimately able to complete his task. The climax of the story follows a battle with his elder Moslem half-brother, which led to their recognition of each other, "an allegorical reference to the two opposed religions of the time, Christianity and Islam: 'two noble sons,' so to say, 'of one father.' "‡ Both are invited to the castle, the king is healed, and Parzival takes his place. The elements of this adventure match those required in our own day for any who would heal the division between the church as a powerful institution and as a People of God, thereby making the waste land bloom: confidence in healthy inner impulses, especially that of compassion, and a willingness to recognize the relationship that transcends religious institutional claims to exclusivity of redemptive franchise, between ourselves and all members of the human family.

The spiritual waste land of our own time will flourish, not in response to authoritarian assertions or the implementation of institutional force, but in response to the same profoundly spiritual realizations to which we must finally

---

*Ibid., pp. 167, 168.

†Ibid., p. 169.

‡Ibid., p. 170.

be obedient, that is, to whose whisperings we must listen and respond. All artists and believers are called to heal the wounded king, not through repeating formulas insisted on by others, but through the natural, healthy power of their own loving compassion for others.

The genuine artist and the good person are drawn, as the knights were toward the spiritual meaning of the grail, by an inner sense of direction to the healthy integration of life's elements; they actively seek wholeness. Their non-manipulative commitment to this fullness of being in their lives and work attracts our freely bestowed attention. Although they do not insist on, or perhaps even think much about, their authority, it is theirs as ripeness belongs to the nature of the harvest and grandeur to the sunset spreading itself along the horizon; their authority is indisputable and irresistible and it has nothing to do with controlling other persons. It is easy to tell, in life and in art, when people know what they are doing. The authority of art is linked inseparably to the vision, intention, and skills of artists, no matter what their medium.

Artists take the pieces of life, the shards of good and bad, of love and friendship, of pain, tragedy, and misunderstanding that confront us all, and endow them with a wholeness that allows us to penetrate the mystery in which our lives are set. They heal our wounds with their compassionate perception and rendering of our striving and our falling short. In their work, they address our total personalities, both conscious and unconscious, leading us more deeply into ourselves, into the furthest recesses of our identity, supporting our stance on the ever-shifting ground of existence. Such persons do not strike the great tent of mystery that billows above us but rather allow us to see its intricate folds and webbing, the mysteries coiled within mystery in the great dwelling of life.

Artists make it possible for us to accept and deal with the magnificent, sometimes comforting, sometimes terrifying ambiguities of our experience. In similar fashion, good persons—holy people—pull together the same easily scattered human elements, not cheaply or superficially, but in the authentically generative fashion that flows from their being responsibly human instead of striking shallow angelic poses. These include shaping a consistent and serious moral vision, and a willingness to expose themselves to hurt—to the dangerous possibilities of failure and rejection—in their efforts to love. They are true seekers of the grail, entering the forest every day at its darkest part. The medium of holy persons is life, and, much like artists, they translate it steadily by respecting, perhaps in the painful act of always rediscovering, its ineffable mystery. They have authority not because they solve the mystery but because they understand that nobody ever can. The great German Jesuit theologian Karl Rahner once said that the mystery of the universe that frustrated Einstein was precisely what attracted him.

Religious persons, like artists, have no easy task in making something fresh, unique, and wondrous of these familiar, perennially perplexing materials of our human situation. That willingness to look again at life defines the nature of respect for life (respect, from *respicere,* means *to look again*) and the capacity for compassion. *Respect for Life,* a slogan much used by the institutional church in its campaigns of education against birth control and abortion, cannot be reduced to these few, albeit important, moral issues. Respect for life connotes a richer comprehension of the complex tasks of existence and of the special authority that individuals manifest through the unselfish love by which they impress a distinctive moral configuration on their lives. This authority is one with and inseparable from the healthy obligation of making something whole out of the diverse aspects of life itself. It is therefore totally different from the authoritarianism falsely invoked as authority by ecclesiastical bureaucrats. Genuine authority, as mentioned often, speaks directly to the human imagination and only indirectly to the will.

Confidence in healthy instincts and intuitions, friendliness to the inner self's striving for wholeness: these are concepts that were not readily accepted in the triumphant age of Culture One. It is not surprising to find that art, other than as the affirmation of institutionally acceptable themes, was looked on with enormous suspicion during that period. It was, indeed, a waste land, although its ecclesiastical proprietors seemed pleased with its severe and well-ordered bleakness. Barrenness was what they wanted. George N. Shuster, then editor of *Commonweal,* suggested in 1922, for example, that "the great bulk of American Catholic fiction is unintelligent and unreadable."

In a recent study of Catholic periodical fiction during that high age of Culture One (1930–1950), Joseph M. McShane observes the clear identification of many Catholic writers with institutional purposes. Their stories, for example, sharply criticized women seeking careers outside the home, warned of the dangers of mixed marriages, divorce, and birth control. As he notes,

> The destructive potential of the modern world was not exhausted by its threats against marriage and its temptations . . . the writers also warned . . . about the dangerous moral relativism and agnosticism that could result from any education beyond high school . . . or from pursuing professional careers in scientific or medical research. To counterbalance the corrosive influence of education, the readers were exhorted to lead lives marked by peasant or childlike faith. . . . Fear created a ghetto in which thought and creativity were devalued, and passivity encouraged.*

*U.S. Catholic Historian,* Vol. 6, Number 2/3, Spring/Summer 1987, pp. 188, 189.

While certain redeeming pockets of concern for the artist existed in the shadowed nooks of Culture One, as in the Dominican Fathers' sponsorship of the theater, or in the literary interests of the Jesuits, novelists such as Harry Sylvester and J. F. Powers who bravely explored the psychological interior of Catholicism in the forties, swam against a powerful cultural stream, and won their literary recognition in the world at large rather than within Catholicism itself. Why this bleak reception for the artist, of whose calling the church was once the greatest supporter, and in whose work, as in that of Michelangelo or Raphael, Catholic theology was once so gloriously expressed? The answer, in accord with dynamics to be explored in greater detail later, is found less in the church's concern for the purity of religious truth than in its anxiety to preserve and enhance the effective power of its organizational structures. Institutions suppress the natural response, so healthy and sacramentally significant in the account of Parzival's quest, Everyman's calling. The authority that a church possesses because of its sacramental insight is quickly dissipated when it chooses to follow its institutional reflexes instead of its healthiest instincts.

Artists, by nature, are antagonists of the institutionalization of existence, persons who cannot successfully fulfill their calling under the control of bureaucrats, however benign. The plight of Catholics with artistic souls was, therefore, extraordinarily frustrating and painful in the church until little more than a generation ago. Vatican II began to welcome them back just as it made possible the related development of Culture Two Catholicism. Only in this free environment were artists once again warmly invited, appreciated, and recognized as legitimate explorers of all human experience, who could, as novelists by their very title claim, return from their daily work with "something new" to tell us about its mountains and hidden valleys. That is the grail found and brought back to us by serious artists of every kind.

Culture Two, in part because its members were given rich opportunities for higher education by Culture One, has had the leisure as well as the perspective to appreciate the intimate kinship of art and religion. It was Culture One, as we have noted, that made Vatican II possible, and, within it, put an end to the *Index* of prohibited books that had so tightly controlled Catholics' freedom to read. In this new and congenial atmosphere, art, like a cathedral freed from the grip of massive scaffolding, shoulders its majestic lines in the sunlight and speaks its silent spiritual language across the landscape. Culture Two makes room for artists to pursue their own inner visions. It is impossible to be against art and for religion, unless one or the other is so falsified as to be unrecognizable. That is why the present tension within Catholicism has come to center on the nature of religion itself. That is a waste-land dilemma. The institutionalists perceive religion as a literal, non-artistic, tightly controllable phenomenon. In short, a mirror held far away and at a distorting angle from reality. Catholics not consumed by institutional concerns understand religion as something far different, something timeless beneath the accidents of time, the mysterious that streams from the vents of everyday experience, rich and dappled, sacramental and inexhaustible, bearing as the air bears light every human mood and rhythm.

In his quest for the grail the poet Thomas Merton not only relived the dynamic elements of challenge in the lives of the knights and of monks like Abelard who preceded him, but he worked out a destiny *(wyrd,* that active pursuit of an unfolding fate, as it is called in the classical legends) similar to that of every Culture Two Catholic. It was almost exactly that of many creative, truly spiritual artists (in the broadest sense) who gave themselves to an institutional church that had lost touch with its own poetic strengths. With the best of intentions, the administrative church did not know what to do with him and, puzzled by his creative yearnings and restlessness, attempted to control rather than encourage him in a variety of ways throughout his life. As a Trappist, he became celebrated for his autobiography, *The Seven Storey Mountain,* the narrative of his movement out of his literary Columbia University milieu into the stark calling of the ever-silent monk. It was a pilgrimage that matched perfectly the highly romantic aspects of Culture One's postwar glory.

So far, so good. The real story, brilliantly revealed in Michael Mott's biography, was far different.* Merton the monk lost the freedom to follow his own inner intuitions. He was forced, under obedience, to write explicitly "religious" books, lives of Trappist saints and other works that reinforced the institution and helped greatly to support his monastery. His works were censored by men who did not comprehend them, his desire to live part of the time in a hermitage was represented to Roman authorities by his own abbot as the request of "an emotional, unstable sort of person who was trying to avoid living a normal life."† He was even accused by a leading Catholic psychoanalyst, Gregory Zilboorg, of being, among other things, "a gadfly . . . very stubborn . . . megalomania and narcissism are your big trends."‡

Yet Merton the monk could not overcome Merton the artist, and he gradually made a separate, uneasy peace with the Trappists, moving out of the community into a cabin of his own, as, indeed, Abelard had centuries before him. Merton also moved in many ways back into the world, stumbling, as an artist in such a situation must, making his way out as he wrote again on the subjects that were his own, forging a new extra-institutional life and identity that

---

*The Seven Mountains of Thomas Merton,* Boston, Houghton Mifflin, 1984.

†Ibid., p. 338.

‡Ibid., p. 295.

were in part clumsy, in part poignant, and immensely human. Mott's biography is clearly an account of Merton's search for the grail, that ultimate symbol of spiritual meaning.

Merton was, one might surmise against the overspiritualized Culture One interpretations of his life, making his way by trial and error out of that culture, not wanting to hurt anyone but needing to get out, seeking health according to the authority of his internal sense of balance. His inner sensitivity made him aware of the universality of the religious impulse as well as of contemplation as its rich common thread. So he wrote, as he gradually moved deeper into an appreciation of the bonds between all the great religious traditions, that for him "Catholicism is not confined to one culture, one nation, one age, and one race . . . my Catholicism is all the world and all the ages."* And, if he lamented the crisis that monasticism itself was enduring in a time of renewal, Merton was also searching for some different setting in which to live out his own life and a deeper language in which to sing of it.

Consider Abelard near the end of his life. Half a man, having been castrated by Heloise's uncles, celebrated as an exiled philosopher and poet, finding an audience outside the church rather than in its administrators, he was, as Campbell observes,

> harried from pillar to post for his views, driven throughout his mutilated life from one monastic haven to another. On one occasion he was compelled to burn his own book with his own hands ("So it was burnt," he wrote of this brutal event, "amid general silence"); and to read aloud then the Athanasian Creed ("the which I read amid sobs and tears as well as I might"). He was sent to a convent near Soissons, which had acquired the reputation of a penitentiary . . . only to fall into more trouble, and then more, until at one point he fled to a forest hermitage, to which . . . students flocked. . . . "God knows," he wrote of those terrible years, "that at times I fell into such despair that I proposed to myself to go off and live the life of a Christian among the enemies of Christ."†

So, Merton, near the end of his life, vexed and on the move, finding even his hermitage filled with guests, a celebrity corresponding with the great writers and spiritual thinkers of his time, but a man under suspicion by his superiors for what they could only perceive as his highly irregular activities. In his last, extraordinarily restless years Merton fell in love with a young nurse, involved

---

*Ibid., p. 315.

†*The Masks of God,* p. 397.

himself in clandestine meetings, phone calls from the monastery that were overheard, a consuming relationship, which, like Abelard, he finally abandoned for the monastery. He seemed to resolve the relationship, but he did call the nurse, identified by Merton's biographer only as S., for a last time in the year he died, saying, "We are two half people wandering in two lost worlds."* He became a pilgrim again, seeking something that even as an artist he was not able fully to name. While pursuing an understanding of the limits of contemplation in the Far East, he died, either from a heart attack or through electrocution by a faulty fan cord. His death remains mysterious in a poetically, sacramentally appropriate way a generation after its occurrence. In his final talk, Merton seemed to hint about his long, lonely journey's end, speaking clearly from his unconscious to his colleagues as the morning concluded, "so I will disappear from view . . ."

His biographer observes that "in his journals Merton had talked over and over of disappearing."† Merton's life may be viewed as something composed by the poet within, a true rendering of the contemporary spiritual voyager, who came to feel trapped in the administrative church that had once seemed his romantic salvation, the artist who suffered, in advance as poets always do, what millions of his fellow Catholics would experience in the generation after his death. Perhaps it is not too far off the mark to say of him, as Campbell did of Abelard, that he "was indeed Tristan as the mutilated Grail King, and he stands symbolic for his time and for the sterilization of heart, body, and mind that the Waste Land theme represents."‡

Merton's life was thus the model for legions of creative people who baffled the institution and who paid high prices for being originals who did not fit easily into precut placements. Some suffered enormously, yielding up their untapped creativity to the unresponsive but hugely confident, and, one might add, generally benevolent, if smugly so, institution of Catholicism. Others experienced severe problems in trying to adjust to lives in which they could never feel comfortable or fulfilled. They all bear the wounds of the Grail King known to Abelard and Merton as well, for the administrative church emasculated them in its efforts to control them. Thus, authoritarian instincts to this day, in the name of a pure teaching authority, heap shame on the sexual dimensions of human personality.

Many highly creative persons in the clergy and religious life, as we have discussed, gradually moved out of its central core, toward marginal lives in which, like Merton, they fashioned a ledge just broad enough to stand on outside the

---

*Mott, p. 454.

†Ibid., p. 564.

‡*The Masks of God*, p. 397.

massive walls, a perilous purchase of freedom that the organization did not know how to give them directly. And, for all the struggle and disorder of his long journey, one might ask who now possesses true spiritual authority, Thomas Merton or a generation and more of nameless ecclesiastical bureaucrats who shook their heads at him? Who touches and opens our hearts, Merton or the monk who criticized him to Roman authority for not wanting to live a "normal life"?

Mystery thrives in the lives of the knowing and the loving. Its metaphors are everywhere in the scriptures, as in the psalmist's images of the wondrous creatures of nature, of nestlings under the protective wings of greater birds, of harts panting for living water. In short, the Bible presents mystery loose in the universe, mystery everywhere for those with eyes to see and ears to hear, mystery in the very texture of life, mystery the discernible aura around every truly human event. Joseph Cardinal Ratzinger, now head of the Congregation for the Doctrine of the Faith, has lamented the loss of mystery in Roman Catholicism. As a sensitive and well-trained theologian, Ratzinger may have felt the enormous pressures that a creative person experiences when he must give himself to administrative tasks. He may, in fact, be experiencing mystery deprivation in an office that requires him to control rather than engage in speculative theology. Perhaps in this man, so often perceived as the symbol of the institution, we have a new yet classic example of the creative person surrendering everything for the sake of the institution. Perhaps there is more Merton in him than he knows. He may not even realize that when he speaks of the absence of mystery in contemporary Catholicism he is revealing the depth of his own loss. Cardinal Ratzinger may himself bear wounds that he has not yet realized to be those of the legend of the grail seeker first written down in his own homeland a thousand years ago by von Eschenbach.

Only those with a lively feeling for mystery can grasp the correspondence between the creative process and the essential dynamics of the central Catholic understanding about life. For if we are all caught up in the search for the spiritual grail, we can recognize that the redemptive pattern of life, death, and resurrection is as common in ordinary life as it is, in intensified form, in the work of the artist. This cadenced experience of yielding up the self, that is, passing through death in order to achieve a deeper and fuller life, lies just below the surface of daily existence; its outlines can be found in every human transaction that has any genuine weight or meaning. This sequence is commonplace for spouses and parents, for teachers and pastors, for friends and lovers everywhere. Nothing reveals the identification of art and religion in a more telling manner than a comparison of the creative process with life itself.

Creative artists, whose long line started well before Abelard and continues beyond Merton, are concerned with a vision of the possible. They are, therefore, essentially persons of faith, for they are ever committed to a world that longs to come into being. Religious faith is of the same grain and texture as the faith that couples have in each other, in their families, and in their communities. The act of bringing the possible into existence defines the generative dimension of the authority that we have already explored in detail. What does the nature of the creative artistic process tell us about the generative authority that marks the lives of Culture Two Catholics?

Poets, in the studies of creative persons carried out by psychologist Frank Barron, speak of learning to "throw themselves away," of having to surrender themselves in pursuit of their art. They experience a certain disorganization of their adjustment in order to achieve the new and higher level of integration, the "wholeness" they express in their work. Barron described this as an experience of "diffusion," a breaching of their ego boundaries in order to bring them together again in the fulfillment of poetic achievement. Barron gives the following description of the creative artist's experience:

> . . . the individual is willing to "die unto himself," i.e., to permit an achieved adaptation or state of relative equilibrium to perish. And there are not guarantees that something better will thereby be arrived at. Looking backwards from the end point of the creative process, we are inclined to say, "Ah, yes, it had to be so; the chance had to be taken; the chalice could not be passed; the agony was necessary for the redemption and the resurrection." But facing forward in time we see only risk and difficulty, and if we have not the courage to endure diffusion ("suffer death") we cannot achieve the new and more inclusive integration ("gain the light").*

Works of art that emerge from such a process have the power to speak authoritatively to us; we recognize what we term, in a related word, the authenticity of the work. That always comes from within. The papers and documents of appraisers and art experts do not confer it. When these are reliable, they merely affirm what the work of art possesses in and of itself. So, too, the lives of good people—those who truly enlarge others through their relationships— have an internal strength purchased at the price of embracing the redemptive sequence of death and resurrection. This is the spiritual authority, so enlivening of the imagination, recognized and responded to by Culture Two Catholicism.

It may have been with just such a sense of the relationship between the

---

*"Diffusion, Integration, and Enduring Attention," in *Study of Lives,* ed. by Robert W. White (New York: Prentice-Hall, 1963), p. 247.

authority of true art and true religion that Pope Paul VI resisted the advice he had received to sell off the contents of the Vatican Museum. Instead, he refurbished it, opening a wing for modern art in the area immediately adjacent to the Sistine Chapel. This profound gesture signified a fresh acceptance of the genuine artist as an honored citizen of the Kingdom. Paul VI spoke, at the wing's dedication, of the need for the prophetic voice of the artist to be heard in the heart of the Vatican. In an era marked by institutional rebuilding and reform, Paul fashioned a sign in the fashion of a genuine artist, against the grain of his counselors. So Paul spoke for all the seekers of the spiritual grail, honoring all those who, like legions of Abelards and Mertons, have suffered pursuing the kingdom of God within them. Paul's gesture may one day be understood for what it was, a great act of faith in a church that was coming into being, a church that is more a servant people and less of a dominating institution, a healer of the wounded rather than a wounder of the healers.

# Facing False Charges

### From: *The Gift of Peace*

B Y   J O S E P H   L O U I S   B E R N A R D I N

On Wednesday, November 10, 1993, I was in New York to give the annual Thomas Merton Lecture at Columbia University. Cardinal John O'Connor, with whom I was staying, told me of a disturbing rumor that was circulating: A U.S. Cardinal was to be accused of sex abuse. Its source was uncertain, and its vagueness made it seem unworthy and yet ominous at the same time.

The rumors were growing by the time I returned to my office the next day. I was stunned to learn that some people were speculating that I was the Cardinal to be accused. In phone calls from friends, I discovered that rumors about an impending lawsuit were spreading rapidly across the country and around the world. I would be served papers the next morning charging that, when I was Archbishop of Cincinnati, I sexually abused a seminarian.

The accusation startled and devastated me. I tried to get beyond the unconfirmed rumors and return to my work, but this lurid charge against my deepest ideals and commitments kept consuming my attention. Indeed, I could think of little else as my aides continued to bring me additional details of rumors that were still circulating. I sat quietly for a moment and asked myself a simple question: Was this what the Lord had been preparing me for, to face false accusations about something that I knew never took place? Spurious charges, I realized, were what Jesus himself experienced. But this evolving nightmare seemed completely unreal. It did not seem possible that this was happening to me.

Late in the afternoon, Mary Ann Ahern of the local NBC television affiliate called, saying she had had a copy of the allegations read to her, that the plaintiff's name was Steven and that he was represented by a New Jersey lawyer who specialized in suing the clergy for sexual abuse. The lawsuit was to be filed in Cincinnati the next morning. "They claim to have pictures of Steven and the Cardinal together," the reporter read from the information that was surfacing in newsrooms across the country.

We learned a few minutes later that Steven's last name was Cook. I searched my memory for a face to go with the name Steven Cook. None appeared. "He was a college student at St. Gregory's," a staff member informed me, "and now he's in his mid-thirties and is very ill with AIDS. That's all we know."

*Steven Cook.* I still could not conjure up a face to go with the name of this person who, according to what was now a full-blown storm of rumor, claimed that he was led to my bedroom in 1975 and forced to submit to a sex act. Who, in God's name, was this person, and why was he accusing me of something that he must have known, as I did, never took place? I then recalled hearing that this same person had already brought complaints to the Archdiocese of Cincinnati against a priest who was on the faculty of St. Gregory's Seminary there. I began to surmise that because, in Steven's judgment, he had not received a satisfactory response from Cincinnati, his lawyer had decided to bring me into the case since I was Archbishop at the time. Later, Steven would tell me how this came about.

I thought of my sincere prayer to learn to let go and empty myself. Was God's answer hidden in this lawsuit through which faceless accusers threatened to brand me indelibly as a sex abuser, a charge that has been leveled at many priests in recent years? Before most other dioceses, I oversaw the development of the first comprehensive guidelines for processing sexual abuse charges against priests of the Archdiocese of Chicago. The procedures were widely adopted throughout the country. One of my first actions in the face of this accusation would be to refer these charges against me to the review board that was part of this process.

I felt a deep humiliation as inquiring callers made it clear that the accusation had now circled the world, that millions of people would know only one thing about me, that I was charged with abusing the trust and the body of a minor almost twenty years before. My advisers urged me to issue a statement to the media whose trucks, which I could see from my office window, were crowding against each other on Superior Street below.

But how do you say anything about a charge you have not seen from persons you do not know about something you did not do? As never before, I felt the presence of evil. From deep in my soul, however, I heard the Lord's words that calmed the storm breaking around and within me: "The truth will set you free" (Jn 8:32).

I immediately wrote the following statement: "While I have not seen the suit and I do not know the details of the allegation, there is one thing I do know, and I state categorically: I have never abused anyone in all my life, any-where, any time, any place."

The truth, I decided, was the only defense I had. After giving my statement to the waiting reporters, I drove home through streets that seemed familiar and yet changed, as I myself had been, by the events of the day.

The truth will set you free. I believed that, and I trusted the Lord who, for reasons I could not yet fathom, had permitted this trial to enter my life. But I also wondered if the voice of truth could be heard in a culture in which image making and distortion have almost completely replaced it. My faith reassured me that the truth was all that I had, and all that I really needed. It would be my rod and my staff through the dark valley (Ps 23:4) in the months ahead.

## Sharing the Truth with the World

The simple truth is that I was innocent of the charges against me. This sustained me on a night filled with phone calls and the breaking news on all the Chicago TV channels at 10:00 P.M. that I had been accused of abusing Steven Cook. Only Bill Kurtis of the local CBS television affiliate raised the possibility that an-other story might lie beneath this one, that certain people might be out to "get" Cardinal Bernardin. I had critics, I knew, but I could not imagine who would resort to these tactics to harm me. A friend called that evening and told me he suspected a conspiracy. I told him that this had already crossed my mind.

I was angry and bewildered that people who did not know me would make such destructive charges against me. There seemed to be some calculation involved because these accusations could not be construed as some innocent misunderstanding of facts. My first worry was about the impact that these imputations of my character would have on the Church. The attack was di-rected against the most important thing I had going for me as a religious leader, my reputation. If my credibility was destroyed, so was my ability to lead. If my people believed I could do what I was charged with doing, how could they place their trust in me? And would they trust me during that period in which the charges hung over my head and my office?

I decided to face the next day with faith in the truth. I could not help think-ing that I was not the only one caught up in those false charges. My intuition was that the young man described as my accuser might have been drawn some-how into this himself. I had no facts to support that sense of his being a pawn in this terrible game, but I felt it clearly. If I was right, he needed prayers as much as I did right then. I felt a genuine impulse to pray with and comfort him.

Indeed, I put those heartfelt feelings into a letter written to him a few days after the filing of the case. I learned much later that his lawyer never passed it on to him. It read, in part:

... as I thought it over, I began to think that you must be suffering a great deal. The idea came to me yesterday morning that it would be a good thing if I visited with you personally. The purpose of the visit would be strictly pastoral—to show my concern for you and to pray with you. If you are interested in such a visit, please let me know. I will come to you if you wish.

The next morning, Friday, November 12, the allegations against me were the lead stories in the press of almost every large city in the world. As I prayed the rosary early in the morning, I meditated on the first of the sorrowful mysteries, the Agony in the Garden. I said to the Lord, "In all my sixty-five years, this is the first time that I have really understood the pain and agony you felt that night." And I also asked, "Why did you let this happen?" I had never felt more alone.

I spent most of my morning meeting with my advisers, preparing for the press conference that was scheduled for 1:00 P.M. My morale was boosted by the letters and calls of support that had already begun to arrive, including a supportive statement from the Holy See.

My counselors discussed all aspects of the case as well as the strategies to use in handling them. We learned that CNN was airing promotional pieces every hour for a Sunday night special entitled "Fall from Grace" about priests who were found guilty of sex crimes. The promotional piece promised an interview with Steven Cook. He and the reporter were shown examining what they called "evidence" against me—a book and a picture. Because this interview had already been conducted and the show scheduled to air on the eve of the semiannual meeting of the National Conference of Catholic Bishops, it seemed that a good measure of planning had gone into developing the "case" against me.

At the conclusion of the meeting with my advisers, I decided to take an hour by myself to pray and reflect. I was being emptied of self in a way that I never could have anticipated, and I wanted to let go and place myself and my cares in the hands of the Lord. I was conscious of the blur of everyday life in the great city outside my windows and of the arrival once more of the caravan of media trucks in the street below. Ten minutes before the scheduled press conference I called an old friend and said, "I have been listening to good advice from good people all morning. I have made a decision to follow my own instincts. I am just going to tell the truth."

Electricity filled the conference room of the Pastoral Center where almost seventy reporters were jammed together in a tangle of cameras, lights, and trailing wires. I understood that these journalists, many of whom I knew and liked, had to assume adversarial roles to carry out their work. But I was not there to do battle with them. I just wanted to answer truthfully their questions.

But as I moved behind the brace of microphones, I felt that I was literally standing before the entire world, and I still felt very much alone. The most important thing I had going for me at the moment was my forty-two years of ordained ministry, my name, and my reputation. But there was also an inner strength, and I am convinced that the Lord was giving me that strength. For me, this moment of public accusation and inquiry was also a moment of grace. A moment of pain, but a moment of grace because I felt the great love and support that many people were giving me. Above all, it was a moment of spiritual growth. I felt that I was entering a new phase of my spiritual journey because of the events of those few days.

Midway into the session, the tension in the room lessened somewhat. While the atmosphere remained grave, it appeared that the truth, as the Lord promised, was freeing me and, in turn, changing the attitudes of those asking me questions. They seemed less doubting, less hostile, more ready to believe than to disbelieve me. Still, their job was to probe and provoke.

The tension reappeared in the waning moments of the press conference when a young man in the front row asked me, "Are you sexually active?"

I paused only a moment, feeling briefly the enormous gulf between the reporter's world and my own. "I have always led," I said simply, "a chaste and celibate life." The reinstated tightness in the atmosphere loosened, and I could read in the eyes of the assembled journalists that they believed me. Afterwards, one told me, "We know now that you're telling the truth, Cardinal, but we have to ask these questions. Our job depends on it." The next day's headline in the *Chicago Tribune* read, " 'I've Led a Chaste Life,' Bernardin Says."

After the session ended, I returned to my office. If it was an ordeal, I thought to myself, it was only the first of many. Indeed, I was to hold fourteen press conferences over the next week, all of them governed by the same dynamics. The truth, as faith promises, did earn me a greater sense of freedom at each of these meetings.

## The Case Unravels

It took one hundred days before the false charges against me were resolved. They may be described as an education in law, but I prefer to think of them as a profound education of the soul. The entire matter really served as scenes in the first act of a three-act play that I now believe constitutes my spiritual pilgrimage over the past three years. This first act began with the false accusation and concluded with my meeting my accuser and reconciling with him. The other two acts, which I will discuss in detail later in this book, include the diagnosis of my pancreatic cancer and my preparation for death. At the time of the accusation, I was only at the beginning of a three-year schooling of the Spirit, but as the year drew to an end I could not fully foresee that.

From the very beginning, even though I knew that I would have to defend myself and the Church in a way that would be successful, I told my lawyers that I wanted no countersuit, that we would not pursue a "scorched earth" policy. The reason was that I did not want to deter persons who had really been abused from coming forward.

I also determined early on that I would not spend any archdiocesan money in my defense for fear that they would be used by some people as an excuse *not* to contribute to the Church. As soon as this became known, a number of prestigious law firms came forward, offering to defend me on a *pro bono* basis, including the firm we were already using for various legal matters.

As soon as the alleged "evidence" was examined, the case against me began to collapse from within. Indeed, the "picture" of me and the plaintiff turned out to be a group photograph taken at a Cincinnati seminary function at which, along with many others, we were both present. The book I allegedly autographed and gave to him bore no signature of mine. The "hypnotist" who supposedly helped the plaintiff, just a month before, to recall memories of my sexually abusing him was found to be someone who had taken only a few hours of training in hypnotism. Moreover, I later learned that she was unaware of the real reason Steven had been sent to her.

It became clear to me that certain critics of mine had played a role in urging Steven Cook to take on the role of plaintiff against me. Indeed, almost as soon as the news broke, some people, including a priest from out of state, expressed the opinion on a local radio talk show that I was guilty, that finally the facts had caught up with me. Also, the night between the publication of the rumor and the filing of the case, a significant section of the telephones at the archdiocesan Pastoral Center was "invaded." Six different messages were left on the phones and were heard the next morning by the staff in the various offices affected. The theme of all six was that I was guilty of the rumored charge and that it would not be to the advantage of the Archdiocese to defend me. Later efforts to find out who did this were not successful.

Under the professional discipline of my lawyers, principally John O'Malley and James Serritella, the true nature of the case against me quickly became apparent. Despite its unfounded nature, this lawsuit possessed the power both to disrupt and to change the direction of my life.

As the disturbing allegations did not stand the test of truth, I began to understand how Steven Cook had been a victim of this whole tawdry episode. My initial intuition of his being used was gradually confirmed. On February 28, 1994, Steven on his own initiative asked a judge at the federal court in Cincinnati to drop the charges against me.

More striking to me than the fact that a troubled priest at St. Gregory Seminary had unwittingly played a role in promoting my false indictment was what we gradually learned of Steven Cook's own difficult life. His brief unhappy period in the Cincinnati seminary had been followed by an estrangement from the Church and a drift into a promiscuous lifestyle. He was suffering from AIDS and was being cared for by a friend at an apartment in Philadelphia whose address they kept secret. He was the sheep who had been lost, and, as a shepherd, I knew that I had to seek him out.

## Meeting My Accuser:
## Forgiveness and Reconciliation

Indeed, after the case was dropped and my final press conference on the matter was covered by the same CNN that had played such a prominent part in publicizing the initial accusation, I plunged back into my crowded schedule. Nonetheless, I thought often of Steven in his lonely, illness-ridden exile from both his parental home and the Church. By mid-December I felt deeply that this entire episode would not be complete until I followed my shepherd's calling to seek him out. I only prayed that he would receive me. The experience of the false accusation would not be complete until I met and reconciled with Steven. Even though I had never heard from him, I sensed he also wanted to see me.

Not knowing his address or phone number and not wanting to take him by surprise, I made contact with Steven's mother, Mary, through Father Phil Seher, her pastor in Cincinnati and a friend of mine. She sent back word that Steven was not only willing but also had a real desire to meet with me. I flew to Philadelphia with Father Scott Donahue on December 30, 1994. Monsignor James Malloy, the rector of St. Charles Borromeo Seminary, where the meeting was to be held, picked us up and drove us to its campus in suburban Overbrook.

I was a bit anxious as we entered the snow-patched seminary grounds. The campus, with its traditional granite structures, was quiet—the seminarians were on Christmas vacation. In the large, tall-windowed room on the second floor of the main building, we waited patiently for Steven and his companion. It was hard to refrain from asking myself an unwelcome question: Would Steven be able to keep the appointment or not?

Within a few minutes he arrived with his friend, Kevin. We shook hands, and I sat with Steven on a couch as Father Donahue and Kevin sat in the wing chairs at either end of it. Steven looked only slightly gaunt despite his grave illness. I explained to him that the only reason for requesting the meeting was to bring closure to the traumatic events of last winter by personally letting him know that I harbored no ill feelings toward him. I told him I wanted to pray with him for his physical and spiritual well-being. Steven replied that he had decided to meet with me so he could apologize for the embarrassment and hurt he had caused. In other words, we both sought reconciliation. However, Steven said he wanted to tell me about his life before we continued.

With a tone and gestures that indicated Steven had bottled up his story for a long time, he told me that as a young seminarian he had been sexually abused by a priest he thought was his friend. He claimed that the authorities did not take his report of the priest's misconduct seriously. He became embittered and left the Church. Much later, he came into contact with a New Jersey–based lawyer with a reputation for bringing legal actions against priests accused of sexual abuse. This lawyer, Steven said, put him in touch with a priest in another state to advise him spiritually.

Although Steven was pursuing a case only against his seminary teacher, his priest adviser began mentioning me, Cardinal Bernardin, suggesting that, if I were included in the case, Steven would surely get back what he wanted from the Church. This "spiritual guide" pushed my name, urging Steven to name me along with the other priest in the legal action. He also urged Steven's mother to cooperate in this plan, sending her flowers as part of his effort to persuade her to support Steven's action. This was the very same priest who expressed his opinion during a Chicago radio talk show on November 12, 1993, that I was guilty.

It became difficult for Steven to explain how, with what he described as a poorly trained therapist, he thought that he had recaptured memories of my abusing him and went along with including me in the suit. He seemed confused and uncertain about this. His friend Kevin broke in to say that he was always suspicious of the lawyer and the priest adviser.

I looked directly at Steven, seated a few inches away from me. "You know," I said, "that I never abused you."

"I know," he answered softly. "Can you tell me that again?"

I looked directly into his eyes. "I have never abused you. You know that, don't you?"

Steven nodded. "Yes," he replied, "I know that, and I want to apologize for saying that you did." Steven's apology was simple, direct, deeply moving. I accepted his apology. I told him that I had prayed for him every day and would continue to pray for his health and peace of mind. It became increasingly clear that he was in precarious health.

I then asked whether he wanted me to celebrate Mass for him. At first, he hesitated. "I'm not sure I want to have Mass," he said haltingly; "I've felt very alienated from God and the Church a long time." He said that on several occasions while in a hotel he threw a Gideon Bible against the wall in anger and frustration. "Perhaps," he said, "just a simple prayer would be more appropriate."

I hesitated for a moment after that, unsure of how he would react to the gift I removed from my briefcase. I told him that I would not press the issue but did want to show him two items I had brought with me. "Steven," I said, "I have brought you something, a Bible that I have inscribed to you. But I do understand, and I won't be offended if you don't want to accept it." Steven took the Bible in quivering hands, pressed it to his heart as tears welled up in his eyes.

I then took a hundred-year-old chalice out of my case. "Steven, this is a gift from a man I don't even know. He asked me to use it to say Mass for you some day."

"Please," Steven responded tearfully, "let's celebrate Mass now."

Never in my entire priesthood have I witnessed a more profound reconciliation. The words I am using to tell you this story cannot begin to describe the power of God's grace at work that afternoon. It was a manifestation of God's love, forgiveness, and healing that I will never forget.

Kevin, Steven's friend, asked if he, a non-Catholic, could attend, and I told him that it would be fine. We all went to the seminary chapel where, with great joy and thanksgiving, Father Donahue and I celebrated Mass for the Feast of the Holy Family. We all embraced at the greeting of peace, and, afterwards, I anointed Steven with the sacrament of the sick.

Then I said a few words: "In every family there are times when there is hurt, anger, or alienation. But we cannot run away from our family. We have only one family and so, after every falling out, we must make every effort to be reconciled. So, too, the Church is our spiritual family. Once we become a member, we may be hurt or become alienated, but it is still our family. Since there is no other, we must work at reconciliation. And that is what we have been doing this very afternoon."

Before Steven left, he told me, "A big burden has been lifted from me today. I feel healed and very much at peace." We had previously agreed to keep our meeting secret, but Steven now said to me, "I'm so happy, I want people to know about our reconciliation." He asked me to tell the story, which I did a few weeks later in *The New World*, our archdiocesan paper. When I read it to him beforehand on the phone, he told me, "Cardinal, you're a good writer. Go with it."

As we flew back to Chicago that evening, Father Donahue and I felt the lightness of spirit that an afternoon of grace brings to one's life. I could not help but think that the ordeal of the accusation led straight to this extraordinary experience of God's grace in our sacramental reconciliation. And I could not help but recall the work of the Good Shepherd: to seek and restore to the sheepfold the one that has been, only for a while, lost.

Steven and I kept in touch after that and, six months later, when I received a diagnosis of pancreatic cancer, his was one of the first letters I received. He had only a few months to live when he wrote it, filled with sympathy and encouragement for me. He planned to visit me in Chicago at the end of August, but he was too ill. Steven died at his mother's home on September 22, 1995, fully reconciled with the Church. "This," he said, smiling from his deathbed at his mother about his return to the sacraments, "is my gift to you." The priest in Cincinnati who attended him told this to me soon afterwards.

# PART III

# IN THE

# NEW

# WORLD

*Immigrant and Ethnic Experiences*

# Introduction

The melting pot that is known as the United States of America has had a profound effect on modern Catholicism. For some reason the phenomenon associated with Vatican II has taken on a very "American" cast to it, much in the same way that Europe is referred to by Americans as the Old World, pre–Vatican II is often referred to as either the old Church or (very inaccurately) as the old religion. To a certain extent in the days of yore the Church and its language, Latin, provided a glue that held all Catholics together despite their varied national/ethnic differences. Enter the American melting pot, the product of an amalgam of cultures and ethnicities of diverse natures, and the universality of the Church yields to a universality of the American pluralism.

Whereas before the maxim was "though we may be Spanish, Irish, Italian, etc., we are all members of the Catholic Church," an identity strengthened by a common belief and a common tongue, it has now been replaced by "though we may be Spanish, Irish, Italian, etc., we are all still Americans." Thus even before Pope Paul convened the ecumenical council, a certain amount of secular ecumenicism had already taken place in America, an ecumenicism that preached an even diversity within a single gestalt. Thus by the late sixties the smart set had sequestered the followers of the old Church to the ranks of the absurd cliché such as old Italian women who attend early morning mass each day, rosary beads firmly in hand, and the Hispanic matron with her face covered by a black lace mantilla (both of whom are obviously fluent in Latin despite their lack of a full command of "American English"); the devout yet poor Irish family of many children (obviously shunning birth control no matter what the economic hardship of yet another mouth to feed), and the Asian refugee convert who "your mission donations" can save from the ravages of godless Communism. In the spirit of ecumenicism the smart set was obviously allowed to deride these virtuous archetypes which no longer fit into a philosophy that preached all Americans on one hand, but a Church of many tongues on the other.

In essence as the Catholic Church made a fledgling move from the Indo-European fixation of its early years toward a more globally diverse philosophy as irreversibly (at least for a time) set in motion by Pope John XXIII, the American culture moved in the opposite direction toward a more homogenized concept of an America which, though it did acknowledge its melting pot roots, seemed to strive for a single identity/single tongue much in the manner of the old Church.

As with many movements, the homogenized America has been thankfully only partially successful, and in recent years there has been renewed support for the ethnic and immigrant diversity that has made the United States a forward-moving entity . . . and in a similar manner the American Catholic Church has come along for the ride.

Where the immigration wave of 1890–1910 lead to the formation of such ethnic immigrant enclaves as "Little Italy," "Irish Town," and "German Town," which usually started as ghettos and grew into neighborhoods or in some cases Roman Catholic parishes, the Church aiding in the assimilation of the American experience, lending a hand, occasionally a leg up, and a sense of community, the immigration wave of 1975–1999 has repeated this paradigm with an even more diverse mix including refugees from the fallen Soviet Union, Asia, and the Third World. As a result of this, a record number of multilingual parishes have sprung up across America with the possibility today that in certain cities there may be more masses said in a tongue other than English rather than in America's alleged native tongue (with Spanish and Asian languages leading the way). Curiously enough the resurgence of the presence of an immigrant tongue has not led to a cultural identity within Catholicism for these new immigrants. This is probably primarily due to the elasticity of the ecumenical movement that already existed here prior to these late arrivals.

Once again the melting pot has surfaced as the equalizer even though its present contents might taste slightly different to each taster at hand. These slight differences, the acquired tastes, provide more of an insight on one's culture prior to one's Americanization.

These acquired tastes can sometimes cause conflicts that might seem paradoxical to someone from a different part of the melting pot. Sometimes it leads to a moltenization of an aspect of the religion which the more progressive wing of Catholicism might label as superstitious (an unfair label for mystical faiths such as Santeria, which tried to meld Roman Catholicism with Caribbean mysticism) or old-fashioned (such as senior citizens still praying to St. Christopher and treasuring their medals of him as the patron saint of travelers).

It is impossible to reconcile many of these different beliefs—and in the long run we really don't have to. In a Catholic church down in New Orleans there is a statue (and religious medals available for purchase) for a nonexistent Catholic saint by the name of Saint Expedite whose mysterious presence in the church is generally agreed to have been the product of the misinterpretation of a shipping label by a recently converted immigrant. The story is absurd, but it is also true, and the presence of this statue does not weaken the Christian resolve/legitimacy of the parish. It is in fact part of the parish's identity.

To embrace an American Catholicism without its ethnic and immigrant influences is to deny its full heritage. The miracle at Fátima, the sighting of Our Lady of Guadalupe, and the mysterious carpenter who built a spiral staircase in a desert chapel are all modern mysteries of our Church, and all hopelessly ethnic in origin. Modern American myths like that of the son of penniless Irish Catholic immigrants who goes on to become President of the United States are just as absurd, and also just as credible, thanks to the likes of John Fitzgerald Kennedy.

John XXIII's insights have made way for a stronger and more diverse American Catholic Church than was ever possible before, but perhaps such a Church is only really possible in America. True, other nations have a stronger/more dominant Catholic population, and in most cases these nations are further to the right in their politics and less permissive in their policies. It is only in America that full diversity can take place—where Native American converts to Catholicism can still protect their mystical Indian heritage while being members of the modern Church, much in the same way that Italian immigrants of the last century could protect their own ethnic traditions within the Church. An example is the present existence of Befana societies during the Christmas holidays. Culturally, Befana the witch is the Italian equivalent of Santa Claus, but with a much more theological twist. As the so-called legend goes, Befana was a witch whose path crossed with that of the astrologers from the East (also known as the Three Kings from the Orient). She too had seen the star and realized that God's son had been born, and was invited to join the astrologers' caravan on the journey to Bethlehem. Unfortunately, she was delayed, quickly fell behind, lost track of the caravan, and never made it to the manger. As a result, the witch visits all of the world's households where there are children present on Christmas Eve leaving a present behind in hopes that she will eventually come across the Christ Child.

Thus, our own ethnic diversity predates ecumenicism, and it is entirely possible that the so-called American experiment, the melting pot of the civilized world, is in fact partially responsible for it. Just as the lifting of the requirement of the Latin language from the liturgy was meant to strengthen the Church, the multihued faith of American Catholicism will strengthen the Church unto the following centuries, setting an example for maybe a more liberal but no less faithful world Catholic Church.

# Ellis Island

## From: *The Story of the Trapp Family Singers*

### BY MARIA AUGUSTA TRAPP

✛

## In Sight of the Statue of Liberty

From the day in March when we left on the *Normandie* to that day in October when we set foot on American soil again we learned a lesson, the greatest of them all. In Bible English it is called: "Be not solicitous," and translated into everyday language, it means: "Don't worry."

We started out by worrying.

"What shall we eat, what shall we drink, what shall we put on?" These must be the very elements of human worries, as Our Lord picks them out when He says: "Be not solicitous for your life, what you shall eat, nor for your body, what you shall put on." Then He explains how useless it is if we do worry, how it gets us nowhere; "Can any of you for all his fretting add an inch's growth to his height? And if you are powerless to do so small a thing, why do you fret about your needs?" After having told us how senseless it is to worry, He tells us what to do. We should look at the lilies, how they grow. They don't work, nor do they spin, but not even King Solomon in all his glory was clothed like one of them. Now—if God clothes the grass, which lives today in the fields and tomorrow is cast into the oven, will He not be much more ready to clothe you, oh you of little faith? You should not be asking then what you shall eat or what you shall drink and worrying about them. The heathens may do that, who don't know about God. You, however, must know that your Heavenly Father knows well that you need all these things. Therefore, seek first the Kingdom of God and all these things shall be added unto you.

And this half year was set apart for teaching us this lesson, that we should never forget it in the future.

There we were, a group of twelve people and a little baby who, for the next seven months, had no home, and except for six concerts, which would provide for three weeks' living, did not know the answer to the question:

What shall we eat, what shall we drink? The political horizon was filled with dark clouds; the outbreak of the war seemed imminent; the atmosphere in Europe was full of suspicion and mistrust; we didn't know a soul in the Scandinavian countries, nor any of the languages; the permission to stay was carefully restricted by every country to the time necessary to give our concerts. Europe was just waking up to recognizing "tourists" as "fifth columnists."

It would have been easy for God to show us the plan for this period, as He had it all fixed up, how there would be enough concerts, enough money, extensions of our stay, helpful people, generous invitations, new friends, and new love. But then we again would not have learned that most valuable lesson, so He left us in the dark, and gave us only one thing at a time. We always spent the cent before the last before we got a new engagement.

In this way we passed the time until the end of May in Denmark, Sweden, and Norway. When our prolonged extension had almost expired, an invitation from Holland with permission to stay for twenty-eight days at the country home of friends took care of the month of June. In July we dared to pay a short visit to Austria. The men of our group, however, stayed away. Back in the old home we learned with horror what one short year can do to an invaded people, how it had embittered the ones while it changed, imperceptibly to themselves, the others, and falsified their way of thinking and living. We learned the shocking truth that "home" isn't necessarily a certain spot on earth. It must be a place where you can *feel* at home, which means "free" to us. Soon we met the men in St. Georgen, south of the border, where I fulfilled my promise and carried little Johannes up the hill and lit a big candle in the shrine of Our Lady. For August and September we had our engagements in Sweden. But, mind you, not all of them were neatly put down on a list in advance. No, each concert brought forth the next one, when an excited member of the audience invited us to his home town for a performance. By then we were well advanced in our course: "Don't worry." It really would have been a waste of time. All the practicing and rehearsing of this new art we needed badly when in September, 1939, the war broke out. All borders were closed, foreigners were asked to depart, concerts already promised were canceled. But we had learned by then that the Heavenly Father knows what we need. More than before, we tried to concentrate on "Seek ye therefore *first* the Kingdom of God" in doing our daily duties, rehearsing the program for the next American tour, taking care of all the little chores of everyday life, and trying most conscientiously *not to worry*. At the moment before our last permission to stay in Sweden expired, Mr. Wagner again advanced the money on the next concerts and sent the tickets for the SS. *Bergensfjord*.

* * *

When, on October 7, 1939, we finally docked in Brooklyn, Hedwig said with disappointment in her voice:

"In spite of the war, this crossing was not dangerous and not a bit exciting. Nothing unusual happened."

Photographers and newspaper men crowded on board, searching for sensational stories. Our picture was taken, too: The Trapp Family Alone, and The Trapp Family With Kirsten Flagstad, who also happened to be on the *Bergensfjord.* Then we saw Mr. Snowden, our friendly guide of the first year, in the crowd. He waved and called, "Welcome home!" and then it was our turn with the Immigration Officer. Rupert had an immigration visa this time, whereas the rest of us were all on visitors' visas.

I was so relieved and so grateful after all these months of uncertainty to have reached the haven again, that when my turn came and the Immigration Officer asked me the fatal question: "What time do you intend to spend in America?" I didn't answer as I was supposed to: "Six months, Sir, as my visa says," but I simply blurted out: "Oh, I am so glad to be here—I want never to leave again!"

Their whole attitude changed. The members of the Trapp Family were held for the very last, and then they were questioned and questioned again; but nothing we said could undo the dangerous impression my most unwise outburst had created: these people don't want to leave again.

Everybody was gone; we were the only passengers on board. But we were not allowed to leave. A tall policeman came and watched us, and all we could do for the rest of the day was play shuffleboard among ourselves and admire beautiful Brooklyn. We didn't understand yet why, but we were prisoners, and so Hedwig had gotten her highlight for this trip after all: tomorrow we should be taken to Ellis Island.

A large motorboat came, and our policeman took us over to the island with the large prison building, where the doubtful people from foreign countries were scrutinized. Lucky Rupert went to the Hotel Wellington and started from there to try to get his family out of jail, because jail it was. When the huge door was closed behind us, the door which had no knob on the inside, we were led into a hall as big as the main waiting room in Grand Central Station.

It was one of those beautiful, hot October days, Indian Summer; but tradition on Ellis Island has it that on October 1 the central heating has to be started. The windows, high up and barred, could not be opened, and the temperature was around eighty degrees.

"Could I get out with the little ones into the fresh air?" Martina approached a warden.

"Every day for half an hour after lunch," was the answer.

We still didn't understand what we were doing there. We had been told by some officer of the ship that our papers were not quite clear, and it was only for some formality that we were being taken to this place. But we couldn't remember having done anything wrong. It must be a misunderstanding, and Rupert would come in the afternoon and get us out. So we tried to make ourselves at home on two large benches facing each other. With the help of our suitcases we boarded up a corner, and as there was absolutely nothing else to do, we started to sing. It is always good to rehearse. Soon people grouped around us, and it seemed that their strained faces looked less worried after listening for an hour to our music. Then we started to talk. There were Spaniards, Jews, Greeks, and a large group of Chinese. We learned that the Chinese had been here already for eight months. Most of the people had been here for weeks. Goodness—and our first concert was supposed to be on the fifteenth. A lady from Poland said:

"At least it doesn't cost anything; it's all paid by the State. And if America doesn't let you in, the ship line on which you came has to take you back in the same class, at its own cost, to the port where you started out. It won't cost you a cent."

How terribly consoling! That meant another third-class passage on the *Bergensfjord* to Oslo!

"And if that country in Europe doesn't let us in, what then?" asked Werner.

"Well," said the lady cheerily, "then the ship has to keep you. There is an Italian family on the ocean traveling for the eleventh time between Le Havre and New York. And it doesn't cost them a cent."

What a prospect!

One of the wardens came, a fat lady with greasy hair and a stern look, and handed each one of us a sheet of paper where it said in German:

"Information: You have been asked to come to Ellis Island as there is some doubt concerning your passport. You will come before the special hearing as soon as possible, and you can plead your cause. If you can't speak English, you will get an interpreter. There is no reason to get excited. You will be treated very politely." Then it said in capitals: "DON'T TALK ABOUT YOUR AFFAIRS WITH YOUR FELLOW PRISONERS"; and at the end it added: "Please be patient. We don't want to keep you a moment longer than we absolutely have to."

Then it was time for lunch. We were lined up by twos and filed through the door, which was opened with a special key from the inside. As we passed by, the fat lady tapped each one of us on the shoulder, counting. Georg disliked this extremely.

On long tables the food was served in tin plates, everything on one plate.

After lunch we were taken out into the yard by twos. The yard was closed in by a very tall wire fence, and what should we see greeting us through the bars from a very short distance, but the Statue of Liberty! The half hour was very short; the whistle blew and we had to go back in.

Finally Rupert came, and he didn't look very cheerful.

"One of you must have made the remark that she wants to stay in this country. That makes you all suspicious, and the authorities don't want to let you in. That's what Mr. Wagner was told."

Soon Rupert had to leave. The visiting hour was over. We asked him to call our different friends to help us out.

Johannes had started to walk while we were alone on the *Bergensfjord* on that last day. Now he practiced walking all day long. He was not quite nine months old, but was very strong. Between singing and playing around with Johannes the long hours passed. We filed through the door again for supper, and right afterwards we had to take all our luggage and were led upstairs into a large dormitory. The windows were small slits high up on the wall, and the door had no knob on the inside. The very bright lights were left on the whole night, which made sleeping hard, and every so often the door opened and the warden came in and counted noses. Each time Johannes woke up and cried unhappily.

Next morning we were awakened at six o'clock. The newspapers had heard of the Trapp Family at Ellis Island and sent reporters and photographers. From time to time a policeman came in and called a name, the name of the lucky one who should go to his hearing. In the afternoon Rupert reported that he had called Mr. Drinker, who had promised to do what he could. How quickly one gets used to things: to be marched by twos, to eat from tin plates, to be counted numberless times day and night, to windows next to the ceiling and doors without knobs. Father Wasner could say Mass each morning, but only we were allowed to attend, no one else.

Mr. King, the big boss of Ellis Island, came to visit us. He was especially nice and said that even Toscanini had been here briefly, and many other famous artists, and we should not worry. In the afternoon Elizabeth, Carleton Smith's wife, came with a big basket of fresh fruit and newspapers with our picture: The Trapp Family Playing Recorders on Ellis Island. What publicity! Elizabeth assured us that our friends were working busily to get us out.

We were singing a good deal now, because the people were so happy about it. It took their worried thoughts away from their own problems. We were getting very popular on Ellis Island.

On the fourth day we were pretty much at home, with a daily routine: *ora et labora*. Mass in the morning and rosary in the evening, during the day rehearsals, recorder practice. Father Wasner was working on a new composition. We wrote letters back to Sweden, letters of thanks. Quietly we waited for our hearing. We had been told from all sides that this was merely a formality;

we just had to wait for our turn. An extremely nice letter from Mr. Drinker helped a great deal to cheer us up. In the afternoon the door opened again, and this time *our* name was called. The policeman led us over to the courtroom. There we took a solemn oath that we would tell the truth, the whole truth, and nothing but the truth, and then the long questioning started. For two and a half hours we (I particularly) were questioned. Why had we come? What did we intend to do? Where did we intend to live? On what boat did we intend to leave again? We didn't know? Didn't we have return tickets? How come? Didn't we intend to leave? And so on. After we had told the truth, the whole truth, and nothing but the truth for two and a half hours, the judge said he didn't believe us, and we were dismissed.

"And the *Bergensfjord* is sailing tomorrow," went through my mind.

Our companions were eagerly awaiting the outcome, and when they heard what had happened, all looked very gloomy. Each time a prisoner is released, they all gather around him and applaud heartily while he is let out the door. This they had intended to do with us. But quietly we all sat down again and—started to sing. It was the only thing to do if we didn't want to cry. In the middle of a song Georg was called out. He came back shortly afterwards, and his beaming countenance spoke the word: we were FREE. Our friends had approached their senators and congressmen, vouched for our honesty, and word had come back from Washington to Ellis Island and the misunderstanding was cleared up.

It was touching how our fellow prisoners selflessly shared in our joy. First endless applause while we got hold of our bags; then one more song; more applause; another song, and finally our best *Jodler* at the end. Outside Rupert was waiting, and in the motorboat we waved over at the Statue of Liberty, this time from the other side of the fence. The second dove had returned into the ark with a branch from an olive tree. It was safe to set foot on land. And this must have been the feelings of Noah, his wife, his daughters and sons, when they sang their hymn of thanksgiving after the tempest was over.

## Learning New Ways

Now we were really in America, and although I wouldn't even have dared to whisper it to myself on the top of the Empire State Building or in the middle of Central Park at midnight, for fear the Immigration Officer could hear it again, I knew this was for good.

A touching reunion with the Hotel Wellington! For the first time I noticed that there were green carpets in the lobby and the nice bell captain with his bellboys and elevator boys wore a handsome purple uniform.

A great many other things I seemed to discover all anew, and many times my family exclaimed:

"But, Mother, don't you remember from last year?"

No, honestly, I didn't. It seems that an expectant mother is more occupied within herself, taking in from the outside world merely the bare essentials.

The first concert was in Town Hall, New York, on a Saturday afternoon. It was a weekend, and what is more, it was one of those balmy days in the fall where the foliage in the country is a riot of color, and people simply didn't feel like staying in town on such a day and listening to Palestrina. Result: a small audience. Further result: a disappointed manager, who had thought we were a better "drawing card" than the box office receipts showed.

For the weekend of our Town Hall concert our Philadelphia friends had come to New York. How wonderful to see them again! The Crawfords offered most kindly to take the little ones into their home. Rosmarie and Lorli could go to their old Academy again, which was not too far from the Crawfords' home. The parting was always a very bitter moment for all of us; but at that time I still thought children had to go to school, and everything else had to be sacrificed to this fact. Later I should learn better.

That was the year of the World's Fair, and we spent some most exciting days on the grounds, which seemed like a whole book of fairy tales.

What that word "drawing card" meant, we should discover in a painful way during the next weeks.

In a short time we learned to know some of the largest auditoriums in this country with a seating capacity of between 2,500 and 4,000, and we always had ample chance to meditate on the color of the upholstery; in one place, a silvery gray, in another, a deep red, or a warm golden yellow; because it was not disturbed by human forms—the huge halls seemed practically empty. (And the artist said to his audience: "Come into the front row, both of you.")

An otherwise large audience of eight hundred or nine hundred got almost entirely lost in that vast space. What was the matter? Well, Grandpa Wagner had "invested quite some money in the Trapp Family Choir," and now he wanted it back. That's why he had them sing in large halls; but he forgot to tell the people about it. From our short meeting with publicity we had learned sentences like this: "You can't tell the people often enough. You just have to rub it in, or they forget." For these people in Hartford, Connecticut; Harrisburg, Pennsylvania; Raleigh, North Carolina; or Washington, D.C., it was not a question of forgetting, but of getting acquainted with the fact that their presence was requested at the first concert of the Trapp Family Choir in their town. But aside from a meager notice in the rear of the local paper, we couldn't find any window cards or photographs, no "three-sheets" glared from the walls; no interviews, no photographers made our life miserable. Quietly we came and quietly we left, and Mr. Wagner got more and more disgusted. At that time he used pink stationery. At each hotel and at each concert hall those pink envelopes awaited us, filled with gentle reproaches about how badly we had done the last time. This is not exactly a tonic before a concert.

We got more and more nervous and discouraged. We knew we had rehearsed very conscientiously. This "Missa Brevis" by Palestrina *was* a masterpiece, and we *did* sing it well. You just feel such a thing. We also knew that the people who had come to our concerts went away deeply moved, and their words of appreciation were sincere. But something seemed to be wrong with us—what was it? We tried so hard, even if ever so tired, to be nice and peppy at the receptions—to please everybody; still, the pink envelopes came in greater numbers.

At our first visit at his office Mr. Wagner had received us with the news that so far he had been able to arrange only twenty-four concerts out of the forty. This time it was due to the war. But there wouldn't be any difficulty to book the rest as soon as we had started to sing. Now the pink letters threatened there would be no more dates if the halls continued to remain empty. It was very disheartening.

Otherwise, we had a wonderful time. There was the big blue bus again with the same driver, who continued in his friendly way: "Let me explain something to you." But this time with our advanced English we understood much more of what he explained.

He noticed with satisfaction that in another point, too, we were advanced: that was our luggage. In vain he had tried to explain to us that when he had driven the Don Cossacks from coast to coast, each one of these grown-up men had carried only one suitcase.

"And these kids don't seem to get along without three bags every night," he had sighed.

I hadn't argued more about this with him for the simple reason that I hadn't enough English words to argue with. Otherwise I would have tried to make him understand that I had to unpack my three suitcases every night, put the little stacks of nightgowns, shirts, panties, etc., neatly into the drawers, my different framed photographs, alarm clock, New Testament, Missal, rosary, candle holder, and little vase with flowers (fresh ones if we could pick any from the bus, otherwise a little bunch of pussy willows and evergreens, which had to be packed carefully in tissue paper)—on my night table; hang the dresses in the closet, and so on. It is just as well I didn't even try. I am sure he would never have understood that. But now with the help of the Crawfords' attic, a lot of stuff was left behind, and each one of us made his entry into and exit out of the daily hotel with only one big, and one small bag. And the big one didn't even get emptied every evening any more; only when we were in a place more than one night. Well, and the driver didn't even know that my little overnight bag was only one-fourth the size of the one which had accompanied me over Europe, that expensive, heavy leather affair, in the lid of which were the two score crystal flasks with silver tops, containing everything from a toothbrush to shoeshine equipment, with heavy silver mirrors, tortoise-shell comb, jewelry box. He also didn't know that our neighbor at home in Salzburg couldn't possibly travel without taking her own bed and night table along with her. She couldn't fathom the idea of how one could sleep in a strange bed. Baroness M. M.—was a widely traveled lady. When she went to India tiger-hunting, among other things she took along three of her own milk cows, which saved her from the strain of getting used to different milk, and about seventy hats, to be up to every occasion. Compared with all this, we were fast approaching the example of the Saint of Assisi.

This time my camera was not packed away, but at my right hand always.

"Please—stop!" I could cry at the most inopportune moments, when the driver was just overtaking a big truck on a well-populated highway. Then when we finally managed to halt, I ran back and took a picture of such an exciting item as a huge roadside advertisement, shouting to the world that you can't live without a Ford. I asked my family to pose in front of it. We would send the photograph back to Europe, where they would gasp at such a thing, which was four times as high as Rupert, and wider than the row of Trapps holding hands with outstretched arms in front of it.

Or I took an American graveyard on the roadside: simply stones stuck into the grass—no little hills covered with flowers, no shrines, no iron or carved-wood crosses; these cemeteries didn't look as if they were frequently visited and tended. There were no seats or benches beside the graves. There was no wall around the graveyard, and no tender love hovered around the place, all of which made Martina exclaim:

"I wouldn't want to be buried in America."

Then there were the rows and rows of cars. When entering a city on a weekend, time and again I had to take a picture of the four-lane highways filled with solid rows of cars with people leaving for the weekend; or a parking place near a factory or a big school. In Salzburg we could count the people who owned a private car, and one of the spectacles of the Festivals had always been the strangers driving up in their limousines to the opera. No one seemed even to waste a look or a thought on this pageant of cars here. They had become a piece of daily necessity, but not yet for us; that's why I took their pictures.

In Gettysburg we took snapshots of the battlefield. Of the monuments and cannons. In Europe every ancient town has such a memorial as this, but in America it is the only one we remember.

In the South we were enchanted with the Spanish moss and the cypress trees growing out of the water. And with the Negroes. Bashfully and embarrassedly at first, later more and more encouraged by the always hearty and kind reception, I asked whether I might take a picture of this old grandma rocking on the porch with the cutest little darky on her lap, or of that group of sturdy colored boys picking cotton or harvesting peanuts.

What a different kind of sight-seeing! This time it was not cathedrals, galleries, or museums. This spectacle was prepared directly by the hand of God: these huge oak trees, these cypress swamps, these endless woods in the Blue Ridge Mountains. They were not man-made, and neither was the Natural Bridge, nor the caves in Virginia, nor Niagara Falls.

"How does it happen," mused Agathe thoughtfully one day while we were riding through the endless pine forests in North Carolina, admiring the bright red soil, "that I feel fine and at peace and quite at home here in America as long as I am in the wilds? The minute, however, traces of men show up, these roadside advertisements, for instance, these ugly wooden houses with their scales [she meant clapboards, completely unknown in Europe], the dump heaps around the huts, the car cemeteries [she meant auto dumps]—oh, it makes me so unhappy! It spoils the countryside, it doesn't fit; then I don't like America."

Funny—I felt the same way, and we found out the others did, too. There was some disharmony which man had brought into the ravishing beauty of this country.

"If I think of the villages in Europe," Rupert entered the conversation, "in the Alps or in France or England or Scandinavia, there the houses fit into the landscape, and the people do, too. They seem to be a part of it."

"Yes," said Werner, "that's true; and those old farms at home look so nice and homey and well-kept, with flowers all around. Look!" and he pointed through the window. We were just passing a run-down farm with rickety barns. "Why don't these people take better care of their houses for their children and grandchildren?"

"Ah," put in our driver, who had listened to our spirited conversation, "that's where you make a mistake. Who wants to live in the country with children and grandchildren? They just want to make some money, for instance, cut a wood lot or get a few good crops, and then move back to town and take it easy."

"You mean," gasped Hedwig, "that the people on these farms won't live there forever?"

"Sure not," he laughed, and his mere tone of voice said "you crazy Europeans."

"Who wants to work hard from dawn to dusk if you can make more money much easier in a factory in the next town?"

Well, of course, that solved the riddle why so many houses were not painted.

Anyway—this side of America was very strange to us. We had to learn much more about this country and its people before we could fit the many little pieces together. At the moment it was puzzling.

Our next stop was Hartsville, North Carolina. There we would learn some more. There was no Catholic church at the place, but on Sunday morning the priest came from the next parish in his car and said Mass in a private home, and we assisted at it. Afterwards we all had breakfast together, and Father Plicunas, the friendly priest of Lithuanian extraction, wanted to show us his church.

"Come on, let's run over. It's just around the corner," he insisted, and packed his car full of as many Trapps as possible. Off we went at hair-raising speed, forty-five miles to his rectory.

"But you said it was . . ."

"Yes, just around the corner. Why—that's nothing. My parish is . . ." and he quoted a fabulous number of miles, length and width, which would have taken care of at least three dioceses in Europe.

More and more as we rode along we were impressed by the foremost quality of America; its terrific size.

One day in December as we drove through the most beautiful winter woods and were admiring the increasing beauty of the landscape as we came farther north, the "Let me explain something to you," was heard again all over the bus.

"Now we are entering the State of Vermont. No use looking out the window. This is not a progressive State. All they raise is gravestones."

        •      •      •

The last of our twenty-four concerts was in Philadelphia in the Academy of Music in the afternoon. It was two days before Christmas. Afterwards we were invited to dinner at the Drinkers'. Harry Drinker received us radiantly.

"I have a house for you right across the street."

After supper we all went to look at the house. It was furnished, and he really meant it, we could move in immediately.

"Instead of paying me in cash, pay me in music." And so it happened: a most perfect exchange of goods. Each one gave what he had; and we sang for him and with him the master works of the sixteenth and seventeenth centuries which he hadn't discovered yet, and both parties were truly happy.

# Penance

## From: *The Godfather*

### BY MARIO PUZO

The bloody victory of the Corleone Family was not complete until a year of delicate political maneuvering established Michael Corleone as the most powerful Family chief in the United States. For twelve months, Michael divided his time equally between his headquarters at the Long Beach mall and his new home in Las Vegas. But at the end of that year he decided to close out the New York operation and sell the houses and the mall property. For that purpose he brought his whole family East on a last visit. They would stay a month, wind up business, Kay would do the personal family's packing and shipping of household goods. There were a million other minor details.

Now the Corleone Family was unchallengeable, and Clemenza had his own Family. Rocco Lampone was the Corleone *caporegime*. In Nevada, Albert Neri was head of all security for the Family-controlled hotels. Hagen too was part of Michael's Western Family.

Time helped heal the old wounds. Connie Corleone was reconciled to her brother Michael. Indeed not more than a week after her terrible accusations she apologized to Michael for what she had said and assured Kay that there had been no truth in her words, that it had been only a young widow's hysteria.

Connie Corleone easily found a new husband; in fact, she did not wait the year of respect before filling her bed again with a fine young fellow who had come to work for the Corleone Family as a male secretary. A boy from a reliable Italian family but graduated from the top business college in America. Naturally his marriage to the sister of the Don made his future assured.

Kay Adams Corleone had delighted her in-laws by taking instruction in the Catholic religion and joining that faith. Her two boys were also, naturally, being brought up in that church, as was required. Michael himself had not been too pleased by this development. He would have preferred the children to be Protestant, it was more American.

To her surprise, Kay came to love living in Nevada. She loved the scenery, the hills and canyons of garishly red rock, the burning deserts, the unexpected and blessedly refreshing lakes, even the heat. Her two boys rode their own ponies. She had real servants, not bodyguards. And Michael lived a more normal life. He owned a construction business; he joined the businessmen's clubs and civic committees; he had a healthy interest in local politics without interfering publicly. It was a good life. Kay was happy that they were closing down their New York house and that Las Vegas would be truly their permanent home. She hated coming back to New York. And so on this last trip she had arranged all the packing and shipping of goods with the utmost efficiency and speed, and now on the final day she felt that same urgency to leave that long-time patients feel when it is time to be discharged from the hospital.

On that final day, Kay Adams Corleone woke at dawn. She could hear the roar of the truck motors outside on the mall. The trucks that would empty all the houses of furniture. The Corleone Family would be flying back to Las Vegas in the afternoon, including Mama Corleone.

When Kay came out of the bathroom, Michael was propped up on his pillow smoking a cigarette. "Why the hell do you have to go to church *every* morning?" he said. "I don't mind Sundays, but why the hell during the week? You're as bad as my mother." He reached over in the darkness and switched on the tablelight.

Kay sat at the edge of the bed to pull on her stockings. "You know how converted Catholics are," she said. "They take it more seriously."

Michael reached over to touch her thigh, on the warm skin where the top of her nylon hose ended. "Don't," she said. "I'm taking Communion this morning."

He didn't try to hold her when she got up from the bed. He said, smiling slightly, "If you're such a strict Catholic, how come you let the kids duck going to church so much?"

She felt uncomfortable and she was wary. He was studying her with what she thought of privately as his "Don's" eye. "They have plenty of time," she said. "When we get back home, I'll make them attend more."

She kissed him good-bye before she left. Outside the house the air was already getting warm. The summer sun rising in the east was red. Kay walked to where her car was parked near the gates of the mall. Mama Corleone, dressed in her widow black, was already sitting in it, waiting for her. It had become a set routine, early Mass, every morning, together.

Kay kissed the old woman's wrinkled cheek, then got behind the wheel. Mama Corleone asked suspiciously, "You eata breakfast?"

"No," Kay said.

The old woman nodded her head approvingly. Kay had once forgotten that it was forbidden to take food from midnight on before receiving Holy Communion. That had been a long time ago, but Mama Corleone never trusted her after that and always checked. "You feel all right?" the old woman asked.

"Yes," Kay said.

The church was small and desolate in the early morning sunlight. Its stained-glass windows shielded the interior from heat, it would be cool there, a place to rest. Kay helped her mother-in-law up the white stone steps and then let her go before her. The old woman preferred a pew up front, close to the altar. Kay waited on the steps for an extra minute. She was always reluctant at this last moment, always a little fearful.

Finally she entered the cool darkness. She took the holy water on her fingertips and made the sign of the cross, fleetingly touched her wet fingertips to her parched lips. Candles flickered redly before the saints, the Christ on his cross. Kay genuflected before entering her row and then knelt on the hard wooden rail of the pew to wait for her call to Communion. She bowed her head as if she were praying, but she was not quite ready for that.

It was only here in these dim, vaulted churches that she allowed herself to think about her husband's other life. About that terrible night a year ago when he had deliberately used all their trust and love in each other to make her believe his lie that he had not killed his sister's husband.

She had left him because of that lie, not because of the deed. The next morning she had taken the children away with her to her parents' house in New Hampshire. Without a word to anyone, without really knowing what action she meant to take. Michael had immediately understood. He had called her the first day and then left her alone. It was a week before the limousine from New York pulled up in front of her house with Tom Hagen.

She had spent a long terrible afternoon with Tom Hagen, the most terrible afternoon of her life. They had gone for a walk in the woods outside her little town and Hagen had not been gentle.

Kay had made the mistake of trying to be cruelly flippant, a role to which she was not suited. "Did Mike send you up here to threaten me?" she asked. "I expected to see some of the 'boys' get out of the car with their machine guns to make me go back."

For the first time since she had known him, she saw Hagen angry. He said harshly, "That's the worst kind of juvenile crap I've ever heard. I never expected that from a woman like you. Come on, Kay."

"All right," she said.

They walked along the green country road. Hagen asked quietly, "Why did you run away?"

Kay said, "Because Michael lied to me. Because he made a fool of me when he stood Godfather to Connie's boy. He betrayed me. I can't love a man like that. I can't live with it. I can't let him be father to my children."

"I don't know what you're talking about," Hagen said.

She turned on him with now-justified rage. "I mean that he killed his sister's husband. Do you understand that?" She paused for a moment. "And he lied to me."

They walked on for a long time in silence. Finally Hagen said, "You have no way of really knowing that's all true. But just for the sake of argument let's assume that it's true. I'm not saying it is, remember. But what if I gave you what might be some justification for what he did. Or rather some possible justifications?"

Kay looked at him scornfully. "That's the first time I've seen the lawyer side of you, Tom. It's not your best side."

Hagen grinned. "OK. Just hear me out. What if Carlo had put Sonny on the spot, fingered him. What if Carlo beating up Connie that time was a deliberate plot to get Sonny out in the open, that they knew he would take the route over the Jones Beach Causeway? What if Carlo had been paid to help get Sonny killed? Then what?"

Kay didn't answer. Hagen went on. "And what if the Don, a great man, couldn't bring himself to do what he had to do, avenge his son's death by killing his daughter's husband? What if that, finally, was too much for him, and he made Michael his successor, knowing that Michael would take that load off his shoulders, would take that guilt?"

"It was all over with," Kay said, tears springing into her eyes. "Everybody was happy. Why couldn't Carlo be forgiven? Why couldn't everything go on and everybody forget?"

She had led across a meadow to a tree-shaded brook. Hagen sank down on the grass and sighed. He looked around, sighed again and said, "In this world you could do it."

Kay said, "He's not the man I married."

Hagen laughed shortly. "If he were, he'd be dead now. You'd be a widow now. You'd have no problem."

Kay blazed out at him. "What the hell does that mean? Come on, Tom, speak out straight once in your life. I know Michael can't, but you're not Sicilian, you can tell a woman the truth, you can treat her like an equal, a fellow human being."

There was another long silence. Hagen shook his head. "You've got Mike wrong. You're mad because he lied to you. Well, he warned you never to ask him about business. You're mad because he was Godfather to Carlo's boy. But you made him do that. Actually it was the right move for him to make if he was going to take action against Carlo. The classical tactical move to win the victim's trust." Hagen gave her a grim smile. "Is that straight enough talk for you?" But Kay bowed her head.

Hagen went on. "I'll give you some more straight talk. After the Don died, Mike was set up to be killed. Do you know who set him up? Tessio. So Tessio had to be killed. Carlo had to be killed. Because treachery can't be forgiven. Michael could have forgiven it, but people never forgive themselves and so they would always be dangerous. Michael really liked Tessio. He loves his sister. But he would be shirking his duty to you and his children, to his whole family, to me and my family, if he let Tessio and Carlo go free. They would have been a danger to us all, all our lives."

Kay had been listening to this with tears running down her face. "Is that what Michael sent you up here to tell me?"

Hagen looked at her in genuine surprise. "No," he said. "He told me to tell you you could have everything you want and do everything you want as long as you take good care of the kids." Hagen smiled. "He said to tell you that you're his Don. That's just a joke."

Kay put her hand on Hagen's arm. "He didn't order you to tell me all the other things?"

Hagen hesitated a moment as if debating whether to tell her a final truth. "You still don't understand," he said. "If you told Michael what I've told you today, I'm a dead man." He paused again. "You and the children are the only people on this earth he couldn't harm."

It was a long five minutes after that Kay rose from the grass and they started walking back to the house. When they were almost there, Kay said to Hagen, "After supper, can you drive me and the kids to New York in your car?"

"That's what I came for," Hagen said.

A week after she returned to Michael she went to a priest for instruction to become a Catholic.

*     *     *

From the innermost recess of the church the bell tolled for repentance. As she had been taught to do, Kay struck her breast lightly with her clenched hand, the stroke of repentance. The bell tolled again and there was the shuffling of feet as the communicants left their seats to go to the altar rail. Kay rose to join them. She knelt at the altar and from the depths of the church the bell tolled again. With her closed hand she struck her heart once more. The priest was before her. She tilted back her head and opened her mouth to receive the papery thin wafer. This was the most terrible moment of all.

Until it melted away and she could swallow and she could do what she came to do.

Washed clean of sin, a favored supplicant, she bowed her head and folded her hands over the altar rail. She shifted her body to make her weight less punishing to her knees.

She emptied her mind of all thought of herself, of her children, of all anger, of all rebellion, of all questions. Then with a profound and deeply willed desire to believe, to be heard, as she had done every day since the murder of Carlo Rizzi, she said the necessary prayers for the soul of Michael Corleone.

# Anarchy in Boston

## From: *Mortal Friends*

### BY JAMES CARROLL

◈

When the phone rang on Curley's desk the dust flew. His office was like an open-air stall at Haymarket, a chaos of tables, jars, old cane chairs, boxes of books and papers, stacks of handbills, and fallen piles of folders. A gaudy velour shamrock, framed in gold, hung on one of the dark paneled walls. Old campaign posters with torn corners covered panels on another. An old whale-oil lamp which had been electrified stood on a corner of the desk next to the phone. It rang again.

James Michael Curley seemed not to hear it. He was standing at the high bay window, dressed in faded black broadcloth trousers and a defeated white shirt with frayed cuffs. His face was thick and slightly pitted. His hair was a mat of fine brown curls, parted sharply on the left side of his head. It was August of 1927. He was fifty-two.

Curley was the president of the South Boston Democratic Club when, as now, he was not the mayor of Boston. His office was on the second floor of a musty Victorian relic that sat like an aging clerk across from the big new courthouse on Dorchester Heights. His window opened on the slope of Southie as it ran down to the Fort Point Channel and the harbor and across to downtown. It seemed to Curley that he spent hours at that window. He refreshed his gaze continuously on its vista. That he was temporarily out of the city office—he had been defeated narrowly for his third term the year before—meant that he surveyed his domain from this window instead of from the one on School Street. The view from the Heights was spectacular, and, though he was counting the days until the next election, in some ways he preferred it.

The phone's bell was cut short in the middle of its third ring. That would be Alice Mahon, his secretary, answering from the small anteroom where she worked the typewriter. She would put him off, whoever it was, and Curley was relieved. The day had bloomed into crisp August perfection, and he wanted to look at his city sparkling there.

The Irish were concentrated in three sections of Boston: Charlestown, East Boston, and South Boston. But the latter was their stronghold. A mile-wide peninsula reaching four miles out into the harbor, it had been laid out a hundred years before as a summer retreat for wealthy Bostonians, but it fell by default to the droves of famine Irish who had no place else to go. By the end of the nineteenth century it was a booming phenomenon of tenements, wharves, ships, churches, graveyards, and factories. The mass production of cheap nails and the development of balloon-framing enabled the construction of hundreds of three-deckers which just kept pace with the influx of immigrants.

At its Broadway Station end, South Boston was a rough and merciless district where tenement flats with lamplight and cellar toilets rented for two dollars a week. There were howling families next to rowdy boarding-houses filled with the micks who were digging the city's subway tunnels. The buildings there were dilapidated. Warehouses and stables made the streets dark and dirty, fearsome at night. In daylight there was noise and dust from the truck and cart traffic in and out of Gillette's razor factory and between downtown and the wharves lining the north shore of the peninsula. That end of South Boston, closest to the city proper, was ugly, weighed down by poverty and crime. Outsiders took it to be typical of the entire ward; Southie was an Irish slum.

But the farther half of the peninsula, from Dorchester Heights out, was not like that at all. On East Broadway were the grand bowfront mansions the old families had built before the Irish came. Now they were the neatly divided dwellings of self-respecting working people who paid, typically, fourteen dollars a month for five rooms with all improvements: kitchen stove, penny heater, inside toilet, and gas piped in for lighting. Having avoided the "shanty," they mocked their own relative affluence by referring to themselves as "Steam-heat-and-nothing-to-eat Irish." Their section of Southie was called City Point, and in 1927 it was home to ten thousand people, all of whom knew that they had the choicest part of Boston. Their parents and grandparents had abandoned the crowded and crumbling North End to the Italian eel-eaters. Back Bay and Beacon Hill, where the Brahmins lived, were regarded as sterile, eerie places for their lack of children playing and their lack of old men watching from the corners. South Boston was the farthest thing from a slum to those who lived there. It was, as Curley himself always said, the citadel of a people who had come into their own.

The door to his office opened behind him.

"Mayor?" Alice Mahon said timidly. She was not supposed to disturb him until noon.

Though he was irritated, Curley cracked his face into a merry grin. "Yes, dearie, what is it?"

"It's Chief McGrath calling from Precinct One. An emergency, he says."

Curley nodded and Alice left.

He crossed to his desk in two lanky steps, picked up the phone, and put its pieces to his mouth and ear.

"Hello, Brian!" he said grandly. "What's up?" Curley had engineered McGrath's appointment himself.

"Mayor, I knew you'd want to know. We're going to clear out those anarchists today."

"From in front of the State House?"

"Yes, sir. Their leaders are bringing in Reds from New York and Chicago and all over. The judge said picketing's to be allowed, but not a demonstration."

"What's the difference?"

"Sixty. Judge Thayer says sixty makes a demonstration. We know a bus of thirty will be pulling in shortly. There's already forty or fifty of them up there. At sixty we move. I got the mounted unit behind the Senate wing and then the stick squads will cuff them."

"When do you expect to go?"

"An hour. The boys would sure appreciate it, Mayor, if you could be there. These anarchists are a tough lot and, well, the boys would like to see you there. You never know."

"Sure, Brian, sure. I'll come right over."

"Thanks, Mayor. I knew we could count on you. This Peters fellow don't give a rat's fart about the boys."

"Forget Peters, Brian. I'm your mayor, no matter what the *Transcript* says."

"Damn right, Mayor. I'll be glad when this is over. Wish they'd plug those two dagos right now and get done with it."

"Just a few days, Brian. The execution's set for Tuesday, eh? You can hold."

"Not if the Bolshies come up from Charlestown at the jail. If the whole crowd marches on Fuller's office we'll need the Marines."

"You *are* the Marines, Chief," Curley said. "You'll have those runts on the first boat to Moscow by supper. I'll see you in an hour. Don't do anything till I get there."

"Thanks a lot, Mayor."

Curley clicked the phone together and put it down with a bang. "Alice," he hollered; "Alice!"

Alice Mahon opened the door.

"Get Brady in here!"

Colman Brady was the treasurer of the South Boston Democratic Club and an associate in Curley's insurance business. He had started out as a foreman on the Castle Island landfill four years before, a city project which had Curley's special interest, and he had impressed the mayor with his energy and easy way with the men. Brady was bright and quick and Curley had liked him instantly. During the campaign the year before, Curley had made good use of Brady's brogue, and he made him treasurer afterward because he wanted him locked into the next campaign as well. Brady was great with the Irish and Curley was too smart to take them for granted. The cops loved the big Mick. He'd be just the fellow to have along if there was trouble.

While he waited for Brady to come down from the fourth floor, Curley went back to the window. He had to imagine the lines of Beacon Hill and the State House dome on its pinnacle because it was obscured by the large commercial buildings just west of South Station. But Curley had no trouble picturing the Bulfinch masterpiece or the rows of Federal mansions below it. It was turf he was very familiar with, but it was not his own. He was familiar with it the way a soldier is familiar with the terrain of his enemy.

Brady knocked politely on the door and waited for the loud grunt. It came. He went in.

"Well, Colman, me lad of gold, how goes it?" The emphatic intimacy of his greeting had its effect on Brady despite his knowing that the warm grin and open affection were chief tools of the man's trade. Curley could endear himself instantly to his own kind.

"Hello, Jim."

"Oh, laddo, am I glad to see you! We got a hot potato. They expect big trouble from the Sacco-Vanzetti crowd. The boys are going to round them up and I want you to come with me."

"To Charlestown, the jail?"

"No, Beacon Hill. Come on."

"Wait a minute, Mayor. I don't get it. That Sacco-Vanzetti stuff is dynamite. You want to keep your distance. It's Fuller's problem. And Peter's. Not yours."

"Fuller and Peters ain't going to be on that street this afternoon with a bunch of looney-bin Bolsheviks. McGrath just called. The boys need me, and by God, whatever the peril, political or otherwise, they'll have me. Come on."

The former mayor grabbed his tired black coat from the back of a chair and strode out of the office. Brady put both hands in the pockets of his trousers and stared after him for a moment. He understood exactly what was happening. Curley loved a crowd. He would play it the way musicians played their instruments. And, even better, he would play it in front of the State House, in front of the Brahmin Temple, in front of Mayor Peters, who had defeated him, in front of Governor Alvan T. Fuller. With their mealy-mouth ambivalent foot-dragging on the case—for six years they had put up with these anarchist protests—they had invited the notoriety and chaos and world-wide attention that was on them now as they prepared to put the two Italians to death. Curley wanted to gloat. The mob was theirs. The Boston police were his.

Colman had to hurry to keep up with Curley. It never occurred to the mayor to take a car to Beacon Hill. It would take them three quarters of an hour to walk it, but that was no problem. McGrath had said an hour. The promenade was one of the best-used routines in Curley's kit, and this one would display the mayor's urgent response to the call of his people. The two men cruised down Broadway. Brady frankly admired Curley's knack for moving quickly while still greeting shoppers and storekeepers and mothers at their carriages. When Curley waved at you and called your name and remembered your sick aunt or your brother's lost job, by God that was something! That James Michael, what a fellow!

Brady waved and greeted friends too, but not so grandly. He was a step behind Curley, and that was exactly where he wanted to be. Curley was the master and Brady was his best student. In the five years since he'd left Ireland, he had mustered sufficient nerve and luck to win a place in the snug of Curley's shadow. After Michael Collins, Brady had considered himself a connoisseur of shadows, and he knew the mayor's was a worthy one. Brady had come to understand Curley's genius as if it was his own. No one had ever embodied the yearnings of a people better than the mayor did those of his own. But Brady saw clearly too that what made Curley a giant on his own turf made him a midget, a circus figure, off it. Colman Brady was learning what to do and what not to do from James Michael Curley. Curley's end would be Brady's beginning. Brady was going to be mayor and more, and with a difference. In the way that Southie was Curley's, the whole city would be Brady's. His people would be the harp immigrants among whom he already moved so easily, but not only them. His people would be the North End Italians too, and the South Cove Chinese and the Roslindale Greeks. And more. His people, before he was through, would be the Beacon Hill Brahmin elite, whom Brady intended to defeat finally, as if they were British, by forcing them to love him. And once he had them all as his own, then he would do wonderful things for them. There was nothing simply self-interested about his ambition. He wanted to be of great and lasting service to Boston. At twenty-nine Colman Brady was a man who wanted everything.

And he dressed like it. He wore a fashionable white linen suit and sported a bright red tie. He flourished a thin cigar at his friends and knew that, when he passed, people feasted on the sight of him. Brady was not cocky, exactly, but he believed in posture and he walked as if he brushed his sand-colored bushy hair against the sky itself.

Terry Griffen, who pumped gas at the Socony on D Street, fell into step with the mayor. "Thanks, Your Honor, for coming to Amy's wake."

"Sorry for your troubles, Terence." Curley let his arm drape the man, who was stooped and red-faced.

"Honest to Pete, Mayor, Ma nearly died when you showed up."

"Now, Terence, we can't have folks dying at funerals. Give a bad name to the Irish wake."

Brady watched Terry Griffen drift off, shaking his head, delighted—that Curley was a card!—anxious to repeat the mayor's crack to the boys. He slid into the speakeasy at Miller's flower shop.

Curley turned to Brady. "Laddo, it startles me at times, how little they want. Just a mere hint or two of your friendship."

"It's more than a hint, Jim, when you help them bury their dead."

Brady's remark pleased Curley, as it was intended to. Brady knew where to touch him, as Curley did them. Curley nodded. It was a sad thought, which was why he loved it.

They crossed the Broadway bridge into downtown, where the lunchtime crowds swirled in and out of stores and foodstands. Curley waved to these strangers as if they were his neighbors too. Everybody was his crony. His large, full figure, that endearing grin—how could they not notice? His loud, glad "Halloo!"—how could they not like him?

Through all this, they were making good time. They crossed through South Cove, by the movie houses on Washington, and past the musical instrument stores on Boylston. They entered the Common, cut by the Parkman Bandstand, in the shade of which salesgirls and clerks were eating their sandwiches, and onto the paved path which cut diagonally across the park up to the State House.

The first pickets they came upon were milling at the foot of the Shaw Memorial stairs at the State House edge of the Common and below Beacon Street.

"They Shall Not Die," a placard read.

Curley and Brady brushed past the picketers, up the stairs and onto the street. A large line of fifty or more protesters moved slowly in their oval on the sidewalk.

"Ladies Full Fashioned Hosiery Workers," another sign read. "Support Sacco and Vanzetti."

A squad of red-faced Boston policemen stood with folded arms on the lowest of the grand stairs that swept up from Beacon Street to the Capitol, the golden dome of which flashed the August sun back at itself. The police eyed the oval line.

Curley crossed to them, pressed their shoulders, pinched their forearms, let everybody see that they were his. Brady hung back. His instinct was a bit different from the mayor's at that point. The police were about to make themselves some real enemies—and not just the Reds and the *artistes* who were going to get it.

Gusts of shouting from the picketers greeted the arrivals of new protesters, little dark men with eyeglasses and seamstresses with their long braids piled on top of their heads. A pair of women in summer dresses and big hats arrived in a large Packard, which drove off without them. Brady remembered that well-heeled Yankee matrons and Harvard professors as well as Communist agitators and Italian peddlers were outraged at the impending execution. Brady was afraid that Curley was seeing the thing a bit too simply. The cops would make many enemies, he was sure.

"Please, Governor, Pardon Them!" read a sign. "The World Waits!" It was carried by a small old man whose hair was white as paper and whose skin had the moist sticky look of paste. He looked unwell, but he walked his line with a determination that made others clear the way for him.

Automobile traffic passed slowly by, drivers staring. A Ford coupe honked—whether in protest or support—before turning down Park Street. State House workers began coming outside in pairs and threes to eat their bag lunches on the Common.

"Join us! Join us!" the picketers chanted.

The girl secretaries giggled and hurried down the Memorial Stairs into the park. But an old lady, a civil service veteran who had rubber thimbles on her forefingers—even at lunchtime—sneered at the marchers.

Curley spotted Chief McGrath standing between the pillars of the State House portico. The mayor took the stairs casually, greeting cops as he went. Brady saw and hurried after him; he wanted the scoop too. He didn't understand why McGrath should be so worried. The picketers were numerous, and a few of them had the fanatic's eye, but mainly they were orderly and quiet, not a particularly threatening lot. As he followed Curley up the stairs Brady reflected again that he himself had no position on the heated question of the two anarchists. Maybe they were guilty. Maybe they were victims of the bias against foreigners—he had felt blasts of that himself in Boston. But the debate seemed futile to Brady. He was certain the men would be put to death. The Lowell Commission had sealed that sentence.

Abbott Lawrence Lowell, president of Harvard, had chaired a special committee appointed by Fuller to review the trial, its verdict, and Judge Webster Thayer's sentence. Lowell found no reason to recommend any leniency whatsoever. Some had argued that Lowell's refusal represented the final proof that Sacco and Vanzetti were classic victims of Beacon Hill bigotry. But it wasn't that simple to Brady. Their lawyer had been Arthur Dehon Hill, a leading member of the bar Establishment. Their great defender in print had been Felix Frankfurter of the Harvard Law School. Brady'd never heard of any harp having free legal weight like that. If Harvard couldn't get them off nobody could. They were probably guilty.

But as far as Brady was concerned there was no point in expressing an opinion on the matter. The affair was poison from start to finish. Everyone who touched it would be infected. There would only be loser in this one. That was why Brady was sorry to see Curley rushing into it. It seemed he wanted to make a fool of himself too, just because Peters, Fuller, Lowell, Hill, Frankfurter, Thayer, and all the others had.

"So how goes it, Chief?" Curley asked loudly. He wanted everyone to hear him. If Fuller was in his State House watching, he'd be furious to see the former mayor's strut.

"A problem, Mayor, a problem. Mayor Peters is in with the governor right now. Peters wants to give them a permit for the demonstration."

"What's that all about?" Curley asked. "Peters can't want this riffraff out here any more than we do."

"It's Mr. Lowell, Mayor. He's asking for the permit himself."

"Lowell? What the hell does he have to do with it?"

"He says they have a right to peaceable assembly. He says this is not Spain or Russia." McGrath smirked as he said this.

"Hell, it was his gang said they're guilty. It's time to stop this lollygagging about."

"That's what I told him, which is why the mayor told me to wait outside."

"The mayor?" Curley asked. He scored the point with McGrath silently; James Michael Curley was the Mayor.

Brady sensed the drive of Curley's arrogance and wanted, for Curley's own sake, to deflect it. He turned and looked down on the picket line. Three young skylarking toughs in tweed caps and knickers were attempting to join it, but a young woman was standing them off.

"You can't walk here with that sign," she said loudly. Several pickets joined her.

One of the boys carried a placard which read, "Two Fried Wops Coming Right Up."

Brady nudged Curley and pointed to it.

Curley strained to read the sign.

The toughs started dancing on the edge of the oval line and chanting. The boy with the "Fried Wops" sign led them, waving his placard rhythmically.

"There, Brian," Curley said. "Look at that. There's a scuffle brewing for sure. Your boys still behind the Senate?"

"Yes, sir. All mounted up and ready."

"Well," Curley said, "I'd sure hate to see you wait too long." Curley was staring at the sign and the shoving that was going on around it.

"What can I do, Mayor?"

"You're the chief of police, McGrath. You uphold the Law. Have they got a permit to demonstrate like that?"

"Not yet, no sir."

"There must be a hundred and fifty of them."

"Mr. Lowell said that . . ."

"Don't you worry about Lowell, Chief, I'll take care of Lowell."

Brady read Curley; he'd love a head-to-head with Lowell right there on the street. He seemed to expect it. But Brady understood the difference between Curley and Lowell. Curley loved the display of power. He was desperate for signs of everybody's deference. Lowell exercised his power almost invisibly. He wanted deference so total that there were no hints of it. Curley take care of Lowell? Not likely. Curley would never see him.

The boy with the sign inserted himself between two pickets. They seized the sign, broke its stick and ripped the cardboard. They shoved the boy to the ground.

His companions jumped on the pickets and flailed away.

Curley had McGrath by the elbow and was yelling, "Stop them! Stop them!"

McGrath blew his whistle sharply three times.

Horses' hoofs clattered on the street.

Bystanders screamed and fled down the stairs into the Common. The picketers tried to link arms, some of them going limp and falling with covered heads as they'd been trained. The police swarmed over them, swinging their clubs, which whacked down viciously.

Bars of the "Internationale" rose and broke off as the cops honed in on the singers.

Patrol wagons with their eerie sirens could be heard coming up from the stationhouse on lower Joy Street.

One protester, bleeding badly from the head, was singing, "Mine eyes have seen the glory of the coming of the Lord."

A mounted policeman ran his horse up the stairs halfway to the State House entrance to club down a bespectacled radical who had been screaming, "Comrades! Comrades!"

Curley was not pleased by the scene, though he'd goaded McGrath into it. He loved his city, and the quick brutal chaos of the police swarming down on the pickets besmirched it. Still, the Law had to be upheld.

Brady thought the whole business unnecessary and he was shocked by it, if not openly. People were being banged about and bloodied more for the sake of Curley's vanity than for the peace of the city. Brady lit a cigar and backed into the shade of the portico. He watched the melee alone. It seemed to him a kind of contest. The horsemen were too aggressive and, by not allowing an orderly retreat, they were forcing the protesters to resist, and some were determined fighters. Stones were hurled. At least two policemen were pulled from their horses and pummeled with their own nightsticks. But most of the pickets were writhing in the street in panic and anger. Horses stepped on some, tearing open red wounds.

At the sight of the tumbled policemen, McGrath ran down the stairs to bark orders at his men, and Curley followed. Brady stayed where he was. There was nothing to be done.

He watched as demonstrators were hauled roughly into paddy wagons, but after a moment he noticed a man coming up the broad stairs and he had, unaccountably, the feeling the man was coming to him.

He was right. The man, dressed in a black serge suit that must have been suffocating, walked into the shaded portico and took up a position right next to Brady. He turned and looked down on the melee. It seemed at first as if he was going to say nothing.

He was Sergio Capelli, a North End second-stringer who worked a small corner of the home-brewed wine business. Brady recognized him as one of Gennaro Anselmo's boys.

"Mr. Brady," Capelli said, but without looking at him. Both men stared down at the street.

Brady said nothing. It was unusual for the likes of Capelli to be on the Hill and extraordinary for him to be near such a massive police action. The North End hoodlums were invisible people. It occurred to Brady that perhaps it was sympathy for the two anarchists. Was Capelli part of the demonstration? Not a chance. North Enders had mastered a remarkable stoicism about Sacco and Vanzetti. The public protests were more the work of Jewish lefties and Brahmin do-gooders than of Italians.

"What brings you out of the old neighborhood, *amico?*" Brady asked. He drew on his cigar and smiled at Capelli.

Capelli replied, "You," and stared at him.

"Me?" Brady laughed. "I don't get it."

"I would like you to come with me." Capelli spoke without a strong accent, but, as the son of immigrants, he had a formal, stilted cadence in his manner of speech. He was about twenty-five.

Brady knew that Capelli himself had nothing for him. He had to be on somebody else's errand. Whose? The answer was obvious. Anselmo: Gennaro Anselmo was a North End comer who ran a large garbage collection business which had started out carting residue from the home stills and which now had a city contract to clean up Haymarket every Sunday. Brady had obtained the contract for Anselmo from Curley, having first met him when he hired his trucks for the Castle Island land fill. Curley had not wanted to hire an Italian outfit for the land fill job since it was in Southie, but Brady'd insisted. He needed the trucks. For Anselmo, that job had provided exactly what he was looking for—a connection outside the North End and a foot inside the door of city contracts. It wasn't that Anselmo needed the trucking business, but that he wanted the cover for his efforts to start a bootleg distribution system outside the Italian neighborhood. He was a ground-breaker. He was the first North End hood to work in tandem with the Irish.

"Why should I go with you, *amico?* For what?"

"A friend wants to see you."

"My friends speak for themselves. Why'd he send you?"

Capelli shrugged. He did not know. Anselmo was a discreet man. Capelli waited.

Brady had to go with Capelli and he knew it. One of the key factors in Curley's loss to Peters the year before had been the Democrats' failure to get the North End vote out. Curley had little use for Italians, and that was one of his mistakes. Any politician who expected to carry and keep more than his own yard had to have a hand inside the Italian district. Anselmo was far from being one of the North End powers, but he was young. He was first-generation and appreciated the value of cooperation with other ethnic elements. And he was damned ambitious. One could do worse, Brady thought, than tie his tail to that kite. If Gennaro Anselmo wanted to see Colman Brady, then he would. Brady knew what it was to be used and to use.

He dropped his cigar and stepped on it. He looked down at the street and saw Curley heading off to the precinct house with McGrath. Nothing else was going to happen there. "All right," he said. "Lead on, friend."

      *      *      *

The North End was the oldest residential section of the city and looked it. The streets were crooked and narrow, following the contours of the land abutting the old wharves. Men clustered on corners and argued. Women with bundles pushed by on the narrow walks. The cobbled streets were jammed with trucks, pushcarts, the ranting hawkers of figs on strings and the day's fish catch. The old brick buildings were tall; their height prevented sunlight from falling anywhere but in the middle of the streets. Old people, elbows on pillows, watched everything like eagles from their windows, and below them slain rabbits and yearling lambs hung from the hooks of butcher shops dripping blood into gutters. Fire escapes slashed down the sides of buildings like wrought lightning, but the landings held mattresses, where the men slept on the summer nights.

Along Hanover Street all of the signs on the doors and store windows were in Italian, and Brady felt even more the foreigner than he did on Beacon Hill. At Fleet Street, Capelli turned east and, though the difference was lost on Brady, by the time they walked two blocks, all of the signs were in Sicilian.

Capelli stopped at the corner of Fleet and North streets.

"If you wait here," he said, and then he was gone.

Brady lit a cigarette, using the business of it to stiffle his uneasiness. He had rarely been in the North End, and never alone. It felt more like Italy than Boston.

"Hello, Brady."

The voice from behind startled Brady. He turned quickly. Gennaro Anselmo was there, a short, stocky man with a delicate face that seemed the foil to his powerful body. He looked at Brady intently, displaying confidence and purpose in his steady, strong gaze.

"Hello, Gennaro. Fancy meeting you here. I was waiting for a friend." Brady cracked his face into a grin and held out his hand, a politician's offer.

Anselmo shook Brady's hand firmly. He had known that Brady would come. Didn't every outsider long to be invited in? Anselmo trusted his intuitions absolutely. He thought he understood exactly what was stirring in the Irishman and he was prepared to risk nearly everything that he was right. That was not unusual. Anselmo continually gambled on his own intuitions. What made this different was that he was about to gamble that Brady's intelligence and ambition were as large as his instinct told him they were.

"North Street!" Brady said. "Did you know that Honey Fitz was born here? On North Street!"

"Who?"

"Never mind."

"One of my sisters was born . . ."—Anselmo pointed to a building halfway down the block—". . . there."

"Used to be Irish over here, they say." Brady could not conceal the faint disgust he felt at the cramped, smelly, steamy neighborhood. *"Dearo,* they called it. Dear Old North End. And before the Irish, the Yankees, Paul Revere, right?" Brady was thinking the Italians got what the Irish didn't want who got what old Boston didn't want.

"I want to talk to you about something else, not the neighborhood." Anselmo studied Brady carefully.

Brady inhaled smoke and said, "Curley's out of office, you know. I'm not sure what we can do for you."

"It is not business I had in mind." Anselmo paused. His eyes flicked up and down the street. "This is not a good place. Come with me."

"You have to give a clue first. What's up?"

"You were at the demonstration?"

"Yes."

"About that."

"The anarchists?"

"They did not kill those men."

Anselmo turned on his heel and walked halfway down the block and stopped in front of a low door.

Brady stared after him. What the hell was this? Every damn leftie in America had been hollering that for six years. But Anselmo was no leftie. There was not a frivolous cell in him. He was serious and he wanted Colman Brady's ear. Brady followed him down the sidewalk and through the door.

Anselmo closed it and faced Brady. They were in a cramped, shadowy vestibule.

"I want to ask your help," Anselmo said. He spoke with a weighty deliberation that communicated his dead seriousness to Brady.

"Lots of people claim they didn't do it," Brady said. "Mainly girls and college kids."

Anselmo didn't reply to that, and Brady wondered if he'd offended him. "So tell me."

"I will prove to you that the two are innocent, and then you must go to the governor."

"Fuller? He hates my guts."

"He hates Curley, not you. You represent Curley to him. You have met with him twice in the last month."

"On a couple of things left over from last year. But you do know your civics, don't you? You studying to be a citizen?"

Anselmo smiled faintly. He had been born in Worcester. Brady's gibe was at the fact that even first-generation Italians were foreigners to old Boston, more foreign even than recently-over Irish like Brady. "I know what you do, Brady," Anselmo said. "You carry the mayor's discreet messages to the governor. Both men talk to you."

"How do you know that?" Brady asked.

Anselmo nodded as if Brady had confirmed what he said. And then he stated a new fact. "The city of Boston bought two hundred heavy trucks from Fuller before he was governor. You brought the bid to Curley."

"Don't make me laugh!" Brady began to move away. "I didn't handle deals like that."

"Fuller paid you one thousand dollars in cash. Discreet."

Brady halted again and slammed Anselmo with a look. "You wouldn't be implying that I was bribed?"

"No. I say these things only to show I appreciate your position. You are a man of great ambition, I think."

"Do you now?"

"If you were to be the source of the much-sought evidence . . ." Anselmo let the sentence hang. It was true. The execution of the two Italians was to take place on August 22, barely a week away. There were reporters from all over the world in Boston. Fuller, squirming in his position as hangman, had practically begged the Lowell Commission to give him reason to commute the sentences to life. Lowell, Samuel Stratton, head of the Massachusetts Institute of Technology, and Robert Grant, a blue-blooded judge of probate court, had not done so. But new evidence might.

"What do you know?" Brady asked.

"I know who hit that payroll."

"Who did it?"

"It is not for me to say."

Brady studied him. Anselmo was totally serious. And he was right. If there was evidence, if Brady could get it, if he could be the source of it—that would be the first rung up on his ambition. He had to play this very carefully. "All right," he said. "But listen, one doesn't just walk into the governor's office and say the two geeks didn't do it, honor bright! What do you have?"

"I need your word first. Your solemn word." Anselmo fixed his stare more inside Brady than on him. He was making a fresh and last assessment before going further. Could he trust him? Were his intuitions reliable? If he was wrong on this one, Anselmo knew, he was dead. "Your oath that you will not mention my name in connection with this to anyone."

Brady nodded immediately. He caught the menace of Anselmo's request. The man lived by the subtlety of his threats. "You have it, my word. But that won't be enough for Fuller."

Anselmo turned and led the way down a dark narrow corridor that wound around a front room to a curving staircase. Brady stifled a wave of nausea at the rancid smell rising from the cellar. It was the odor of boiling wine, and it was piercing and indelible like vinegar. The home brewing of wine had become, with Prohibition, the most ubiquitous and profitable business in the North End.

The staircase seemed to rise forever. At every turn Colman tried to avoid touching anything with his white suit, but there was no light and he kept bumping the walls.

Finally they went through a low door and out onto the roof of the building. Laundry hung from lines strung between chimneys. The adjacent buildings were taller, and so the only view was of brick walls. Anselmo ducked under a line of bedclothes. When Brady found him he was halfway up a filthy rickety ladder that led to the rooftop of the next building.

"Jesus, Anselmo! Where now?"

But Anselmo ignored him and, with considerable agility, climbed to the top of the ladder, vaulted over a high ledge, and disappeared again.

Brady followed, ruining his suit.

When he came over the ledge he was shocked and thrilled.

There, on the next rooftop, was an elegant, manicured garden. It was evident at once that someone had taken infinite pains to haul soil bit by bit up to the roof and to cultivate fruit trees and flowers with great skill. As Brady brushed dirt from his sleeve, he stared at the garden. It was practically an orchard, full-blown, running the entire length of the roof, thirty yards at least, and across by ten. There were fig trees, orange trees, and a lemon tree with a ready crop of five or six lemons. Brady walked into their midst, touching the leaves and smelling the fruit.

"How wonderful!" he said aloud. "How wonderful!"

An old man appeared suddenly from behind a shrub. He was tiny and stooped. His skin was the color of olives, but wrinkled as stewed figs. He was smiling at the tall Irishman.

"You have a wonderful garden," Brady said formally.

Anselmo stepped to the old man's elbow and spoke to him in Sicilian. The old man smiled again at Brady and nodded like a drinking bird. *"Grazie, grazie."* And then he said something which Brady did not understand. Brady looked at Anselmo, who said, "He bids you welcome to his house."

"Thank you," Brady said. "I never heard of a garden on a roof like this. I used to be a farmer myself."

Anselmo translated.

The old man nodded and smiled. Most of his teeth were gone.

After an awkward silence, Brady said, "All right, Anselmo, what's the story?"

Anselmo touched the old man gently on the elbow and spoke confidentially to him. Brady watched as the old man's expression changed. Suddenly he stepped closer to Brady and seized his lapels and began speaking rapidly and urgently. His eyes brimmed and he rushed through whatever he was saying with such great feeling that Brady felt himself drawn to the man and moved. When he finished speaking he did not release his grip on Brady's suit, but lowered his head until it nearly touched Brady's chest. The man seemed exhausted and ashamed.

"It is not Gennaro Anselmo who says this," Anselmo began; "it is Giuseppe Tucci."

"What does he say?"

"He says it was not the two who robbed the factory in Braintree. It was a group of seven men from this neighborhood, including Enrico Zorelli."

"Zorelli!" Brady knew the name and showed it. Enrico Zorelli was the head of the Unione Siciliana, the disciplined North End organization that controlled the tenement district and the citywide marketing of its bootleg wine. Zorelli was known to Brady because he had been competing with Jerry MacCurtain from South Boston for control of whiskey smuggling on the waterfront. Zorelli was a typical Old World don; he was ruthless, devious and contemptuous of outsiders. He had, above all, refused to put his organization to work for Curley during the election the year before.

"Including Enrico Zorelli," Anselmo repeated, "and his own son, Antonio Tucci."

"His own son?" Brady stared at the old man.

"Yes."

Brady lifted the old man's face and looked at him. Tears were streaming down his cheeks but he made no sound.

"Sacco?" Brady asked.

The man shook his head: No!

"Vanzetti?"

Again, no!

"Antonio Tucci?" Brady asked.

The man nodded. *"Mi figlio."*

"I have a son too," Brady said gravely, feeling older than he was, feeling like a father.

Brady looked at Anselmo.

"His son is at Concord prison. He asked his father to make it possible for him to tell the truth."

"Why is he there?"

"A bank robbery in Lynn."

"And he's willing to admit murder?"

"He wants to arrange . . ."

"You need a lawyer, not me. I sell insurance."

"He's willing to tell how it was Zorelli's soldiers who did that, not Sacco. Not the other one. He was there. He has nothing to hide."

"Zorelli will kill him."

Anselmo did not respond to that.

Brady studied him carefully. "I would have guessed that you're in the Unione yourself, Anselmo."

Again Anselmo did not reply. Brady understood then how bold a stroke this was. Anselmo was delivering himself into Brady's hands. It seemed a rash and careless move, a foolish one unless the bet was for the entire house. Brady guessed what Anselmo's moves were aimed at, but he pressed him. "What's your interest in this? Justice for your compatriots?" Brady smiled and thought,

*Here you tell me I'm ambitious.* He wanted not to be Curley's lackey for longer than he needed to be, that was true. But it seemed to Brady that his ambition paled by comparison to Anselmo's who wanted nothing less, Brady saw, than to bring down Zorelli. "I admire your nerve," he said.

Anselmo shrugged. "What Tucci says is the truth." Anselmo looked at the old man, who stood there as if *he* were guilty. "Many of our people know the truth. That's why the picket lines are of bohemians and college boys, not Italians. We know and we are afraid, most of us."

Brady could not take his eyes from the old man. He put his hand on his shoulder and pressed it with warmth and fondness, almost forgiveness.

"If you arrange for the governor to see him, young Tucci will provide details of the holdup that only a participant could know. He will provide names of others who can be persuaded to support him. Sacco and Vanzetti are innocent."

Anselmo paused. Brady took his arm away from the old man, who had withdrawn into his own sadness; his body had gone wooden.

"You can be the one to save them," Anselmo said.

Brady nodded. He was thinking, *Nice for me and nice for the two bastards. If they're innocent they should get off, even if they are Reds.*

"The discussion is ended now," Anselmo said. He took old Tucci by the arm and led him away between the fruit trees. It took the Irishman some moments to realize that neither of them was coming back. He made his way off the roof, down to the street, and out of the North End the way he'd come.

Colman Brady walked down Atlantic Avenue, across the pier, up Summer Street, and into South Boston. On the hill at Dorchester Heights he went into the Democratic Club. At the entrance an old porter sat at his table with a row of dominoes.

"Mr. Nagle, good day!" Brady said cheerfully. "Is himself back yet?"

"Hello, Mr. Brady. Indeed he is. I just brought up the paper."

Brady took the winding wooden stairs two at a time and went to Curley's office. Alice Mahon was not at her desk, so he knocked quickly and breezed in. "Hello, Mayor!"

"Colman, damn it!" Curley ranted. "They're crucifying me!"

"Who?"

"Goddamn *Transcript!*" Curley slammed his hand down on the newspaper open on his desk. "This afternoon's, just out! Listen to this! 'With the former mayor himself standing by, the troops assaulted the picketers without provocation. The reaction of the police was extreme and irresponsible, even allowing for the fact that the former mayor—disregarding the City Charter and the will of the people—was himself directing the operation.'" Curley looked up. "Goddamn *Transcript!* Goddamn Prescott! They ought to make up their minds.

Are they for these Reds or not? It's Fuller, I tell you, trying to drain this Sacco-Vanzetti pus off on me!"

"That's what I wanted to talk to you about."

"Oh, Christ, never mind. I don't want to talk about it. Let's go to Fenway. The Sox are playing the Yanks."

"No, Jim, I must talk to you."

"Goddamn Yankees, all of them."

"I've come across something important."

"What, are the Reds going to march again?"

"No . . ."

"I can hear your heart thumping from here. What is it?"

"Do you recall meeting a fellow name of Gennaro Anselmo?"

"Garbage trucks, right? He bootlegs that terrible dago hooch."

"Right. He does the Haymarket and worked for us on the land fill at the Island."

"For *you*, not me. I told you not to hire him. Wops building the Irish Riviera! What does he want now? Another city contract?"

"No." Brady paused, letting the weight of his silence draw Curley's attention. "He says they didn't do it. Sacco and Vanzetti."

"Oh, Jesus H. Christ, Brady! Not you too! I don't care *who* did it! I just want the goddamn thing over with. Reds from all over the damn world swarming down on Boston like maggots. You think those State House coachmen have to deal with this crap? You think that ass Peters will? No! It's *my* boys on the line! My city!"

"Jim . . ."

"Don't you 'Jim' me. I'm going to the ballgame."

Curley grabbed his suit coat from a chair, fuming, "That wop don't know a bee from a bull's balls!"

Brady grabbed Curley's arm. "Maybe not, but I do!"

Curley's sail fell and he stopped. He stood looking at Brady, waiting. He was on the verge of an explosion and Brady knew it.

"I don't care who did it either, Jim." Brady's face wasn't six inches from the mayor's. He would out-cynic him. "I don't care any more about 'justice' than you do. I'm talking about a stick of dynamite with names on it—Alvan T. Fuller. J. J. Peters. How would you like to blow them out of the water? And not only them, but a fellow name of Enrico Zorelli?"

"I'm listening."

"Here's the scene. Sit down, Mayor." Curley sat. Brady went on melodramatically. He was going to use Curley's method against him; he was going to talk to him as if he were a crowd. "Here's the scene. For Sacco and Vanzetti, it's two minutes to midnight. Boston, America—no, the world—is holding its breath waiting for the switch to be thrown by Governor Alvan T. Fuller of Massachusetts, who regrets he has no choice under law but to send ten thousand volts of electricity into the emaciated bodies of two misguided immigrant slobs who couldn't even spell the word *anarchist!* When suddenly, the former mayor of the great city of Boston announces that what the U.S. Department of Justice and the entire court system of the Commonwealth and a team of blue-ribbon lawyers and even the commission chaired by the president of Harvard University itself could not do, he—out of his own modest zeal for justice and love of the little guy—*has done!* On his own! Without government funds! Namely, uncovered the true culprits and produced one of them to confess and name the others!"

"I'm still listening."

Brady smiled. "I can hear you listening—with your heartbeat."

"So go on."

"That's it. I go to Fuller, present the evidence, and get him to issue the executive order for stay. Then I alert you, and before the news breaks you call the boys in and take credit for it."

"But what . . . ?"

"Jim, Anselmo's fingered the bird for us. He's at Concord right now, waiting to sing. *He* did the payroll job in Braintree. *He was there.* And guess who else was?"

"Zorelli."

"Your North End nemesis."

"Oh, my God, Colman. Oh my God!" Curley pulled away from Brady and walked around behind his desk to sit. "Do you know what this is?" Curley was allowing himself the faintest grin. "This is the luck of the goddamn Irish! Peters, Fuller, *and* Zorelli! Oh my God! I'd save the good name of Boston!"

"Anselmo's given us a wedge, all right, but we have to hit it square on."

Curley sat forward. "What if it's a put-up job?"

"It could be. Anselmo's out to get Zorelli. He wants the Unione for himself. It's the young kicking up against the old, same as everywhere. But it won't matter. If the mate in Concord is willing to swear *to his own part in it,* the public will buy it. What better proof of a man's truthfulness than the willingness to incriminate himself? Fuller would have to pardon S. and V. after that, and the world would thank *you!*"

"And you too, of course." Curley's glance was knowing, not disrespectful. "What's the bird's name?"

"Tucci. I talked to his father."

"Why would he do it?"

"I don't know. Anselmo has a hand in his bowels. Hell, maybe the guy wants to tell the truth."

"Not likely. But you're right. It doesn't matter as long as the last couplet rhymes."

"Anselmo wants no part of the whistle. In fact he asked me not to mention him to anyone, including you, for obvious reasons. I gave him my word on that."

Curley nodded. He knew that Brady wouldn't break his word lightly, but also that Brady would never keep a secret from him. "It's better for us that way. We can take the credit."

"And Anselmo gets the north corner on poteen for the rest of Prohibition."

"Fair enough," Curley said. "Jerry MacCurtain can work with him. Zorelli won't even talk to Neapolitans, much less the Irish mob. Oh, it'll just kill Fuller and Peters and Lowell and the goddamn *Transcript*. We can make it look like a Brahmin cabal!"

Brady shook his head. "Not so. The Brahmin split on this one. The *Transcript*'s been out front for S. and V. all along, and don't forget Hill and Frankfurter and Gardner Jackson. They've been solidly behind them."

"Tokens! Tokens! It *has* been a Brahmin plot, by God. They just hate foreigners!"

"So do you."

"Not if they'll vote for me! I'll *love* 'em! I'll love the goddamn *Reds* if they'll vote for me!"

"After this they will."

"After this they'll get a chance. You're looking at the first four-term mayor this city ever had."

"Four! You're not in your third yet."

"You got to think big, Colman. You got to think big."

"You're right, Jim." But Colman was thinking, not for the first time, that the mayor thought too small.

# Thursday Night at the Rectory

From: *Ordained*

BY ROBERT LECKIE

T he joy of Thursdays was made complete for Father Cullen by his night-
time obligation to be "on call" at the rectory. To hear the rectory bell ring
and to open the door and find a hungry or unhappy person on the doorstep
was for Robert Emmet Cullen the fulfillment of his priestly ministry. He very
seldom made a distinction between those who were deadbeats or truly
destitute, those who were in genuine anguish or those who just wanted to chat,
giving to all freely of his money and his time in the fear that, by refusing an
apparent counterfeit, he might in truth be rejecting one of the "little ones" of
the Lord. Perhaps an even greater joy was to bring the Viaticum to the dying.
Only two weeks ago Father Cullen had been summoned by telephone to the
side of a blind man, and he had been horrified to discover what extremes of
comfort and degradation existed within the cathedral parish. The dying old
man lived with a sister in two rooms ankle-deep with filth. The moment he
entered the flat, Father Cullen's nostrils had been filled with a nauseating
stench so powerful that the young priest quickly put his hand to his mouth for
fear that he might vomit. Before him was the sick man, seated in a chair. For a
moment, Father Cullen thought that the gaunt old face and sightless eyes had
brightened when he said, "I'm Father Cullen." In the next instant, a second
wave of revulsion came over him. The poor man was stuck to the chair by his
own dried excrement! Yet, Father Cullen would never forget the expression of
joy that had illuminated the features of this wretched human husk when he
had opened the pyx and placed the Host in his hungry mouth. He had been
glad, too, that the man had asked him the meaning of the Latin formula, and
he had translated: "Receive, my brother, this food for your journey, the body
of our Lord Jesus Christ, that he may guard you from the wicked enemy and
lead you into everlasting life."

"Oh, that's beautiful," the blind man said, and then: "I hope you're dressed warmly, Father. I hated to bring you out on a cold night like this." It was then that Father Cullen had decided to call for the ambulance, doing so over the weeping protests of the blind man's sister. When the attendants came in, holding their noses, they found that they could not detach the old man from his filthy chair, and were compelled to carry him out in it. Father Cullen learned later that the blind man not only had to be cleansed but also deloused. His frail old body was so covered with lice bites that in some places it was difficult to put a pin between them. But, oh, how his face had shone with gratitude when Father Cullen brought him the Body of Christ! Reflecting on it, Father Cullen had wondered about the strangeness of the spirit. He had never been fond of St. Simeon Stylites up there on his pillar, all stench and sanctity; yet, Simeon had had his sight and God's fresh air to comfort him. But the blind man! Think of it: years and years of darkness and filth, never complaining, and then, with your dying breath to apologize for bringing a priest out on a cold night. Truly, "The Spirit breatheth where it will."

Not all of Father Cullen's Thursday nights had been so uniquely inspiring. The week before, the bell had rung and opening the door he had found a young woman standing outside. She was tall, not especially pretty, but very shapely. At least she dressed in a style calculated to show off every curve of her figure. Seeing the tall young redhead in the black soutane, her eyes brightened with interest.

"I'd like to speak to a priest," she said, and Father Cullen beckoned her into the hall, closing the door and looking at her inquiringly. "I, I'm interested in your religion, Father," she said, glancing around as though searching for a place to sit. Watching her carefully, Father Cullen had decided not to invite her into the waiting room. Nor did he offer her a chair, although she very quickly sank into one beside the wall, carelessly crossing her silken legs.

"You're not a Catholic?" he had asked.

"No. Actually, I'm not anything. But I do love to go into a Catholic church and watch the candles on the altar flicker."

Oh, Lord, Father Cullen had thought: a romantic! Wondering unhappily if she was going to quote from *The Lost Chord,* he was startled to hear her say: "I've always wondered about Catholic priests."

"Why?"

"Well, that stuff about staying away from women," she said, shifting suggestively in her chair. She looked up at him invitingly. "I don't believe you can do it."

In two long strides, Father Cullen was at the door. Trembling with rage, he flung it open and bellowed: "Get out!" Jumping to her feet, the young woman hurried outside, averting her face from the brown eyes blazing in Father

Cullen's white face. Still shaking, Father Cullen had slammed the door shut with such force that the rectory's front windows rattled. Afterward, however, he had felt remorseful. Perhaps he should not have been so angry. On the following morning, he had revealed his qualms to Father Krause, and had been relieved when the old priest shook his head gently and murmured: "Don't worry about it, Bob. You did the right thing. You should never be kind to temptation; or, worse, try to reason with it."

It had been on that morning that the odd odor on Father Krause's breath had been particularly noticeable. Father Cullen remembered it now, sitting in the hall office of the rectory, waiting for the doorbell or the telephone to ring. He still could not place the odor. He wondered if Father Krause was fond of foreign cooking. Perhaps he went to French restaurants on his night off, he thought, remembering reading somewhere of how an American priest in the World War heard confessions in Southern France and was nearly overpowered by the garlicky breath of his penitents. Suddenly, the seductive gaze of his temptress of the previous Thursday swam into his mind. He began to pray. How hard it was to conquer the "natural man" in him! As much as you might pray or avoid St. Bernard's "second look," he always lay in ambush. In your dreams, he had you at his mercy, Father Cullen thought; and he quickly rose from the desk and went to the bookshelf to take down one of John Henry Newman's works.

Cardinal Newman was Father Cullen's favorite writer. How often he had bathed his troubled spirit in those calm and soothing waters. Newman had been dead for nearly fifty years, yet Robert Emmet Cullen found him as modern as the new buses replacing the trolley-cars in Hudson City; and when the buses gave way before the next superior means of transportation, John Henry Newman would be modern still; modern because he was timeless. Coming back to his desk, Father Cullen opened the book and began to read: "Now, the phenomenon, admitted on all hands, is this:—that great portion of what is generally received as Christian truth, is in its rudiments or in its separate parts to be found in heathen philosophies and religions. For instance, the doctrine of a Trinity is found both in the East and in the West; so is the ceremony of washing; so is the rite of sacrifice. The doctrine of the Divine Word is Platonic; the doctrine of the Incarnation is Indian; of a divine kingdom is Judaic; of Angels and demons is Magian; the connexion of sin with the body is Gnostic; celibacy is known to Bonze and Talopoin; a sacerdotal order is Egyptian; the idea of a new birth is Chinese and Eleusinian; belief in sacramental virtue is Pythagoraean; and honors to the dead are a polytheism. Such is the general—"

The telephone rang. Reaching for it, Father Cullen saw that the little desk clock said eleven o'clock. "Father Cullen speaking," he said, marking his place in the book with his finger. The voice on the other end was shocked and urgent. "Father, this is the Shamrock Bar. A man in here just had a heart attack."

"Is he a Catholic?"

"Yes, Father. Can you hurry? He looks like he's a goner."

"I'll be right over," Father Cullen said, hanging up and getting quickly to his feet. Going into the chapel he took a host from the ciborium, placing it in a pyx used especially for such occasions. Returning to the hall, he put the pyx in the inside pocket of his old raincoat, took down the short purple and white stole from a hook and draped it around his neck, after which he put on the raincoat, picked up his missal and went outside to start the old Oakland reserved for priests on call.

Father Cullen reached the Shamrock Bar in five minutes. Parking the Oakland at the curb, he went inside, reverently holding his right hand over the Sacrament at his breast. Blinking to accustom his eyes to the dim light issuing from two dirty brass lamps hanging from the ceiling, he saw a narrow room with an oblong bar running out from one wall and a cluster of tables and chairs up against another. Four or five men and a policeman gathered around an inert figure on the floor near the bar dropped to their knees and crossed themselves when they saw the tall young priest in the black raincoat enter with his hand at his breast. Father Cullen came quickly to the prostrate figure in the rumpled gray business suit. He knelt beside the man, and as a familiar yet strange odor filled his nostrils, his heart turned to stone.

It was Father Krause.

Father Cullen thought that he would weep, but he could not. He could only stare in disbelief at the beloved features: the bulbous nose and wispy bald head, the kindly mouth now red with blood already dull and drying, the old eyes screwed shut in the last grimace of agony. For a moment, Father Cullen was reminded of Jesus being taken down from the cross, and then he reached hurriedly for the pyx. Careful not to handle the Host with his cut finger, Father Cullen opened the little gold case with his left hand; and as he did, he became conscious of a sturdy pair of legs in uniform blue beside him and heard a gruff voice trying to be gentle declare:

"It's no use, Bob. He's gone."

Looking up, Father Cullen saw that the policeman beside him was Jake Golarski, and he experienced a second shock, like the reverberating temblor that follows the earthquake. Jake had his hat off, and Father Cullen noticed that his boyhood friend's blond hair had begun to thin. Otherwise, the square, handsome, slightly brutal face was unchanged. "I've already called the morgue," Jake said, and Father Cullen nodded sadly and put away the pyx. Still kneeling, he raised his hand in conditional absolution. Father Krause might be dead, as Jake Golarski insisted, but because Catholic theology holds that the soul does not depart the body until several hours after death, it was still possible to absolve Father Krause's soul of its sins. Sins? Father Cullen wondered, sadly lifting his hand and pronouncing the absolution while the workingmen around him bowed their heads: what sins could Father Krause have committed? But, oh!, he must have been so lonely, Father Cullen thought, getting to his feet. What else could have compelled him to change his clothes on Thursday nights and seek the rough companionship of neighborhood bars? Yet, he had truly found a safe harbor. In the end, they had brought him a priest.

Turning to Jake Golarski, Father Cullen asked, "What happened?" and the policeman put a hand on his arm, drawing him away from the men who had also gotten to their feet and were crowding around the priest and the stricken man. "He'll tell you," he said, pointing to the bartender and leading him to the bar. Glancing sharply at the men, Jake Golarski attempted to frighten them off to a respectful distance, but they were not to be intimidated out of their rightful share in the event, and trailed doggedly after Father Cullen, pressing in around him as he spoke to the bartender.

"He'd just got off his stool and was heading for the men's room," the bartender said. "All of a sudden, he let out a yell and grabbed at his shoulder and then he went down. Before we could do anything, he got up on his knees like he was fighting something, and then he went down again and rolled over and I guess that was it." The bartender paused as though waiting for confirmation from the men gathered around the priest and the policeman, and when they nodded their heads approvingly, he continued. "Lucky for us, Jake was in—" Momentarily flustered by Jake's heavy frown, the bartender halted, and then went on: "Jake was passing by and he was able to put in a call to the station house. Then I called you, Father."

"How did you know he was a Catholic?" Father Cullen asked, trying to make his voice sound casual, striving to conceal his recognition of Father Krause.

"Him?" one of the men exploded. "What else could he be? Whenever he was in here and we was having an argument about the Church, we'd ask him for the answers."

"Yeah," another man said. "The little guy knew so much about religion we figured he was a pr—" He caught himself, and flushed, retreating to the outer rim of onlookers, and the bartender coughed warningly and said: "He was such a nice little guy, Father. He'd come in here on Thursday nights. Not every Thursday. He'd miss maybe once or twice a month. But he never came in any other night. He'd just sit there at the end of the bar, sippin' his shandy-gaff—you know, Father, half beer an' half birch?, he never drunk nothin' stronger—and listenin' to the guys argue. He'd never talk himself, only when somebody asked him about something." The bartender shook his head sadly. "Just before he'd leave, he'd have a hard-boiled egg and a coupla blind robins—"

"Blind robins?" Father Cullen asked, and the bartender nodded, turning to lift one of a cluster of cellophane-wrapped objects out of a bowl on the counter behind him. Dropping it on the bar before the priest, he said: "That's a blind robin, Father. Dried herring and garlic. The little guy loved 'em." He grinned fondly. "I'd sure hate to've been working in the same office with him the next day. The way those things stink, I'd've—"

The wail of a siren interrupted him. Growing louder, the sound trailed off into silence directly outside the Shamrock Bar. Jake Golarski quickly put on the uniform cap he had been holding, and went to open the door and admit two patrolmen carrying a stretcher. A police physician in civilian clothes with a stethoscope in his coat pocket came in next. Going briskly to the body, the physician knelt down and fumbled for a pulse. Finding none, he opened Father Krause's shirt, put the stethoscope terminals in his own ears and searched the prostrate frail body for a heartbeat. Again failing, he removed the stethoscope and roughly grasped Father Krause's chin with one hand while peeling back the eyelids with the other.

"Please!" Father Cullen called imploringly, and the doctor looked up in surprise. Shrugging, he released his grasp and rose to his feet. "Coronary," he murmured. "Probably massive." The policemen nodded, put the stretcher alongside the body, and then, with deferential glances at the tall young priest, gently rolled the corpse onto the stretcher. Arising, they carried it outside. Jake Golarski and the doctor followed, and Father Cullen called, "Wait for me, Jake," before turning to the bartender to say, "Thank you. Thanks for calling the rectory."

"Glad to do it, Father," the bartender said, beginning to draw beer for the customers once again seated at the bar. "You sure didn't lose any time getting here." Nodding to the men, Father Cullen went outside, just as the ambulance rolled away, its siren muted, its flashing red light extinguished. Jake Golarski was waiting for him.

"Here, Bob," he said, handing him a worn black wallet. Father Cullen took it, guessing at once that it had belonged to Father Krause. "You knew he was a priest, Jake?" he asked.

"Yeah," Golarski said, moving his shoulders eloquently. "Soon as I got a look at his wallet I told the bartender he better call the rectory."

"Thanks, Jake. Right now, you've got a pretty good friend in Heaven."

Jake Golarski fingered the brim of his cap in embarrassment. "Forget it," he said. "Don't worry none about the report either. It won't mention the Shamrock. I'll just say he got the seizure on the corner here." Now it was Father Cullen who looked away in embarrassment. He nodded in gratitude, yet he was ashamed of his own conniving at the truth. Who would understand a priest dying in a bar, he thought, trying to rationalize the deception; but he still felt a sense of betrayal. "Let's not stand here," he said. "Let's go sit in the car and talk a while."

"Okay," Jake Golarski said, looking at his wristwatch. "I'm through in fifteen more minutes." Inside the car, Jake removed his cap again and loosened his tight-fitting uniform collar. "It's sure been a long time, Bob," he said, running a thick, powerful hand over his thinning blond hair.

"Five years, anyway," Father Cullen said, closing his eyes thoughtfully. "No, it's more like six! Last time I saw you was at the Loyola-Cleveland game in nineteen thirty. Of course, I've seen you a couple times since then, but never to talk to. So that was October nineteen thirty, and this is April nineteen thirty-six," he said, drumming off the months on his fingertips. "That makes it five and a half years. Boy, oh, boy, Jake," he said with a warm grin, "it's sure great talking to you again. What've you been doing with yourself?"

Jake Golarski smiled sourly. Even as childhood playmates, his had been the sullen disposition which drew constantly on the gaiety of his friend. "Just bummin' around, I guess. I never got my diploma, you know. The Depression finished that." Reaching inside his tunic, Jake drew out a crumpled pack of cigarettes, shook one free and bent to light it, the flare of his match making points of light on his hard, chiseled features. Blowing smoke forcefully, he turned to examine his friend. "I nearly flipped when you came through that door," he said. " 'Course, I always knew you wanted to be a priest. But it was funny, really seeing you with your collar on backwards." Jake Golarski studied the cigarette in his hand. "You really meant it, after all," he said slowly.

"Why not?"

"Well, you know how I feel about it. It's a sucker's life. No dough, no fun—you can't even call your life your own."

Father Cullen grinned. "That wasn't what you said when I transferred to Loyola. You said then that priests were nothing but a bunch of fat capons. Remember?"

Jake Golarski scowled. "That was my old man talking again. But I was mad as hell, you leaving Cleveland like that. If you'd've stayed, we'd've won the city title." Jake wound down his window. Plucking the cigarette from his lips, he seized it between thumb and middle finger and flicked it outside in a red arc. Winding the window up again, he said: "It was two years or more before I got a steady job. There wasn't much in those days. Christmas you could help peddle Christmas trees or work a couple hours in the post office. Summers I used to mow lawns in Juergen County. There was a guy out there had an outfit called Man Friday. He'd contract for all kinds of odd jobs around people's houses." Jake's voice was bitter. "He'd pay you all of thirty cents an hour. I don't know what he charged his customers, the cheap son of a bitch, but all we got was thirty cents. And he'd make us buy our uniforms off him, too." Jake Golarski glanced sideways at Father Cullen. "One summer was all I could take from that crumb," he grunted. "So I tried Organized Baseball. One year with the Pony League and then I wound up in Class C with Portsmouth in the Piedmont League."

"You were always a good catcher, Jake."

"Yeah, mebbe so. But I never could hit a curve. And lemme tell you somethin', Bob. In those days, some of the guys playing Class D ball, there's bums in the majors now couldn't carry their glove." Rolling down the window again, Jake coughed and spat. "So then I went to sea," he said.

"No kidding? I never knew you went to sea, Jake. That must have been fun, anyway."

"Nah. I was only a wiper on a coastal tanker. I never even got across the big pond. Galveston and back, Galveston and back, a hundred, hundred-ten degrees in the engine room, and maybe if you're lucky you get on deck a few times to see the sun go down. Believe me, it was a rotten life. And hot! Soon's I heard Roosevelt was starting the CCC, I come ashore for good and signed up." A note of fondness came into Jake's rasping voice. "It wasn't a bad life in the CC's," he said. "They shipped me out to a camp in Montana. The chow wasn't bad, better'n the slop they fed you at sea, and I kind've got to like the outdoor livin' . . . Fightin' forest fires, plantin' trees, diggin' dams, that kind've stuff. I must've put on fifteen pounds in the CC's, Bob, and lemme tell you, it was all muscle." Leaning back against his seat, Jake Golarski began to rebutton his tunic. "But they don't let you stay in too long. So when I came out, I had a few bucks saved and I got my diploma and then I joined the boys in blue." The bitterness came back into his voice. "Joined!" he sneered. "It cost me five hundred bucks to wear this suit. Every goddam penny I had, the dirty, grafting bas—" The door of the Shamrock Bar opened, emitting a dim shaft of light that illuminated the faces of both the men in the automobile. Turning, they saw one of the customers standing in the doorway to wave his farewell. When he shut the door, Father Cullen and Jake Golarski were in darkness once more. "Those guys in there," Jake said, jerking his head toward the bar, "they knew he was a priest."

"They *did?*"

"Sure. How can you hide something like that? After the first couple times, everybody tumbled. They never let on though." Jake Golarski lit another cigarette. "He wasn't the first padre to change his suit on his night off."

"I know," Father Cullen said softly. "But Father Krause was a holy man."

"Yeah, they all are," Jake jeered.

"No, they aren't," Father Cullen persisted. "But he was." He touched his friend gently on the shoulder. "When are you coming back to church, Jake?"

he asked, and Golarski snapped: "You let me worry about that, huh, Bob?" Settling back in his seat with a sigh, Father Cullen asked: "How do you like being on the force?"

"It ain't bad. It's a living, anyway. Better'n mowin' lawns or shovelin' shit." Golarski looked sideways at the priest beside him. "You think I'm bluffing, don't you?" he said, his voice harsh. "But I did shovel shit. Ash cans full of it." He drew on his cigarette, inhaling so ferociously that the coal glowed and crept up its stem like a red worm. "When I was at sea, one of my duties was cleaning out the head. At the seminary, I guess you'd call it the lavatory. But at sea they call the shithouse the head. They weren't very fancy heads, either, and sometimes they'd get stuck, and when that happened I'd have to unstick 'em." Winding down the window again, he sent his second cigarette spinning through the night.

"Jake, Jake," Father Cullen said gently, "it's me you're talking to. Your old friend from Dixon Street. You know you can't shock me with a four-letter word. I've heard them all before. What's eating you, Jake? Am I your enemy now, just because I'm a priest?"

"It ain't that," Jake growled. "Ah, mebbe I'm feelin' sorry for myself. I dunno." He scowled heavily and put his cap back on. "Today I heard about a guy gettin' promoted who can't hardly write his name. I guess that's it. It's me!" He turned fiercely on Father Cullen. "Where's a guy with a name like Golarski gonna get in a burg like Hudson City? Mebbe if I had a mick or an O in front of it, it'd be different, but with a ski on the end I'm walking down a dead-end street." Jake lit a match to look at his watch. "Seeing you and everything," he muttered, "knowing how much better educated you must be, I guess that's what got me burned up." He blew out the match, and fastened his uniform collar. "You going past the station, Bob?"

"Sure," Father Cullen said, leaning forward to start the motor. "How about a cup of coffee after you check in?"

"Nah, I ain't got time. I gotta be up early tomorrow. I got the duty at the Navy Yard." Jake Golarski glanced sheepishly at his friend. "I'm a sergeant in the Marine Corps Reserve," he said.

"Marine Corps!" Father Cullen exclaimed, letting out the clutch. "Boy, you sure do get around, Jake. Why the Marines?"

"Who knows?" Jake Golarski murmured, gazing out the window as they rolled past the darkened shops of Cranberry Street. "There could be another war, you know. And then Jake Golarski might be somethin' a little better'n a pavement-pounder."

"If you mean Hitler and Mussolini and all that, I'd say sure. But over there. Not us, Jake. We're never going over there again. We got our fingers burned the last time, pulling England's chestnuts out of the fire." Shaking his head, Father

Cullen drove slowly between the dark bulks of the pro-cathedral on his right and the archbishop's residence on his left, turning carefully to his right when he came to Eighth Street.

"You could be right, and you could be wrong," Jake Golarski said with huge indifference. "Anyway, I kind've like the action in the Marines. Not full time, of course, not in peace time. But we drill only once a month and two weeks in the summer and you pick up a few extra bucks." He fell silent while Father Cullen brought the Oakland to a halt outside the doorway flanked by green electric globes. "And the Marines don't give a damn how you spell your name either," he said, opening the car door. "If you pass the exam for sergeant, you make it, and nobody gives a sh—, nobody cares if you drank your milk from Mrs. O'Leary's cow." Jake Golarski got out of the car, almost cheerful as he leaned inside the door to grasp Father Cullen's hand and say: "Thanks for the lift, Bob. See you soon, huh?" Then he slammed the door shut and went inside.

Turning his car around on the deserted street, Father Cullen drove back to the pro-cathedral rectory, his mind full of Jake Golarski: his bitter voice, the hard lines in his face, his ambitions and frustrations. Clearly, Jake Golarski had lived a little. Robert Emmet Cullen felt like a puppy in comparison.

It was not until he was inside the rectory and in bed that Father Cullen remembered the face of Father Krause, and when he did, grief seized him in long sorrowing sobs that convulsed his long body and broke from his nose in bubbles of phlegm. When he finally fell asleep, his pillow was wet with tears.

# Visions of Gerard

### From: *Visions of Gerard*

#### BY JACK KEROUAC

When my father comes home from his printing shop and undoes his tie and removes his 1920's vest and sits himself down at hamburger and boiled potatoes and bread and butter of the prime with the kiddies and the good wife, the proposition is put up to him why men be so cruel and mice betrayed and cats devour the rest—Why we were made to suffer and be harsh in return, one the other, and drop turds of iron on brows of hope, and mop up sick yards and sad—"I'll tell you, Ti Gerard, little one, in life it's a jungle, man eats man either you eat or get eaten—The cat eats the mouse, the mouse eats the worm, the worm eats the cheese, the cheese turns and eats the man— So to speak—It's like that, life—Dont cry and dont bother your sweet lil head over these things—All right, we're all born to die, it's the same story for everybody, see? We eat the cow and the cow gives us milk, dont ask me why."

"Yes, why—why do men make traps for little mice?"

"Because they eat their grain."

"Their old grain."

"It's grain that's in our bread—Look here, you eat it your bread? I dont see you throw it on the floor! and you dont make *passes* with the dust in the corner!"—*Passes* were the name Gerard had invented for when you run your bread over gravy, my mother'd do the soaking and throw the *passes* all around the table, even to me in my miffles and bibs at the little child flaptable—But because of our semi-Iroquoian French-Canadian accent *passe* was pronounced *PAUSS* so I can still hear the lugubrious sound of it and comfort-a-suppers of it, *M'ué'n pauss,* as you'd expect Bardolph to remember his cock-walloping heigho's of Eastcheap—My father is in the kitchen, young and primey, shirtsleeves, chomping up his supper, grease on his chin, bemused, explaining moralities to his angels—They'll grow 12 feet tall in the grave ere

the monstrance that contains the solution to the problem be held up to shine
and make true belief to shine, there's no explaining your way out of the evil
of existence—"In any case, eat or be eaten—We eat now, later on the worms
eat us."

Truer words were not spoken from any vantage point on this packet of
earth.

"Why? *Pourquoi?*" cries lil Gerard with his brows forming woe and inabili-
ties—"I dont want to be like this, me."

"Though you want or not, it is."

"I dont care."

"What you gonna do?"

He pouts; he'll go to heaven, that's what; enough of this beastliness and
compromising gluttony and compensating muck—Life, another word for mud.

"Come, come, little Gerard, maybe there's something you know that *we*
dont know"—My father always did concede, Gerard had a deep mind and deep
things to think that didnt find nook in insurance policies and printer's bills—
They'd never write Gerard a policy but in eternity, he knew we were here a
short while, and pathetic like the mouse, and O patheticker like the cat, and O
worse! like the father-cant-explain!

"Awright," he'll go to bed and sleep it off, he'll tuck me in too, and kiss Ti
Nin goodnight and the mouse be no lesser for her moment in his hands at
noon—Together we pray for the Mouse. "Dear Lord, take care of the little
mouse"—"Take care of the cat," we add to pray, since that's where the Lord'll
have to do his work.

Ah, and the winds are cold and blow forlorner dust than they'll ever be able
to invent in hell, in Northern Earth here, where people's hopes though warm
fail to conceal the draft, the little draft that works all night moving curtains over
radiator heat and sneaks around your blanket, and would bring you outdoors
where russet dawn-men with cold-chapped ham-hands saw and pound at wood
and work and stream with horses and curse the Satan in the air that made all
Russias, Siberias, Americas bare to the blasts of infinity.

Gerard and I huddle in the warm gleeful bed of morning, afraid to get
out—It's like remembering before you were born and your hap was at hand and
Karma forced you out to start the story.

"Where is she the little mouse now?"

"This morning. The cat has shat her in the woods *(Le chat l'a shiez dans
l'champ)*—with the little pipi yellow you see in the snow down there, see it?"

"*Oui.*"

"*Voilà* your fly of last summer, she's dead too—"

We think it over in motionless trance, as Ma prepares Pa's breakfast in the
fragrant kitchen below.

"Angie," says Dad at the stove, "that kid'll break my heart yet—it hurt him so much to lose his little mouse."

"He's all heart."

"With his sickness inside—Ah, it busts my head—Eat or get eaten—not men?—Hah!—There's a gang downtown would, if their guts were big enough."

*       *       *

Gerard's feeling of the holiness of life extended into the realm of romance.

A drunkard under an ample tent was never more adamant concerning how his little sister should behave—"Mama, look what Ti Nin's doing she's going to school with her overshoes flopping and throwing her behind around like a flapper!" he yelled one morning looking out the window—It was one of those days when he was suffering a rheumatic fever relapse and had to stay in bed, weeks sometimes, some days worse than others—"Aw look at her!—" He was horrified—He refused to let her do it, when she came home at noon he had a speech worked out for her—"I'm telling you Gerard, you'll be a priest some day!" my mother'd say.

Meanwhile the kids at church did the sign of the cross some of them with the following words:

> *"Au nom du père*
> *Ma tante Cafière*
> *Pistalette de bois*
> *Ainsi soit-il"*

Meaning

> *"In the name of the Father*
> *My Aunt Cafière*
> *Pistolet of wood*
> *Amen"*

There's my pa—Emil Alcide Duluoz, at that time, 1925 a hale young printer of 36, dark complexioned, frowning, serious, hardjawed but soft in the gut (tho he had a gut so hard when he oomfed it and dared us kids butt our heads in it or punch fists off it and it felt like punching a powerful basketball)—5:7, Bretonsquat, blue eyed—He had a habit I cant forget, even now I just imitated it, lighting a small fire in the ashtray, out of cigarette pack paper or tobacco wrapping—Sitting in his chair he'd watch the little Nirvana fire consume the

paper and render it black crisp void, and understand, mayhap, the bigger kin-
dling of the 3,000 Chillicosms—That which would devour and digest to
safety—A little matter of time, for him, for me, for you.

Too, he'd take fresh crisp MacIntosh apples of the Fall and sit in his easy
chair and peel em with his pocket knife, making long tassels around and around
the fruitglobe so perfect you could have hung them like tassels' canopies from
chandelier to chandelier in the Hall Tolstoy, the which we'd take and sling
around and I'd eat em in like great tapeworms and they'd end up flung out in
the garbage can like coils of electric wire around and around—After which
he'd eat his peeled apple at the gisty whitemeat cut-surface with great slobber-
ing juicy bites that had all the world watering—"Imitate the roar of a lion!
Imitate a tiger cat! Imitate an elephant!"—Which he'd do, in his chair, for us,
evenings in New England, Gerard on one knee, me on the other, Nin on his
lap—That is, when ever there was no poker game to speak of downtown.

"And you my little Gerard, why do you look so pensive tonight? What's
goin on in that little head?" he'd say, hugging his Gerard to him, cheek against
soft hair, as Nin and I watched rave lip't and rapt in the happiness of our childhood, little dreaming what quick work the winds of outside winter would do
against the timbers and tendons of his poor house. In the name of the father,
the son, and the Holy Ghost, amen.

•     •     •

But Gerard had his holidays, they bruited before his wan smile—New
Year's Eve we're all in bed upstairs under the wall-papered eaves listening to the
racket horns and rattlers below and out the window the dingdong bells and sad
horizon hush of all Lowell and towards Kearney Square where we see the red
glow embrowned and aura'd in the new (1925) sky and we think: "A new
year"—A new year with a new number and a new little boy with candlelight and
*kitchimise* standing radiant in the eternities, as the old, some old termagant with
beard and scythe, goes wandering down the darkness field, and on the sofa arms
of the parlor chairs even now the fairies are dancing—Gerard and Nin and I are
sitting up in the one bed of conclave, with a happy smile he's trying to explain
to us what's really happening but by and by the drunks come upstairs with wild
hats to kiss us—Some sorrow involved in the crinkly ends of pages of old
newspapers bound in old readingroom files so that you turn and see the news
of that bygone New Year's day, the advertisements with top hats, the crowds in
Hail streets, the snow—The little boy under the quilt who will have X's in his
eyes when the rubber lamppost ushers in his latter New Years Eves, one scythe
after another lopping off his freshness juices till he comes to bebibbling them
from corny necks of bottles—And the swarm in the darkness, of an ethereal
kind, where nobody ever looks, as if if they did look the swarms ethereal would

wink off, winking, to wink on again when no one's watching—Gerard's bright explanations about dark time, and cowbells—Then we had our Easter.

Which came with lilies in April, and you had white doves in the fields, and we went seesawing thru Palm Sunday and we'd stare at those pictures of Jesus meek on the little *azno* entering the city and the palm multitudes, "The Lord has found that nice little animal there and he got up on his back and they rode into the city"—"Look, the people are all glad"—A few chocolate rabbits one way or the other was not the impress of our palmy lily-like Easter, our garland of roses, our muddy-earth Spring sigh when all in new shoes we squeaked to the church and outside you could smell the fragrant cigarettes and see men spit and inside the church was all dormant and adamant like wine with white white flowers everywhere—

We had our Fourth of July, some firecrackers, some fence sitting spitting of sparks, warm trees of night, boys throwing torpedoes against fences, general wars, oola-oo-ah popworks at the Common with the big bomb was the finale, and popcorn and Ah Lemonade—

And Halloween: the Halloween of 1925, when Ma dressed me up as a little Chinaman with a queu and a white robe and Gerard as a Pirate and Nin as a Vamp and old Papa took us by the hand and paraded us down to the corner at Lilley and Aiken, ice cream sodas, swarms of eyes on the sidewalks—

All the little children of the world keep quickly coming and going to the holidays that only slowly change, but the quality of the brightness of their eyes monotonously reverts—Seeds, seeds, the seed sown everywhere blossoming the fruit of our loom, living-but-to-die—There's just no fun in holidays when you know.

All the living and dying creatures of the endless future wont even wanta be forewarned—wherefore, I should shut up and close up shop and bang shutters and broom my own dark and nasty nest.

●    ●    ●

At this time my father had gotten sick and moved part of his printing business in the basement of the house where he had his press, and upstairs in an unused bedroom where he had some racks of type—He had rheumatism too, and lay in white sheets groaned and saying *"La marde!"* and looking at his type racks in the next room where his helper Manuel was doing his best in an inkstained apron.

It was later on, about the time Gerard got really sick (long-sick, year-sick, his last illness) that this paraphernalia was moved back to the rented shop on Merrimack Street in an alley in back of the Royal Theater, an alley which I visited just last year to find unchanged and the old graywood Colonial one storey building where Pa's pure hopeshop rutted, a boarded up ghost-hovel not even fit for bums—And forlorner winds never did blow ragspaper around useless rubbish piles, than those that blow there tonight in that forgotten alley of the world which is no more forgotten than the heartbreaking and piteous way Gerard had of holding his head to the side whenever he was interested or bemused in something, and as if to say, "Ay-you, world, what are our images but dust?—and our shops,"—sad.

.     .     .

Nonetheless, lots of porkchops and beans came to me via my old man's efforts in the world of business which for all the fact that 't is only the world of adult playball, procures tightwad bread from hidden cellars the locks of which are guarded by usurping charlatans who know how easy it is to enslave people with a crust of bread withheld—He, Emil, went bustling and bursting in his neckties to find the money to pay rents, coalbills (for to vaunt off that selfsame winter night and I'd be ingrat to make light of it whenever trucks come early morning and dump their black and dusty coal roar down a chute of steel into our under bins)—Ashes in the bottom of the furnace, that Ma herself shoveled out and into pails, and struggled to the ashcan with, were ashes representative of Poppa's efforts and tho their heating faculties were in Nirvana now 'twould be loss of fealty to deny—I curse and rant nowaday because I dont want to have to work to make a living and do childish work for other men (any lout can move a board from hither to yonder) but'd rather sleep all day and stay it up all night scrubbling these visions of the world which is only an ethereal flower of a world, the coal, the chute, the fire and the ashes all, imaginary blossoms, nonetheless, "somebody's got to do the work-a the world"—Artist or no artist, I cant pass up a piece of fried chicken when I see it, compassion or no compassion for the fowl—Arguments that raged later between my father and myself about my refusal to go to work—"I wanta *write*—I'm an *artist*"—"Artist shmartist, ya cant be supported all ya life—"

And I wonder what Gerard would have done had he lived, sickly, artistic— But by my good Jesus, with that holy face they'd have stumbled over one another to come and give him bread and breath—He left me his heart but not his tender countenance and sorrowful patience and kindly lights—

"Me when I'm big, I'm gonna be a painter of beautiful pictures and I'm gonna build beautiful bridges"—He never lived to come and face the humble problem, but he would have done it with that *noblesse tendresse* I never in my bones and dead man heart could ever show.

.     .     .

It's a bright cold morning in December 1925, just before Christmas, Gerard is setting out to school—Aunt Marie has him by the hand, she's visiting us for a week and she wants to take a morning constitutional, and take deep breaths and show Gerard how to do likewise, for his health—Aunt Marie is my father's favorite sister (and my favorite aunt), a talkative openhearted, teary bleary lovely with red lipstick always and gushy kisses and a black ribbon pendant from her specs—While my father has been abed with rheumatism she's helped somewhat with the housework—Crippled, on crutches, a modiste—Never married but many boyfriends helped her—The spittin image of Emil and the lover of Gerard's little soul as no one else, unless it be the cold eyed but warm hearted Aunt Anna from up in Maine—"Ti Gerard, for your health always do this, take big clacks of air in your lungs, hold it a long time, look" pounding her furpieced breast, "see?"—

"*Oui,* Matante Marie—"

"Do you love your Matante?"

"My Matante Marie I love her so big!" he cries affectionately as they hug and limp around the corner, to the school, where the kids are, in the yard, and the nuns, who now stare curiously at Gerard's distinguished aunt—Aunt Marie take her leave and drops in the church for a quick prayer—It's the Christmas season and everyone feels devout.

The kids bumble into their seats in the classroom.

"This morning," says the nun up front, "we're going to study the next chapter of the catechism—" and the kids turn the pages and stare at the illustrations done by old French engravers like Boucher and others always done with the same lamby gray strangeness, the curlicue of it, the reeds of Moses' bed-basket I remember the careful way they were drawn and divided and the astonished faces of women by the riverbank—It's Gerard's turn to read after Picou'll be done—He dozes in his seat from a bad night's rest during which his breathing was difficult, he doesnt know it but a new and serious attack on his heart is forming—Suddenly Gerard is asleep, head on arms, but because of the angle of the boy's back in front of him the nun doesnt see.

Gerard dreams that he is sitting in a yard, on some house steps with me, his little brother, in the dream he's thinking sorrowfully: "Since the beginning of time I've been charged to take care of this little brother, my Ti Jean, my poor Ti Jean who cries he's afraid—" and he is about to stroke me on the head, as I sit there drawing a stick around in the sand, when suddenly he gets up and goes to another part of the yard, nearby, trees and bushes and something strange and gray and suddenly the ground ends and there's just air and supported there at the earth's gray edge of immateriality, is a great White Virgin Mary with a flowing robe ballooning partly in the wind and partly tucked in at the edges and held aloft by swarms, countless swarms of grave bluebirds with white downy bellies and necks—On her breast, a crucifix of gold, in her hand a rosary of gold, on her head a star of gold—Beauteous beyond bounds and belief, like snow, she speaks to Gerard:

"Well my goodness Ti Gerard, we've been looking for you all morning—where were you?"

He turns to explain that he was with . . . that he was on . . . that he was . . . that . . . —He cant remember what it is that it was, he cant remember why he forgot where he was, or why the time, the morning-time, was shortened, or lengthened—The Virgin Mary reads it in his perplexed eyes. "Look," pointing to the red sun, "it's still early, I wont be mad at you, you were only gone less than a morning—Come on—"

"Where?"

"Well, dont you remember? We were going—come on—"

"How'm I gonna follow you?"

"Well your wagon is there" and Oh yes, he snaps his finger and looks to remember and there it is, the snow-white cart drawn by two lambs, and as he sits in it two white pigeons settle on each of his shoulders; as prearranged, he bliss-remembers all of it now, and they start, tho one perplexing frown shows in his thoughts where he's still trying to remember what he was and what he was doing before, or during, his absence, so brief—And as the little wagon of snow ascends to Heaven, Heaven itself becomes vague and in his arm with head bent Gerard is contemplating the perfect ecstasy when his arm is rudely jolted by Sister Marie and he wakes to find himself in a classroom with the sad window-opening pole leaning in the corner and the erasers on the ledges of the blackboards and the surly marks of woe smudged thereon and the Sister's eyes astonished down on his:

"Well what are you doing Gerard! you're sleeping!"

"Well I was in Heaven."

"What?"

"Yes Sister Marie, I've arrived in Heaven!"

He jumps up and looks at her straight to tell her the news.

"It's your turn to read the catechism!"

"Where?"

"There—the chapter—at the end—"

Automatically he reads the words to please her; while pausing, he looks around at the children; Lo! all the beings involved! And look at the strange sad desks, the wood of them, and the carved marks on them, initials, and the little boy Ouellette (suddenly re-remembered) as usual with the same tranquil unconcern (outwardly) whistling soundlessly into his eraser, and the sun streaming in the high windows showing motes of room-dust—The whole piti-ful world is still there! and nobody knows it! the different appearances of the same emptiness everywhere! the ethereal flower of the world!

"My sister, I saw the Virgin Mary."

The nun is stunned: "Where?"

"There—in a dream, when I slept."

She does the sign of the cross.

"Aw Gerard, you gave me a start!"

"She told me come on—and there was a pretty little white wagon with two little lambs to pull it and we started out and we were going to Heaven."

*"Mon Seigneur!"*

"A little white wagon!" echo several children with excitement.

"Yes—and two white pigeons on my shoulder—doves—and she asked me 'Where were you Gerard, we've been waiting for you all morning' "—

Sister Marie's mouth is open—"Did you see all this in a dream?—here now?—in the room."

"Yes my good sister—dont be afraid my good sister, we're all in Heaven—but we dont know it!"—"Oh," he laughs, *"we dont know it!"*

"For the love of God!"

"God fixed all this a long time ago."

The bell is ringing announcing the end of the hour, some of the children are already poised to scamper on a word, Sister Marie is so stunned everyone is motionless—Gerard sits again and suddenly over him falls the tight over-powering drowsiness around his heart, as before, and his legs ache and a fever breaks on his brow—He remains in his seat in a trance, hand to brow, looking up minutes later to an empty room save for Soeur Marie and the elder Soeur Caroline who has been summoned—They are staring at him with tenderest respect.

"Will you repeat what you told me to Sister Caroline?"

"Yes—but I dont feel good."

"What's the matter, Gerard?"

"I'm starting to be sick again I guess."

"We'll have to send him home—"

"They'll put him to bed like they did last year, like before—He hasnt got much strength, the little one."

"He saw Heaven."

"Ah"—shrugging, Sister Caroline—"that"—nodding her head—

Slowly, at 9:30 o'clock that morning, my mother who's in the yard with clothespins in her mouth sees him coming down the empty schooltime street, alone, with that lassitude and dragfoot that makes a chill in her heart—

*"Gerard is sick—"*

For the last time coming home from school.

When Christmas Eve comes a few days later he's in bed, in the side room downstairs—His legs swell up, his breathing is difficult and painful—The house is chilled. Aunt Louise sits at the kitchen table shaking her head—*La peine, la peine,* pain, pain, always pain for the Duluozes—I knew it when he was born—his father, his aunt, all his uncles, all invalids—all in pain—Suffering and pain—I tell you, Emil, we havent been blessed by Chance."

The old man sighs and plops the table with his open hand. "That goes without saying."

Tears bubbling from her eyes, Aunt Louise, shifting one hand quickly to catch a falling crutch, "Look, it's Christmas already, he's got his tree, his toys are all bought and he's lying there on his back like a corpse—it's not *fair* to hurt little children like that that arent old enough to know—Ah Emil, Emil, Emil, what's going to happen, what's going to happen to *all* of us!"

And her crying and sobbing gets me crying and sobbing and soon Uncle Mike comes in, with wife and the boys, partly for the holidays, partly to see little Gerard and offer him some toys, and he too, Mike, cries, a great huge tormented tearful man with bald head and blue eyes, asthmatic thunderous efforts in his throat as he draws each breath to expostulate long woes: "My poor Emil, my poor little brother Emil, you have so much trouble!" followed by crashing coughs and in the kitchen the other aunt is saying to my mother:

"I told you to take care of him, that child—he was never strong, you know—you've always got to send him warmly dressed" and et cetera as tho my mother had somehow been to blame so she cries too and in the sickroom Gerard, waking up and hearing them, realizes with compassion heavy in his heart that it is only an ethereal sorrow and too will fade when heaven reveals her white.

*"Mon Seigneur,"* he thinks, "bless them all"—

He pictures them all entering the belly of the lamb—Even as he stares at the wood of the windowframe and the plaster of the ceiling with its little cobwebs moving to the heat.

.     .     .

Hearken, amigos, to the olden message: it's neither what you think it is, nor what you think it isnt, but an elder matter, uncompounded and clear—Pigs may rut in field, come running to the Soo-Call, full of sowy glee; people may count themselves higher than pigs, and walk proudly down country roads; geniuses may look out of windows and count themselves higher than louts; tics in the pine needles may be inferior to the swan; but whether any of these and the stone know it, it's still the same truth: none of it is even there, it's a mind movie, *believe* this if you will and you'll be saved in the solvent solution of salvation and Gerard knew it well in his dying bed in his way, in his way—And who handed us down the knowledge here of the Diamond Light? Messengers unnumerable from the Ethereal Awakened Diamond Light. And why?—because is, is—and was, was—and will be, will be—t'will!

Christmas Eve of 1925 Ti Nin and I gayly rushed out with our sleds to a new snow layer in Beaulieu street, forgetting our brother in his sack, tho it was he sent us out with injunctions to play good and slide far—

"Look at the pretty snow outside, go play!" he cried like a kindly mother, and we bundled up and went out—

I still remember the quality of that sky, that very evening, tho I was only 3 years old—

Over the roofs, which held their white and would hold them all night now that the sun was casting himself cold and wan-pink over the final birches of griefstricken westward Dracut—Over the roofs was that blue, magic Lowell blue, that keen winter northern knifeblade blue of winter dusks so unforgettable and so cold and dry, like dry ice, flint, sparks, like powdery snow that ss'ses at under doorsills—Perfect for the silhouetting of birds heading darkward down their appointed lane, hushed—Perfect for the silhouetting presentations of church steeples and of rooftops and of the whole Lowell general, and always yon poor smoke putting from the human chimneys like prayer—The whole town aglow with the final russet adventures of the day staining windowpanes and sending pirates to the east and bringing other sabers of purple and of saffron scarlot harlot rage across the gashes and might ironworks of incomprehensible moveless cloud wars frowned and befronting one another on horizon Shrewsburies—Up there where instead of thickening, plots thinned and leaked and warrior groups pulled wan expiring acts on the monstrous rugs of sky areas with names in purple, and dull boom cannons, and maw-mouth awwp up-clouds far far away where the children say "There's an old man sleeping in the north with a big white mouth that's open and a round nose"—These mighty skies bending over Lowell and over Gerard as he lay knowing in his deathbed, rosaries in his hands, pans on papers by the bed, pillows under his feet—The sides and portion wedges of which sky he can barely see thru the window shade and frame, outside is December's big parley with night and it's Christmas Eve and his heart breaks to realize that it will be his last Christmas on our innocent mistaken earth—"Ah yes—if I could tell them what I knew—but now I *know* it—just like my dream—poor people with their houses and their chimnies and their Christmases and their children—listen to them yelling in the street, listen to their sleds—they run, they throw themselves on the snow, the little sled takes them a little ways and then that's all—that's all—And me, big nut, I cant explain them what they're dying to know—It's because God doesnt wanta—"

God made us for His glory, not our own.

Nin and I have our sleds and mufflers and we have wrangled dramas with the other kids over the little dispositions of activity among snowbanks and slide-lanes, it all goes on endlessly this world in its big and little facets with no change in it.

# The Power to Heal

### From: *Bless Me, Ultima*

B Y   R U D O L F O   A N A Y A

There is a time in the last few days of summer when the ripeness of autumn fills the air, and time is quiet and mellow. I lived that time fully, strangely aware of a new world opening up and taking shape for me. In the mornings, before it was too hot, Ultima and I walked in the hills of the llano, gathering the wild herbs and roots for her medicines. We roamed the entire countryside and up and down the river. I carried a small shovel with which to dig, and she carried a gunny sack in which to gather our magic harvest.

"¡Ay!" she would cry when she spotted a plant or root she needed, "what luck we are in today to find la yerba del manso!"

Then she would lead me to the plant her owl-eyes had found and ask me to observe where the plant grew and how its leaves looked. "Now touch it," she would say. The leaves were smooth and light green.

For Ultima, even the plants had a spirit, and before I dug she made me speak to the plant and tell it why we pulled it from its home in the earth. "You that grow well here in the arroyo by the dampness of the river, we lift you to make good medicine," Ultima intoned softly and I found myself repeating after her. Then I would carefully dig out the plant, taking care not to let the steel of the shovel touch the tender roots. Of all the plants we gathered none was endowed with so much magic as the yerba del manso. It could cure burns, sores, piles, colic in babies, bleeding dysentary and even rheumatism. I knew this plant from long ago because my mother, who was surely not a curandera, often used it.

Ultima's soft hands would carefully lift the plant and examine it. She would take a pinch and taste its quality. Then she took the same pinch and put it into a little black bag tied to a sash around her waist. She told me that the dry contents of the bag contained a pinch of every plant she had ever gathered since she began her training as a curandera many years ago.

"Long ago," she would smile, "long before you were a dream, long before the train came to Las Pasturas, before the Lunas came to their valley, before the great Coronado built his bridge—" Then her voice would trail off and my thoughts would be lost in the labyrinth of a time and history I did not know.

We wandered on and found some orégano, and we gathered plenty because this was not only a cure for coughs and fever but a spice my mother used for beans and meat. We were also lucky to find some oshá, because this plant grows better in the mountains. It is like la yerba del manso, a cure for everything. It cures coughs or colds, cuts and bruises, rheumatism and stomach troubles, and my father once said the old sheepherders used it to keep poisonous snakes away from their bedrolls by sprinkling them with oshá powder. It was with a mixture of oshá that Ultima washed my face and arms and feet the night Lupito was killed.

In the hills Ultima was happy. There was a nobility to her walk that lent a grace to the small figure. I watched her carefully and imitated her walk, and when I did I found that I was no longer lost in the enormous landscape of hills and sky. I was a very important part of the teeming life of the llano and the river.

"¡Mira! Qué suerte, tunas," Ultima cried with joy and pointed to the ripe-red prickly pears of the nopal. "Run and gather some and we will eat them in the shade by the river." I ran to the cactus and gathered a shovelful of the succulent, seedy pears. Then we sat in the shade of the álamos of the river and peeled the tunas very carefully because even on their skin they have fuzz spots that make your fingers and tongue itch. We sat and ate and felt refreshed.

The river was silent and brooding. The *presence* was watching over us. I wondered about Lupito's soul.

"It is almost time to go to my uncles' farms in El Puerto and gather the harvest," I said.

"Ay," Ultima nodded and looked to the south.

"Do you know my uncles, the Lunas?" I asked.

"Of course, child," she replied, "your grandfather and I are old friends. I know his sons. I lived in El Puerto, many years ago—"

"Ultima," I asked, "why are they so strange and quiet? And why are my father's people so loud and wild?"

She answered. "It is the blood of the Lunas to be quiet, for only a quiet man can learn the secrets of the earth that are necessary for planting—they are quiet like the moon—and it is the blood of the Márez to be wild, like the ocean from which they take their name, and the spaces of the llano that have become their home."

I waited, then said. "Now we have come to live near the river, and yet near the llano. I loved them both, and yet I am of neither. I wonder which life I will choose?"

"Ay, hijito," she chuckled, "do not trouble yourself with those thoughts. You have plenty of time to find yourself—"

"But I am growing," I said, "every day I grow older—"

"True," she replied softly. She understood that as I grew I would have to choose to be my mother's priest or my father's son.

We were silent for a long time, lost in memories that the murmur of the mourning wind carried across the treetops. Cotton from the trees drifted lazily in the heavy air. The silence spoke, not with harsh sounds, but softly to the rhythm of our blood.

"What is it?" I asked, for I was still afraid.

"It is the *presence* of the river," Ultima answered.

I held my breath and looked at the giant, gnarled cottonwood trees that surrounded us. Somewhere a bird cried, and up on the hill the tinkling sound of a cowbell rang. The *presence* was immense, lifeless, yet throbbing with its secret message.

"Can it speak?" I asked and drew closer to Ultima.

"If you listen carefully—" she whispered.

"Can you speak to it?" I asked as the whirling, haunting sound touched us.

"Ay, my child," Ultima smiled and touched my head, "you want to know so much—"

And the *presence* was gone.

"Come, it is time to start homeward." She rose and with the sack over her shoulder hobbled up the hill. I followed. I knew that if she did not answer my question that that part of life was not yet ready to reveal itself to me. But I was no longer afraid of the *presence* of the river.

We circled homeward. On the way back we found some manzanilla. Ultima told me that when my brother León was born that his mollera was sunken in, and that she had cured him with manzanilla.

She spoke to me of the common herbs and medicines we shared with the Indians of the Rio del Norte. She spoke of the ancient medicines of other tribes, the Aztecas, Mayas, and even of those in the old, old country, the Moors. But I did not listen, I was thinking of my brothers León, and Andrew, and Eugene.

When we arrived home we put the plants on the roof of the chicken shed to dry in the white sun. I placed small rocks on them so the wind wouldn't blow them away. There were some plants that Ultima could not obtain on the llano or the river, but many people came to seek cures from her and they brought in exchange other herbs and roots. Especially prized were those plants that were from the mountains.

When we had finished we went in to eat. The hot beans flavored with chicos and green chile were muy sabrosos. I was so hungry that I ate three whole tortillas. My mother was a good cook and we were happy as we ate. Ultima told her of the orégano we found and that pleased her.

"The time of the harvest is here," she said, "it is time to go to my brothers' farms. Juan has sent word that they are expecting us."

Every autumn we made a pilgrimage to El Puerto, where my grandfather and uncles lived. There we helped gather the harvest and brought my mother's share home with us.

"He says there is much corn, and ay, such sweet corn my brothers raise!" she went on. "And there is plenty of red chile for making ristras, and fruit, ay! The apples of the Lunas are known throughout the state!" My mother was very proud of her brothers, and when she started talking she went on and on. Ultima nodded courteously, but I slipped out of the kitchen.

The day was warm at noonday, not lazy and droning like July but mellow with late August. I went to Jasón's house and we played together all afternoon. We talked about Lupito's death, but I did not tell Jasón what I had seen. Then I went to the river and cut the tall, green alfalfa that grew wild and carried the bundle home so that I would have a few days of food laid in for the rabbits.

Late in the afternoon my father came whistling up the goat path, striding home from the flaming-orange sun, and we ran to meet him. "Cabritos!" he called. "Cabroncitos!" And he swung Theresa and Deborah on his shoulders while I walked beside him carrying his lunch pail.

After supper we always prayed the rosary. The dishes were quickly done, then we gathered in the sala where my mother kept her altar. My mother had a beautiful statue of La Virgen de Guadalupe. It was nearly two feet high. She was dressed in a long, flowing blue gown, and she stood on the horned moon. About her feet were the winged heads of angels, the babes of Limbo. She wore a crown on her head because she was the queen of heaven. There was no one I loved more than the Virgin.

We all knew the story of how the Virgin had presented herself to the little Indian boy in Mexico and about the miracles she had wrought. My mother said the Virgin was the saint of our land, and although there were many other good saints, I loved none as dearly as the Virgin. It was hard to say the rosary because you had to kneel for as long as the prayers lasted, but I did not mind because while my mother prayed I fastened my eyes on the statue of the Virgin until I thought that I was looking at a real person, the mother of God, the last relief of all sinners.

God was not always forgiving. He made laws to follow and if you broke them you were punished. The Virgin always forgave.

God had power. He spoke and the thunder echoed through the skies.

The Virgin was full of a quiet, peaceful love.

My mother lit the candles for the brown madonna and we knelt. "I believe in God the Father Almighty—" she began.

He created you. He could strike you dead. God moved the hands that killed Lupito.

"Hail Mary, full of grace—"

But He was a giant man, and she was a woman. She could go to Him and ask Him to forgive you. Her voice was sweet and gentle and with the help of her Son they could persuade the powerful Father to change His mind.

On one of the Virgin's feet there was a place where the plaster had chipped and exposed the pure-white plaster. Her soul was without blemish. She had been born without sin. The rest of us were born steeped in sin, the sin of our fathers that Baptism and Confirmation began to wash away. But it was not until communion—it was not until we finally took God into our mouth and swallowed Him—that we were free of that sin and free of the punishment of hell.

My mother and Ultima sang some prayers, part of a novena we had promised for the safe delivery of my brothers. It was sad to hear their plaintive voices in that candle-lit room. And when the praying was finally done my mother arose and kissed the Virgin's feet, then blew out the candles. We walked out of la sala rubbing our stiff knees. The candle-wick smoke lingered like incense in the dark room.

I trudged up the steps to my room. The song of Ultima's owl quickly brought sleep, and my dreams.

*Virgen de Guadalupe, I heard my mother cry, return my sons to me.*

*Your sons will return safely, a gentle voice answered.*

*Mother of God, make my fourth son a priest.*

*And I saw the Virgin draped in the gown of night standing on the bright, horned moon of autumn, and she was in mourning for the fourth son.*

"*Mother of God!*" *I screamed in the dark,* then I felt Ultima's hand on my forehead and I could sleep again.

# PART IV

# INTERIOR LIVES

## Catholic Memories

# Introduction

The Catholic childhood has fallen victim to the desecration of cliché even though it has often been done in both an affectionate and well-intentioned manner. The works of John R. Powers, humor books such as *Growing Up Catholic, Once a Catholic,* etc., and films like *Heaven Help Us,* though perhaps factually as accurate as *Washington Post* reporting, nonetheless stigmatize the Catholic childhood with an aura and mystique of Naïveté balanced with absurdity. Such childish concerns as whether the accidental chewing of the Eucharist wafer will result in the breaking of all your teeth, the moral and spiritual virtues of rote memorization of catechism, and the evils unto damnation of adolescent sexuality (and the timeless question of whether patent leather shoes really *do* reflect up and whether or not any real person ever invoked this use) all tend to invoke a giggle and a nostalgic look back at an alleged simpler time (which didn't seem so simple back then) while also giving short shrift to the assets and benefits that this socialization was actually incurring.

Even for the Catholics involved, it was easier to laugh when looking back than to try to be objective and discerning . . . and Catholic school and confraternity training was only one part of the growing-up-Catholic process, though its long-term effects have been surprisingly beneficial and not just in terms of matters of the faith. (Case in point—literacy has become a major problem in U.S. society; prior to the decline of the availability of Catholic schools, the faithful student body in these institutions would be treated to twice the amount of reading instruction—one class with a "reader" as a text, one class with a "catechism" as a text. The demands of rote memorization of all matters of the faith, though not necessarily training the soul, did indeed train the mind for similar necessary academic endeavors such as remembering the network of cranial nerves for doctors or precedents of law for attorneys.)

We look back and laugh, remembering the good parts and the funny parts without really understanding the socialization that was taking place. Today we may make reference to having lost our faith, having fallen away from the ritual and rote that had been so much a part of our growing up.

Part of this loss is due to the melting pot cycle that is so much a part of

American life. First- and second-generation immigrants hold on to the familiar, in this case "the faith," when confronted by the confusing miasma of the
great society that they wish to become a part of. Ultimately one holds on to the
strengths of one's faith while at the same time weakening it through one's own
desire for assimilation, or, as Dunce points out in a slightly different context,
"the first generation makes it, the second generation enjoys it, and the third
generation loses it." The pious Catholic student who never missed mass on
Sunday (usually the nine o'clock and usually in Latin) observed First Fridays
(plus every Friday during Lent), collected for the missions, and memorized ten
questions a week from the Baltimore Catechism has eventually been assimi-
lated into what is sadly referred to as a Christmas and Easter Catholic, or simply someone whom our old Irish grandmother would have referred to as a
damnable Protestant.

Yet even within this era of laxness, one remains Catholic.

Part of this is because of the impression that being different has made on
us from our earliest years. The childhood neighborhood question of what one
is—a Jew, a Protestant, a Catholic. If one didn't have an answer, one was a
nothing, not an enviable designation. Catholic becomes the identity, partly
based on our training, and partly based on the course of elimination as to what
we weren't, no different than such popular prejudices as black and white, and
haves and have-nots.

Some choose to remember only the good parts.

Others only recall the bad parts.

How could we be so silly?

How could we endure such pain and debasement?

Some choose to return to the memories and apply the same sort of dis-
cernment that was applied to the catechetical studies by Vatican II, seeking at
least justification if not in the long run a satisfying understanding.

Others choose to revolt, to reject, or try to exclude their experiences and
teachings as no longer relevant, and then quickly change the subject because
even an exclusionary and defiant decision does not provide comfort or assurity.

In the end, these Catholic memories have provided us with a crucible that
has helped to shape our character. For some it incurs doubt (which if handled
correctly only makes one stronger), for others comfort, and for some just stability. No matter what one remembers, one is left with an unconscious sense of
one's faith, as distinctive as one's ethnic, genetic, or racial makeup.

The faith has been instilled and cultivated within us, even if we can't notice
it as part of our own daily makeup . . . and is still there even if we deny it.

It still waits within, ready to be tapped in our times of darkest needs, even
if it's just the glimpse of a memory of the past which succors us with a chuckle
or perhaps the celestial light that might lead us toward salvation.

# How I Grew

## From: *How I Grew*

### B Y   M A R Y   M c C A R T H Y

I was born as a mind during 1925, my bodily birth having taken place in 1912. Throughout the thirteen years in between, obviously, I must have had thoughts and mental impressions, perhaps even some sort of specifically cerebral life that I no longer remember. Almost from the beginning, I had been aware of myself as "bright." And from a very early time reasoning was natural to me, as it is to a great many children, doubtless to animals as well. What is Pavlov's conditioned reflex but an inference drawn by a dog? The activities of incessant induction and deduction are characteristically childlike ("Why don't we say 'Deliver us to evil,'" I am supposed to have asked, "the way Mama does in Frederick and Nelson's when she tells them to deliver it to Mrs. McCarthy?") and slack off rather than intensify as we grow older. My "cute" question, quoted by my mother in a letter to her mother-in-law (apparently the last she wrote), may have been prompted by our evening prayers: did we already say the "Our Father" and the "Hail Mary" besides "Now I lay me"? At six, I was too young to have had a rosary.

Someone, of course, was "hearing" our prayers; my father, probably, for I speak of "Mama" in the third person. It is Daddy I must be questioning; Gertrude, our nurse, was too ignorant. And now, writing it down more than sixty-five years later, all of a sudden I doubt the innocence of that question. There was premeditation behind it, surely; play-acting. I knew perfectly well that children could not pray to be delivered to evil and was only being clever—my vice already—supplying my parents with "Mary's funny sayings" to meet a sensed demand.

It is possible (to be fair) that the question "Why don't we . . . ?" had honestly occurred to me in Frederick's listening to Mama order and being surprised to have "deliver," an old bedtime acquaintance, pop up in the middle of a department store. Or, conversely, as we intoned the Lord's Prayer, my mind may have raced back to Mama at Frederick's. Which had priority, which bulked larger in my teeming experience, which name had I heard more often, God's or Frederick and Nelson's? But if, in one way or another, the question had honestly occurred to me, the answer could not have been slow to follow, without recourse to a grown-up. No, that inquiry was *saved up* for an audience, *rehearsed.* For my father's ear, I was not so much reasoning as artfully mimicking the reasoning process of a child. In any case, as far as I know, this is the last of my cute sayings on record. After the flu, there was no one there to record them any more. Nobody was writing to her mother-in-law of the words and deeds of the four of us. With the abrupt disappearance of the demand, the supply no doubt dried up. Soon our evening prayers—we knelt in a row now, wearing scratchy pajamas with feet in them—underwent expansion. To "God bless Mama and Daddy" something new was added: "Eternal rest grant unto them, o Lord, and let the perpetual light shine upon them. . . ."

From an early time, too, I had been a great reader. My father had taught me, on his lap, before I started school—*A Child's Garden of Verses* and his favorite, Eugene Field, the newspaperman poet. But in the new life instituted for us after our parents' death almost no books were permitted—to save electricity, or because books could give us "ideas" that would make us too big for our boots. A few volumes had come with us, I think, from Seattle to Minneapolis; those would have been *Black Beauty,* the "autobiography" of a horse, by Anna Sewell, *Hans Brinker or The Silver Skates, Heidi,* and Dante and *Don Quixote* illustrated by Doré, but these two were for looking at the pictures on the living-room floor while a grown up watched, not for reading. Someone, not our parents, was responsible for *Fabiola, the Church of the Catacombs,* by Cardinal Wiseman, and I remember a little storybook, which soon disappeared, about some Belgian children on a tow-path along a canal escaping from Germans—was it taken away out of deference to the feelings of our great-aunt's husband, the horrible Uncle Myers, who was of German "extraction"? At any rate these are all the books I recall from the Minneapolis household, not counting Uncle Myers' own copy of *Uncle Remus,* Peter Rabbit (outgrown), and a set of the Campfire Girls (borrowed).

Yet the aunts must have had a *Lives of the Saints,* full of graphic accounts of every manner of martyrdom, and where did I come upon a dark-greenish volume called *The Nuremberg Stove,* about a porcelain stove and illustrated with German-looking woodcuts? And another story with a lot about P. P. Rubens and a "Descent from the Cross" in Antwerp Cathedral? Not in school, certainly; the parochial school did not give us books, only readers that had stories in them. I can still almost see the fifth- or sixth-grade reader that had Ruskin's "The King of the Yellow River," with pages repeating themselves and the end missing—a fairly common binder's error, but for a child afflicted with book hunger, it was a deprivation of fiendish cruelty, worse than the arithmetic manual that had the wrong answers in the back. Those school readers also gave you "tastes" of famous novels, very tantalizing, too, like the chapter about Maggie and Tom Tulliver from the start of *The Mill on the Floss,* which kept me in suspense for more than twenty years, Becky and Amelia Sedley leaving Miss Pinkerton's, a sample of *Jane Eyre.*

Oh! Among the books at home I was nearly forgetting *The Water-Babies,* by Charles Kingsley (illustrated, with a gilt-and-green cover), which must have come from my father's library—I can feel a consistent manly taste, like an *ex libris,* marking little Tom, the sooty chimney-sweep who runs away from his cruel master and falls into a river, Don Quixote and his nag, Dante and Virgil, and Wynken, Blynken, and Nod, who "sailed off in a wooden shoe" one night, "Sailed on a river of crystal light, / Into a sea of dew." *(Black Beauty,* on the other hand, which was a bit on the goody side, had surely been our mother's.)

When he died, my father (another Tantalus effect) had been reading me a long fairy tale that we never finished. It was about seven brothers who were changed into ravens and their little sister, left behind when they flew away, who was given the task of knitting seven little shirts if she wanted them to change back into human shape again. At the place we stopped reading, she had failed to finish one little sleeve. I would have given my immortal soul to know what happened then, but in all the books of fairy tales that have come my way since, I have not been able to find that story—only its first and second cousins, like "The Seven Ravens" and "The Six Swans." And what became of the book itself, big with a wine-colored cover? Was it left behind on the train to Minneapolis when we all got sick with the flu? Or did our keepers promptly put it away as unsuitable, like my little gold beauty-pins? In Minneapolis we were not allowed fairy stories any more interesting than "The Three Bears."

But stop! That cannot be true. Certainly I read "The Little Match Girl" and "The Snow Queen," with the little robber girl I loved so and the piece of ice in little Kay's eye that even then I understood to be a symbol, in other words over my head. There was a good deal of that in Hans Andersen—the feeling of morals lurking like fish eyes peering out from between stones in the depths of clear water. Except in "The Snow Queen," where the furs and the sleigh and the reindeer and Gerda and the robber girl made up for everything, I disliked those lurking morals; I hated "The Little Match Girl." And I was not fond of "The Ugly Duckling" either; I sensed a pious cheat there—not all children who were "different" grew up into swans. Was that why I was allowed to have Andersen, like a refined sort of punishment, in my room? And they let me have another book, printed in big type on thick deckle-edged paper and possibly not by Andersen, that contained a frightening tale about a figure

named Ole Luk Oie who threw sand in people's eyes just as they were going to
sleep. Not the same as the sandman; more of a bogey. Burying my head under
the covers, for nights running I used to scare myself in my pillow-less (better
for the posture) bed with this runic fiction, repeating the words "Ole Luk Oie"
like a horrible spell. And in the morning, sure enough, my finger found grainy
particles stuck to my eyelashes showing that he had been there. But maybe, if
you knew Danish, the story was more boring than spooky, and the dread sand
in the eyes was just a symbol of something in society.

Almost no books, but how then, while still in Minneapolis, did I learn
about Loki and Balder the Beautiful and Frey and his golden sister Freya, goddess of love and beauty? That was not the kind of thing the Sisters of St.
Joseph taught, and there were no comic books then to retell myths in strip language with balloons coming out of the mouths of helmeted gods and
heroes—just the funny papers, which showed funny people like Olive Oyl and
Miss Emmy Schmaltz. Probably the answer lies in *The Book of Knowledge,* a
junior encyclopedia that someone finally gave us—proof that prayers were
answered—and that our guardians for some reason let us keep and even use.
They must have thought that it was a collection of known facts and figures and
therefore no more harmful than the diagrams it carried of chemical retorts and
the Bunsen burner. But to me, in that household, that red-bound set was like
a whole barrel of bootleg liquor, cut but still the real stuff. Of course there
were facts in it (there had to be), but you could ignore those; the main point
was that it told you the plots of the world's famous books from the *Iliad*
through *The Count of Monte Cristo.* If the Trojan Horse and the Cyclops were
there (and Roland and Oliver), they would have had to have Thor and his iron
gloves, blind Hoder and his arrow—at least the "basics."

Yet the suggestion leaves me unsatisfied. It does not account for the *intimacy* I formed with those scenes and figures of Norse mythology: how Thor
lost his hammer, Odin's raven, the bad dreams of Balder, Sif's hair—you
would think that I had had an entire "Edda for Children" hidden in the swing
in our backyard.

Nor can I altogether account for the hold this material, however acquired,
had on my imagination, for my so much preferring those gods and goddesses
to the "sunny" Greek ones. Perhaps I liked the strong light-and-dark contrasts
of the Northern tales. I was a firm believer in absolutes: the lack of shadings,
of any in-between, made Asgard a more natural residence than Mount
Olympus for my mythic propensity, just as clear, concise Latin was always
more natural to me than Greek with all its "small, untranslatable words" (as
Mrs. Ryberg at Vassar called them).

But there was more to it than that. For a juvenile half enamored of the
dark principle, fond of frightening herself and her brothers with the stories

she made up (or just a decided brunette with pale skin that she tried to see as "olive"), there was a disappointing lack of evil in Greek mythology. Obviously they did not tell children about the banquet of Thyestes, and all we knew of Jason was the *Argo* and the Golden Fleece, yet the crimes and horrors that were kept from us "till we were old enough" (like the watches my brothers received from our Seattle grandfather) were the work of mortals and titans, not Olympians. Even in his worst moments, no Greek god could approach the twisted cunning of a Loki. I hated his very name, and yet in a way he "made" the story of the Aesir for me.

In fact, the notion of a thoroughly evil creature sharing in the godhead was thoroughly un-Greek, and I suspect that it did not sit well with me either at the age of nine or ten despite the spell of intrigue and danger he cast on those tales. I could not quite fathom why Loki should go virtually unpunished even for the awful act of plotting the slaying of Balder; did it have something to do with his mixed ancestry, half-god and half-giant? You would think the *least* he deserved was permanent expulsion from Asgard, and yet he crept back, assuming new forms. The weakness of the Aesir (even Thor) in dealing with him was mystifying; they seemed to treat him and his relatives as fixtures of the establishment—his deathly daughter Hel ruled over the nether world. Being already a "confirmed" Catholic, I associated gods with goodness and could not take a standpoint that identified them simply with power—as sheer power of evil, Loki merited worship certainly. If I was unable to see that, it was doubtless because my model for badness was Satan. Proud Lucifer (Loki was a real cringer and fawner) was cast out of heaven once and for all, and such power as he retained, below, among men, was helpless before the saving action of God's grace.

Yet now that I consider it, I can see that the appeal of Freya, Balder, Loki, and Company was, precisely, to my Catholic nature. The Prince of Darkness, despite his large handicap, *was* a power for us, a kind of god even if we avoided the Manichean heresy of picturing him as dividing the world in equal shares with God the Father. The only surprise is that the Norse cosmogony should have felt so congenial to me given the prejudice against real Norsemen—the "Scandihoovians" of Minnesota—that Irish Catholics learned at their mother's knee. Evidently I made no connection between the great battle of Ragnarok that was to end the world and the local Olsens and Hansens. In the same way, my grandmother, old Lizzie McCarthy, who was "not over-fond" of Jews, never appeared to notice that Jesus was one, at least on His mother's side.

The sense of being at home among the Aesir, "speaking their language," was all the more natural to a Catholic child in that the Northern myths (though I did not guess it then) show clear traces of Christian impaste overlaying very primitive material. Balder, in particular, their pure-as-snow sun god, is a lot closer to Jesus on Mount Tabor than to Phoebus Apollo in his sky-chariot. The gods and Nature weep tears for him, treacherously slain by an arrow of mistletoe, as he descends like Christ crucified to the lower world, but there is a promise of a Second Coming, when all will live in harmony.

So it "fits," I suppose, that when I left the house in Minneapolis and, before very long, the faith, the gods of Asgard lost their hold on me. I have scarcely thought of them since. Looking them up now, to reaffirm my memory, I am amazed to learn that Balder has a wife (Nanna); I had imagined him as a bachelor like Our Lord or Sir Percival. Otherwise that Northern pantheon has remained surprisingly fresh in my mind, as though deep-frozen in a snow-slide, untouched by any process of wear or tear. I do not think they figure in my writings even metaphorically, unlike King Arthur and his knights, who turn up in the story of Peter Levi *(Birds of America)*. My passion for them was a crush, which I got over so completely that the cure has left me with a perfect immunity to Wagner. Though *The Ring* has been "in" twice during my life, I have never had any interest in it.

.        .        .

But I am digressing in the middle of a digression, piling Ossa on Pelion, we Latinists would say. I was talking about books or, rather, about the scarcity of them that I had to endure between my seventh and my twelfth year. Yet losing the thread (or seeming to) has given me time to wonder about the truth of what I was saying. On reflection I see that I have been exaggerating. I cannot have waited more than a decade to read "Thumbelina" and "Puss in Boots," or "Snow White" or "Rapunzel" or "Rumpelstiltskin." If they were already old friends when I read them aloud to Reuel, it means that in Minneapolis we must have had the usual Grimm and Perrault fairy tales and that secretly or openly I read them.

Aladdin and his lamp, too—I have a distinct memory of a genie, somewhat pear-shaped, emerging from a cloud of smoke—Ali Baba, and Sinbad the Sailor, in one of whose adventures I first learned of the roc and pictured to myself fearfully its huge white fabulous eggs. Then there are books I feel I have read that I cannot remember in the Minneapolis house or "place" in the years just following: *Tanglewood Tales* and a *Pilgrim's Progress* illustrated with dark, Doré-like lithographs. But a Catholic home would not have had Bunyan; still less would the Sisters of St. Joseph have given it to us in school—almost better Foxe's *Book of Martyrs*. And yet I feel sure that I was a child—not a girl—when I saw the words "Apollyon" and "Slough of Despond" and essayed to pronounce them to myself. The volume with its gloomy illustrations "belongs" in the Minneapolis framework, more specifically in the glass-fronted bookcase in the parlor, and I can only suppose that, like the Dante and *Don Quixote,* it had belonged to our father, more catholic in his tastes than the rest of his family, and that our guardians were too ignorant to confiscate it.

It was not till I left Minneapolis, I think, that a book disappointed me. I could not finish Washington Irving's *The Alhambra.* That was in the convent, in Seattle. I doubt that such a thing could have happened in the Minneapolis time, for then I could read just about anything—I had an iron stomach for printed matter, like a goat's. To this day, I have a good digestion in this respect, which I must owe, like my generally good digestion and appetite, to the Blaisdell Avenue regime. The ability to read almost anything was the corollary, obviously, of deprivation, for, exaggerate or not, it is still true that we had very few books.

It is true, too, that at that time children by and large had a far greater power of absorption of the printed word than children do today, and there also scarcity was a factor—children's books were a comparative rarity, so that children "made do" with books written for adults. The change came between my generation and the next: a book like *The Water-Babies,* which I "ate up" as a child, no doubt like my father before me, was utterly resistant to being gulped down or even tasted by my son. And he rebelled against Cooper's *The Prairie,* even though it was being read aloud to him—a kind of spoon-feeding. You could blame that on the Hardy Boys, were it not for Henty and H. Rider Haggard, whom he read straight through and begged for more of.

On the whole, children's taste in books seems to change more slowly than adults'. *Heidi* and *Robin Hood* are still classics, and I have read the Howard Pyle King Arthur books not only to Reuel but to my husband's children, more than fifteen years his junior. But other old books have become inaccessible to young readers, as though placed out of their reach by the modern child's shrunken vocabulary. Stylistic mannerisms are another barrier. They can cause books to date alarmingly, like affected fashions in dress, and this applies equally to old and young. We cannot return to the favorites of our youth. It is as much as I can do to read Meredith now, though I devoured him as a girl, to the point where until recently I supposed that my sentences must sound like him. But when a couple of summers ago I reread *Richard Feverel,* I could not see the shadow of a resemblance; the problem was to get through it at all.

Charles Kingsley, a "muscular Christian," was a contemporary of Meredith's. There is an old copy of *The Water-Babies* (first published in 1863, four years after *Richard Feverel)* in the room where I am writing, inscribed "Harry from Uncle Louis, Christmas 1904." The two names are in my family, "Harry" on both sides of it, but the book is no relation; it came with the house in Maine when we bought it. Nevertheless the bookshelves that face me as I write are confronting me, eerily, with the classics of my childhood: *The Water-*

*Babies,* Andrew Lang's edition of *The Arabian Nights* (same illustrations), *Black Beauty, Heidi, Rebecca of Sunnybrook Farm,* even Manly's *English Poetry,* where I found "Sister Helen" a few years later on a Tacoma boarding-school shelf. It is as if these ghostly volumes that had formed my persona had been haunting the house on the Maine seacoast that my husband was to buy in 1967.

But to return to the point at hand: *The Water-Babies,* which was written as a children's story on a theme of child labor, is extremely arch and fanciful, as much so as anything Meredith ever penned. On opening it yesterday, I felt sympathy with the reluctant Reuel of forty years ago; the only plain sentence in the whole narrative is the first one: "Once upon a time there was a little chimney-sweep and his name was Tom." In the same way a new look at the first chapter of *Vanity Fair,* borrowed from the Bangor Public Library, makes me wonder how this could have figured in the sixth-grade reader of St. Stephen's parochial school. Even if ruthlessly cut and preceded by a vocabulary, the need of which is emphasized by the markings in red ink of a previous borrower underlining the difficult words: "equipage," "bandy," "Semiramis," "incident to," "orthography," "sensibility." . . .

Well! Necessity is the mother of invention: the shortage of books in the Minneapolis house was compensated for by other kinds of reading-matter. We had the funny papers every afternoon and a whole section of them in color on Sunday. There was also the Sunday magazine section, which we were allowed to look at (I can't guess why), spread out on the den rug after church. I remember best the high-society scandals, constituent elements (come to think of it) of Henry James's "international theme"—Anna Gould, Count Boni de Castellane, the much-married Peggy Hopkins Joyce, the Marquise de la Falaise de la Coudray—King Tut, the Kohinoor diamond, the curse of the Carnarvons, and some medical curiosities. Then there were religious periodicals: Grandma McCarthy's blue-and-white *Ave Maria,* which I read in her upstairs sunroom, and old Aunt Mary's more low-brow *Extension,* sepia-toned, which I would "borrow" and keep hidden under my mattress; both of these carried short stories. In *Our Sunday Visitor,* sold after church every Sunday, you could read about the scary burning of crosses by the Ku Klux Klan on Catholic lawns, and there was a gripping Question-and-Answer column that advised you, if you were a doctor, which to save, the mother or the child, in a perilous childbirth—readers seemed to write in the same questions week after week, maybe in the hope of getting a different answer. In church after Sunday Mass there were also free distributions of tracts on foreign missions—that was probably where I learned of Father Damien and the lepers on Molokai—Catholics had a great appetite for reading about gruesome diseases, especially those involving the rotting or falling off of parts of the body. But in general the various tracts, flyers, illustrated brochures on missionary work extended our horizons almost like *The National Geographic* of Protestant homes.

That was all there was to the "media" then; the very word was unknown. There was no equivalent of *The Reader's Digest;* rotogravure sections of the Sunday papers were yet to come; radio was in the crystal-set stage—in our house Uncle Myers' envied toy. We were allowed to watch him listen with the earphones on his head. There was a unique occasion, however, when we were brought to my grandmother's house to listen to a radio "event" on a big set for which you did not need earphones; that was the Dempsey-Firpo fight (September 14, 1923). Unfortunately the knock-out took place early in the second round, almost before the fight had started, and there was nothing to do but tag home to bed, sadly (at least in my case) because Luis Angel Firpo had lost.

My passion for the Bull of the Pampas was a great laugh to the family. They did not understand that I had fallen in love with his name. Names were often the reason for my preferences—what else did I have to go by? And they are not such bad indicators: a man does not choose his name, but he can change it—witness Voltaire and Muhammad Ali. That a little girl should have a passionate crush on a prize fighter may seem odd, but here again the economics of scarcity were at work. It would have been more normal to be "crazy about" a star of the silver screen, but I had never seen one, unless maybe an episode of Pearl White in the days of Mama and Daddy. During the five years in Minneapolis, the only full-length movie I saw was *The Seal of the Confessional,* shown in the church basement. It was about a handsome priest who heard a murderer's confession and so had to keep silent, rather tiresomely, while an innocent man was going to the chair, but there was an exciting sub-plot about an atheist who was struck down by lightning when he defied God to demonstrate His existence. On Saturday mornings our neighborhood movie house let children in free to see the trailer for the coming Western, but those "tastes," while whetting the appetite, were of course not a substitute for the real William S. Hart. By the time I left Minneapolis and could go to the movies, the great days of silent film had passed.

Stage stars we never laid eyes on, nor vaudevillians. The only music we got to hear was a few records, e.g., "Over There," "Listen to the Mocking-bird," occasional band concerts in parks, the church organ, and military brasses in parades; our grandmother's "music room" contained a player piano, with rolls you inserted, but we were forbidden to work it. We knew John McCormack and Harry Lauder from their photos, Caruso, probably, too, and our great-aunts cherished a faded tintype of a figure called Chauncey Olcott, who, Webster's tells me, was "Chancellor John Olcott, 1860–1932, American actor and tenor," surely of Irish descent. In my grandmother's "music room," I eyed a big photograph of Mme. Schumann-Heink and was shocked by the monstrous bellows of her bosom.

No public figures entered our ken, except for Marshal Foch, whom we saw in person—a trim little white-haired figure—being welcomed by the city in front of the Art Institute, across from Fairoaks Park. During the Harding-Cox campaign (1920), I pedaled our little wooden wagon up and down our driveway shouting "Hurrah for Cox!" but the only basis for my support was that he was a Democrat and I thought my father had been one. I was impressed by President Harding's death because Seattle had a part in it. Returning from Alaska, he fell sick (surely from the seafood?) in Seattle and died in San Francisco. It was exciting to see our birthplace "make" the headlines. From the McCarthy aunts, uncles, and cousins we had already heard more than once about the IWW mayor, Ole Hansen, Seattle had elected. The initials, they said, stood for "I Won't Work," but I was less interested by that than by his horrible first name, which I probably identified with Ole Luk Oie, the bogey in the storybook. My happy memories of boulevards and grassy terraces and continual picnics in the backyard got muddied by the McCarthy family's Republican politics and dislike of their in-laws till I came to think of Seattle as a disreputable place that had a dangerous district called Coon Hollow (I remembered that from my father) and an "I Won't Work" Ole for a mayor.

Needless to say, on the visual side we were kept well below the poverty line, just as in politics, reading, entertainment. The house they had put us in was ugly, with an ugly yard and a few ugly bushes like Bridal Wreath. For a while we were allowed to use a stereopticon, with views of the pyramids, and in my room there was a "Baby Stuart" in a blue-and-white boy's dress. In a group of schoolchildren, we could sometimes go to the museum, where, running away from home, I once hid behind the cast of the Laocoon. But our clothes, faded, continually pieced, let out, and let down, the repellent food we ate, my worn, dull black, second-hand rosary were cruelly punishing to a sense of beauty. Yet in this sphere our guardians were less effectual. They could keep books out of our hands, limit the repertory of the phonograph, restrict our intercourse with the neighbors' children by penning us within a wire-net fence, but they could not stop us from using our eyes. The passionate pleasure I got from soap bubbles, rainbows—anything iridescent, including smears of oil on street puddles—from the funny "faces" of pansies, spurs of nasturtiums (which also concealed a nectar), freckles of foxglove, from holy pictures, spider webs, motes of dust riding on a sun ray, "Jack Frost flowers," dew, the white vestments at Easter, Easter lilies around the altar, all that joy was beyond our guardians' power of prevention. No more could they put a halt to it than they could keep us, fenced in our yard, from reading the sky-writing that spelled out "Lucky Strike" on the summer sky while we watched the words form.

Nature finds substitutes in the cultural realm, and how can I regret *Orphans in the Storm, Little Lord Fauntleroy,* Buster Keaton, early Harold Lloyd, the Little Pepper books, the "Patty" books, Jeritza, Mary Garden, when I had Balder and Freya, Thor and Sif, *The Book of Knowledge,* snowflakes, prismatic refractions, the seeds I planted one year on Good Friday that turned into frilly sweet peas?

The wryness I feel on looking back at Uncle Myers and the Sheridan sisters, on that jaundice-colored house with its attendant Golden Glow, Bridal Wreath, and gross rhubarb plant in the backyard, is almost wholly material. I don't mind about the cultural sustenance that was withheld from us—rather, the contrary. They seem to have hit on a formula for child-rearing that virtually forced us to use our imaginations. What I mind is the horrible food we were made to eat, the carrots I dumped out the window, the gristle and fat, the chicken necks I sucked to draw out the little white cord, the prunes, farina, and Wheatena. Here there was no compensation, no sensibilizing of the palate to shadings of taste; the envy with which we watched Uncle Myers put bananas on his corn flakes led only to my devouring thirteen in one fevered session in my grandmother's pantry in Seattle—a *sickening* experience and my last encounter with the fruit.

The beatings with hairbrush and razor-strop I can still resent, but abstractly, as injustice. My body does not remember them as it remembers the carrots and parsnips, still refusing more than sixty-five years later the sweetish taste of the first unless camouflaged with mint, butter, caramelized sugar, and so on, and refusing the second absolutely. As to compensation for the physical abuse I received (and I count being made to stay outdoors in the snow for two hours at a stretch in sub-zero temperatures going down to twenty), I am not sure whether Nature has seen to that or not. Certainly those people, at least in this world, never had to pay for their crimes. Yet I do not think that I have tried to avenge myself on them in what I have written—they were dead long before I could use a typewriter. As far as I can tell, I dd not *feel* vindictive toward them, have not for years, maybe not since I was seated on a train for Seattle with my other grandfather; my escape was my revenge. And if I triumph over them now, still again, recalling details of their regimen, it is because the tale of it makes me smile. Perhaps that is Nature's repair-work: over the years I have found a means—laughter—of turning pain into pleasure. Uncle Myers and Aunt Margaret, my grandmother, too, in her own style, amuse me by their capacity for being awful. It is a sort of talent, really, that people do not have nowadays or not in the same way. And, to the extent that my memory has been able to do justice to that talent in them, they have been immortalized, which is to say that Uncle Myers and his pedometer have been condemned to eternal derision.

Not his razor-strop, mind you. That is not funny. Yet if he had only that to speak for him, I do not think he would "live" as a character. The pedometer humanizes, which is the first step toward immortality. Nevertheless there are moralists who think I ought not to laugh or get an audience to laugh with me during a public reading at the figure of Uncle Myers, my old persecutor. What they overlook is the fact that as the injured party I have earned the right to laugh. My laughter is a victory over circumstances, and insofar as it betokens a disinterested enjoyment I imagine it to be a kind of pardon. I had the choice of forgiving those incredible relatives of mine or pitying myself on their account. Laughter is the great antidote for self-pity, maybe a specific for the malady. Yet probably it does tend to dry one's feelings out a little, as if by exposing them to a vigorous wind. So that something must be subtracted from the compensation I seem to have received for injuries sustained. There is no dampness in my emotions, and some moisture, I think, is needed to produce the deeper, the tragic, notes.

# On the Special Blessings, and Problems, of Catholics

From: *Nearer, My God: An Autobiography of Faith*

BY WILLIAM F. BUCKLEY JR.

I turned to strengths that sustain, and problems that beset, the little circle of converts I brought together to give me their thoughts.

I grew up, as reported, in a large family of Catholics without even a decent ration of tentativeness among the lot of us about our religious faith. Protestants were a majority everywhere we lived and studied, except for the few months I spent at St. John's in England. Our sense of it was that ours was the truly serious exercise of Christianity; an underinformed judgment, obviously, but then that can be held always to be the case. Catholic Christianity was beleaguered in the sense that American traditional culture is Protestant. In this sense, in the thirties and forties, the U.S. Catholic had some sense of it that his culture was alien. But direct anti-Catholicism was rarely expressed in doctrinal terms. Such criticisms as I heard—or thought I had heard, as a boy and teenager— weren't orderly indictments of the anti-Catholic faith. When the subject arose—What are the special disqualifications of American Catholics?—it was usually the political point that was being pursued, the question of divided loyalties.

We all knew that in 1928 many voters who would normally have gone with the Democratic Party did not do so because the party's candidate was Al Smith. Much of Protestant America didn't like the idea of a Catholic in the White House, even feared the idea. When Paul Blanshard's famous book came out *(American Freedom and Catholic Power)*, about which I have made mention, the case was crystallized: American Catholics were burdened with a divided loyalty and for that reason incapacitated from being at once dutiful Catholics and dutiful Democrats. It struck me, when as a freshman I first heard the argument put with some force, that the Blanshard objection was entirely valid. It highlighted, however indirectly, the doctrine that crystallized during my sophomore year. It came to be known as the Nuremberg Defense: The only reason, your honor, I helped to slaughter six million Jews was that Hitler told me to do so, and Hitler was my superior.

The argument hadn't worked in Nuremberg for Göring et al., nor should it have. In the inconceivable event that a majority of Americans decided to end liberty—specifically, religious liberty—a Catholic sheriff would certainly have a problem requiring a synagogue—or a church—to close down after duly authorized instructions to do so had been handed down to him through proper, democratic channels. In such a situation one likes to think that non-Catholics would join the resistance; but there is no question that, in such a situation, a Catholic official true to his faith would heed the authority of Rome, not Washington. If critics then chose to accuse him of divided loyalty, they'd be only half right. *All* loyalty to Washington would have been forfeited.

Most critics were focusing on Christianity at large. The special exposures of the Catholic—divided loyalty, the authority of the magisterium—were surely counterbalanced, I thought, by Catholicism's strengths. What were they? What was it about my faith that especially attracted to it the men who constitute what I have called my Forum, all of them born and raised as Protestants?

For a Catholic to read about another Catholic's journey to Damascus is an exhilarating experience, reminding us of satisfactions that may have become jaded. I wanted to hear about what especially engaged the mind and heart of my Forum. And wanted also—an adjacent question—to know what it was that kept some of them, for so long, at the gates. My inquiry was wonderfully rewarding for me and, I devoutly hope, others. The question exactly as I posed it:

*Was there one feature of the Catholic Church, distinguishing it from other Christian sects, that in particular drew you toward the Church? If so which was it (or them)?*

> Permit me to suggest that it is not accurate (nor is it nice) to speak of "other Christian sects." For one, it suggests that the Catholic Church is one sect among others. The Catholic Church is not a sect. [*American Heritage Dictionary:* "A group of people forming a distinct unit within a larger group by virtue of certain refinements or distinctions of belief or practice."] The reason I became a Catholic is, entirely and alone, because of the ecclesial claims of the Catholic Church, which I have for many years held to be true.

There was no personal narrative in Fr. Neuhaus's account. Later, he would be more revealing.

And then Fr. Rutler, formerly a High Church Episcopalian priest:

* * *

I was drawn by three things. First the papacy (which, as a High Anglican, I had considered the principal error of Rome). The utter consistency of the papal magisterium over against all teleological extremes of every age, combined with the evidently supernatural appearance of a Slav Pope at this tumultuous period in world affairs, made the Petrine office seem essential to Church and culture. Second, I came to appreciate the uniqueness of Catholic "systematic thought," which has no parallel in any philosophical structure and which proved itself by working coherently in our antinomian and highly subjective age.

What you have read is not the complete passage given me by Fr. Rutler. I didn't want to relay the sentences that follow without first making this point, namely that I am not a bit certain that I myself fully understand them. I don't mean to say that I don't understand why Fr. Rutler is taking the position he takes. I mean something else, that I am not confident I understand what exactly he is *saying*. He is using theological concepts that my mind does not fully fathom—maybe can't fathom? I know that I could pick up the telephone and call—how many? three?—friends who would endeavor to explain them to me. But such spelunking for hidden treasure is for explorers and specialists.

I thought also, on deciding whether to reproduce the abstruse sentences, that I shouldn't resist the temptation to expose the reader to far reaches of theological language and speculation. The typical modern academic is quite simply ignorant of theology. Mostly this is because scholars proceed happily on the assumption that theological studies are voodoo, deserving ignorance, condescension, or contempt. But even if God did not exist, were not real, theology would remain a profound philosophical science. Even if trees do make noise when they fall down in a forest out of human earshot, David Hume and George Berkeley are engrossing epistemologists. Fr. Rutler's words, whatever they mean, bring to mind the refinements of the theological mind at work. He is not merely "spinning wheels" (Professor Kendall's term for student papers in which nothing really was being said or thought, merely pages being filled). There are those who scorn the very idea of extra-worldly phenomena, and deem all language devoted to the study of them a philosophical conceit. You will hear it said that it is not surprising that less than the most talented graduate students go on to divinity schools. That last may be so, but it is not a matter of brainpower, but of calling. Just to begin with, it requires a profound ignorance of the achievements of the human mind to ignore all the work of the primary thinkers in the Christian tradition between Augustine and Kierkegaard. Herewith the balance of Fr. Rutler's reply:

•     •     •

This [the uniqueness of Catholic systematic thought] made clear the "scrutability" of paradox, and provided an economy in which natural law and revelation were compatible and effectively defined the use and limits of reason. By the *via negativa* I had to observe that nothing else "worked" and this did. Third, I was converted by the fact of the saints. There is no isolated psychological phenomenology of the saints—the utterly natural supernaturalness of grace *(gratis non tollit naturam sed perficit)* [Grace does not destroy nature, rather, perfects it] in the lives of the saints of heroic virtue is proof positive that there is grace and that it is available. Léon Bloy's line (the only tragedy is *not* to be a saint) seemed to sum up the reason for Christ and the whole meaning of existence. As we enter a "postmodern" age we may consider the neglect of the lives of the saints to have been the single most curious lacuna in modern intellectual life.

What I take away from that is (1) that which was thought impenetrable as a paradox is, by Catholic reasoning, in fact discernible; (2) only by exposure to the incomplete road (presumably to religious thought finally rejected as incomplete—Anglicanism, in this instance) was it possible for Fr. Rutler to acknowledge the true road; (3) the mere existence of the saints, never mind that the exact properties of saintliness have never been absolutely defined, establishes that divine favor is there, and available to us. The striking failure of humankind is to have eschewed a (sufficient) study of saintliness, and aspiration to saintliness; and it is above all strange, given the perspectives we have in postmodern thought, that that failure itself fails sufficiently to engage the attention of modern intellectuals.

There it is. It can be parsed, as here done. But do you fully understand it? I don't. Not fully.

Russell Kirk, by contrast, was plainspoken, and exemplary in dramatizing the necessary end of his tempermental resistance to relativism. He adds a fine paragraph about the lateness of his baptism, the result of a very long series of inferences that finally—but only then—made up his Holy Grail.

What I found in the Church was Authority. Catholicism is governed by Authority; Protestants, by Private Judgment. I had become painfully aware of the insufficiency of Private Judgment in the twentieth century—every man creating his own morals. In my search, over the years, for a sound apprehension of the human condition, I came at last to recognize in the Roman Church the elements of Truth, as sustained by two thousand years of continuity; by the wealth of wisdom in the Church's pronouncements; by the lives and words of St. Augustine of Hippo and St. Gregory the Great, particularly, among the Church Fathers; by Acton's observation, if you will, that no institution purely human could have survived, over the centuries, so many blunders.

I was not "converted" to the Church, but made my way into it through what Newman calls *illation*—fragments of truth collecting in my mind through personal experience, conversations, knowledge of exemplars, and much reading and meditating. (I was not baptized in any church until 1964, when I attained the age of forty-five years.) Mine was the god of the philosophers, Pascal notwithstanding (though I read Pascal, too), rather than the god of Abraham, Isaac, and Jacob. Father Hugh O'Neill, S.J., at the University of Detroit, who gave me some instruction during 1953–54, replied in answer to an inquiry of mine that most people seeking knowledge of Church doctrines came to him out of some psychological distress or want. It was not so with me: rather, I still was seeking the source of wisdom.

Kirk left the impression that people who contemplate conversion and consult priests are driven by psychological disorders. Yes; but psychological distress (or "want") can be the symptom of spiritual hunger. Even if I thought I could competently handle the psychoanalytical vocabulary, I would let it alone, and say simply this: that I know human beings who are unhappier than they would be if they believed that God could give solace, and that He cared.

Jeffrey Hart answered in a single sentence:

The answer here is in the plural: (a) continuous distinguished intellectual tradition stretching back over two millennia; (b) doctrinal coherence; (c) institutional stability, produced by its theory of church government, which is monarchical; (d) universality; (e) liturgical stability, even now.

Wick Allison, a generation younger than the rest of us, gave his own itinerary with simple and, I think, effectively solemn conviction.

Five things attracted me in stages to the Catholic Church:
1. Its understanding of human nature and of human society. I was a student in the sixties when theories about the perfectibility of man and schemes for new utopias were the intellectual air one

breathed. I thought they were all rubbish. But I didn't have a clear sense of why I thought that, and as I looked for intellectual support I stumbled across the Church Fathers, or writings about the Fathers: their clarity, their appeal to the evidence of the senses and, most of all, to common sense, their insistence on the unchanging nature of creation, all these were to me like drinking from a fresh-water spring. I became interested in the religion that seemed to foster such clear thinking.

2. Its antiquity. I became impressed that such views were held and argued with a consistent vigor over the centuries by all sorts of different people who were Catholic. I became interested in such subjects as the apostolic succession and the Church's claim that it is the original Church founded by Jesus. Just as any thinking person in the West sooner or later has to confront the claims of Jesus, sooner or later he has to confront this claim of the Catholic Church.

3. Its universality. I found it interesting, when I read them, that St. Augustine and Cardinal Newman both came to the conclusion that the Catholic faith was the true Christianity by this fact of its ubiquity. I was raised in a denomination (Methodist) where one felt uncomfortable attending a church service in another part of town, much less another part of the country (in another part of the world was inconceivable). When I started getting interested in the Catholic faith I began to attend Mass. I was only an observer, and I really didn't understand the significance of what I was observing, but I liked to go, and it was with a start one Sunday that I realized I was going to Mass in a city I was visiting, that I had been to Masses in lots of different places and that nothing much seemed different about any of them. This probably never occurs to a born Catholic but it comes as a shock to the rest of us.

Part of the universalism is the diversity. In Protestantism a particular church, like a particular magazine or particular retail store, is geared to a demographic segment. It's where like-minded people gather together to worship, so there's no surprise that everyone looks, acts, and thinks the same. The first time I attended a Mass a Mexican gardener in his work clothes knelt down beside me.

At first I was put off; I was raised among people who associated bad smell with unwashed Mexican gardeners. Here was one sitting next to me in church. Then I was dazzled. Of *course* it had to be this way! In the original Christian church the strictures of St. Paul are still followed: "Here you are neither Greek nor Jew. . . ." Of all the things about the Catholic Church I love, this is the thing I love the best.

4. Mary. How does one talk to God? How does one relate to Christ the Savior? For me it was difficult. And so I turned to Mary. To this day I am not at all sure about the theological underpinnings of Mariology, and I suspect I'll never investigate them. I took the concept of Mary as my Mother to heart from the beginning and, as Dante chose Virgil, made her my own personal guide to the Catholic faith. She has been wonderful.

5. The Eucharist. This took a little longer. When my brother lived outside London he took me to see the oldest standing church in England, a squat Saxon building made out of stone. We went inside. The building was still set up as a church, with old wooden pews and altar fixtures. But what struck me immediately was how empty the place felt. And then I realized what was missing: the Eucharist. A church is warm; this place was cold. A church is somehow made alive by the Life inside it; this place was dead. It was sad. The chain of worship that should have united me with the sturdy, sixth-century yeomen who built the church had been broken.

It was that experience that made me understand how important the Real Presence had become for me and what my forefathers had given up when they discarded it.

The thought that the Real Presence should give off emanations is widely dismissed as psychological autohypnosis. If such phenomena are analyzed by strict scientific standards, then the skeptic cannot lose the argument. By strict scientific rules, all sensations related to special presences are self-induced; what you feel while waiting, the heartbeat a little faster, to enter the Oval Office; in the presence of the Pope; in the hotel lounge when the girl—your girl—comes in. But the rules are abundantly violated. They don't seem, to me, to make it. And anyway, how do they account for the sensory perceptions in homing pigeons, let alone in some who think they feel—do feel?—something in the company of the Real Presence?

*     *     *

The next question followed naturally. I put it this way:

*Was there one feature, or more, of the Catholic Church that kept you from joining it sooner than you did? If so, please say which, and (a) explain why they antagonized you; and (b) how you overcame that antagonism, if indeed you did.*

Fr. Neuhaus spoke of the journey from Lutheranism and its "Augustinian Christianity," the devotion to a God of all-encompassing love, who gave the world the Incarnation (the emphasis is otherwise on man's effort to qualify for God's love), and of the three dogmatic pronouncements of the Catholic

Church, made after the Reformation: the Immaculate Conception, that Mary was born without sin (1854); that the Pope cannot mislead in matters of faith and morals when speaking ex cathedra (1870); and that when Mary departed the earth, she ascended into Heaven (1950).

> The key discovery is that I was a Lutheran because I was an Augustinian, notably on the question of God's utterly gratuitous justifying grace in Christ. It was for me a providential coincidence that at the time I was wrestling with these questions, the chief guardian of Catholic orthodoxy was Josef Ratzinger, a thorough Augustinian. For me it is of great importance to emphasize that to be an orthodox Catholic today is to be an ecumenical Catholic. Catholics can afford to be very generous in acknowledging the grace and truth of God in other communions. That is the case at least if the teachings of the Second Vatican Council are right. Those who deny the teachings of the Council have a very hard time making the case that they are orthodox Catholics. (That applies to the Lefebvres on the right, as well as those on the left such as Fr. Richard McBrien, who defy the magisterium in the name of "the Church of John XXIII.")

Fr. Neuhaus grew to accept the three post-Reformation dogmas—Immaculate Conception, infallibility, Assumption—as "all of them understandable in a thoroughly evangelical and Christocentric way." He admits that the question of papal infallibility was difficult:

> At the same time, had I been around then, I expect I would have been, with Newman and many others, an "inopportunist" with respect to infallibility. Its magisterial interpretation, however, makes clear that it is derived from the "indefectibility of the Church" and reflects the Petrine ministry (firmly grounded in the New Testament) and therefore poses no problems. [Might it, sometime in the future?] Conceivably, yes. A Pope could not, for example, "infallibly" define that there are four persons in the Godhead. Such a definition would be invalid on the face of it and would be clear evidence of the incompetence of the Pope who attempted it. To ask about some aberrant exercise of infallibility is like asking what you would think of your wife if you knew she was planning to poison you. It is contrary to fact, and I trust will always remain so.

That is heady stuff. I found most striking the reminder that the Vatican Council acknowledged, if not the legitimacy of the heretical churches, at least the common ground we have with them, from which we deduce that ecumenism is the necessary objective. And Fr. Neuhaus reminds us that it is now as it was always, and throughout history has been. Although the Church is convincingly united, there are, in the current context, both left and right inclinations to heterodoxy. The Lefebvrites—led by Archbishop Marcel Lefebvre (1905–91)—protest the liturgical reforms and the new Mass of Vatican II. But it was only when Lefebvre undertook to ordain another bishop (this only the Pope can authorize) that indocility spilled over to schism. Fr. McBrien, who has been head of the department of theology at Notre Dame, is here mentioned as contumacious because of his continuing advocacy of women's ordination, a noncelibate priesthood, and birth control. It is helpful to remember that many priests considered deviant at this or another point in Church history are in due course restored. The distinction has surely to be between defective disciplinary compliance and the teaching of subversive doctrine. The structure of the papacy, as observed early on, requires final doctrinal authority; the institution of the Church, effective administrative authority. I was beyond measure happier with the old than with the new liturgy, I am relieved that the advocacy of birth control is less than an excommunicable offense, and I am serene, as a matter of faith, that the Church is not materially misguided. I like what Fr. Neuhaus says about the promulgation of infallibility in 1870. He has to admit that back then he'd have opposed it, but he has to admit now that it was there all the time.

Fr. Rutler remains difficult exactly to understand. Better put, he uses language both poetic and provocative, inviting us to parse his thoughts to the end of the night. He gives me a compelling view of the pilgrim seeking utter authenticity, going to Catholic Christianity to find it, but weighed down with sorrow by so much of what he finds in the modern Church, however irrelevant to its singularity.

> The chief obstacle was the failure of the Catholic Church to be herself in practice. I do not mean being "holy" enough because she is always that and most conspicuously so, in a chiaroscuro way, when most corrupt in the material order. I do mean that Church's tendency to compromise with the most dismal conceits of progressivism just when they were proving to be philosophical and aesthetic phantoms.
>
> The Catholic Church had ceased being properly universal and had in the West become bourgeois. This hit me as particularly evident in her liturgical life. Used as I was to the aesthetic "form without substance" of Anglican externals I did not enjoy the prospect of substance without form. English in "ghastly bad taste" had its

drawbacks but that "gaudy meretriciousness" [the designation of a seventeenth-century Anglican theologian] of the post-Vatican II Church seemed revolting. Worse, this symbolized a loss of the sacramental vision and a petit-bourgeois surrender on the part of the Church which is properly the shared communion of kings and peasants, knaves and saints. I would be happy with both the Sainte-Chapelle of Louis IX and the hovel of the Curé d'Ars but not with a suburban church glorifying the shopping mall.

I overcame that, I daresay, by the grace which makes conversion possible. This was aided in the natural order by the realization that Anglicanism was over and done for having always been an illicit compromise between a truth and a lie, and the sheer desperation of realizing that the crises of our times are crises of saints and saints are the products of the Catholic fact.

For the most part, Russell Kirk resisted the confessional requirement of the Church, though he acknowledges that the institution was more offensive to his nature than to others'.

Although nothing in doctrine or dogma in any way repelled me, I was not attracted by the rite of confession—not that in my unchurched years I was much given to committing deadly sins, mine being the sins of omission, chiefly. (One thinks of a line from an Edwardian comedy: "I'm afraid I was a very *good* young man; but I'm not sorry; for that has enabled me to be a very wicked old one.") Shy and self-sufficient, I resented being expected to open my smug heart to anybody. My wife remarks that I do not let anyone into my secret garden.

My attitude toward confession has not much improved since my baptism in the Church, although requirements for frequency of confession have diminished since then. But more repugnant than the old sort of confession in some antique carven confessional is the latter-day notion—popular with "advanced" priests, especially those who rejoice in what they call the Jesus-centered liturgy (actually the priest-centered liturgy)—of the public, or open, or collective confession, reducing the sacrament to absurdity and hypocrisy.

I recognize now that confession fulfills a most important psychological function, as did the ritual ablutions of the ancient Greeks in some sacred river, washing away the haunting consciousness of grim guilt. But I refrain from confessing the outrageous sin of wandering thoughts at Mass; that failing of mine is incurable.

* * *

The public confessional formula (every member of the congregation recites to himself his sins, summons up contrition, and the priest grants corporate absolution) was one of those excesses of the Vatican II sixties, and after a little while was all but discontinued (penance services are still performed twice a year, in preparation for Christmas and Easter). In some dioceses the practice was never permitted.

Jeffrey Hart had no specific problem, Ernest van den Haag the problem of ignorant clergy, Wick Allison the problem of the "priest":

> While most of the priests I've known have been warm and affable types, the priesthood itself is an intimidating institution to the outsider. I can't say that it is antagonizing; just intimidating.

Yes, the priesthood is intimidating, and so are individual priests. On that subject I thought Fr. Andrew Greeley said exactly the right thing in an essay I stumbled upon during my research:

> The reader can make up his own litany of injuries the Catholic Church has done to him. I do not care how horrendous that litany may be, it does not provide a valid excuse for disengaging from the Catholic Christian heritage. Indeed, it is irrelevant. I attempt no justification and offer no excuse for what the Church may have done to you: I simply assert that the failures of Christians and the failures of Christian leadership have nothing to do with the validity of the Catholic Christian heritage. If you use those failures as an excuse for not facing the essential religious demands of the Catholic Christian heritage, you are engaged in an intellectually dishonest cop-out. The question is not whether the Catholic leadership is enlightened but whether Catholicism is true. A whole College of Cardinals filled with psychopathic tyrants provides no answer one way or another to that question.
>
> [And then a killer of a closing line.] Search for the perfect church if you will; when you find it, join it, and realize that on that day it becomes something less than perfect.

# Memories of a Catholic Boyhood

From: *Bare Ruined Choirs: Doubt, Prophecy, and Radical Religion*

BY GARRY WILLS

INTROIBO AD ALTARE DEI.
AD DEUM QUI LAETIFICAT JUVENTUTEM MEAM.

We grew up different. There were some places we went, and others did not—into the confessional box, for instance. There were also places we never went, though others could—we were told, from youth, to stay out of non-Catholic churches. Attendance there would be sinful, a way of countenancing error. It was forbidden territory—though tasted by some *because* prohibition gave tang to the experience: we were assisting at evil rites. Even those who feel they long ago outgrew that tabu have residual feelings of wickedness, now and then, when attending non-Catholic services—like men who go with self-assuring mockery (mocks just a little too loud) into a dark house said to be haunted. We "born Catholics," even when we leave or lose our own church, rarely feel at home in any other. The habits of childhood are tenacious, and Catholicism was first experienced by us as a vast set of intermeshed childhood habits—prayers offered, heads ducked in unison, crossings, chants, christenings, grace at meals; beads, altar, incense, candles; nuns in the classroom alternately too sweet and too severe, priests garbed black on the street and brilliant at the altar; churches lit and darkened, clothed and stripped, to the rhythm of liturgical recurrences; the crib in winter, purple Februaries, and lilies in the spring; confession as intimidation and comfort (comfort, if nothing else, that the intimidation was survived), communion as revery and discomfort; faith as a creed, and the creed as catechism, Latin responses, salvation by rote, all things going to a rhythm, memorized, old things always returning, eternal in that sense, no matter how transitory.

Such rites have great authority; they hypnotize. Not least by their Latinity.

It is not certain, philologists say, that "hocus-pocus" is derived from *"Hoc est Corpus"* in the Mass; but the Latin phrases, often rhythmed, said in litanies and lists of saints' names, replicated, coming at us in antiphonies and triple cries *(Sanctus, Sanctus, Sanctus),* had a witchery in them, to hush or compel us as by incantation.

We spoke a different language from the rest of men—not only the actual Latin memorized when we learned to "serve Mass" as altar boys. We also had odd bits of Latinized English that were not part of other six-year-olds' vocabulary—words like "contrition" or "transubstantiation." Surely no teenager but a Catholic ever called an opinion "temerarious." The words often came imbedded in formulae ("imperfect contrition"), and the formulae were often paired in jingles (imperfect contrition and *perfect* contrition). Theology was a series of such distinctions: *ex opere operato* and *ex opere operantis,* homoousion and homoiousion, mortal sin and venial sin, matter of sin and intention of sin, parvity of matter and gravity of matter, baptism of water and baptism of desire, Mass of the Catechumens and Mass of the Communicants, the Church Teaching and the Church Taught, infallible and authoritative, valid and invalid, invalid by reason of the minister and invalid by reason of the material. Matter and form. *Materialiter et formaliter.* Black and white. The mode of theology was constant—a simultaneous linking and severing in the Scholastic *distinguo.* To know the terms was to know the thing, to solve the problem. So we learned, and used, a vast terminology.

That terminology haunts a Catholic's speech in ways he is often unaware of. One could tell, after a certain amount of talk with Senator Eugene McCarthy, that he was a Catholic, though theology had not formally been brought up or discussed. He uses casually such giveaway phrases as "occasion of sin," and "having scruples," and "particular friendship," and "rash judgment," and "special dispensation"—not terribly exotic expressions, but each with a special meaning for Catholics.

Even when we did not use different words, we pronounced them in a different way, a possessive way that took the words from others and made them, exclusively, ours. We said "doc-*trine*-al" because doctrine was ours. And "con-*temp*-late" because monks belonged to us. And "con-*sum*-mated" because what was con-*sum*-mated on the Cross was not the same as what is consum-*mate*-ed in the marriage bed. Though other Christians were devoted to our saints, they did not know how to pronounce their names. It was Saint Au-*gus*-tin, for instance, not *Aug*-us-teen. Or Saint *Jeh*-rom, not Je-*rome.* We did not pronounce them this way in order to approximate the Latin or medieval forms; in fact we were departing from both. We did it, ultimately, just to be different—to say *our* Augustine was not the same one claimed by Luther, the Augustine recruited into heresy.

The church judged things not out of a deeper antiquity, but from outside time altogether. That was borne in on us by an unanchored, anachronistic style (or mix of styles) in all things the church did. Going into a Catholic church of our day, one might think history was a rummage sale, and this place had been fitted out after visits to the sale. Here one century, there another, and all jumbled together. Here the soutane, there the crozier. In the drone of Latin, sudden gabbles of Greek. Ancient titles *(Pontifex Maximus)* and an ancient familiarity of address *(Paul* our Pope, and *Laurence* our Bishop). The humble pilgrim hat for cardinals, proud miter for bishops, triple tiara for a Pope, and absurd biretta for priests (made absurder, with purple poofs, for monsignors—yes, *monsignori,* for the patina of Italy was on all this merchandise, like the fuzzy encrustations on a shipwrecked cargo).

It all spoke to us of the alien. The church was stranded in America, out of place. And not only out of place here. It belonged to no age or clime, but was above them all; it had a "special dispensation" from history. History was a thing it did not have to undergo. Thus the church could pick and choose from any period, odd bits of all the ages clinging to her as she swept along, but none of them catching her, holding her back; she moved free of them all.

One lived, then, in contact with something outside time—grace, sin, confession, communion, one's own little moral wheel kept turning in the large wheel of seasons that moved endlessly, sameness in change and change in sameness, so was it ever, so would it always be, a repetition like that frequent "always"—*per omnia saecula saeculorum,* through all the ages' roll of ages—punctuating our prayers. The form could be varied, short or long, grand or simple: *per Christum Dominum nostrum Jesum Christum qui vivit et regnat per omnia saecula saeculorum,* or just *qui vivis et regnas per omnia saecula saeculorum.* It could be said or sung by priest or people; or the choir, after freer melodies (God! how free, then, and how trivial), would chant it at the end, predictable end, return to reality, to "always." The real was what *always* was; it was eternal, unchangeable, like the church. Eternity, in those Latin prayers, was ever nagging at us; never, in the flux of change and seasons, letting us go.

We were, thus, a chosen people—though chosen, it seemed, to be second-rate. Still, in that uncompetitive mediocrity we found a certain rest denied to others, those who, choosing themselves, achieving by themselves, were driven and badly in need of being first-rate. Our mediocrity hid superior moral tone, obvious to us, concealed from others, a secret excellence, our last joke on the World (World, dignified by a capital letter, but dumb—Devil and Flesh knew what we were up to, but not blundering, dim-witted World). We were distinguished by spiritual favors that made us just a bit—we had to admit it—odd.

A protective skein was thus woven all around us—not forming a time capsule, since it kept us at a far remove from time; an *un*time capsule, a fibery cocoon of rites and custom in which we were to lie, the chrysalis, till we broke through into promised Reality after death. It is no wonder that, for Catholics, the old childhood sequence of questions took on special promise, or menace:

"What are you?"

"What do you mean?"

"A Catholic, or a Lutheran, or what?"

"Oh, I'm nothing."

"How can you be a Nothing?"

For people brought up inside this total weave of Catholic life, it did seem that departure from one aspect of the faith meant forfeiting all one's connections with religion. A single authority ran through each aspect of one's upbringing. That authority stood behind every practice, endorsing them all. To doubt anywhere was to doubt everywhere. Since the authority was single, so should the acceptance be.

In such a context "losing one's faith" meant a loss of many good things, beginning with one's own past. It meant betrayal, not only a betrayal of grace, of God's gift, but of others—parents, children, all those woven up in the same cocoon. Tear the seamless weave for your own exit, you made a hole through which the world could seep in on dear ones, your friends still left there. Tension was thus established—on the one side, a very human urge to remain, at all cost, within this cradling, this gently nurturing, carefully tended pod, metaphysical womb. This was the home of reality, a seed that was ripening toward ultimate fulfillment. Its membranous covering let only truth's light come through, filtering evil and error out. To leave such a shelter was to fall forever in unchartable darkness.

On the other hand, since the acceptance asked for was total, there was an urge toward total rejection whenever irritants developed. At such a moment, an opposite totalism came over Catholics like a spasm—belief that reality was just outside, one must flail through to it with one blow. One sees this oddly exhilarating *lack* of faith—a suspended-action continuing *loss* of faith—in some ex-Catholics (e.g., in that reverse seminarian, Will Durant), their belief that wisdom lies in one's great rejection, that outside the cocoon there is no further goal to reach, one has taken the great final step.

In the past, D. H. Lawrence claimed, our civilization's "dirty little secret" was sex. But the church's secret, hidden away in official teaching, minimized when it could not be ignored, was *change*. Other things came and went, captive to history. But the gates of hell would not prevail against the church, and the gates of hell often looked like history, or the latest products of history—"modernism," science, rationalism. We did not deal with such fads—what was sound in them the church had always possessed, for what the church is, it always was; what it could accept now, it could and did accept then (that vague "then" not much explored). The church's past, so far as it could be said to have one, was glimpsed in quick raids made on history, meant to capture proof-texts showing that our sacraments, our doctrines, were all there in the Fathers (though not fully analyzed till St. Thomas Aquinas' time). A book that young Catholics were steered toward, as soon as they seemed bright enough to ingest it, was *The Thirteenth, Greatest of Centuries* (1907, often reprinted) by James J. Walsh. The church could pick one age or other as "the best of times" inasmuch as that time lived up best to the church's demands (which are the same in all times).

The experience of change came to Catholics as a form of personal crisis. As a man grew, his views underwent some alteration, enlargening—even his views of the church. If things he had been taught seemed childish now, it was his own earlier view that had been childish, not anything in the church itself. He had to account for his own development in relation to a fixed thing. When he could no longer do so, he had "lost the faith"—outgrown that fixed thing. It failed him because it did not change—the very fact that reassured and comforted those who stayed.

We have yet to learn all the good wrought by "Vatican Two," and all the damage. But the main point about the Council can be put quite simply: *it let out the dirty little secret.* It forced upon Catholics, in the most startling symbolic way, the fact that *the church changes.* No more endless roll of *saecula saeculorum.* No more neat ahistorical belief that what one did on Sunday morning looked (with minor adjustments) like what the church had always done, from the time of the catacombs. All that lying eternity and arranged air of timelessness (as in Mae West's vestmented and massive pose) was shattered. The house with the arrested clocks, like Miss Havisham's Satis House ("The bride within the bridal dress had withered like the dress, and like the flowers") collapsed, by reverse dilapidation, out of death's security into uncertain life.

Some, of course, rejoiced at this entry of the incalculable into areas that had seemed too clearly lit and solid, like endless marble corridors. They saw in this uncertainty a pledge of truthfulness—or, better, of adequacy. Nothing can be very deep unless troubled by mysteries, partaking of the mysterious, of dark things to be undergone, risks to be taken—intellectual risk, as well as moral.

But however bracing this experience of change has been to some, to the mass of Catholics it came as a shock, engendering disillusion. It threatened psychic ruin to them personally, as well as institutional jeopardy for the church. Such people recall the broken old woman in Mauriac's novel, *Maltaverne:*

> She was stepping out firmly along the road, returning the greetings
> of those she met with nods and smiles proportionate to their
> importance, and yet what she chiefly suggested to me at this point

in her life was that fly which a schoolfellow of mine, pretending to degrade Dreyfus, had gradually dismembered. Thus Mother was being stripped, day by day, of all her certainties. Nothing was true of all that she had believed, but the falsest thing of all was what she had mistaken for revealed truth.

Not only had such people conceived of their church as timeless; they tried to approximate that state themselves. The readjustment all men undergo when there is growth was, for them, reorientation back to one immutable thing.

Catholics inhibited change, so far as they were able, in themselves and in their world. Perfect faith and trust would quiet the soul in a peaceful attitude of rest. After all, if one possesses the Truth already, any change is liable to be a departure from that truth, diminution of one's treasure. "Mysteries" remained, but were well posted—things one does not solve (or even, therefore, think much about). It would be the sin of presumption to ask for understanding of them. In heaven it would all be clear. Man's poor mind cannot grasp the high and deep things. A peasant's or old woman's faith was the ideal for which one should strive. There is an element of truth in this "wise peasant" school of thought; but that element is exaggerated and perverted by non-peasants striving back toward intellectual rusticity. Jacques Maritain calling himself "the peasant of the Garonne" is a bit like Marie Antoinette playing shepherdess to imbibe arcadian virtue.

The church looked, on one side, like the last guardian of reason in a world of unfounded and shifting impressions. It held to a logical view of things, full of studied distinctions, its doctrine spelled out, endlessly examined in technical language. Yet its learning was formal, opposed to intellectual initiative or exploration. The reasons for this go far back, to Wittenberg, to Antioch—indeed, to Eden. But the form the obscurantism took in America is easily grasped by those who remember Bing Crosby's movie, *Going My Way*.

That movie was, under its cassocks and other disguises, the classic melodrama based on a mortgage foreclosure. But the mortgage there was not on an ancestral home; it was on the church, St. Dominic's. The old father (Barry Fitzgerald), debilitated by his own building program, was about to lose his parish. The heroine (Ingrid Bergman) would thus lose, not her Virtue, but her children—in the school. (No, come to think of it, she came into the Crosby series with *The Bells of St. Mary's*—but the plot assumptions were the same, with a school to be built instead of a church to be saved.) The young romantic lead arrives ("Toora-loora-loora"), staves off ruin, gives his home back to old Father Fitzgibbon, gives her children back to the heroine, then "goes his way" to Rainbow's End.

It was, for all its shmaltz, surprisingly true to Catholic life, and to Catholic blindness about that life. The film celebrated all the church's faults as if they were virtues—right down to Father O'Malley's practiced golf game. There was a bit of hard truth at the film's soft core because the plot turned on the central fact of American parish life—the mortgage on St. Dominic's. . . .

•        •        •

Since the sermon was so bad, the best Mass was the early one on a weekday when there was no sermon, only the odd mixed rites so familiar we could mumble proper responses in our sleep. Much was written, in the Sixties, of "the underground church," a strangely visible one (as if the catacombs had been reconstructed in air, some streamlined new "El"). But eight o'clock Mass on a Monday "in the old days" did have a feel of the catacombs about it, of underground good rendered to a world still bound in sleep. We came in winter, out of the dark into vestibule semidark, where peeled-off galoshes spread a slush across the floor. We took off gloves and scarves, hands still too cold to dip them in the holy water font. Already the children's lunches, left to steam on the bare radiator, emanated smells of painted metal, of heated bananas, of bologna and mayonnaise. Inside, we had an almost furtive air about our cramped genuflection and inhibited first crossings of the day—as if virtue were a secret we feared to confess even here. The priest's words came to us disjointedly through a hiss and protest of harshly awakened pipes. Girls without hats hairpinned Kleenex to their heads—it fluttered as they strode to the communion rail, like a raffish dove ill-perched on these sharers in the mystery. At the rail, as one knelt on the hard marble step, there was first the priest's quick murmur over each communicant *(Corpus Domini Nostri Jesu Christi custodiat animam tuam in vitam aeternam),* then the touch of his thumb wetted down the line from tongue to pious tongue.

The whole thing clearly did not mesh with what we did afterward. It stood apart in shadow, as if we re-entered some oracular cave to puzzle meaning out of phrases both foreign to us and familiar. Isolated so, apart from the world, we could almost believe this was our own "last supper"—or, in John Donne's phrase, "the world's last night." But then the scuffling resumed; all the coughs and sniffs held in during consecration and communion formed a firecracker series of soft percussions. Back into the vestibule. And when, galoshes resumed, we came out, day had broken after all. The world was saved again.

To remember such mornings is to start one pigeon of a muffledly screeching flock. Memories throng back, each of them stirring others:

Altar-boy assignments at odd hours, when God was a morning woozily begun under candles, a sweaty afternoon of games ended in the incense-tessitura of preprandial Benediction—the crusty and unwieldy monstrance, spangled cope, and *Tantum Ergo.*

Or midnight Mass—the first time one has been out so late, and farewell to

Santa Claus—a pompous affair served with twenty or so other altar boys: endless high candles to light (the long lighting-tree makes young arms ache), biretta of the celebrant to dispose of (it drops on the marble step with a cardboardy pop), as the organ undulates "When flowers blossomed in the snow . . ." The crib is dimmed-blue, suggesting Christmas night, and banked evergreen trees give off a rare outdoors odor inside the church as one extinguishes candle after high candle. The three kings will come in pine-needled silence (Epiphany is not a holy day of obligation), hooves of their camels unheard—already they inch over the sanctuary; they must arrive punctually by Twelfth-night.

A lenten procession, cross carried in front (swathed in purple), no organ to support the *a cappella* groan of "Pange lingua." The purple cloth is folded back, exposing the feet on the crucifix for people to kiss (priest making quick passes with a clean handkerchief, wiping the feet between each kiss).

An oddly jazzy lilt to *Flectamus genua,* sung over and over on Holy Saturday. All our food-chiseling during Lent *(ne potus noceat)* will end in a Saturday afternoon orgy of candy and stored-up sweets.

May procession in the warm night air of summer, "Hail Holy Queen enthroned above," as a girl in her prom "formal" teeters up a ladder with flowers to crown the plaster brow.

It was a world of quaint legalisms. Looking up a movie in the Legion of Decency list (if one had to look, it was probably "Condemned"). Wild surmise on the contents of a Friday soup—did it have gravy or meat products in it? Long debate, as midnight approached on Saturday, over using Mountain Standard Time to begin the precommunion fast. Priests groping their way to the Pullman lounge, for light to finish the breviary. *Dies Irae* on All Souls' Day as J. P. Morgans of the soul accumulate indulgences in purgatorial vaults by ducking in and out of church all day.

The bigger churches, with windows of a richly muddied color—fine gloom up behind the altar, busy commerce near the front doors. Unobtrusive boxes to be shriven in; baptismal font close to the pamphlet racks—a bigger holy water font; side-altar statues, stations of the cross, candled shrines where one could priest it over private liturgies.

Bells at the consecration—one was taught by the nuns to look up, murmur "My Lord and my God," and look down again. Heads buried in hands after communion (grade-schoolers peeking through their fingers). Breasts thumped quietly three times at the Confiteor ("through my fault, through my fault, through my most grievous fault"); one could tell a good deal about a person by his thumping style—lordly sweep of hand, favored by priests and more prominent laymen (a sinner here, but an important one); sneaky soft beats (one would not guess what the rustle was all about, but for prior knowledge); the slow-motion laying of hands on oneself much favored by women, or Tarzan strokes done in Victor McLaughlin seizures of contrition, producing audible chest echoes. Genuflections were just as revealing—from the skip, the fluid mere *nod* of the body (sacristans were expert at this, because of frequent passage by the tabernacle) to the crumpled abasement of total inner surrender (would she *ever* get up?).

Baptism in the spittle of repeated *Exorcizo*'s. Car blessings, name-saint days, letters dated by the church feast. Plastic holy water dips at bedroom doors, the Sacred Heart dark and Hispanic in a heavy frame. Scapulars like big postage stamps glued here and there on kids in swimming pools. "JMJ" at the top of schoolwork. The sign of the cross before a foul shot. Fishing pennies and dimes out of pockets pebbled with the fifty-nine beads and assorted medallions of a rosary. One's white first-communion suit, worn again and again on summer Sundays till winter darkened the year and one's clothes (and by next spring it would not fit). Awkward preadolescent girls in the first-communion line, all dumpiness made partly delicate with veils. Nuns who moved in their long habits with stately calm, like statues rocking. The deferential "-ster" pinned to all sentences "Yester" for "Yes, Sister").

Holy cards of saints with eyes so strenuously upturned as to be almost all white. The Infant of Prague bulkily packaged in "real" clothes. The sight, in darkened churches, of a shadowy Virgin with hands held palm-out at the level of her hips, plaster cape flowing down from those hands toward blue votive lights unsteady under her like troubled water. Sand under the votive candles for putting out tapers; and a box of kitchen matches, for lighting tapers, stuck into the sand. The momentary waxen strangle of St. Blaise day, as crossed candles bless one's throat.

Certain feelings are not communicable. One cannot explain to others, or even to oneself, how burnt stuff rubbed on the forehead could be balm for the mind. The squeak of ash crumbled into ash marked the body down for death, yet made this promise of the grave somehow comforting ("Rest, rest, perturbed spirit").

There were moments when the weirdest things made a new and deep sense beyond sense—when Confession did not mean cleaning up oneself (the blackboard erased again) but cleansing a whole world, the first glimpse of sky or grass as one came out of church. When communion was not cannibalism but its reverse, body taken up in Spirit. Being inwardly shaken by unsummoned prayers, as by muffled explosions. Moments of purity remembered, when the world seemed fresh out of its maker's hands, trees washed by some rain sweeter than the world's own.

All these things were shared, part of community life, not a rare isolated joy, like reading poems. These moments belonged to a *people,* not to oneself. It was a ghetto, undeniably. But not a bad ghetto to grow up in.

# Confession

### From: *A Drinking Life*

### BY PETE HAMILL

I tried very hard to believe in God, but I had almost no success. From the first grade on, I studied religion at Holy Name. I memorized endless pages of the Baltimore Catechism and even won religion prizes for reciting in a singsong way the questions and answers of the text. Who made the world? *God made the world.* Who is God? *God is the creator of heaven and earth, and of all things.* What is man? *Man is a creature composed of body and soul, and made to be the image and likeness of God.* Why did God make you? *God made me to know Him, to love Him, and to serve Him in this world, and to be happy with Him forever in the next.* Where is God? *God is everywhere.*

The problem was that I didn't believe any of this. On the surface, I was a reasonably good Catholic boy. I took my first communion, was confirmed, finally became an altar boy, memorizing the Latin responses for the whole Mass. *Ad Deum qui laetificat, juventutum meum.* . . . I loved the glazed baroque paintings on the walls of the church. I loved the statues of the flayed Jesus and his grieving mother. I loved the music most of all, with the great booming hymns filling the church on Sunday mornings. I even loved the smell of guttering candles, palm leaves at Easter, pine needles at Christmas. I just couldn't believe in God.

This was one of the heaviest secrets that I carried through those years. I couldn't talk to my mother or father about my terrible failure to imagine God; I certainly couldn't discuss it with the Xaverian Brothers at Holy Name; and down on the street I was afraid that the other kids would think I was weird. So I kept silent. To be sure, the religious education I received taught me some valuable lessons. I didn't care much about the Holy Ghost (though I loved his cartoony name), the Blessed Trinity, or Original Sin. But I did understand the catechism's definition of a mortal sin; it had to be a grievous matter, committed with sufficient reflection and full consent of the will. That is, a mortal sin was a felony. And the Baltimore Catechism taught us that certain mortal sins cried to heaven for vengeance: willful murder, the sin of Sodom, oppression of the poor, defrauding laborers of their wages. For a long time, I didn't know what the sin of Sodom was and couldn't get anyone to explain it to me (not to mention whatever it was they did in Gomorrah). But the rest of the Church's list of abhorrent sins was certainly admirable.

One trouble was that the Church in New York didn't follow its own list of rules, as laid out in the catechism. It certainly didn't seem to care very passionately about the poor. It shamed us into contributing money every Sunday by publishing our names in the church bulletin along with the amounts of the donations. But while altars were heavy with gold chalices and monstrances, and priests drove cars and grew fat, I never saw them down on Seventh Avenue. A Big Shot from the political club helped my father get a job; no priest ever did the same. I never saw priests on picket lines outside the Factory, joining in the fight against the bosses who were defrauding the workers. After sex, most of their negative passion was reserved for communism, which had absolutely nothing to do with life in the tenements of Seventh Avenue. The priests would never try to help a drunken man; all they ever did was judge him.

Still, the Xaverian Brothers at Holy Name tried hard to make me a good Catholic. I was taught the chief sources of sin: Pride, Covetousness, Lust, Anger, Gluttony, Envy, and Sloth. But again, most of the focus seemed to be on Lust. In the sixth grade, Brother Eliot kept me after school one afternoon and tried to explain sex to me. I knew some of the mechanics now from Arnold, the boys at Fox Lair Camp, and the kids from Seventh Avenue. But somehow, in the vague, reverent, whispering way Brother Eliot described it, sex became even more awesome and darkly attractive. It was, Brother Eliot said, a wonderful gift from God. But that didn't prevent the Baltimore Catechism from trying to make it a felony. "Lust," the catechism said, "is the source of immodest looks and actions, which lead to blindness of intellect, hardness of heart, the loss of faith and piety, the ruin of health, and final impenitence." Obviously, this was written by men with a well-developed sense of horror. But they didn't understand that an experience so colossally ruinous could never truly be avoided by the young. Even at the risk of hardness of heart and the ruin of health. In a way, they were offering another dare.

I listened in religion class, and to the fearful whisperings of Brother Eliot, but I just didn't understand it. There were people all over the Neighborhood who were bone poor. Night and day, there was violence on the streets. And I had seen those movies about the concentration camps. Why were the priests and brothers so crazy and fierce about sex? I was a virgin. I had no idea how it felt to fuck a woman. But I just couldn't imagine that someone as all-powerful as God was sitting around heaven on some throne, pissed off about what I might do at night on Seventh Avenue. The good brothers made God sound like some glorified scorekeeper, endlessly filling in box scores and then punishing those who made errors. Since there were billions of people on the earth, it seemed to me that He would have almost nothing else to do. Just writing down the sins of the Tigers would keep him busy; and if he had to do all of Asia, all of Russia, all of Europe, every man and every woman committing sins of Lust, all the movie stars and all the baseball players and all the wise guys in the Mafia, when would He ever get around to noticing what Noona Taylor was doing on the roof with Millie from the Tigerettes?

None of it made any sense. So I carried my disbelief with me, even as an altar boy. I didn't ask to be an altar boy; I was chosen by the brothers in the sixth grade. They probably believed that boys with good grades were also good Catholics; or perhaps they chose us only because we could remember all the Latin responses in the Mass. For whatever reason, I was drafted. But if anything, my time as an altar boy widened my separation from the Church. I learned the Latin; I got up on time every morning, winter and summer, draped my starched surplice over my arms and traveled up the hill to Holy Name. But from the beginning I felt part of a show, giving a rehearsed performance in which the lines never varied. I loved the sound of Latin, the roll of vowels, the way words changed according to their meaning; Latin was another code to be cracked. But even for the priests, it was all an act.

I did like some of the priests, particularly a kind man named Father Ahearn, and another named Father Kavanaugh, who said the fastest Mass in the parish, the Latin falling from his lips as if he were a tobacco auctioneer. But watching them get dressed in priestly garments or smoke cigarettes after Mass, being subjected to their scorn when I made a mistake, I saw them as human beings, not as officers in the army of Christ. I lost whatever sense of awe that I once felt during the Mass. They were men like other men.

At least one of them was like the men of Seventh Avenue, or like my father: a drunk. He had a sweet, smooth, baby's pink face, and eyes without irises. Sometimes he staggered onto the altar. He often forgot some of the Latin, repeated other parts at least twice. His superiors seemed to know he had a problem and gave him the earliest, most sparsely attended Masses. Even at six-thirty in the morning, he was shaky, his breath reeking. The sight of him filled me with pity and anger. It was bad enough that he staggered around; he was forced by his work to do so before an audience. I was angry that nobody from the Church tried to save him from this humiliation.

There was another personal element to the ceremony of the Mass. Wine was central to the ritual. We were taught that during the Mass, bread and wine were transformed into the body and blood of Christ. As an altar boy, I held the wine cruets while the priest blessed them and then poured the sweetish liquid across his fingers during the Offertory. That was the "first act" of the Mass, the section when the priest offered up to God the wine and the small unleavened wafers called hosts. In the second act of the drama, the consecration, he transformed these banal elements, saying his magic words in Latin, holding the host up for all to see; it was the custom in Holy Name to hide one's eyes and bow the head, refusing to look directly at the offered host because that little wafer had become God. Natives often did this in Tarzan movies, when facing their gods, and in *Gunga Din,* the murder cultists did the same with the image of Kali. Then the priest turned his back on the parishioners of Holy Name, ate the host, who was God, and washed Him down with the wine, or His blood. The more I learned, the more I thought that it was all very strange.

# Do Black Patent Leather Shoes Really Reflect Up?

From: *Do Black Patent Leather Shoes Really Reflect Up?*

By JOHN R. POWERS

## Retreat Retreat

Although I can't remember it, I'm sure it happened shortly after I was born. Perhaps it occurred the first time I knocked over my cup of milk. Or maybe it was when I tried to pull my sister's nose off. Someone much bigger than me said, "Don't do that, it's not nice. Now aren't you sorry?" Those were the first words to water that seed of solid guilt, buried deep within my cranium, which would shortly grow into a full-size Catholic conscience.

What started as a drizzle quickly swelled to a torrent. "No, don't touch that." "No, you can't eat now." "No, you can't go outside." "No, it's too early." "No No No No No." Presumably, those who rained around me hoped that my conscience would mushroom to such a size that it would eventually snuff out my brain.

The biggest cloudburst was my religion. Going through eight years of Catholic grammar school and Sunday morning sermons was like sitting for all those years in the courtroom of a hanging judge. *Guilty! Guilty! Guilty!* Catholicism was always having to say, "I'm sorry."

When the words of parents, the nuns, priests, and any other adult weren't hailing down on us kids in the neighborhood, we'd rain on each other. One summer day when I was nine years old, Lanner and I were walking down the street when we saw a group of kids, including Cookie Vlitsew, sitting on her front porch. In the middle of the group was an eleven-year-old known as the Cut-Rate Liquor Girl. Her mother ran the Cut-Rate Liquor Store up on 111th

Street. The girl had lived in the neighborhood only for six months. For some reason nobody seemed to be able to remember her real name. She and her mother moved out of the neighborhood a few months later with everyone still referring to her as the Cut-Rate Liquor Girl.

Oddly enough the Cut-Rate Liquor Girl was built just the way a girl with such a name should have been. She had a shot-glass head and a six-pack body.

As Lanner and I walked up to the porch, I noticed an ant colony between one of the cracks in the sidewalk. Normally I'm a rather tame person and I don't go out of my way to inflict pain on anyone, mainly because I'm not too crazy about it myself. But that day, without even thinking about it, I stepped on the ant colony. I guess we all like to play God occasionally.

By the way, the Cut-Rate Liquor Girl was not one of your great humanitarians. What I had just done to the ants, she had done to kids in the neighborhood.

The Cut-Rate Liquor Girl was horrified. "What did you do that for?"

"I don't know. I just did it," I said. Everyone else on the porch stopped talking to listen.

"You think you're going to get away with something like that?"

"What are you talking about?"

"You think God's going to let you get away with it?"

"I don't think God worries too much about ants."

"God worries about everything that lives."

"Well, yeah, maybe. But I don't think He spends a lot of His time on ants."

"What if God is an ant?"

"You're crazy."

"Did anyone ever tell you that He wasn't?"

"No. But nobody ever told me that He was."

"So there. I might be right. He came down here once as a human being. Why not as an ant?"

"Yeah, you might be right. No, no, I don't think so."

"Well, if I am, God help you."

"God help me? If He's an ant, He's not gonna help me."

"You're right. You're outta luck."

For the rest of the summer I felt guilty about stepping on that anthill, and I had more than one nightmare where I heard God saying to me just after I died, "So you're the clown who squashed my son."

Compared to my younger years, the religion classes at Bremmer High School were a drought. Every member of the faculty who was a religious brother had to teach one section of Religion a day. During the other four periods the brother would teach whatever his subject was, English, History, Science. Since Religion wasn't any faculty member's "subject," very few of the brothers spent any time preparing for their religion classes.

My religion teacher in freshman year was Brother Sash, who had us read the textbook during the first half of class. In the second half of class he would ask us questions on what we had read. Occasionally Brother Sash would skip all of this and lecture to us on the evils of sex.

He told us that our sex drive was like a tank of gas in a car. "Your tanks may be full to the brim now, boys, but if you're sexually overactive at this age, by the time you reach your thirties you may just run out of gas. You'll be impotent."

Danny Budswell, a Jolly Numbers boy, thought that was a good deal until someone explained to him that Brother Sash wasn't mispronouncing the word "important."

Brother Sash's favorite topic was "self-abuse." The biggest danger of this practice, he said, was that if you did it often enough you would go blind. We knew that wasn't true. If it had been, half the population of the school would have had seeing-eye dogs.

I had Brother Sofeck, the Biology teacher, for Religion in sophomore year. Everyone in that class spent most of his time trying to keep his breakfast down. Brother Sofeck had a pet rabbit named Lazarus, whose cage was our classroom. Every morning we had to tiptoe through the rabbit droppings to get to our desks.

Brother Sofeck spent most of his Religion classes talking about Biology. On those rare occasions when he did get into Religion, he would resort to terror tactics. One morning, for instance, Brother Sofeck showed us how to avoid mortal sin.

"Now, boys, if you don't want to commit a mortal sin, the kind of sin that sends you straight to hell, all you have to do is carry a pack of matches around with you." As he continued to talk he pulled a pack of matches out of his pocket, yanked a match loose from the binding, and lit it. "If you feel like committing a mortal sin, just light a match and stick your finger in it. . . ." He held the flaming match in front of his eyes. ". . . because that would be just a slight taste of what hell is like. Go ahead. The next time you want to commit a mortal sin, light a match and stick your finger in it. If you like it, if it feels good on your finger, go ahead and commit that mortal sin. Commit all the mortal sins you want. You'll just love it in hell. There, your entire body is engulfed in flames for all eternity."

Brother Sofeck was the first one to so graphically demonstrate to me that tactics of the Mafia and the Catholic Church were so alike: Step out of line with either one and you'd get burned.

He also told us about eternity. "How long is eternity, boys? How long? I'll tell you how long. Imagine that there is a solid steel ball the size of the sun. Not the earth but the sun. The sun, as you know, is one million, three hundred thousand times larger than the earth. Now every thousand years a bird flies up

to this massive steel ball and flicks its wing against it. When that bird wears that
steel ball into nothingness, eternity is just beginning."

After class, Timmy Heidi gave me a better definition of eternity: listening
to Brother Sofeck talk about it.

My Religion teacher in junior year was Brother Falley. He never mentioned
the subject. Every day when we came to class he'd tell us to take out a book to
study and he'd be with us in a moment. Then he'd pick up a book from his desk
and start reading. The "moment" never arrived.

The only Religion classes we had that year came during the two weeks
when Brother Sens, the Typing teacher, substituted for Brother Falley. Brother
Falley had walked through a glass door and had nearly cut his head off. At this
time, he was reading a book.

One thing that annoyed me about religion classes was that if a class got
into a debate with the teacher and managed to logically back him into a corner,
he'd get out of that corner with the same old statement. "Well, boys, it is, after
all, a matter of faith. You either believe it or you don't." End of argument.

We were discussing, with Brother Sens, the idea of the infallibility of the
Pope; that is, the Catholic Church's article of faith that when the Pope speaks
on matters of faith and morals he is always right. Sure enough, just as Brother
Sens was beginning to lose the argument, he said, "Well, boys, it is an article of
faith. Either you believe it or you don't. I can't prove it to you logically. It's not
a question of logic." His statement was greeted by a chorus of moans backed
up by scatterings of "Come on, brother."

"Granted," retorted Brother Sens, "sometimes it doesn't make sense to
believe. But there are other times when it makes even less sense not to believe.
Faith is a very strange thing. If you haven't got it, it's tough to get. And if you
have got it, it's tough to lose."

We could feel a "Brother Sens" story coming on. When he told a story,
everyone automatically gathered around the fireplace.

"I have a younger brother named Oliver," said Brother Sens. "Years ago,
when we were both very young, we got up early one Easter Sunday morning
and went around our yard, looking for the eggs that the Easter Bunny had hidden. Oliver was walking toward a small bush when, suddenly, a rabbit shot out
from behind the bush and bounded away. My little brother couldn't believe it.
But when he ran behind the bush there it was, an Easter egg. Oliver is now
sixty-four years old. Though all the years he's lived have carried evidence to the
contrary, Oliver still isn't quite sure about the Easter Bunny."

Brother Mandeau, my Religion teacher in senior year, was one of the few
who, every day, taught Religion to his Religion class. One morning Brother
Mandeau advised us about the truly desirable assets of a prospective dating
partner. He said that we should look for a girl whom we could respect, one

who dressed modestly and liked old people. "If you want to know what a girl is really like," said Brother Mandeau, "notice how she treats the other members of her family. That's where the true personality comes out. Don't be fooled by that plastic personality she shows you on dates."

Although we all knew that what Brother Mandeau said was true, I'm sure only the purest of souls among us ever followed his advice. It didn't seem like a very sane idea to go out with an ugly girl and, every time someone looked at her, jump to her defense by saying, "But you should see how she treats her little brother."

In the month of March, senior-year Religion teachers were required to spend at least one class talking about the facts of life. We wondered how Brother Mandeau, who blushed when he had to mention the Immaculate Conception, was going to achieve such a feat.

Since he was a History teacher, Brother Mandeau's classroom was equipped with numerous pull-down maps that were fastened to the walls above the blackboards. As we walked into his room one morning, we saw that all the maps had been completely pulled down. After prayers Brother Mandeau quickly walked past the maps, not even stopping as he gave each one a sharp tug that sent it scampering back up into its metal cylinder. As each map rolled up, it exposed the sexual information that had been written on the blackboard behind it. Brother Mandeau refused to look at any of us as he repeatedly yelled out, "No questions, no questions."

Although Religion classes at Bremmer provided only a trickle of water to help our consciences grow, we were, each year, subjected to a three-day downpour: our annual retreat.

A retreat is when you spend a number of days immersed in spiritual activities. During a retreat day, you attend Mass and other religious services such as the Stations of the Cross. You listen to sermons, which are often identified in the schedule as "conferences," do spiritual readings in the library, and endure a few meditation sessions, which consist of kneeling in the chapel for thirty minutes at a time.

The purpose of a retreat is to offer the individual a spiritual reprieve from the materialistic world he daily lives in. Although many do not, Catholics are encouraged to go on at least one retreat a year.

Some retreats, which run from Friday through Sunday afternoons and require staying overnight, are offered by various religious orders at their monasteries. Retreats are often held at parishes for those Catholics who can't or don't want to attend a retreat that requires boarding. A priest from a religious order will come to a parish and conduct the retreat during the evening hours of a particular week. Then there are school retreats, such as the ones that were given at Bremmer High School.

Retreats at Bremmer were no big thrill, but they certainly beat the alternative, three days of regular classes. When you came to school on the morning of a retreat day, you didn't have to worry about homework, surprise quizzes, getting jugged, or any of the other billions of bristles that threatened to stick you during an ordinary school day.

A retreat day contained a very exact schedule: 8:00 A.M., Mass; 9:00 A.M., Conference; 10:00 A.M. Meditation; 10:45 A.M., Stations of the Cross . . . You would walk into school and the retreat schedule would scoop you up and, like an assembly-line belt, automatically carry you through the day.

School retreats were like Holiday Inns. No matter where or when you found them, they were always the same. Even the stories the priests told at the conferences were the same. Two perennial favorites were the "God, this is Jimmy" story and the "Don't get in an accident with dirty pictures in your wallet" monologue.

I first heard the "God, this is Jimmy" story at a retreat that was given to my seventh-grade class.

"There was once a boy named Jimmy," the priest began. "He was an average child, just like any of you. The only thing that he did, that most of you probably never thought of doing, was that every day on his way to school he would step into his parish church, kneel down for a moment in one of the pews, and simply say, 'God, this is Jimmy.' Then he would go out and spend his day doing the same things that you do. He would attend school, play outside with his friends, and help his mother with work around the house. One day as he was crossing the street in front of the church on his way to giving his daily greeting to God, a car came out of nowhere and ran Jimmy over, killing him instantly. As Jimmy lay in the street, people rushed to his side. And do you know what those people heard coming from the sky as they knelt beside him?"

The room was silent. Even our breathing had shied away to a whisper so as not to interfere with the words that the priest was about to drop on us.

"Jimmy heard a voice say, 'Jimmy, this is God.' "

I was impressed. I really was. I planned, the very next morning, to apply its moral to my own life. I would step into church and whisper from the first pew, "God, this is Eddie." It never hurts to be on a first-name basis.

An hour later I was walking home with Timmy Heidi, whose words quickly pulverized my awe for the anecdote.

"That sure was a dumb story that Father Brennan told us this afternoon," Heidi said.

"Why do you say that?" I was hardly about to admit to Heidi that I had been duped.

"Let's just say that I never go in and say hello to God, okay?" said Heidi.

"Okay."

"What happens when I die? As my soul heads toward heaven and I yell out, 'God, this is Heidi,' what's He gonna yell back? *Who?* Some God. He's just like any other person who's in a position to screw you. You gotta brown nose."

At my junior-year retreat I heard the "God, this is Jimmy" story for the fifth time.

The "dirty pictures in the wallet" monologue was about this kid who also got run over by a car and ended up in the hospital with a skull fracture, two broken arms, and two broken legs. His biggest problem, however, was that when he got run over he had dirty pictures in his wallet. I first heard the story during my freshman-year retreat.

"Oh, the anguish that boy must have experienced," groaned the priest, "when his parents walked into that hospital room and he realized that they knew he was carrying around such disgusting pictures in his wallet. Being good parents, they eventually forgave him. But that kind of hurt, boys, a parent carries in his heart forever. Ah, the sorrow that must have filled his mother's mind. What his father must have thought of him. Can you imagine how that boy must have felt?"

We certainly could. It was a very squeamish story. The kind you didn't like to think about. Actually the only person I knew who carried dirty pictures around all the time was Felix Lindor. After he heard the talk, Felix took the dirty pictures out of his wallet and put them in an envelope along with a letter, which he stuck in his back pocket. The letter read: "Dear Charlie, I found these pictures in the science book you lent me. They are disgusting. If I were you, I'd tear them up. Signed: Felix Lindor."

The priest hinted that even if the kid had died, it would still have been a very embarrasing situation. Such a fact could hardly be deleted from the eulogy. "Johnny was a good student, was popular among both his teachers and his fellow classmates, was cheerful, kind, and considerate. He led an exemplary Christian life, except for the fact that when he died he had dirty pictures in his wallet."

The only student who relished retreats was Louie Schlang. Louie was thoroughly enchanted by the sound of his own voice. He loved to ask dumb questions. During regular school days he didn't often get the opportunity to serenade himself because his habit was too well known among the faculty. But our retreats were held by priests from various religious orders who came to Bremmer for only three days out of the year. For Louie, those retreat days were orgies of idiotic inquiries.

"Father, is it a sin to eat meat on Friday if I'm on a ship out in the ocean and we're crossing the date line, well, the front part of the boat is but I'm on the back part of the boat and I'm about to eat a hot dog, but it's not an all-meat hot dog, it's got a lot of filler . . ."

"Say, Father, if God is all-powerful, can He create a rock so big that He can't lift it Himself? But then, if He can't lift it, how can He be all-powerful?"

"Is it a sin to miss Mass on Sunday, Father, if when I get up I have a headache, not a big one just a small one, and I feel like I'm gonna throw my guts up, but when I take my temperature, I find I'm normal . . ."

It would have taken more than a 98.6 body temperature to make Louis Schlang normal.

We were only a few months away from graduation when we went on retreat in senior year. Convinced that many of us were going to walk straight from the graduation stage to the altar, the priests who conducted the retreat spent most of their time talking about marriage.

Father Blenzy, who was in charge of the retreat, gave the first talk. As expected, he spent the opening minutes trying to convince each of us that we probably had a religious vocation but were just refusing to listen to God's calling. That's the way it always went. Whenever priests, religious brothers, or nuns talked to you about what you were going to do with your life, they tried to convince you to do with it what they had done.

"But if you feel that you must get married," Father Blenzy continued, "that you absolutely need the release that marriage provides, then by all means, get married.

"Now there are, as you boys know," (we didn't) "three purposes of marriage, one primary and two secondary. Let's first talk about the two secondary purposes. The first secondary purpose is companionship. The other secondary purpose is the curbing of concupiscence."

None of us knew what "concupiscence" meant, but since it was preceded by "curbing" we knew it must have something to do with sex.

"The primary purpose of marriage," said Father Blenzy, "is, of course, children. That is why God has given us our sexual powers. In order that we may create, with His assistance, souls that may share with Him forever the joys of Heaven. Looked at in those terms, the marriage act is truly beautiful, truly holy. I knew one Catholic couple who confided to me that when they performed the marriage act, they say the rosary together. Isn't that beautiful?"

At the next conference there was a young married couple who were supposed to talk to us about their married life. They first told us about the things they did that annoyed one another. "You know what George does that bothers me? In the morning, he leaves the cap off the toothpaste." She followed up that remark with a few titters as if she had just told you something that was quite personal but at the same time very funny. A few school-spirit nuts tittered back at her. He said something about how she always wanted to watch hour-long television programs while he preferred half-hour shows.

The married couple then talked about the little things they did for one another. For instance, he'd get her flowers for no reason at all. She'd set up the morning newspaper for him on the breakfast table. That kind of stuff. They also said that they thought the marriage act was the most beautiful way of saying they loved each other and that, even if she wasn't in the mood, she was still willing to perform her marital duties.

I thought their entire act was putrid. Any two people who would stand up in front of a few hundred high school seniors and talk about their married life had to be crazy.

After the married couple finished, they asked if there were any questions. Not even Louie Schlang raised his hand. Who would want to ask two crazies a question?

I looked over at Felix Lindor. He wasn't going to ask it, but as he looked her over I could see the question slithering in his mind. "How often do you say the rosary together?"

During the last day of my senior-year retreat, small group conferences on a variety of topics were held in the classrooms. Tom Lanner, myself, and about twenty other guys were listening to Father Rinsbury tell us about Christ's trial before Pontius Pilate. Besides being a priest, Father Rinsbury was also an attorney. He was explaining to us the historical background and personality of Pontius Pilate, the political and legal options that were open to him, and why he acted as he did. It was all very interesting stuff we had never heard before.

Ernie Kogan, the center on the football team, was sitting in the last row. Ernie liked to sit in the front row but he had arrived late, just as we were all sitting down, so he didn't have any choice.

As Father Rinsbury spoke I could hear Ernie Kogan shuffling his feet under the desk. Whenever Ernie was in a place where he didn't feel comfortable, he started pacing, even if he was sitting down. Gradually the sound of Ernie's shuffling feet subsided.

Toward the end of the presentation Father Rinsbury became very dramatic. "As I've already told you, Pilate, who was the Roman governor, didn't care one way or the other about the Jews or this man Christ, who claimed to be their king. He just wanted to keep things quiet. If word got back to Rome that the Jews were raising a fuss, Pilate would be held responsible.

"There was a large crowd of Jews outside Pilate's palace demanding that Christ be crucified for claiming to be their king. But Pilate didn't believe that Christ had done anything to warrant crucifixion. To appease the crowd Pilate had Christ viciously whipped. The guards who inflicted the punishment also placed a crown of thorns on Christ's head. Afterward Pilate presented the brutally beaten Christ before the crowd. Pilate thought they would feel sorry for Christ and want Him released. But they didn't.

"Pilate stood before the crowd and spoke to them. 'I find no reason to condemn this man. I'm going to release Him.' But the crowd yelled back, 'Crucify Him, crucify Him.' 'Crucify Him yourselves,' Pilate replied. But the crowd persisted. 'We haven't the power; you must.' 'What?' said Pilate mockingly, 'crucify your king?' 'We have no king but Caesar,' the crowd replied. 'If you do not do this,' they shouted, 'you will not be a friend of Caesar's. Anyone who claims to be a king isn't a friend of Caesar's.'

"Pilate was getting scared. The Jews were implying that if he didn't have Christ executed, he'd be committing treason against Caesar. Pilate washed his hands before the crowd to show that Christ's death would be their doing and not his. Then Pilate gave the order, 'Crucify this Christ.' "

"The dirty sonofabitch."

It was Ernie Kogan's voice. His words froze Father Rinsbury's face. What a lousy time to try and be funny, I thought, as I, along with the others, spun my head around to stare at Ernie Kogan. It was then we saw that Ernie Kogan wasn't trying to be funny.

Uncomfortable because of all the unwanted attention he was receiving, Ernie began shuffling his feet again. Our heads turned back toward Father Rinsbury to see what he was going to do.

He stared at Ernie. "Thank you," he said, "for your act of faith." Then Father Rinsbury quietly continued.

# Martyrs

BY MICHAEL DORRIS

I lived to die. At any moment, the Red Chinese might sweep across the Pacific, through California, ravaging the continent until they reached Kentucky and surrounded Holy Spirit Church while terrified, hymn-singing parishioners cowered bravely within.

I was well aware of the Communists' ultimate goal: the ciborium, full of spare Eucharists, locked behind the carved golden door in the alcove at the center of the altar. Host-defilement was known to be a major motivator for nonbelievers of all stripes, and it had to be anticipated as adjunct to any invasion. The protection of sacred wafers, however, presented a problem for Defenders of the Faith because it entailed a tricky stipulation: with the exception of priests, consecrated hosts could only be manipulated or touched by the tongues of post–First Holy Communion persons (in the state of grace, naturally), and, to complicate matters even further, but one tiny disk could be consumed per capita per day.

What was a Catholic boy to do when at last the polished mahogany doors were battered down and enemy soldiers charged past the imported Italian marble holy water fonts and up the center aisle? I projected the ensuing scene as a vision reminiscent of Donald Duck's avaricious uncle cavorting with wild abandon in his money vault, except in this instance Scrooge was a *Peking* duck and each silver dollar was transformed into a miniature Body of Christ.

How to forestall this abomination without, in the process, committing a Mortal Sin by swallowing multiple wafers? Did the end justify the means? Could omnipotent God make a rock so big He couldn't lift it? In 1950s Irish-American Catholicism, paradox abounded.

We debated such philosophical topics in grade school, pausing even in the cafeteria over our sloppy joes and Jell-O. Timing, it seemed, played a key role—always implicated by a delicate system of checks and balances. Even when the intention was good, if the act was bad it was still a Sin, whether one realized it or not. There were fine-print rules governing almost everything: the recitation of the names (in proper sequence) "Jesus, Mary, and Joseph" was good for a 300-day commutation of one's eventual Purgatory sentence, *but only if they were vocalized.* Simply *thinking* a rote litany gained one no time at all (unless Communists were listening and would torture your parents if they overheard the magic words; under such circumstances, it was provisionally okay to simply mouth an invocation of the Holy Family without sound—unless there was a *deaf* Communist present who could lip-read, in which case . . . and so on and so forth).

You could sin by omission and commission, by desiring to do something bad you didn't actually do, or by begrudging something good you did. The Ten Commandments, in their various interpretations and subclauses, pretty much excluded all but a tightrope of permitted behavior toward your family, teachers, associates, and self, and God never, ever blinked or looked away in indulgent amusement. When I was nine—two years into the Age of Reason and therefore eternally, cumulatively responsible for every transgression—confessing my sins and doing Penance twice weekly hardly seemed often enough, the list of slips and slides was that long.

There was, joyfully, one surefire escape hatch, one soul-bleaching rinse that erased even the most persistent stains. All was absolutely forgiven and forgotten in the event that—even if positively stuffed with unleavened bread, even having at one time or another given Scandal to a Protestant by making a joke about a nun, even with a record as a prideful, self-abusing Friday hamburger-user—I managed to be persecuted for my Faith and perish in the process. Martyrdom, that just-like-new Baptism of Blood, automatically canceled all debits.

*Treasure Chest* magazine and the *Junior Catholic Messenger* offered a weekly parade of historical and virtually contemporary child saints who earned their wings through suffering. Maria Goretti succumbed intact to a pornographycrazed handyman. St. Martin was roasted on a spit rather than worship false gods. Father Brébeuf watched benignly while Iroquois tormentors ate his heart. St. Peter, even after thrice denying that he so much as knew the Lord ("Jesus *who?*"), ascended to heaven without detour after having been crucified upside down. Beheaded saints-to-be politely carried their own skulls to the graveyard, blessed their executioners with their final breaths, eschewed every "This is your last chance to dance naked before a Golden Calf statue" offer of reprieve. The message was clear: the road to Heaven is filled with bamboo spikes, and the fastest route is to run barefoot.

Okay: I believed. I was ready. Test me. I wore a scratchy Scapular against my bare skin and caused a rash on my chest. I did without—you name it: chocolate, pie, *I Love Lucy*—during Lent. I self-castigated, I regretted. I unfavorably compared my innate miserableness to every anti-Catholic reprobate from Attila the Hun to Henry VIII. I knelt on pebbles, gladly. Along with the rest of my family, I boycotted *Your Hit Parade* on television when one of its stars, the famously Catholic Gisele MacKenzie, got a divorce. A year or so later, we collectively stopped speaking to an old friend when she paid admission to see the "condemned" film *The Moon Is Blue*. I put up with, accepted, denied, prepared myself for the day the Communists underestimated my resolve. I was so ready I became impatient, then disappointed, then bored. The moment of truth passed and I was left unscathed, yet I yearned to be scathed! It was like training and stretching before a race, then never hearing the gun go off.

In spite of my ambitions, unlike Dominic Savio, the preteen role model saint who uttered the fateful phrase, "Death Rather Than Sin," and then conveniently died, I lived into the complexity of adulthood. The innocent right-and-wrong view of the world I had been offered by Sister Stanislaus Kostka shaded into layered ambiguity. Once removed from the regimen of Catholic-approved textbooks, issues that had once seemed simply religious blurred into politics, psychology (as in paranoia), and ethnocentric or misogynist bias. Like Adam and Eve, who, after eating of the Tree of Knowledge, lost their comfortable digs in Paradise, I found myself awash in a permanent state of unsureness—an emotion for which I had no preparation.

The popular survivor-saints in my grade school pantheon were hard to imagine emulating. St. Francis of Assisi talked to animals—and they answered! St. Theresa didn't eat anything but a daily host. St. Ann, an aged primipara, produced the Mother of God, while in the next generation St. Joseph remained on the sidelines while his wife, ever a virgin, gave birth to God Himself.

Without the drama of martyrdom, normal longevity—unless one possessed magic powers—seemed positively dull, an endless succession of Canaan conferences, compromise, toil without glory, and boring, predictable imperfection. Real life didn't hold a candle to old-fashioned Catholic boyhood, which, for me, had a swashbuckling kick, a dizzy aura of danger and flamboyance and possibility—provided that it didn't last too long.

# The Brooklyn Dodgers and the Catholic Church

### From: *Wait Till Next Year*

B Y  D O R I S  K E A R N S  G O O D W I N

⊕

My early years were happily governed by the dual calendars of the Brooklyn Dodgers and the Catholic Church. The final out of the last game of the World Series signaled the approach of winter, bringing baseball hibernation, relieved only by rumors of trades and reports of contract negotiations. Even before the buds had appeared on the trees of Rockville Centre, players had sloughed off their winter weight and prepared to reconvene for spring training, bringing the joyous return of the box score (whose existence my father had finally revealed). Excitement mounted as the team returned to Brooklyn for opening day, a day of limitless promise. As spring yielded to summer, the pennant race began to heat up, reaching a peak of intensity—of mingled hope and apprehension—during the sultry days of August, when the hopes of many teams were still alive. By mid-September, a chill in the air of shortening days, the scales began to tip, depressing the hopes of many teams. For fans of contending teams, however, like the Dodgers of my childhood, it was Indian summer, a glorious respite before the last out of the last game opened the door once more to winter.

Analogous to the seasonal cycles of baseball were the great festivals of the Catholic Church. A month before Christmas we hung the Advent wreath, and each week we lit one of the four candles that presaged the coming of the Christ child. The fulfillment of Christmas followed, symbolized by the decoration of our Christmas tree, the exchange of gifts, and the mystery and wonder of Midnight Mass. When I was five or six, I would lie awake in bed, listening as the thunder of church bells at midnight announced the coming of the Savior, and dream of the day I would be permitted to stay up late enough to accompany my sisters to Midnight Mass. When I was finally allowed to go, none of my imaginings prepared me for the splendor of the church, its marble altars bordered with garlands of white and red poinsettias and dotted with red flames from clusters of small white candles surrounding the central one that symbolized Christ, the Light of the World. My parents worried that I wouldn't last through the two-hour service, but the sight of the altar, the priests' gold vestments, the sounds of the Latin ritual, and the soaring choir music over-whelmed fatigue until long after the service was completed.

The last weeks of winter brought Ash Wednesday and the beginning of Lent, commemorating the period of Jesus' fast in the desert. We knelt before the priest, who traced in ash the sign of the cross on our foreheads. "Remember," the priest intoned, his thumb touching each brow, "that thou art dust and unto dust shalt thou return." How much nearer death seemed to me when I was a child, when, kneeling like millions of other children, I said the nightly prayer: "Now I lay me down to sleep, I pray the Lord my soul to keep. If I should die before I wake, I pray the Lord my soul to take." But symbols of death were more than matched by symbols of rebirth, renewal, and resurrec-tion, as the Lenten feast led up to Palm Sunday, marking the triumphal return of Jesus to Jerusalem. Holy Week—windows opening to the onrushing spring—continued through the solemnity of Holy Thursday and the deep mourning of Good Friday, when the church stood desolate and bare, its altar draped in black, its statues covered in purple, giving way to the joyful triumph of Easter Mass, when the church was bedecked in white lilies. As Easter had been preceded by forty days of sorrow, it was followed by fifty days of rejoic-ing, leading up to Whitsunday, the feast of the Pentecost, and the gift of the Holy Spirit. Through these seasonal festivals, so firmly embedded in the rou-tine of our lives, I developed a lasting appreciation of the role that pageantry, ritual, and symbolism play in tying together the past and the present.

I took great pride in the commanding beauty of my church, St. Agnes. Built in the thirties to resemble a fifteenth-century Gothic cathedral, St. Agnes was furnished with oak pews that could seat over twelve hundred people. Its luminous windows made of antique stained glass had been imported from England and Germany, and its bell tower, surmounted by an aluminum cross, was visible for miles. I regarded with awe the serene darkness of the interior, a vast clear space illuminated by the soft amber light of two dozen iron chande-liers, hanging in two rows on long chains from the vaulted ceiling. Like some-thing out of the Arthurian Legend, richly colored banners honoring the saints were mounted on lines of decorated poles projected from the side walls. These colorful lines converged at the sanctuary, with its white marble altar and its enormous crucifix suspended on chains from the canopy.

The scale of the church was the result of the vision of one man, Father Peter Quealy. He had arrived in Rockville Centre at the turn of the century, only two decades after six families had organized a tiny Roman Catholic parish and celebrated Mass in a blacksmith's shop. Under Father Quealy's inspired guidance, the pastorate increased to hundreds and then thousands, outgrowing two churches until the present St. Agnes was built, covering an entire block in the center of the village, with the church, rectory, convent, and a parochial school. When the foundation was laid in 1935, many thought Father Quealy's reach had exceeded his grasp, but in 1957 the church built on the scale of a cathedral actually became a cathedral: Pius XII announced that a new Catholic diocese, encompassing Nassau and Suffolk counties on Long Island, was to be formed out of the existing Brooklyn Diocese, with St. Agnes Church as its seat. By then Father Quealy's health was failing, but he lived to witness the celebratory Mass, attended by six hundred priests, one hundred monsignori, three archbishops, twenty-five bishops, and nine hundred nuns, at which Bishop Walter Kellenberg assumed the throne and officially made St. Agnes a cathedral.

•          •          •

When I was seven years old, my twin passions for the church and baseball collided. It was 1950, the year of my First Holy Communion. Every Wednesday afternoon at two-thirty, all Catholics who attended second grade in public school, as I did, were released early to attend the classes at St. Agnes that would prepare us for First Communion, admitting us into the congregation of the Catholic Church. Whereas the parochial-school students were allowed to receive their First Communion in the first grade, the rest of us had to wait an extra year, so that the nuns could compensate for all the rigorous hours of instruction that were lost. Our class was held in a dark room in the parochial school, the large map of the forty-eight states that adorned the back wall of our public-school room supplanted by a gallery of the saints. There was the infant St. Ambrose, on whose mouth a swarm of bees had settled, causing his elders to predict great oratorical gifts; St. Patrick, the apostle of Ireland, brandishing a staff as he expelled the serpent of sin and paganism from Ireland. My favorite saint was the Jesuit, Aloysius Gonzaga, the patron of youth, whose name my father had taken at his own confirmation, completing the full name I loved to say aloud—Michael Francis Aloysius Kearns.

Our teacher, Sister Marian, was a small Dominican nun who seemed ancient at the time but was probably in her fifties, with a gentle manner, a flowing white habit with a wimple pulled so tight her forehead was stretched smooth, and cheeks that bore such deep lines that the bottom and top of her face appeared the composite of two different people. Sister Marian introduced us to the text familiar to generations of Catholic schoolchildren: the blue-covered Baltimore Catechism with a silver Mary embossed on a constellation of silver stars. The catechism was organized around a series of questions and answers we had to memorize word for word to help us understand the meaning of what Christ had taught and, ultimately, to understand Christ Himself. "Who made us? God made us." "Who is God? God is the Supreme Being who made all things." "Why did God make us? God made us to show forth His goodness and to share with us His everlasting happiness in heaven." Although it was learned by rote, there was something uniquely satisfying about reciting both the questions and the answers. No matter how many questions we had to memorize, each question had a proper answer. The Catholic world was a stable place with an unambiguous line of authority and an absolute knowledge of right and wrong.

We learned to distinguish venial sins, which displeased our Lord, from the far more serious mortal sins, which took away the life of the soul. We memorized the three things that made a sin mortal: the thought or deed had to be grievously wrong; the sinner had to know it was grievously wrong; and the sinner had to consent fully to it. Clearly, King Herod had committed a mortal sin when, intending to kill the Messiah, he killed all the boys in Judea who were two years old or less. Lest we feel too far removed from such a horrendous deed, we were told that those who committed venial sins without remorse when they were young would grow up to commit much larger sins, losing their souls in the same way that Herod did.

Every Tuesday night, the day before my class in religious instruction, my mother would drill me on the weekly lesson. She never betrayed the slightest impatience, and she made it fun by playing games with me. She held up playing cards numbered one through seven for the seven gifts of the Holy Ghost—wisdom, understanding, counsel, fortitude, knowledge, piety, and fear of the Lord—placing the appropriate card on the table as I recalled each one. In similar fashion, I learned the three theological virtues, the ten commandments, and the seven sacraments. And when I had to memorize various prayers—the Our Father, the Hail Mary, and the Apostles' Creed—she put a glass of milk and a box of Oreo cookies on the table so I could savor my success at the completion of each prayer.

In class, Sister Marian explored each commandment with us in fuller detail. To understand the eighth commandment—"Thou shalt not bear false witness against thy neighbor"—we were told to imagine emptying a feather pillow from the roof of our house, then trying to pick up every feather. If it seemed impossible for us to imagine gathering all the feathers back into the pillow, Sister explained, "so would you never be able to get the rumor you told about someone back from everyone who heard it."

My imagination was kindled by the concept of baptism. We learned that we were all born with souls that were dead in original sin under the power of the devil, but that baptism gave us new life and freed us from Satan's grasp.

Without baptism, one could not receive any of the other sacraments or go to heaven. The part that particularly aroused me, however, was the thought that, if an unbaptized person was dying, and no priest was present, it was up to us—i.e., me—to perform the sacrament by pouring ordinary water on the forehead of the dying person and saying aloud: "I baptize thee in the name of the Father, and of the Son, and of the Holy Ghost." More than once, I used my unbaptized doll to practice the sacrament of baptism. I would make her comfortable on my pillow, run into the bathroom directly across the hall, fill a plastic cup with water, and very solemnly launch her toward salvation.

Sister Marian told us stories about the early Christian martyrs who were willing, sometimes even eager, to die for their faith when put to the test by the evil Roman emperor, Nero. After a great fire destroyed much of Rome six decades after Christ, Nero's people began to suspect that he had started the fire himself to clear a site for his proposed "Golden House" and had celebrated the conflagration on his fiddle. To deflect the people's wrath, he made the Christians of Rome his scapegoats, sending them into the jaws of lions if they insisted on professing their Christian faith. Many a night I lay awake worrying whether I might lack courage to die for my faith, fearing that when the test came I would choose instead to live. Lions began populating my dreams, until visits to the Bronx Zoo found me standing in front of the lion's cage, whispering frantically to the somnolent, tawny beast behind the bars in hopes that, if ever I were sent as a martyr to the lions' den, my new friend would testify to his fellow lions that I was a good person. Evading the terrible choice, I could exhibit courage, affirm my faith, and still manage to survive.

. . .

So rich were the traditions and the liturgy of my church that I could not imagine being anything other than Catholic. Though there were Jews and Protestants on our block—the Lubars and the Barthas were Jewish, the Friedles and the Greenes Protestant—I knew almost nothing about these other religions. I could not describe what distinguished an Orthodox Jew from a Reform Jew, or say what made someone a Methodist rather than a Presbyterian or Episcopalian. I understood that our neighbors were devoted to their religions, lighting Sabbath candles on Friday or attending services Saturday or Sunday. Their church or synagogue was central to their social lives. The Friedles were very active in the Mr. and Mrs. Club at the Congregational church, which sponsored dances, pot-luck dinners, and card-playing evenings, and their children attended Sunday school every week. I knew that the Lubars were active in their temple and that the Greenes, who had been the Greenbergs before converting to Protestantism, were equally involved in their church. Indeed, in my neighborhood, everyone seemed to be deeply involved in one religion or another. Although I observed the fellowship that other religions provided, I had no inkling of what beliefs they inculcated in their followers. We were taught only that these people were non-Catholics and that we should not read their literature or inquire about their beliefs. Furthermore, it was, we thought, a grievous sin for us to set foot in one of their churches or synagogues.

It was this last admonition that produced my first spiritual crisis. In early February 1950, our newspaper, the *Long Island News and Owl,* reported that Dodger catcher Roy Campanella was coming to Rockville Centre. He planned to speak at a benefit for the local black church, then under construction, the Shiloh Baptist Church. The program was to be held in the Church of the Ascension, an Episcopal church one block from St. Agnes.

The son of an Italian American father and an African American mother, Campanella had joined the Baltimore Elite Giants, one of the great teams in the Negro League, when he was only fifteen. In short order, his skill in calling pitches, his ability to fathom the vulnerability of an opposing hitter, his strong arm, his prowess at the plate, and his endurance became legendary. He once caught four games in a single day: a twin bill in Cincinnati on a Sunday afternoon, followed by a bus ride to Middletown, Ohio, and another doubleheader that evening. Unlike Jackie Robinson, who considered his experience in the Negro League demeaning, Campanella claimed to have thoroughly enjoyed his years in black baseball. Less combative and more conciliatory than Robinson, Campanella repeatedly said that he thought of himself as a ballplayer, not a pioneer; that, when he was catching or hitting, he focused only on what the pitcher was throwing, not the color of his opponent. Since his rookie season with the Dodgers in 1948, he had established himself unequivocally as the best catcher in the National League. In 1949 he led all catchers with a .287 batting average, twenty-two doubles, and twenty-two home runs.

I couldn't wait to tell my father that his favorite player would be coming to our town, so he would get tickets and take me with him. I begged my mother to take me to the train station so I could tell my father the dramatic news as soon as he stepped off the platform. As our car passed St. Agnes on the way to the station, however, it dawned on me that Campanella was scheduled to speak in the *Episcopal* church. "Oh, no!" I said. "It can't be." "What?" my mother asked. Close to tears, I announced that there was no hope of my going after all, since I was forbidden to set foot in the Episcopal church. Campanella was coming to my town and I could not even go to see him. To my surprise, my mother simply said, "Well, let's see, let's wait and talk to Daddy." When I explained the dilemma to my father, he said that he understood the church's prohibition against participating in the service of another church, but he didn't really believe it extended to attending a lecture by a baseball player in the parish hall. He was certain it would be proper for us to go and would get the tickets the following day.

Reassured, I put my qualms aside until the big night arrived and the moment came to cross the threshold of the white clapboard church. A sudden terror took possession of me, and my knees began to tremble. Fearing that we would be struck dead in retaliation for our act of defiance, I squeezed my body against my father and let his momentum carry me past the door, through the sanctuary, and into the parish hall. At first, I tried to keep my eyes on the ground, but I soon found myself surveying the simple altar, small windows, and plain wooden pews, so much less ornate and imposing than ours. A podium had been set up in the hall with about 150 folding chairs, and we were lucky enough to find seats in the second row.

The program opened with choral singing, which subsided as the black Baptist minister, Reverend Morgan Days, came forward to introduce the squat, powerful Campanella, dressed in a black shirt and a light jacket with broad lapels. His topic was not baseball, but "Delinquency and Sportsmanship." Nonetheless, I tried to absorb every word. Children, he argued, were not born with prejudice but were infected with it by their elders. The only way to combat this cycle of bigotry was to bring kids of different races together early on in social and recreational programs. He had a surprisingly squeaky voice for a powerful-looking man, but his message rang with such conviction that he received a standing ovation. When his presentation ended, Campanella stood around for half an hour shaking hands with everyone. There were a dozen things I wanted to say, but when he turned and took my hand, I managed only to thank him for being a Dodger and for coming to our town. The warmth of his broad smile was all I needed to know that this was a night I would never forget.

My earlier fear returned, however, as I climbed into bed that night. The warnings of the nuns tumbled through my head, convincing me that I had traded the life of my everlasting soul for the joy of one glorious night when I held Roy Campanella's strong hand in a forbidden church. Jumping out of bed, I got down on my knees and repeated every prayer I could remember, in the hope that each would wipe away part of the stain that the Episcopal church had left on my soul. I was distracted in school the following day, and again that night had difficulty falling asleep. It was a Friday night, and my parents were playing bridge with three other couples in the dining room, so I could not run downstairs and curl up on the porch sofa, as I sometimes did when I could not fall asleep.

I must have dozed off, because the long-drawn-out squeal of a siren awakened me. Three times the siren wailed, paused, then started again, summoning members of the volunteer fire department. I ran downstairs to find my worried parents and their friends. "They're calling *all* the surrounding towns!" my father exclaimed, listening to the pattern of the alarm. "Not just Rockville Centre," said my mother. At that moment, my sister Jeanne ran into the house with her friends. "There's been an awful train wreck!" she announced, breathless. "Two trains—it's gruesome!" Shaking, she burst into tears. We found out from her friends that they had followed the crowd to the station after a basketball game at the high school, but the scene was so appalling that they had to turn around and come home. My parents and their friends debated whether they should go into town; I remember my mother remarking that it was ghoulish to be a spectator to misery and unable to do anything about it.

As I eavesdropped, I began to discern in this calamity an opportunity for my own redemption. If there were no priests present, if I could locate a dying person and baptize him "in the name of the Father, and of the Son, and of the Holy Ghost," thus granting his entrance to heaven, I would earn considerable points toward purging my sin. I grabbed my coat and slipped undetected out the front door while my parents were still absorbed by the catastrophic news. Although it was cold and dark, I wasn't afraid as I set forth on the familiar route to my grammar school, knowing the train station was in the same direction. Once I rounded the corner at Brower, the pitch-darkness scared me and I considered returning home, but just then one of my sister's friends offered me a ride, and soon we were joined by hundreds of people, all moving in the same direction. Emergency floodlights and car headlights leached the color from faces as the crowd surged forward. My heart hammered with excitement. I was ready. Though I had no water to pour on the forehead of my convert, I figured I could find some clean snow that would serve the same purpose.

My zeal gave way to horror as I approached the station. The fitful lights picked out people huddled in shock and misery, bandaged heads and limbs, men hustling with difficulty up the embankment carrying a stretcher on which lay a motionless blanketed body. I fought the impulse to flee. Pushing my way toward the tracks, I was small enough to maneuver through the immense crowd that had gathered around the carnage.

It was the worst wreck to date in the history of the Long Island Rail Road, a head-on collision of two trains, one eastbound for Babylon, the other westbound for New York. The collision occurred on a short temporary stretch of single track set up to run trains in both directions while a construction project was under way. The engineer of the eastbound train had inexplicably failed to heed a stop signal and plowed straight into the oncoming train. Most of the casualties were from the front cars on both trains, which were split down the middle by the force of the collision. "It looked like a battlefield," one policeman said later. "I never heard such screams. I'll hear them till I die."

More than forty doctors were at the scene, some still dressed in the tuxedos they had worn to a big event at the local hospital. It was hard to see at first through the haze of the blue light from the acetylene torches used to cut away the steel that was trapping bodies inside the cars. Scores of volunteer firemen aided the doctors in amputations performed by flashlight with only local anesthesia.

Ambulances arrived from as far away as twenty miles. In the glare of their floodlights, I saw at once that I wasn't needed. A half-dozen priests were moving through the wreckage, bending down to minister to those in pain, giving last rites, providing comfort to stricken relatives who had converged on the scene. This grotesque and terrifying scene was not the one I had rehearsed with my doll propped up on my pillow. My missionary theatrics completely vanished. My pretensions suddenly seemed ugly and absurd, and I longed for my orderly bedroom, for my glass cabinet of dolls and the set of Bobbsey Twins books beside my bed. I turned away and started home, running as fast as I could. Quietly, I let myself in through the front door, tiptoed carefully upstairs so as not to disturb the conversation of my parents and their guests in the dining room, put my coat under my bed, and fell into a troubled sleep.

The next morning, the collision was the talk of the village. Large headlines and photographs of the wreckage covered the front pages of the newspapers, along with a list of the twenty-nine people who had died. Obsessively, I tried to read each story. I repeated the names of the dead with grim curiosity: John Weeks, thirty, a graduate of Yale and an editor of *Time;* Harry Shedd 3d, a senior at Harvard who had temporarily suspended his studies to work at Simon & Schuster; Jefferson Allen, twenty-four, a glass-blower killed along with his father, Charles; and Martin Steel, thirty-one, a veteran of nine campaigns in Italy and Germany during the Second World War. Their concise biographies seemed disconnected from the frightful scene that filled my mind. Images of mangled bodies pursued me, and every time I thought of that night, I squeezed back tears. Nor could I explain my inordinate fixation with the horrible night to my parents. Not only had I sneaked out of the house in the middle of the night, but I had made myself something they detested: a spectator to misery. My secret heaped yet another sin on my already endangered soul.

# PART V

# FAiTH

## AND

# FANTΔSY

*A Catholic Imagination*

# Introduction

Fiction is the province of the storyteller, and Christianity has always been rich in storytelling—not just parables and Bible stories, but legends and miracle tales as well. Medieval mystery plays have given way to Christmas pageants, the yearly ritual of any Catholic grammar school or confraternity group worth its salt. Bible stories and Gospel chronicles have been reworked on the big screen and on the printed pages, and the lives of the apostles have been "fictionalized" in such memorable epics as Lloyd C. Douglas's *The Robe* (dramatizing the effect that Christ's crucifixion robe has on one of the centurions charged with executing him) and Taylor Caldwell's *Great Lion of God* (about the conversion of St. Paul from persecutor to apostle), and who can make it through Lent or Advent without a viewing of *King of Kings* or *The Greatest Story Ever Told?* One is drawn to Morris West's fictional account based in fact on the election of the first Slavic pope in *The Shoes of the Fisherman,* where a fictional character is used to illuminate the innermost workings of the Vatican.

But fiction writers are not limited in their scope to telling, or more precisely retelling, tales of faith, as our ancestors were. Just as the Kingdom of God is one of Mystery and the Fantastic (no matter how well documented in the works of Augustine and Aquinas) and far beyond the true ken of mortal man, the imagination it can inspire is equally unlimited.

The actual designation of what a Catholic writer is (or at least for the purposes of this section a Catholic fiction writer) is by necessity vague. Two of the noted men of letters whose nonfiction appears elsewhere in this book have also successfully dabbled in the fictional realm, and they and their work can be used to more fully illustrate the expansiveness of the designation. Noted theological scholar Father Andrew M. Greeley has authored numerous novels in a wide variety of genres ranging from historical romance to international thriller to mystery to fantasy and science fiction. In addition to providing his reader with a rollicking good read, the good father also uses his craft to illustrate to the laity what used to be thought of as a sermon or more simply a moral. Sometimes it is a story of a priest struggling with his faith, or perhaps a procedural mystery that doubles as a morality tale, or even an angelic visitation that helps the faithful maintain their path . . . but in all cases it is some ele-ment of the Catholic faith upon which all plot and characters must turn. At the other end of the spectrum is the noted man of letters and political pundit William F. Buckley Jr. and his Blackford Oakes series of spy novels. Curiously, the main character of Oakes, an early agent of Allen Dulles before the CIA was up and ready, appears to all practical purposes to be Anglican, and the nov-els themselves do not venture into the realms of church and state relations and matters of theological import.

This noted, Buckley's novels are quite simply spy stories (exceptionally good and entertaining ones at that). They do not illustrate doctrine or dogma, theological crises of faith and morality, or any of the things that form the centers of the Greeley entertainments—yet the author's Catholicism comes shining through, making these works and the author himself a clear brother in fiction with the good Father Greeley.

All of the pieces contained within the following section pretty much fall between the two extremes that are illustrated by Greeley and Buckley. Roman Catholic dogma is neither as blatantly focal as in the Greeley nor as tangetially incidental as in the Buckley. In some cases the pieces illustrate a scene out of Catholic life as a backdrop (as in several popular mystery series) or as a focus, whether pertaining to the life (day-to-day or career) of a member of the clergy or perhaps to a member of a parish or even to one who has fallen away from the Church but maintains his memories and—to a certain extent—his faith (that class of Catholic referred to by theologians and sociologists alike as being "lapsed"). Sometimes in these works of fiction, members of the clergy are called upon to do double duty, sometimes as a detective, sometimes as a scientist, and in one case as quite literally a vanquisher of ultimate evils, yet a careful reexamination of their roles might merely suggest that they are simply fulfilling their priestly duties to their greatest extent.

After the decadent revolutions of the sixties, there was a common fallacy that all traditional religion, let alone Roman Catholicism, had fallen out of fashion and had become the purview of old fogies, neurotics, and "scary peo-ple" (like the poor demented fellow in James Leo Herlihy), but this belief, and/or any evidence to its validity, quickly went the way of the Nehru jacket. Nowhere is this more evident than in the realm of fiction, where two novels, one published in the late sixties, the other published in the mid-seventies, each dealt with crucial Catholic issues within the confines of commercial fiction; each went on to become one of the bestselling novels in publishing history. Even more blatantly, both novels take as their title specific role-designations within both the Catholic faith and the hierarchal Catholic Church itself.

Perhaps the most effective works of Catholic fictioneering are the most subtle, where themes and details embroider Catholicism into the fabric of the storytelling in a way that may or may not be the focus of the plot itself. By following this maxim it becomes obvious that it would be unnecessary for Buckley's spy, Blackford Oakes, to be a Roman Catholic at all in order for the books themselves to be Catholic. Likewise, the Catholic clergy are not a necessary part of the fictional world portrayed within Catholic fiction. Obviously they exist in "that world," but their presence need not be blatantly mentioned on the printed page, as numerous events of a character's "real life in that world" are also overlooked in favor of the necessary economy of time and storytelling. Furthermore, one must remember that in addition to serving as nuns and priests, these members of God's chosen on Earth are also normal men and women who can be portrayed with or without vestments and habits, as the laity is just as important as the clergy in making the Church work.

There are obviously no clear-cut models to follow. I dare say that authors do not usually sit down to "write a Catholic piece of fiction," as such labels are usually thrust upon the works by others who feel the need to differentiate a given work in a given way. Likewise, it is entirely possible that there can exist a clear piece of Catholic fiction that might be authored by a non-Catholic or even an atheist (as I remember a certain holiday mystery play that was authored by existentialist Jean-Paul Sartre at the behest of a Catholic fellow concentration camp inmate of his during World War II who just happened to be a priest). Probably this is a genre best defined, like most genres, with an active tendency toward inclusion rather than exclusion. A partial listing of such elements/motifs/aspects would include obviously Catholic dogma, as well as acts of both faith and doubt. Theological matters of history beg for inclusion as well as metaphoric depictions of Christ and his works (the term "Christ figure" having already been overly watered down by countless overuse in academia and other realms of criticism). Yet even these designations are insufficient, as Catholic fictioneering can include reactive works that seem to illustrate/support an opposing view, while also managing to—"between the lines"—support the Catholic view (again I am drawn to refer to Herlihy's despairing denizens of Times Square in *Midnight Cowboy,* where one nut's ravings in reality express hope for redemption and salvation, or perhaps Greene's noble sinners in *The Heart of the Matter* and *The Power and the Glory).*

A liberal might go so far as to include *A Tale of Two Cities* as a Catholic work (after all, isn't the alcoholic lawyer, Sidney Carton, emulating the Son of God in his actions when he decides to die in the place of one of his brethren?), but such extrapolations eventually become just silly.

The maxim "you know it when you see it" is probably best. It neither limits the field nor includes all the universe. The characters, qualities, rifts, and innovations are as infinite as the universe, and the variety available is only as limited as the extent to which an individual's soul and faith might soar.

# The Curate

From: *The Cardinal*

BY  HENRY  MORTON  ROBINSON

⊕

With feast, fast, and changing color of vestments, the ecclesiastical year wore on. September brought crisper weather and the Nativity of Our Blessed Lady. October slipped past in an ocher haze: All Souls' Day trod upon the eve of All Saints'; the long Pentecostal cycle drew to a close, and the blessed season of Advent began. With purple vestments the coming of the Infant was celebrated—the beginning of a new cycle of joy to the world, and the Incarnation of new hope for man.

How frail that hope seemed under the assault of war! From the Baltic to the Mediterranean, men faced each other at bayonet length. In Flanders, the poppy fields ran red before their season; in the Masurian Lakes, armies perished. The trenches grew longer; the deadlock of Europe dragged on.

In blood-red vestments, on December 26, Stephen celebrated the feast of his name saint, Stephen the first martyr. The Epistle for the day recounted the age-old story of that earlier Stephen who, full of grace and fortitude, saw the heavens open and the Son of Man standing on the right hand of God. But even in that younger age, when the personal splendor of Christ still illuminated the world, men could not sustain the vision. They ran violently upon Stephen, stoned him to death. He fell asleep in the Lord, forgiving his persecutors in words of loving severity. And then, from the Gospel, Father Stephen read Christ's lament: *"How often would I have gathered together thy children, as the hen gathereth her chickens under her wings, and thou wouldest not?"*

Smiling at the homely tenderness of the hen-and-chicken simile, Stephen was unvesting after Mass, when young Jeremy Splaine came up. Jeremy had become Stephen's favorite altar boy. Nothing clownish these days about Jeremy's handling of the Book and bells. He was a little master of liturgy now, and a daily joy to Stephen at early-morning Mass.

There was a troubled query in Jeremy's blue eyes, and one of them was black. "Father," he began, "is it true like it says in the Collect for today that we should love even our enemies?"

"That's what it says, Jemmy."

"Does that mean I ought to love some Episcopal kids that make fun of the skates my father gave me for Christmas?"

"I think it includes Episcopalians, Jem. But why should anyone make fun of your skates?"

"Because they've got straps," said Jemmy.

"And what," inquired Steve, "do other skates have?"

Jemmy burst forth. "These sissy Episcopals have aluminum skates that fasten right onto their shoes. The blades are hollow—they go like blazes. Well, yesterday afternoon me and some other altar boys went up to Spot Pond to play hockey, and these St. Jude kids—they've got a choir team—began to laugh at my skate straps . . ."

"That got your Irish up, eh?"

"It sure did. But I came right back at them. 'My skates ain't screwed onto my shoes,' I said, 'but me and my brother and Dave Foley here, we'll beat you playing hockey.' "

"You played them?"

"Yeh, we played them all right, Father."

"And," suggested Steve, "they beat the pants off you. Those St. Jude sissies skated all around St. Margaret's tough guys?"

Jeremy Splaine nodded. "They goose-egged us, fourteen–nothing."

Stephen pretended to mull over the tragedy. "Did you have a little disagreement afterwards?"

"Well, we sort of threw snowballs"—Jeremy hung his head—"with rocks inside."

Still stoning each other, thought Stephen. Aloud he said, "Fourteen–nothing is quite a trimming. Still, it's not a matter for a religious war. Seems to me that what St. Margaret's needs is a little coaching."

"Yeh, I guess we could use some, Father. Dr. Lethbridge, the Episcopal minister, coaches *his* kids."

The Groton touch. "Well," said Stephen, "I haven't been on skates for four or five years. But when I played forward for Holy Cross—"

"You played for Holy Cross! Geez, Father. I mean gee, Father—would you coach us?"

"I'd do anything to back up that Collect for St. Stephen's Day. Get your gang up at Spot Pond this afternoon at three-thirty. I'll be there with skates on."

The next month was one of the happiest times in Stephen Fermoyle's priesthood. Full of grace and fortitude, he did great wonders among the skaters of St. Margaret's. He showed them how to nurse a puck across the ice in the crook of a hockey stick, how to pass the hard-rubber disk in team play from man to man instead of dashing down the pond with it alone. The boys took on style—but no amount of style could keep their cheap strap skates from falling off at critical times. Stephen dreamed of fitting out his squad with hollow-tubed shoe skates; he priced these desirable items at Troland's Sport Shop, and found that six pairs of shoe skates would stand him two weeks' salary. Whereupon he called up Cornelius J. Deegan and said to that knightly gentleman:

"Corny, I need thirty dollars to buy shoe skates for six little hockey-playing demons."

"Shoe skates, is it? When your dad and me were boys, we slid across Liffey ice on the seat of our pants."

"I know, Corny. But my altar boys are playing the Episcopal hockey team."

"Episcopals!" exploded Corny. "Why didn't you say so in the first place?"

The next day St. Margaret's swarmed onto the ice in aluminum shoe skates, while the Knight of St. Sylvester stamped up and down the edge of the pond warming himself with the fire of Irish pride. The ragged jackets of Stephen's boys troubled Corny. "You'll be needing sweaters with a big gold ST. M on the breast of each and every one," he burst out—and straightway the team had sweaters.

"Arrange the game, Jemmy," said Stephen, after two weeks of practice. "St. Margaret's as ready as she'll ever be."

The game was played on a day of iron New England cold. Sharp skates rang against blue ice as hard-muscled boys, inheritors of the world's toughest tradition of play, struggled against each other. It was strictly a North American clash; as Stephen watched the two teams play he knew that no Greek or Italian boys had ever moved so rapidly or with equal grace. With the score 6–6 and a minute to play, Stephen saw Jeremy Splaine snatch the puck from a scuffle of hockey sticks and streak down the pond like a zigzag wind. But now the St. Jude captain, a long-shanked blond youth, shot in obliquely, hooked the puck away from Jemmy, and was off toward St. Margaret's goal for a heartbreaking score.

Episcopals, 7; Catholics, 6.

But no religious war broke out. When the game was over, Jeremy Splaine shook hands with the St. Jude captain. Even Corny Deegan, setting up hot chocolates for both teams at Morgan's Drug Store, had to admit that the Protestant lads had an honest bit of an edge somehow.

Dog-tired when he went to bed that night, Stephen turned back the pages of his Missal to the Gospel of St. Stephen's Day. *"How often,"* he read, *"would I have gathered together thy children, as the hen gathereth her chickens under her wings, and thou wouldest not?"*

Would it ever be otherwise? Would men one day drop the stones of hatred, forget the names of sect and nationality, and join in praising one Name forever and that Name alone? Stephen Fermoyle doubted that they ever would, but the last image in his mind before he fell asleep was that of a red-cheeked Jeremy Splaine extending his hand in a sportsman's embrace to the St. Jude hockey captain.

# The Presence of Grace

From: *The Presence of Grace*

BY J. F. POWERS

O n a fine Sunday morning in June, Father Fabre opened the announce-
ment book to familiarize himself with the names of the deceased in the
parish for whom Masses would be offered in the coming week, and came upon
a letter from the chancery office. The letter, dated December, dealt with the
Legion of Decency pledge which should have been administered to the people at that time. Evidently Father Fabre was supposed to read it at the nine-
thirty and eleven o'clock Masses that morning. He went to look for the pastor.

Father Fabre, ordained not quite a year, had his hands full at Trinity. It
wasn't a well-run parish. The pastor was a hard man to interest in a problem.
They saw each other at meals. Father Fabre had been inside the pastor's bedroom, the seat of all his inactivity, only once; Miss Burke, the housekeeper,
never. The press of things was very great in the pastor's room, statues,
candlesticks, cases of sacramental wine, bales of pious literature and outdated
collection envelopes, two stray pews and a prie-dieu, the implements and furniture of his calling. There was a large table-model radio in his bed, and he
obviously slept and made the bed around it. That was about it.

Father Fabre found the pastor in the dining room. "Little late for this, isn't
it?" he said. He held out the letter which had wintered in the pastor's room.

"Don't watch me eat," said the pastor, a graying dormouse. He had had
the six-thirty and eight o'clocks, and was breaking his fast—not very well,
Father Fabre thought, still trying to see what was in the bowl. Shredded wheat
*and* oatmeal? Something he'd made himself? Not necessarily. Miss Burke could
make dishes like that.

The pastor shifted into a sidesaddle position, bending one of his narrow
shoulders over the bowl, obstructing the curate's view.

Father Fabre considered the letter in his *hand. . . . immoral motion pictures /*

272

*demoralizing television / indecent plays / vulgar radio programs / pernicious books / vicious papers and periodicals / degrading dance halls / and unwholesome taverns* . . . Was this the mind, the tongue of the Church? "Little late for this, isn't it?"

"No."

"I thought we were supposed to give it a long time ago." On the Sunday within the Octave of the Immaculate Conception, in fact. On that day, Trinity, pledgeless, had been unique among the churches of the diocese—so he'd bragged to friends, curates who were unhappy about the pledge, as he was, and he hadn't really blamed them for what they'd said out of envy, that it had been his duty to repair the omission at his Masses. "Weren't we?"

"No."

*"No?"*

The dormouse shook his head a half inch. The spoon in his right hand was a precision instrument, scraping up the last of whatever had filled the bowl. Grain.

"I don't feel right about this," Father Fabre said, going away with the letter. He went to the sacristy to vest for the nine-thirty, talking to himself. It *was* a little late for the pledge. *No.* The Sunday within the Octave *had* been the day for it. *No.*

The white fiddleback chasuble he was putting on had been spoiled on Christmas. He'd been vesting, as now, when the pastor, writing out a Mass card for a parishioner, had flicked his pen at the floor to get the ink flowing. Father Fabre had called his attention to the ink spots on the chasuble. " 'S not ink," he'd said. Asked what it was, he'd said, " 'S not ink," and that was all he'd say. For a time, after that, Father Fabre wondered if the pastor's pen could contain some new kind of writing fluid—not ink—and thought perhaps the spots would disappear. The spots, the *'s not ink* spots, were still there. But a recent incident seemed to explain the pastor's odd denials. "Not a ball point, is it?" he'd said to Father Fabre, who was about to fill his fountain pen from the big bottle in the office. *"No,* Father," said Father Fabre, presenting his pen for inspection. "Takes ink," said the pastor. *"Yes,* Father." The pastor pointed to the big bottle from which Father Fabre customarily filled his pen, and said, "Why don't you try that?" "Say, that's an idea," said Father Fabre, going the pastor one better. "Better go and flush your pen with water first," said the pastor. And the funny part was that Father Fabre had gone and flushed his pen before filling it from the big bottle that time. "I think you'll like *that,*" said the pastor. *That* was *Quink.* The dormouse had the casuist's gift, and more.

He escaped much of man's fate. Instead of arguing his way out of a jam, or confessing himself in error, the pastor simply denied everything. It was simple—as simple as when he, as priest, changed the bread and wine into the body and blood of Christ. But he had no power from his priesthood to deny the undeniable, for instance that he'd spoiled a good chasuble. When he said " 'S not ink," nothing was changed. He could really slow you up, though, if you were inclined to disagree with him and to be rational about it.

When the pastor entered the sacristy before the nine-thirty, Father Fabre was ready for him. "Father," he said, "I can't give this pledge in conscience—not as it's given in some parishes. I can't ask the people to rise as a body and raise their right hands, to repeat after me words which many of them either don't understand the full meaning of, or don't mean to abide by. I don't see anything *wrong* with giving it to those who mean to keep it." He'd wrangled against the pledge in the seminary. If it was "not an oath," as some maintained, wasn't it administered by a priest in church, and didn't it cheapen the clergy to participate in such a ceremony, and one which many merely paid lip service to? Didn't the chancery use the word "invite" and wasn't "demand" the word for the way the thing was rammed through in some parishes? Couldn't outsiders, with some justice, call the whole procedure totalitarian? What *did* Rome think of it? Wasn't it a concession to the rather *different* tone in America, a pacifier?

But the pastor had gone, saying, "Just so you give it."

Father Fabre got behind his servers and started them moving toward the altar. He saw the pastor in front of a battery of vigil lights, picking up the burned matches. Parishioners who had used them would be surprised to know that the pastor blew out all the lights after the last Mass. "Fire hazard," he'd said, caught in the act.

.        .        .

Before the eleven o'clock, after resting a few minutes between Masses in his room, he went to the bathroom and called down the laundry chute to Miss Burke in the kitchen. "Don't set a place for me. I'm invited out for dinner." He stood ready at the chute to cut her off but heard only a sigh and something about the pastor having said the same thing. He hadn't expected to get away with it so easily. They were having another critical period, and it was necessary, as before, to stand up to her. "I hope I let you know soon enough," he said. She should be happy, with them both gone. She wouldn't have to cook at all. And he was doing her the honor of pretending that she planned their meals ahead.

"Father!"

"Yes, Miss Burke."

"Is it Mrs. Mathers' you're going to?"

He delayed his reply in the hope that she'd see the impertinence of the question, and when this should have been accomplished, he said, "I hope I let you know in time."

He heard the little door slam at the other end of the chute. Then, as always in time of stress, she was speaking intimately to friendly spirits who, of course, weren't there, and then wailing like the wind. "Sure she was puttin' it around she'd have him over! But we none of us"—by which Father Fabre assumed she meant the Altar and Rosary Society—"thought he'd go *there!* Oh, Lord!"

He'd lost the first fall to the pastor, but he'd thrown Miss Burke.

Going downstairs, he heard the coin machines start up in the pastor's room, the tambourines of the separator, the castanets of the counter. The pastor was getting an early start on the day's collections. He wore a green visor in his room and worked under fluorescent tubes. Sometimes he worked a night shift. It was like a war plant, his room, except that no help was wanted. The pastor lived to himself, in a half-light.

In the hallway downstairs, John, the janitor, sitting in the umbrella chair, was having coffee. The chair had a looking-glass back, and when John turned his head he appeared to have two faces.

"Thought you had the day off," said Father Fabre.

"Always plenty to do around here, Father."

"I suppose." They knew each other well enough now for John not to get off that old one about wanting to spend the day with his family.

"She's really rarin' in there," John said. "I had to come out here." He glanced down at the floor, at the cup of muddy water cooling there, and then fearfully in the direction of the kitchen. This did not impress Father Fabre, however, who believed that the janitor and the housekeeper lived in peace. "Not her responsibility," John said.

Father Fabre, knowing he was being tempted, would not discuss the housekeeper with the janitor. Curates came and went, and even pastors, but the janitor, a subtle Slav, stayed on at Trinity.

"I told her it was none of her business."

"*What* isn't?"

"If you want to go there, that's your business," John said. "I had to come out here." John reached down for his cup, without looking, because his hand knew right where it was. "I don't blame you for being sore at her, Father." ("I'm not," Father Fabre murmured, but John, drinking, smiled into his cup.) "I told her it's your business what you do. 'He's old enough,' I said."

"What's she got against Mrs. Mathers?" Father Fabre asked, wondering if Mrs. Mathers was any match for the housekeeper. A natural leader vs. a mental case. It might be close if the Altar and Rosary Society took sides. But the chances were that Miss Burke would soon be fighting on another front. Impossible for her to wage as many wars as she declared.

"Hell, you know how these old maids are, Father," John was saying. "Just needs a man. *You* can understand that."

Father Fabre, calling it a draw with John, turned away and left.

The other guests at Mrs. Mathers' didn't act like Catholics. Mr. Pint, a small man in his sixties, was surprisingly unfriendly, and his daughter, though rather the opposite, went at Father Fabre the wrong way. It might have been the absence of excess respect in her manner that he found unsettling. But Mrs. Mathers, a large motherly but childless widow with puffy elbows, had baked a cake, and was easy to take.

They were all on the back porch of her second floor flat, watching Mr. Pint make ice cream.

"Let me taste it, Dad," Velma said.

"I can't be standin' here all day with this cream gettin' soft on me," Mr. Pint said.

Velma pouted. She had on a purple dress which reminded Father Fabre of the purple veils they'd had on the statues in church during Passiontide. Otherwise there was nothing lenten about Velma, he thought.

"If you taste it now," he said, "it'll just take that much longer to harden."

Mr. Pint, who might have agreed with that, said nothing. He dropped a handful of rock salt into the freezer, a wood-and-iron affair that must have been as old as he was, and sank again to his knees. He resumed cranking.

Father Fabre smiled at Mrs. Mathers. Parishioners expected a priest to be nice and jolly, and that was how he meant to be at Mrs. Mathers'. With Mr. Pint setting the tone, it might not be easy. Father Fabre hadn't expected to be the second most important person there. The cake, he believed, had not been baked for him.

"Your good suit," said Mrs. Mathers. She snatched a *Better Homes and Gardens* from a pile of such magazines and slid it under Mr. Pint's knees.

"Sir Walter Reilly," said Velma, looking at Father Fabre to see if he followed her.

He nodded, doubting her intelligence, wondering if she was bright enough to be a nurse. Mrs. Mathers was a registered nurse.

"Aw, come on," Velma said. "Let me taste it, Dad."

Mr. Pint churned up a chunk of ice and batted it down with the heel of his hand. "By Dad!" he breathed, a little god invoking himself.

Mrs. Mathers wisely retired to the kitchen. Velma, after a moment, ingloriously followed.

Father Fabre gazed over the porch railing. With all the apartment buildings backed up together, it was like a crowded harbor, but with no sign of life—a port of plague. Miss Burke, he remembered, had warned him not to go. John, however, had said go. Mr. Pint's shirt had broken out in patches of deeper blue, and his elastic suspenders, of soft canary hue, were stained a little. Pity moved Father Fabre to offer the helping hand, prudence stayed it, then pity rose again. "Let me take it awhile," he said quietly.

But Mr. Pint, out to deny his size and years, needed no help, or lost in his exertions, had not heard.

Father Fabre went inside, where he found the women, by contrast, laughing and gay. Velma left off tossing the salad, and Mrs. Mathers' stirring spoon hung expectantly in mid-air. "I'm afraid I wasn't much help out there," he said.

"That's just Dad's way," Mrs. Mathers said. "Come in here a minute, Father, if you want to see something nice."

Mrs. Mathers led him into a little room off the kitchen. She wanted him to see her new day bed. He felt the springs as she had and praised the bed in her terms. He meant it when he said he wished he had one, and sat down on it. Mrs. Mathers left the room, and returned a moment later whispering that she believed in flushing the toilet before she made coffee. That was the quickest way to bring fresh water into the house. Father Fabre, rising from the day bed, regretted that he wouldn't be able to pass this household hint on to Miss Burke.

Then, leaving the room, they met Mr. Pint, all salt and sweat, coming in from the back porch. He came among them as one from years at sea, scornful of soft living, suspicious of the womenfolk and young stay-at-home males.

The women followed Mr. Pint, and Father Fabre followed the women, into the dining room.

"You're a sight," said Velma.

"Your good blue shirt," said Mrs. Mathers. She went down the hall after Mr. Pint.

"We're going to eat in a minute," Velma said to Father Fabre. "You want to wash or anything?"

"No, thanks," he said. "I never wash."

He had tried to be funny, but Velma seemed ready to believe him.

Mrs. Mathers, looking upset, entered the dining room.

"Should I take off her plate?" Velma asked.

"Leave it on in case she does come," Mrs. Mathers said.

"Father, you know Grace."

"No, I don't think so."

"Grace Halloran. She's in the Society."

"Of course." Of course he knew Grace, a maiden lady. He saw her almost daily, a shadow moving around the sanctuary, dusting the altar rail and filling vases with flowers—paid for by herself, the pastor said. Her brother was a big builder of highways. She wasn't the kind to use her means and position, however, to fraternize with the clergy. "Maybe she's just late," he said, rather hoping she wouldn't make it. The present company was difficult enough to assimilate.

Mr. Pint appeared among them again, now wearing a white shirt. Had he brought an extra? Or had Mrs. Mathers given him one which had belonged to her late husband? Father Fabre decided it would be unwise to ask.

They sat down to eat. It was like dining in a convent, with Velma in the role of the nun assigned to him, plying him with food. "Pickles?" He took one and passed the dish to Mr. Pint.

"He can't eat 'em," Velma said.

"That's too bad," said Father Fabre.

Mrs. Mathers, brooding, said, "I can't understand Grace, though heaven knows she can be difficult sometimes."

"If she'd only come," said Velma.

"Yes," said Father Fabre.

"Vel had to work last Sunday and didn't get a chance to meet her," said Mrs. Mathers.

"That's too bad," said Father Fabre.

"Grace was my best friend," Mrs. Mathers said. "In the Society, I mean." Father Fabre frowned. *Was?*

"I was dying to meet her," said Velma, looking at Father Fabre.

"Very nice person," he said.

"I just can't understand it," declared Mrs. Mathers, without conviction. Then: "It's no surprise to me! You soon find out who your friends are!"

Father Fabre applied his fingers to the fried chicken. "Well," he said, "she doesn't know what she's missing." Grace's plate, however, seemed to reject the statement. "Did she know I was coming?"

"Oh, indeed, she did, Father! That's what makes me so blamed mad!"

Velma went to answer the telephone. "Yoo-hoo! It's for you-hoo!" she called.

"She means you," Mrs. Mathers said to Father Fabre, who wondered how she could have known.

He went to the bedroom, where Mrs. Mathers, never knowing when she'd be called for special duty, had her telephone. When he said "Hello" there was a click and then nothing. "Funny," he said, returning to the table. "Nobody there."

"Vel," Mrs. Mathers asked, "was *that* Grace?"

"She didn't say, Mildred. Wouldn't she say who she was if she was Grace?"

"It was Grace," said Mrs. Mathers quietly. She looked unwell.

There was a rattle of silverware. "Eat your dinner, Mildred," said Mr. Pint, and she did.

.          .          .

After dinner, they retired to the living room. Soon, with Mrs. Mathers and Mr. Pint yawning on the sofa, Velma said, "I met some Catholic priests that were married, once." She had taken the chair near Father Fabre's. They were using the same ash tray.

"Were they Greek or Russian?"

She seemed to think he was joking. "They were with their wives, two of them—I mean they were two couples—but they said the ones that weren't married could have dates with girls if they wanted to."

He nodded. "It's only been observed among us since the eleventh century—celibacy." Velma looked doubtful. "It may be overrated," he added, smiling.

"I never tried it," Velma said.

"Yes, well . . . in some parts of the world, even now, there are married Catholic priests."

"That's what these were," Velma said.

"Maybe they were *Old* Catholics," he said.

"No, they weren't, not at all."

He looked across the room at the couple on the sofa. Mr. Pint appeared to be asleep, but Mrs. Mathers was trying to fight it with a *Good Housekeeping*. "That's a sect," he said, getting back to Velma. "They go by that name. Old Catholics."

"I wouldn't say they were that," she said.

He was ready to drop it.

"I met them in Chicago," she said.

"I understand Old Catholics are strong there," he said. "Comparatively."

There was a lull during which Velma loaded her cigarette case and Father Fabre surveyed the room—the bookcase with no books in it, only plants and bric-a-brac, and the overstuffed furniture rising like bread beneath the slipcovers, which rivaled nature in the tropics for color and variety of growing things, and the upright piano with the mandolin and two photographs on top: one would be the late Mr. Mathers and somewhere in the other, a group picture of graduating nurses, would be the girl he had married, now stout, being now what she had always been becoming. Mrs. Mathers was openly napping now. The room was filled with breathing, hers and Mr. Pint's in unison, and the sun fell upon them all and upon the trembling ferns.

"Mildred says you can't have dates."

Father Fabre looked Velma right in the eye. "That's right." He'd drifted long enough. He'd left the conversation up to her from the beginning, and where had it got him? "I take it you're not a Catholic."

"Oh, no," she said, "but I see all your movies."

"I beg your pardon."

"I liked *The Miracle of the Bells* the best. But they're all swell."

He felt himself drifting again.

"I enjoyed reading *The Cardinal*," she said.

So had he. He wondered if a start could be made there.

Mrs. Mathers, whom he'd thought asleep, said, "Why don't you tell Father what you told me, Vel?"

"Mildred!" cried Velma.

Father Fabre blushed, thinking Velma must have remarked favorably on his appearance.

"About the church of your choice," said Mrs. Mathers.

"Oh, that. I told Mildred *The Miracle of the Bells* made me want to be a Catholic."

Mr. Pint came to and mumbled something.

Father Fabre decided to face up to him. "Do you like to go to the movies, Mr. Pint?"

"No, sir." Mr. Pint was not looking Father Fabre in the eye, but it was as though he didn't think it necessary—yet.

"Why, Dad," Mrs. Mathers said, "you took me last Sunday night."

"Not to those kind, I didn't. Whyn't you let me finish? By Dad, I ain't so old I can't remember what I did a week back."

"Who said anybody was old?" Velma asked.

"Stop showin' off," Mr. Pint said. "I heard who said it."

Mrs. Mathers clucked sadly, too wise to defend herself.

Mr. Pint blinked at her. "You made me go," he said.

Mrs. Mathers saw her chance. "Ho, ho," she laughed. "I'd just like to see anybody *make* you do anything!"

"You can say that again! Tell him about your office, Dad," Velma said, but Mr. Pint would not.

From the women, however, Father Fabre learned that Mr. Pint had asked "them"—his employers, presumably—to build him an office of glass so that he could sit in it, out of the dirt and noise, and keep an eye on the men who worked under him.

"Why shouldn't they do it," said Mrs. Mathers, "when he saves them all the money he does?"

Father Fabre, about to address Mr. Pint directly, rephrased his question. "He has men under him? I mean—many?"

"Five," said Mrs. Mathers. "Before he came, they had six. He gets more out of five men than they did out of six."

"Two he brought with him," Velma said. "They've been with Dad for years."

Father Fabre nodded. Mr. Pint, with his entourage, was like a big-time football coach, but what was Mr. Pint's work?

Velma, who had switched on the radio, cried, "Lee!"

Father Fabre watched the women closely. Evidently "Lee" was the announcer and not some entertainer to follow on the program. His sponsor, a used car dealer, whose name and address he gave, dispensed with commercial announcements on Sunday, he said, and presented music suited to the day. They sat quietly listening to *How Are Things in Glocca Morra?* Then to *The Rosary,* one of Mrs. Mathers' favorite pieces, she said. Then to *Cryin' in the Chapel.* Father Fabre wanted to go home.

Lee came on again with the business about no commercials and also threw in the correct time. (Mr. Pint pulled out his watch.) Lee warned motorists to be careful on the highways.

"Don't judge by this. You should hear him on weekdays," Velma said. "Does he ever kid the sponsors!"

"He's a good disc jockey or he wouldn't be on the air," Mrs. Mathers said tartly. "But he's no Arthur Godfrey." It sounded to Father Fabre as though she'd been over this ground with Velma before. "Do you ever get Arthur, Father?"

"Can't say that I do, Mrs. Mathers."

"He might give you some ideas for your sermons."

"My radio isn't working."

"I'll take Lee," Velma said. She rose and went down the hall to the bathroom.

Mrs. Mathers whispered, "Father, did I tell you she wanted to call in for them to play a song for you? *Our Lady of Fatima* or something. She wanted it to come over the air while you were here. A surprise."

"No," he said. "You didn't tell me about that."

"I told her not to do it. I said maybe you wouldn't want it."

"No, I wouldn't." He was grateful to Mrs. Mathers.

Showing a little interest, Mr. Pint inquired uneasily, "What do you think of this disc jockey business?" He got up and turned off the radio.

"I'm afraid I don't know much about it," Father Fabre said, surprised to find himself engaged in conversation with Mr. Pint.

"Sounds kind of fishy to me," said Mr. Pint, sitting down again. He had opened up some, not much, but some. "You know it's just playing phonograph records?"

"Yes," said Father Fabre, and then wondered if he'd said the right thing. Mr. Pint might have wanted to tell him about it. Fearing a lull, he plunged. "Certainly was good ice cream."

"Glad you liked it."

After the long winter, gentle spring, the sap running.... "That's a good idea of yours when you make ice cream—bringing an extra shirt, I mean."

There was a bad silence, the worst of the afternoon, crippling every tongue. Even Velma, back with them, was quiet. Mr. Pint was positively stony. Finally, as if seeing no other way, Mrs. Mathers explained:

"Mr. Pint lives here, Father."

"He does?"

"Yes, Father."

"I guess I didn't know."

"I guess I didn't tell you."

"No reason why you should've," he said quickly. "You do have quite a bit of room here." He seemed to be perspiring. "Certainly do get the sun." He never would have thought it. Was there a chance that Mr. Pint, who acted so strangely, was not her lover? He took a good look at Mr. Pint. Was there a chance that he was? In either case, Mrs. Mathers had planned well. Father Fabre, taking out his handkerchief, blew his nose politely and dabbed at his cold, damp neck. He was in very good health and perspired freely. The fat flowery arms of the overstuffed chair held him fast while the hidden mouth devoured him. The trembling ferns frankly desired him. He just never would have thought it.

"You should see my little room at the Y," Velma said. "So dark." She was looking at Father Fabre, but he could think of nothing to say.

Mrs. Mathers sighed. "Vel, you *could* stay here, you know. She could, too." Mrs. Mathers appealed to Father Fabre. "The day bed is always ready."

"Oh, well," said Velma.

"So I had this extra bedroom," Mrs. Mathers said, as if coming to the end of a long explanation, "and I thought I might as well have the income from it—what's your opinion, Father?"

"Swell," he said. In the future he ought to listen to Miss Burke and stay away from John, with his rotten talk against her. A very sound person, Miss Burke, voices, visions and all. He ought to develop a retiring nature, too, stick close to the pastor, maybe try to get a job in his war plant. "I hate to rush off," he said, rising.

"Don't tell me it's time for devotions," said Mrs. Mathers.

.          .          .

They went down the street together. "You know, Father," said Mrs. Mathers, "I almost asked them to come along with us."

"You did?" Mrs. Mathers was hard to figure. He'd heard that hospital life made iconoclasts.

"What'd you think of Vel?"

"Who? Oh, fine." He didn't know what he thought of Vel. "What does she do?"

"She's with the telephone company, Father. She thinks she's in line for a supervisor's, but I don't know. The seniority system is the one big thing in her favor. Of course, it wouldn't come right away."

"I suppose not," Father Fabre said. "She seems quite young for that."

"Yes, and they're pretty careful about those jobs."

"What I understand." He was in line for a pastor's himself. They were pretty careful about those jobs too. "What does Mr. Pint do?"

"Didn't I tell you?"

"No," he said bleakly.

Mr. Pint was an engineer. "But he never touches a wrench. He's like an executive."

"Where?"

"At the hospital, Father."

"At City?"

"At Mercy, Father."

Oh, God he thought, the nuns were going to be in on it too. They walked the next block in silence.

"Who plays the mandolin?" he asked.

"He does."

They walked another block in silence. "I don't want to get TV," she said plaintively. She brightened at the sight of a squirrel.

"Don't care for TV?"

"No, it's not that. I just don't know how long I'll keep my apartment."

Was Mrs. Mathers saying that she'd get out of town, or only that she'd move to another parish? If so, she was a little late. By feasting at their board, he had blessed the union, if any, in the eyes of the parish. What a deal! It was too late for him to condemn the enamored couple, one of whom was out of his jurisdiction anyway (in parting, he had shaken Mr. Pint's hand). It was a bad situation, bad in itself and bad because it involved him. Better, though, that they live in sin than marry in haste. That was something, however, that it would take theologians (contemplating the dangers of mixed marriage, the evil of divorce) to see. He knew what the parishioners would think of that.

And the pastor . . .

At the church, at the moment of parting, he said, "You're going to be early for devotions." That was all. To thank her, as he wanted to, for the good dinner would be, in a way, to thank her for compromising him with parish and pastor. It was quite enough that he say nothing to hurt her, and go.

"I've got some things to do around the side altars," Mrs. Mathers said.

He nodded, backing away.

"You suppose Grace'll be inside?" she called after him, just as if all were now well between her and her best friend in the Society.

He had his back to her and kept going, plowed on, nodding though, vigorously nodding like one of the famous yes-horses of Odense. For a moment he entertained the idea that Mrs. Mathers was a mental case, which would explain everything, but it wouldn't do. Mrs. Mathers remained a mystery to him.

In the rectory, he started up the front stairs for his room. Then he went back down, led by sounds to the converts' parlor. There he found a congregation of middle-aged women dressed mostly in navy blues and blacks, unmistakably Altar and Rosary, almost a full consistory, and swarming.

"Could I be of any service to you ladies?"

The swarming let up. "Miss Burke said we should wait in here," someone said.

He hadn't seen who had spoken. "For me?" he said, looking them over. He saw Grace sorrowing in their midst.

"No, Father," said someone else, also hidden from him. "We're here to see the pastor."

"Oh," he said.

"*He* went out on a sick call," said someone else.

"Oh," he said, and escaped.

One minute later he was settling down in the garage, on the bottom rung of a folding ladder, the best seat he could find. He picked up a wrench, got grease on his fingers, and remembered that Mr. Pint never touched a wrench. He wondered where he'd gone wrong, if there was anything he might have done, or might yet do. There was nothing. He attributed his trouble to his belief, probably mistaken, that the chancery had wanted a man at Trinity to compensate for the pastor. Father Fabre had tried to be that man, one who would be accessible to the people. The pastor strenuously avoided people. He was happy with the machines in his room, or on a picnic with himself, topped off perhaps with a visit to the zoo. The assistant was the one to see at Trinity. Naturally there were people who would try to capitalize on his inexperience. The pastor gave him a lot of rope. Some pastors wouldn't let their curates dine out with parishioners—with good reason, it appeared. The pastor was watchful, though, and would rein in the rope on the merest suspicion. Father Fabre was thinking of the young lady of charm and education who had come to him after Mass one Sunday with the idea of starting up a study club at Trinity. He'd told the pastor and the pastor had told him, "It's under study." You might think that would be the end of it. It had been, so far as the young lady was concerned, but that evening at table Father Fabre was asked by the dormouse if he knew about young ladies.

"Know about them?"

"Ummm." The dormouse was feasting on a soda cracker.

"No," said Father Fabre, very wise.

"Well, Father, I had them all in a sodality some years ago." (Ordinarily untalkative to the point of being occult, the pastor spoke now as a man compelled, and Father Fabre attended his every word. The seminary professors had harped on the wisdom of pastors, as against the all-consuming ignorance of curates.) It seemed that the pastor, being so busy, didn't notice how the young ladies showed up for induction during the few years of the sodality's existence at Trinity, but from the day he did, there had been no more of that. *(What?* Father Fabre wondered but did not interrupt.) The pastor was not narrow-minded, he said, and he granted that a young woman might wear a bit of paint on her wedding day. But when sodalists, dedicated to the Blessed Virgin, the Mother of God, Mary Immaculate, presented themselves at the communion rail in low-necked evening gowns, wearing lipstick, stuff in their eyes, and with their hair up in the permanent wave, why then, Gentlemen—the pastor used that word, causing Father Fabre to blink and then to realize he was hearing a speech the pastor must have given at a clergy conference—there was something wrong somewhere and that was why he had suppressed the sodality in his parish.

By God, thought Father Fabre, nodding vigorously, the pastor had a point! Here was something to remember if he ever got a church of his own.

It must have touched the pastor to see his point so well taken by his young curate, for he smiled. "You might say the scales dropped from my eyes," he said.

But by then Father Fabre, gazing at the cracker flak on the pastor's black bosom, had begun to wonder what all this had to do with a study club.

"A study club's just another name for a sodality," the pastor prompted. "See what I mean?"

Father Fabre did not, not unless the pastor meant that young ladies were apt to belong to either and that, therefore, his curate would do well to steer clear of both. Hear their sins, visit them in sickness and prison, give them the Sacrament. Beyond that, there wasn't much to be done for or about them. In time they would get old and useful. The pastor, for his part, had put them away in the cellar part of his mind to ripen like cheese. But the good ladies of the Altar and Rosary were something else again. Nuns could not have kept the church cleaner, and the good ladies, unlike nuns, didn't labor under the illusion that they were somehow priests, only different, and so weren't always trying to vault the communion rail to the altar.

"You want to be one of these 'youth priests,' Father?"

"I haven't thought much about it."

"Good."

But, as the pastor must have noticed, Father Fabre had wanted to get some "activities" going at Trinity, believing that his apostolate lay in the world, with the people, as the pastor's obviously didn't. Well, he had failed. But he wasn't sorry. Wasn't there enough to do at Trinity, just doing the regular chores? For the poor, the sick and dying, yes, anything. But non-essentials he'd drop, including dining out with parishioners, and major decisions he'd cheerfully hand over to the pastor. (He still thought the man who rented owls to rid you of pigeons might have something, for that was nature's way, no cruel machines or powders. But he'd stop agitating for the owls, for that was another problem for the pastor, to solve or, probably, not to solve.) Of course the parish was indifferently run, but wasn't it a mistake to keep trying to take up *all* the slack? He'd had himself under observation, of late. It seemed to him his outlook was changing, not from a diminution of zeal, not from loss of vision, but from growing older and wiser. At least he hoped so. He was beginning to believe he wasn't the man to compensate for the pastor—not that he'd ask for a transfer. The bishop was a gentle administrator but always seemed to find a place in one of the salt mines for a young man seeking a change. Father Fabre's predecessor in the curate's job at Trinity had been anti-social, which some of the gad-about clergy said could be a grievous fault in a parish priest, but he hadn't asked for a change—it had come to him—and now he was back in the seminary, as a professor with little pocket money, it was true, but enjoying food and hand-ball again. That afternoon, sitting in the garage, Father Fabre envied him.

．　　　．　　　．

The pastor handed a wicker basket to Father Fabre, and himself carried a thermos bottle. He showed no surprise at finding his curate waiting for him in the garage and asked no questions. Father Fabre, the moment he saw the basket and bottle, understood that the pastor was returning from a picnic, and that Miss Burke, telling the ladies he'd gone on a sick call, thought it part of her job to create a good impression whenever possible, part of being loyal, the prime requisite. Who but the pastor would have her for a housekeeper?

They walked to the back door at the pastor's pace.

"Some coffee in here for you," the pastor said, jiggling the thermos bottle.

"Thanks," said Father Fabre, but he'd not be having any of that.

"One of the bears died at Como," the pastor said. "One of the babies."

"That's too bad," said Father Fabre. He pushed in the door for the pastor, then stood aside. "Some women to see you in the converts' parlor," he said, as the pastor passed in front of him.

The pastor nodded. Women in the converts' parlor; he would see them.

"I don't know," Father Fabre said. "It may concern me—indirectly." Then, staring down at the kitchen linoleum, he began an account of his afternoon at Mrs. Mathers'. At the worst part—his chagrin on learning of the setup there— the pastor interrupted. He filled an unwashed cup from the sink with the fluid from the thermos bottle, gave it to Father Fabre to drink, and watched to see that he did. Father Fabre drank Miss Burke's foul coffee to the dregs and chewed up a few grounds. When he started up his account again, the pastor interrupted.

"That's enough," he said.

Father Fabre, for a moment, thought he was in for it. But when he looked into the pastor's eyes, there was nothing in them for him to fear, nor was there fear, nor even fear of fear, bravado. The pastor's eyes were blue, blank and blue.

Father Fabre followed the pastor at a little distance, out of the kitchen, down the hallway. "Will you need me?" he said.

With an almost imperceptible shake of his head, the pastor walked into the converts' parlor, leaving the door ajar as always when dealing with women.

Father Fabre stayed to listen, out of sight of those inside. He soon realized that it had been a mistake to omit all mention of Velma in his account, as he had, thinking her presence at Mrs. Mathers' incidental, her youth likely to sidetrack the pastor, to arouse memories of so-called study clubs and suppressed sodalists. Why, if the pastor was to hear the details, didn't they tell him that Grace had been invited to dinner? Then there would have been five of them. The pastor was sure to get the wrong impression. To hear the ladies tell it, Mr. Pint and Father Fabre were as bad as sailors on leave, kindred evil spirits double-dating a couple of dazzled working girls. The ladies weren't being fair to Father Fabre or, he felt, even to Mr. Pint. He wondered at the pastor's silence. When all was said and done, there was little solidarity among priests— a nest of tables scratching each other.

In the next room, it was the old, old story, right from Scripture, the multitude crying, "Father, this woman was taken in adultery. The law commandeth us to stone such a one. What sayest thou?" The old story with the difference that the pastor had nothing to say. Why didn't he say, She that is without sin among you, let her first cast a stone at her! But there was one close by who could and would speak, who knew what it was to have the mob against him, and who was not afraid. With chapter and verse he'd atomize 'em. *This day thou shouldst be pastor.* Yes, it did look that way, but he'd wait a bit, to give the pastor a chance to redeem himself. He imagined how it would be if he hit them with that text. They, hearing him, would go out one by one, even the pastor, from that day forward his disciple. And he alone would remain, and the woman. And he, lifting up himself, would say, Woman, where are they that accused thee? Hath no one condemned thee? Who would say, No one, master. Neither will I condemn thee. Go, and sin no more.

"Think he can handle it?"

Whirling, Father Fabre beheld his temper. "Be gone, John," he said, and watched the janitor slink away.

Father Fabre, after that, endeavored to think well of the pastor, to discover the meaning in his silence. Was this forbearance? It seemed more like paralysis. The bomb was there to be used, but the pastor couldn't or wouldn't use it. He'd have to do something, though. The ladies, calmed at first by his silence, sounded restless. Soon they might regard his silence not as response to a grave problem but as refusal to hold council with them.

"We don't feel it's any of our business to know *what* you intend to do, Father, but we would like some assurance that something will be done. Is that asking too much?"

The pastor said nothing.

"We thought you'd know what to do, Father," said another. "What would be best for all concerned, Father. Gosh, I don't know what to think!"

The pastor cleared his throat, touched, possibly, by the last speaker's humility, but he said nothing.

"I wonder if we've made ourselves clear," said the one who had spoken before the last one. She wasn't speaking to the pastor but to the multitude. "Maybe that's what comes from trying to describe everything in the best possible light." (Father Fabre remembered the raw deal they'd given him.) "Not *all* of us, I'm afraid, believe that man's there against Mildred's will."

"*'S not so.*"

Father Fabre gasped. Oh, no! Not that! But yes, the pastor had spoken.

"Father, do you mean to say we're lying?"

"*No.*"

Father Fabre shook his head. In all arguments with the pastor there was a place like the Sargasso Sea, and the ladies had reached it. It was authority that counted then, as Father Fabre knew, who had always lacked it. The ladies hadn't taken a vow of obedience, though, and they might not take "'S not so" for an answer. They might very well go to the chancery. At the prospect of that, of the fine slandering he'd get there, and realizing only then that he and the pastor were in the same boat, Father Fabre began to consider the position as defined by "'S not so" and "No." The pastor was saying (a) that the situation, as reported by the ladies, was not so, and (b) that the ladies were not lying. He seemed to be contradicting himself, as was frequently the case in disputations with his curate. This was no intramural spat, however. The pastor would have to make sense for a change, to come out on top. *Could* the dormouse be right? And the ladies wrong in what they thought? What if what they thought was just not so? *Honi soit qui mal y pense?*

One said, "I just can't understand Mildred," but Father Fabre thought he could, now. At no time had Mrs. Mathers sounded guilty, and that—her seeming innocence—was what had thrown everything out of kilter. When she said Mr. Pint lived with her, when she said she was thinking of giving up her apartment, she had sounded not guilty but regretful, regretful and flustered, as though she knew that her friends and even her clergy were about to desert her. Mrs. Mathers was a veteran nurse, the human body was her work bench, sex probably a matter of technical concern, as with elderly plumbers who distinguish between the male and female connections. It was quite possible that Mrs. Mathers had thought nothing of letting a room to a member of the opposite sex. She could not have known that what was only an economy measure for her would appear to others as something very different—and so, in fact, it had become for her, in time. Mrs. Mathers and Mr. Pint were best described as victims of their love for each other. It was true love, of that Father Fabre was now certain. He had only to recollect it. If it were the other kind, Mrs. Mathers never would have invited him over—and Grace—to meet Mr. Pint. Mr. Pint, non-Catholic and priest-shy, had never really believed that Mrs. Mathers' friends would understand, and when Grace defaulted, he had become sullen, ready to take on anybody, even a priest, which showed the quality of his regard for Mrs. Mathers, that he meant to marry her willy-nilly, in or out of the Church. There must be no delay. All Mrs. Mathers needed now, all she'd ever needed, was a little time—and help. If she could get Mr. Pint to take instructions, they could have a church wedding. Velma, already Catholic in spirit, could be bridesmaid. That was it. The ladies had done their worst—Father Fabre's part in the affair was criminally exaggerated—but the pastor, the angelic dormouse, had not failed to sniff out the benign object of Mrs. Mathers' grand plan. Or what would have been its object. The ladies could easily spoil everything.

One of the ladies got sarcastic. "Would it be too much to ask, then, just what you do mean?"

The pastor said nothing.

Then the one who earlier had succeeded in getting him to clear his throat said, "Father, it's not always easy for us to understand everything you say. Now, Father, I always get a lot out of your sermons—why, some I've heard on television aren't half as good—but I don't kid myself that I can understand *every* word you say. Still waters run deep, I guess, and I haven't got the education I should have. So, Father, would you please tell us what you mean, in words we can all understand?"

It would have surprised Father Fabre if, after all that, the pastor had said nothing.

" *'S not so,*" he said.

Father Fabre had to leave then, for devotions.

In the sacristy, he slipped into his cassock, eased the zipper past the spot where it stuck, pawed the hangers for his surplice, found it on the floor. The altar boys had come, but he wasn't in the mood for them, for the deceptive small talk that he seemed to do so well, from ballplayers to St. John Bosco in one leap, using the Socratic method to get them to do their own thinking and then breaking off the conversation when he'd brought out the best in them. It wasn't necessary with the two on hand—twins who were going to be priests anyway, according to them at the age of ten. They had fired the censer too soon, and it would be petering out after the rosary, when it would be needed for benediction. He stood at the door of the sacristy and gazed out into the almost empty church. It was the nice weather that kept people away from devotions, it was said, and it was the bad weather that kept them away in the wintertime. He saw Mrs. Mathers kneeling alone in prayer. The pastor had done well for her, everything considered, but not well enough, Father Fabre feared. He feared a scandal. Great schisms from little squabbles grew . . .

•        •        •

And great affirmations! He'd expected the pastor to dismiss the ladies in time for devotions, but he hadn't expected them to come, not in such numbers, and he took it as a sign from heaven when they didn't kneel apart from Mrs. Mathers, the woman taken in adultery, or thereabouts, a sign that the pastor had triumphed, as truth must always triumph over error, sooner or later, always: that was heaven's promise to pastors. Life was a dark business for everyone in it, but the way for pastors was ever lit by flares of special grace. Father Fabre, knowing full well that he, in spirit, had been no better than the ladies, thanked God for the little patience he'd had, and asked forgiveness for thinking ill of the pastor, for coveting his authority. He who would have been proud to hurl the ready answer at Mrs. Mathers' persecutors, to stone them back, to lose the ninety-nine sheep and save not the one whose innocence he would have violated publicly then as he had in his heart, in his heart humbled himself with thoughts of his unworthiness, marveled at the great good lesson he'd learned that day from the pastor, that Solomon. But the pastor, he knew, was zealous in matters affecting the common weal, champion of decency in his demesne, and might have a word or two for his curate at table that evening, and for Mrs. Mathers there would certainly be a just poke or two from the blunt sword of his mercy.

Father Fabre, trailing the boys out of the sacristy, gazed upon the peaceful flock, and then beyond, in a dim, dell-like recess of the nave used for baptism, he saw the shepherd carrying a stick and then he heard him opening a few windows.

# Wise Blood

From: *Wise Blood*

BY FLANNERY O'CONNOR

✚

Hawks kept his door bolted and whenever Haze knocked on it, which he did two or three times a day, the ex-evangelist sent his child out to him and bolted the door again behind her. It infuriated him to have Haze lurking in the house, thinking up some excuse to get in and look at his face; and he was often drunk and didn't want to be discovered that way.

Haze couldn't understand why the preacher didn't welcome him and act like a preacher should when he sees what he believes is a lost soul. He kept trying to get into the room again; the window he could have reached was kept locked and the shade pulled down. He wanted to see, if he could, *behind* the black glasses.

Every time he went to the door, the girl came out and the bolt shut inside; then he couldn't get rid of her. She followed him out to his car and climbed in and spoiled his rides or she followed him up to his room and sat. He abandoned the notion of seducing her and tried to protect himself. He hadn't been in the house a week before she appeared in his room one night after he had gone to bed. She was holding a candle burning in a jelly glass and wore, hanging onto her thin shoulders, a woman's nightgown that dragged on the floor behind her. Haze didn't wake up until she was almost up to his bed, and when he did, he sprang from under his cover into the middle of the room.

"What you want?" he said.

She didn't say anything and her grin widened in the candle light. He stood glowering at her for an instant and then he picked up the straight chair and raised it as if he were going to bring it down on her. She lingered only a fraction of a second. His door didn't bolt so he propped the chair under the knob before he went back to bed.

"Listen," she said when she got back to their room, "nothing works. He would have hit me with a chair."

"I'm leaving out of here in a couple of days," Hawks said, "you better make it work if you want to eat after I'm gone." He was drunk but he meant it.

Nothing was working the way Haze had expected it to. He had spent every evening preaching, but the membership of the Church Without Christ was still only one person: himself. He had wanted to have a large following quickly to impress the blind man with his powers, but no one had followed him. There had been a sort of follower but that had been a mistake. That had been a boy about sixteen years old who had wanted someone to go to a whorehouse with him because he had never been to one before. He knew where the place was but he didn't want to go without a person of experience, and when he heard Haze, he hung around until he stopped preaching and then asked him to go. But it was all a mistake because after they had gone and got out again and Haze had asked him to be a member of the Church Without Christ, or more than that, a disciple, an apostle, the boy said he was sorry but he couldn't be a member of that church because he was a Lapsed Catholic. He said that what they had just done was a mortal sin, and that should they die unrepentant of it they would suffer eternal punishment and never see God. Haze had not enjoyed the whorehouse anywhere near as much as the boy had and he had wasted half his evening. He shouted that there was no such thing as sin or judgment, but the boy only shook his head and asked him if he would like to go again the next night.

If Haze had believed in praying, he would have prayed for a disciple, but as it was all he could do was worry about it a lot. Then two nights after the boy, the disciple appeared.

That night he preached outside of four different picture shows and every time he looked up, he saw the same big face smiling at him. The man was plumpish, and he had curly blond hair that was cut with showy sideburns. He wore a black suit with a silver stripe in it and a wide-brimmed white hat pushed onto the back of his head, and he had on tight-fitting black pointed shoes and no socks. He looked like an ex-preacher turned cowboy, or an ex-cowboy turned mortician. He was not handsome but under his smile, there was an honest look that fitted into his face like a set of false teeth.

Every time Haze looked at him, the man winked.

At the last picture show he preached in front of, there were three people listening to him besides the man. "Do you people care anything about the truth?" he asked. "The only way to the truth is through blasphemy, but do you care? Are you going to pay any attention to what I've been saying or are you just going to walk off like everybody else?"

There were two men and a woman with a cat-faced baby sprawled over her shoulder. She had been looking at Haze as if he were in a booth at the fair. "Well, come on," she said, "he's finished. We got to be going." She turned away and the two men fell in behind her.

"Go ahead and go," Haze said, "but remember that the truth don't lurk around every street corner."

The man who had been following reached up quickly and pulled Haze's pantsleg and gave him a wink. "Come on bach heah, you folks," he said. "I want to tell you all about *me.*"

The woman turned around again and he smiled at her as if he had been struck all along with her good looks. She had a square red face and her hair was freshly set. "I wisht I had my gittarr here," the man said, " 'cause I just somehow can say sweet things to music bettern plain. And when you talk about Jesus you need a little music, don't you, friends?" He looked at the two men as if he were appealing to the good judgment that was impressed on their faces. They had on brown felt hats and black town suits, and they looked like older and younger brother. "Listen, friends," the disciple said confidentially, "two months ago before I met the Prophet here, you wouldn't know me for the same man. I didn't have a friend in the world. Do you know what it's like not to have a friend in the world?"

"It ain't no worsen havinum that would put a knife in your back when you wasn't looking," the older man said, barely parting his lips.

"Friend, you said a mouthful when you said that," the man said. "If we had time, I would have you repeat that just so ever'body could hear it like I did." The picture show was over and more people were coming up. "Friends," the man said, "I know you're all interested in the Prophet here," pointing to Haze on the nose of the car, "and if you'll just give me time I'm going to tell you what him and his idears've done for me. Don't crowd because I'm willing to stay here all night and tell you if it takes that long."

Haze stood where he was, motionless, with his head slightly forward, as if he weren't sure what he was hearing.

"Friends," the man said, "lemme innerduce myself. My name is Onnie Jay Holy and I'm telling it to you so you can check up and see I don't tell you any lie. I'm a preacher and I don't mind who knows it but I wouldn't have you believe nothing you can't feel in your own hearts. You people coming up on the edge push right on up in here where you can hear good," he said. "I'm not selling a thing, I'm giving something away!" A considerable number of people had stopped.

"Friends," he said, "two months ago you wouldn't know me for the same man. I didn't have a friend in the world. Do you know what it's like not to have a friend in the world?"

A loud voice said, "It ain't no worsen havinum that would put . . ."

"Why, friends," Onnie Jay Holy said, "not to have a friend in the world is just about the most miserable and lonesome thing that can happen to a man or woman! And that's the way it was with me. I was ready to hang myself or to despair completely. Not even my own dear old mother loved me, and it wasn't because I wasn't sweet inside, it was because I never known how to make the natural sweetness inside me show. Every person that comes onto this earth," he said, stretching out his arms, "is born sweet and full of love. A little child loves ever'body, friends, and its nature is sweetness—until something happens. Something happens, friends, I don't need to tell people like you that can think for theirselves. As that little child gets bigger, its sweetness don't show so much, cares and troubles come to perplext it, and all its sweetness is driven inside it. Then it gets miserable and lonesome and sick, friends. It says, 'Where is all my sweetness gone? where are all the friends that loved me?' and all the time, that little beat-up rose of its sweetness is inside, not a petal dropped, and on the outside is just a mean lonesomeness. It may want to take its own life or yours or mine, or to despair completely, friends." He said it in a sad nasal voice but he was smiling all the time so that they could tell he had been through what he was talking about and come out on top. "That was the way it was with me, friends. I know what I speak," he said, and folded his hands in front of him. "But all the time that I was ready to hang myself or to despair completely, I was sweet inside, like ever'body else, and I only needed something to bring it out. I only needed a little help, friends.

"Then I met this Prophet here," he said, pointing at Haze on the nose of the car. "That was two months ago, folks, that I heard how he was out to help me, how he was preaching the Church of Christ Without Christ, the church that was going to get a new jesus to help me bring my sweet nature into the open where ever'body could enjoy it. That was two months ago, friends, and now you wouldn't know me for the same man. I love ever'one of you people and I want you to listen to him and me and join our church, the Holy Church of Christ Without Christ, the new church with the new jesus, and then you'll all be helped like me!"

Haze leaned forward. "This man is not true," he said. "I never saw him before tonight. I wasn't preaching this church two months ago and the name of it ain't the Holy Church of Christ Without Christ!"

The man ignored this and so did the people. There were ten or twelve gathered around. "Friends," Onnie Jay Holy said, "I'm mighty glad you're seeing me now instead of two months ago because then I couldn't have testified to this new church and this Prophet here. If I had my gittarr with me I could say all this better but I'll just have to do the best I can by myself." He had a winning smile and it was evident that he didn't think he was any better than anybody else even though he was.

"Now I just want to give you folks a few reasons why you can trust this church," he said. "In the first place, friends, you can rely on it that it's nothing foreign connected with it. You don't have to believe nothing you don't understand and approve of. If you don't understand it, it ain't true, and that's all there is to it. No jokers in the deck, friends."

Haze leaned forward. "Blasphemy is the way to the truth," he said, "and there's no other way whether you understand it or not!"

"Now, friends," Onnie Jay said, "I want to tell you a second reason why you can absolutely trust this church—it's based on the Bible. Yes sir! It's based on your own personal interpitation of the Bible, friends. You can sit at home and interpit your own Bible however you feel in your heart it ought to be interpited. That's right," he said, "just the way Jesus would have done it. Gee, I wisht I had my gittarr here," he complained.

"This man is a liar," Haze said. "I never saw him before tonight. I never . . ."

"That ought to be enough reasons, friends," Onnie Jay Holy said, "but I'm going to tell you one more, just to show I can. This church is up-to-date! When you're in this church you can know that there's nothing or nobody ahead of you, nobody knows nothing you don't know, all the cards are on the table, friends, and that's a fack!"

Haze's face under the white hat began to take on a look of fierceness. Just as he was about to open his mouth again, Onnie Jay Holy pointed in astonishment to the baby in the blue bonnet who was sprawled limp over the woman's shoulder. "Why yonder is a little babe," he said, "a little bundle of helpless sweetness. Why, I know you people aren't going to let that little thing grow up and have all his sweetness pushed inside him when it could be on the outside to win friends and make him loved. That's why I want ever' one of you people to join the Holy Church of Christ Without Christ. It'll cost you each a dollar but what is a dollar? A few dimes! Not too much to pay to unlock that little rose of sweetness inside you!"

"Listen!" Haze shouted. "It don't cost you any money to know the truth! You can't know it for money!"

"You hear what the Prophet says, friends," Onnie Jay Holy said, "a dollar is not too much to pay. No amount of money is too much to learn the truth! Now I want each of you people that are going to take advantage of this church to sign on this little pad I have in my pocket here and give me your dollar personally and let me shake your hand!"

Haze slid down from the nose of his car and got in it and slammed his foot on the starter.

"Hey wait! Wait!" Onnie Jay Holy shouted, "I ain't got any of these friends' names yet!"

The Essex had a tendency to develop a tic by nightfall. It would go for-

ward about six inches and then back about four; it did that now a succession
of times rapidly; otherwise Haze would have shot off in it and been gone. He
had to grip the steering wheel with both hands to keep from being thrown
either out the windshield or into the back. It stopped this after a few seconds
and slid about twenty feet and then began it again.

Onnie Jay Holy's face showed a great strain; he put his hand to the side of
it as if the only way he could keep his smile on was to hold it. "I got to go now,
friends," he said quickly, "but I'll be at this same spot tomorrow night, I got to
go catch the Prophet now," and he ran off just as the Essex began to slide
again. He wouldn't have caught it, except that it stopped before it had gone ten
feet farther. He jumped on the running board and got the door open and
plumped in, panting, beside Haze. "Friend," he said, "we just lost ten dollars.
What you in such a hurry for?" His face showed that he was in some kind of
genuine pain even though he looked at Haze with a smile that revealed all his
upper teeth and the tops of his lowers.

Haze turned his head and looked at him long enough to see the smile
before it was thrown forward at the windshield. After that the Essex began
running smoothly. Onnie Jay took out a lavender handkerchief and held it in
front of his mouth for some time. When he removed it, the smile was back on
his face. "Friend," he said, "you and me have to get together on this thing. I
said when I first heard you open your mouth, 'Why, yonder is a great man with
great idears.' "

Haze didn't turn his head.

Onnie Jay took in a long breath. "Why, do you know who you put me in
mind of when I first saw you?" he asked. After a minute of waiting, he said in
a soft voice, "Jesus Christ and Abraham Lincoln, friend."

Haze's face was suddenly swamped with outrage. All the expression on it
was obliterated. "You ain't true," he said in a barely audible voice.

"Friend, how can you say that?" Onnie Jay said. "Why I was on the radio
for three years with a program that give real religious experiences to the whole
family. Didn't you ever listen to it—called, Soulsease, a quarter hour of Mood,
Melody, and Mentality? I'm a real preacher, friend."

Haze stopped the Essex. "You get out," he said.

"Why friend!" Onnie Jay said. "You ought not to say such a thing! That's
the absolute truth that I'm a preacher and a radio star."

"Get out," Haze said, reaching across and opening the door for him.

"I never thought you would treat a friend thisaway," Onnie Jay said. "All I
wanted to ast you about was this new jesus."

"Get out," Haze said, and began to push him toward the door. He pushed
him to the edge of the seat and gave him a shove and Onnie Jay fell out the
door and into the road.

"I never thought a friend would treat me thisaway," he complained. Haze kicked his leg off the running board and shut the door again. He put his foot on the starter but nothing happened except a noise somewhere underneath him that sounded like a person gargling without water. Onnie Jay got up off the pavement and stood at the window. "If you would just tell me where this new jesus is you was mentioning," he began.

Haze put his foot on the starter a succession of times but nothing happened.

"Pull out the choke," Onnie Jay advised, getting up on the running board.

"There's no choke on it," Haze snarled.

"Maybe it's flooded," Onnie Jay said. "While we're waiting, you and me can talk about the Holy Church of Christ Without Christ."

"My church is the Church Without Christ," Haze said. "I've seen all of you I want to."

"It don't make any difference how many Christs you add to the name if you don't add none to the meaning, friend," Onnie Jay said in a hurt tone. "You ought to listen to me because I'm not just an amateur. I'm an artist-type. If you want to get anywheres in religion, you got to keep it sweet. You got good idears but what you need is an artist-type to work with you."

Haze rammed his foot on the gas and then on the starter and then on the starter and then on the gas. Nothing happened. The street was practically deserted. "Me and you could get behind it and push it over to the curb," Onnie Jay suggested.

"I ain't asked for your help," Haze said.

"You know, friend, I certainly would like to see this new jesus," Onnie Jay said. "I never heard a idear before that had more in it than that one. All it would need is a little promotion."

Haze tried to start the car by forcing his weight forward on the steering wheel, but that didn't work. He got out and got behind it and began to push it over to the curb. Onnie Jay got behind with him and added his weight. "I kind of have had that idear about a new jesus myself," he remarked. "I seen how a new one would be more up-to-date.

"Where you keeping him, friend?" he asked. "Is he somebody you see ever' day? I certainly would like to meet him and hear some of his idears."

They pushed the car into a parking space. There was no way to lock it and Haze was afraid that if he left it out all night so far away from where he lived someone would be able to steal it. There was nothing for him to do but sleep in it. He got in the back and began to pull down the fringed shades. Onnie Jay had his head in the front, however. "You needn't to be afraid that if I seen this new jesus I would cut you out of anything," he said. "Why friend, it would just mean a lot to me for the good of my spirit."

Haze moved the two-by-four off the seat frame to make more room to fix up his pallet. He kept a pillow and an army blanket back there and he had a sterno stove and a coffee pot up on the shelf under the back oval window. "Friend, I would even be glad to pay you a little something to see him," Onnie Jay suggested.

"Listen here," Haze said, "you get away from here. I've seen all of you I want to. There's no such thing as any new jesus. That ain't anything but a way to say something."

The smile more or less slithered off Onnie Jay's face. "What you mean by that?" he asked.

"That there's no such thing or person," Haze said. "It wasn't nothing but a way to say a thing." He put his hand on the door handle and began to close it in spite of Onnie Jay's head. "No such thing exists!" he shouted.

"That's the trouble with you innerleckchuls," Onnie Jay muttered, "you don't never have nothing to show for what you're saying."

"Get your head out my car door, Holy," Haze said.

"My name is Hoover Shoats," the man with his head in the door growled. "I known when I first seen you that you wasn't nothing but a crackpot."

Haze opened the door enough to be able to slam it. Hoover Shoats got his head out of the way but not his thumb. A howl arose that would have rended almost any heart. Haze opened the door and released the thumb and then slammed the door again. He pulled down the front shades and lay down in the back of the car on the army blanket. Outside he could hear Hoover Shoats jumping around on the pavement and howling. When the howls died down, Haze heard a few steps up to the car and then an impassioned, breathless voice say through the tin, "You watch out, friend. I'm going to run you out of business. I can get my own new jesus and I can get Prophets for peanuts, you hear? Do you hear me, friend?" the hoarse voice said.

Haze didn't answer.

"Yeah and I'll be out there doing my own preaching tomorrow night. What you need is a little competition," the voice said. "Do you hear me, friend?"

Haze got up and leaned over the front seat and banged his hand down on the horn of the Essex. It made a sound like a goat's laugh cut off with a buzz saw. Hoover Shoats jumped back as if a charge of electricity had gone through him. "All right, friend," he said, standing about fifteen feet away, trembling, "you just wait, you ain't heard the last of me yet," and he turned and went off down the quiet street.

Haze stayed in his car about an hour and had a bad experience in it: he dreamed he was not dead but only buried. He was not waiting on the Judgment because there was no Judgment, he was waiting on nothing. Various eyes looked through the back oval window at his situation, some with considerable reverence, like the boy from the zoo, and some only to see what they could see. There were three women with paper sacks who looked at him critically as if he were something—a piece of fish—they might buy, but they passed on after a minute. A man in a canvas hat looked in and put his thumb to his nose and wiggled his fingers. Then a woman with two little boys on either side of her stopped and looked in, grinning. After a second, she pushed the boys out of view and indicated that she would climb in and keep him company for a while, but she couldn't get through the glass and finally she went off. All this time Haze was bent on getting out but since there was no use to try, he didn't make any move one way or the other. He kept expecting Hawks to appear at the oval window with a wrench, but the blind man didn't come.

Finally he shook off the dream and woke up. He thought it should be morning but it was only midnight. He pulled himself over into the front of the car and eased his foot on the starter and the Essex rolled off quietly as if nothing were the matter with it. He drove back to the house and let himself in but instead of going upstairs to his room, he stood in the hall, looking at the blind man's door. He went over to it and put his ear to the keyhole and heard the sound of snoring; he turned the knob gently but the door didn't move.

For the first time, the idea of picking the lock occurred to him. He felt in his pockets for an instrument and came on a small piece of wire that he sometimes used for a toothpick. There was only a dim light in the hall but it was enough for him to work by and he knelt down at the keyhole and inserted the wire into it carefully, trying not to make a noise.

After a while when he had tried the wire five or six different ways, there was a slight click in the lock. He stood up, trembling, and opened the door. His breath came short and his heart was palpitating as if he had run all the way here from a great distance. He stood just inside the room until his eyes got accustomed to the darkness and then he moved slowly over to the iron bed and stood there. Hawks was lying across it. His head was hanging over the edge. Haze squatted down by him and struck a match close to his face and he opened his eyes. The two sets of eyes looked at each other as long as the match lasted; Haze's expression seemed to open onto a deeper blankness and reflect something and then close again.

"Now you can get out," Hawks said in a short thick voice, "now you can leave me alone," and he made a jab at the face over him without touching it. It moved back, expressionless under the white hat, and was gone in a second.

# Mr. O'Daniel

From: *Midnight Cowboy*

BY JAMES LEO HERLIHY

Walking up Broadway toward Times Square, Joe observed that Rizzo's leg served him well enough in an open stretch. He would catch hold of a certain target with his eye—the next corner, say—and then set himself in motion, falling at once into a kind of crazy-wheel rhythm that rolled him toward his objective at such a hell-bent pace one wondered if he'd be able to stop himself at the traffic light.

At 42nd Street, Rizzo said, "We'll try his hotel first. With fantastic luck, I mean fan*tas*tic luck, we'll find him in his room. Come on." They wove their way through the traffic of people whose complexions appeared never to have seen the real sun, only this topsy-turvy daylight of neon and electricity, a kind of light that penetrated the first layer of skin, even cosmetics, illuminating only the troubled colors under the surface: weary blue, sick green, narcotic gray, sleepless white, dead purple.

"Not that he'll *be* there," Rizzo mumbled. "What I expect, I expect I'll have to drag this leg in and out of every bar in the West Forties; and frankly, I don't know why I bother, I don't need a buck that bad."

As they entered the lobby of the Times Square Palace Hotel, Joe said, "Shee-it, man, this is where I *live!*"

Rizzo brought himself to a halt. He looked at Joe carefully. "You live here?" he said in a small, high voice.

Joe nodded. "Yeah."

"Uh. Do you know anybody *else* that lives here? By any chance?"

"I don't guess. I only checked in today."

"You sure?"

"Hell yeah, I'm sure."

"Well, what do you know." Rizzo's smile was weak. "Coincidence, huh?"

He picked up the house phone. "Mr. O'Daniel, please. I want to talk to Mr. O'Daniel."

During the pause, he winked at Joe, showing him a circle formed by his forefinger and thumb.

"Mr. O'Daniel? How do you do, sir. This is Enrico Rizzo speaking. . . . Oh, but I remember *you*. Yes, sir. . . . Yes sir, many times, it was unforgettable. . . . Mr. O'Daniel, I've got a young man here, a very fine young cowboy. And he's, uh, he's ready to, uh—well, frankly, sir, he's just in from the West and he needs your help—needs it bad. . . . You think you could work out something for him tonight? I've never seen anybody so . . . I was gonna say, he's anxious, anxious to get started. . . . OH, that's wonderful. . . . Yes sir, if you could, I uh—"

He held his hand over the mouthpiece and whispered to Joe: "He's *dying* to get you started tonight. I guess he's up to here with orders, and nobody to send. You sure you want to?"

Joe nodded with such vigor that the entire upper half of his body was used in the gesture.

Into the telephone, Rizzo said, "Yes sir, three seventeen. Thank you sir, thank you very much."

Rizzo hung up the telephone. "He's *very* excited to meet you already."

"W-w-what'll I do? Just go on up?"

"Room three seventeen. Let's see how you look." Rizzo stepped back, appraising Joe from head to foot. "Fine, you look fine. Now, I'm gonna have to have that other ten. Right?"

"Listen, kid." Joe handed Rizzo a ten-dollar bill. Then he took hold of his arm with both hands, one at the wrist, one at the elbow. "I want you to know I appreciate this, and furthermore, when things work out—well, I won't forget you. You can bet your bottom dollar on that, and I mean it."

"Nah, you don't owe me a thing. Look, I'm glad to help already." With a flick of the finger, the money disappeared into Rizzo's side pocket.

"No, no," Joe insisted. "I want to know where I can find you. 'Cause, dammit, I'm gonna make this thing right with you. Now what's your *ad*dress?"

"C'mon, quit it, will you?"

"I want your *ad*dress," Joe insisted.

"All right, I'm at the Sherry-Netherland Hotel, now get your ass up there. He's *waiti*n'!"

Joe released Rizzo's arm. He closed his eyes and pressed his temples with his forefingers, saying, "Cherry Neverlin, Cherry Neverlin, Cherry Neverlin. I got it!" When he opened his eyes, he saw Rizzo passing through the glass door and scuttling toward the street at his usual breakneck speed.

Joe used the mirror next to the elevator door. Finding himself somewhat pale, he leaned forward from the waist, dangling his head and arms toward the floor, hoping to bring some color into his face. Then he combed his hair, stuck in his shirt, fiddled for a moment with his cuffs, made a few reassuring clicks with his boots on the tile floor, smiled at himself and boarded the elevator.

*          *          *

The minute the door opened, Joe began to feel like a small child. For the man in Room 317 was clearly somebody's father; he was the age of a father, old but not *really* old, and he was wearing a fancy, cheap, worn-out bathrobe that looked like a long ago Father's Day present.

Mr. O'Daniel was fat, and the great sagging pouches in his face were those of a man on a diet or one who has recently been sick. His eyes were his most commanding feature. With dark-colored sacs below them and heavy brows above, they were the faded blue of an old sea captain, half blind from questioning the horizon. Standing there in his bathrobe with lips slightly parted and looking at Joe with these searching eyes, he might even have been a survivor of a shipwreck who has not yet heard the fate of his children: *Are they alive?* his eyes demanded. *Are you one of them?*

Joe acted as if he were trying to answer some such question when he said, "How do you do, sir, my name is Joe Buck."

Mr. O'Daniel nodded. He repeated Joe's name and nodded again. His eyes said, *This is an ungodly hour to get home, but thank God you're alive.*

Aloud, he said, "Joe Buck."

Joe felt he was being appraised and tried to squeeze a lot of worth into his face.

"They tell me you're a cowboy, is that the truth?"

"No, sir." Joe surprised himself by telling the truth. Then, somehow inspired to show a touch of humor, he added: "I'm no cowboy, but I'm a first-class fucker."

This didn't earn the response he'd hoped for. Mr. O'Daniel was plainly shocked. "Son." His voice was firm. "They's no reason to use that kind of talk. Now come on in here."

Joe felt at once the dreariness of the room, noticed the dirty green walls, the single window giving on an airless airshaft, with the smell of dampness coming from it and of something that had died at the bottom of it.

It never once occurred to him that Mr. O'Daniel would be staying in such a room out of poverty: Undoubtedly he had some sly motive relating to his profession.

"But then again," said the fatherly man, sitting on the edge of the bed, "why not? It seems to me you're in the mood for plain talk. That's why you come up here in the first place, or I miss my guess."

Joe said, "Yes sir." He felt he only half understood what Mr. O'Daniel was getting at, but it seemed important, especially in view of that first blunder, to appear intelligent and agreeable.

"You're—uh." Mr. O'Daniel was still appraising him. "You're a little different than a lot of the boys't come to me. With most of 'em, they seem to be, well, troubled, confused. Whereas I'd say you knew exactly what you wanted." The man's voice had some old-fashioned element in it—a riverboat orator's elongated vowels, a medicine man's persuasion—but mostly he sounded like a plain person from Chillicothe or some such place.

"You bet I do, sir."

"Well, I'll bet you got *one* thing in common with them other boys: I'll bet you're *lonesome!*" Mr. O'Daniel seemed almost angry now. "Am I right? You're lonesome, aren't you?"

"Well, I, uh . . ." Joe stalled for time. He wasn't certain what was expected of him. "Not *too.* I mean, you know, a *little.*"

"There! I knew it, didn't I? *That's always the excuse:* 'I'm lonesome.' " He mimicked a whining person. " 'I'm lonesome, so I'm a drunk.' 'I'm lonesome, so I'm a drug fiend.' 'I'm lonesome, so I'm a thief, a fornicator, a whoremonger.' *Poop!* I say *Poop!* I've heard it all. And it always boils down to *lonesome, I was lonesome!* Well, I'm sick of it, sick to death!"

Suddenly Joe felt he had a grasp of the situation: the man was no doubt a whopper of a pimp, as Rizzo had promised, but he was also a little bit crazy. Joe wished he had been forewarned.

"Now the Beatitudes is very clear," said Mr. O'Daniel, looking at the ceiling and beginning to recite: " '*Blessèd are the poor in spirit: for theirs is the kingdom of Heaven. Blessèd are they that mourn . . .*' "

I wonder, Joe thought, if maybe he wouldn't appreciate if I said a little something to bring his mind back to business, poor old fella. . . .

" '*Blessèd are they which are persecuted for righteousness' sake: for theirs is the kingdom of heaven.*' There!" said Mr. O'Daniel, proceeding like a man who has already proved his point and can now afford magnanimity: "Did you hear anything in there about *the lonesome?* Even one word? Oh, you heard about the poor in spirit, the meek, the merciful, and you heard about them that do hunger after righteousness. Sure you did. *But.*" He leaned forward on the edge of the bed, elbows resting on his knees, fingers woven together in a tense snarl of thick X's, eyes aflame with confusion, looking at Joe. "You didn't hear a purr, not a *purrrrr!* about the lonesome. And you know why? 'Cause they's no Beatitude for the lonesome. The Book don't say they are blessèd. *Not once!*"

Mr. O'Daniel seemed to have worked himself up into another anger: "Lonesomeness is something you *take! You take it!* You hear me, dammit, I say *you take it, you take it!*"

He sat straight up and hugged himself with both arms like a person taken with a sudden chill. The news had arrived, the word on those children in the shipwreck: all drowned.

"They go do this, and they go do that, and they go do the other thing, and they live the life o' Riley, and they whatnot, and they follow every little whim, and they think it's fine fine fine, oh just *fine*—because they was *lone*some! Hm-mm. Hm-mm. Hm-mm. It's not fine atall."

His voice was suddenly tired: The oration was over. Rising from the bed, he began to pace the room, speaking quickly and quietly: "Read Matthew five it's all in Matthew five. Six won't hurt you either, read Matthew six, now let's get down to business. A cowboy, huh?"

Happy to return to the matter at hand, Joe said, "Yes sir, I'm a cowboy."

"Well, we need cowboys, we need everybody we can get." Mr. O'Daniel looked him over again, then nodded. "A nice-lookin' fella like you, young, strong, presentable, they's no end to what you can do in this work."

Joe was relieved and grateful to be accepted. He burst into a smile and began to relax in the presence of this crazy, fatherly, important person.

"Son, do you know what I think we ought to do?"

"Whatever it is," Joe said, "I'm ready."

"Yes, I believe you are." A heavy hand fell upon Joe's shoulder, and he was gripped by a pair of blue, moist, benign, searching, questioning eyes. "You know, I've got a hunch, Joe Buck. *Just* a hunch: But I think it's gonna be easier for you than most."

"I got that same hunch, sir." Joe nodded and smiled some more. "I think it's gonna be like money from home."

"Money from home." Mr. O'Daniel, impressed by this expression, repeated it over and over again. He looked at Joe as if he had discovered a major poet. "There, you see? That's another part of your power, your strength. You put things in very earthy terms an ordinary man can understand. Son, I'm warnin' you, I'm gonna *use* you! I'm gonna run you ragged! Are you ready for hard, hard work?"

Joe made a fist and drove it into the air. Then he threw his hands up in a gesture that meant: What more can I tell you?

Now Mr. O'Daniel was smiling, too. "You're a wonderful boy," he said. "And I think you and me's gonna have us some fun, dammit! It don't have to be joyless, you know, not atall. Now!" He put his hands up, like a politician waiting for attention. Then, speaking almost in a whisper, he said: "Why don't we git right down on our knees? How does that strike you?"

There followed a moment in which no word was spoken, no motion was made, no breath was taken. Joe knew now what he had begun to know at the moment the door of the room had been opened to him.

The knowledge had been like something sickly green trickling slowly, irrevocably, into his bloodstream, too deadly to acknowledge. And now, even though he knew—and knew for certain—it was still too soon to act as if he knew.

Therefore, after this long moment, he said, "Get down—where?" His lips were dry, his voice small and puny.

Mr. O'Daniel said, "Right here. Why not? This is a church, isn't it? Every square *inch* of this earth of ours is a church. I've prayed in saloons, I've prayed in the streets. I'm not ashamed to pray anywhere. You want to know something?"

"What, sir?"

"I've prayed on the toilet! *He* don't care where. What He wants is that prayer!"

Joe nodded, and not knowing what else to do, he decided to get down on his knees and pray awhile. But he couldn't concentrate on it.

•     •     •

He reviewed in his mind the swindle that had taken place. It didn't seem believable to him, so he went through it all again, and a third time. Then he heard Mr. O'Daniel's words about getting Jesus into his heart and suddenly the reality of what had happened got through to him.

He rose without a word and ran from the room, determined to right the situation. He didn't even look back when Mr. O'Daniel called down the hallway after him: "Boy? Boy? Don't be frightened, don't be frightened, boy!" He didn't wait for the elevator either, but ran down the stairs two at a time, and out onto 42nd Street, all the way over to Sixth Avenue and back again to Eighth, knowing even as he searched that the odds against finding Rizzo were overwhelming. Even as he was trying to remember the name of Rizzo's hotel, he knew it was useless to do so. Joe didn't want his twenty dollars back, not any more; what he wanted now was some kind of revenge that would make him feel less of a fool.

# True Confessions

## From: *True Confessions*

### BY JOHN GREGORY DUNNE

*L avabo inter innocentes . . ."* Bishop O'Dea intoned.

    Appearances. They were very much on Desmond Spellacy's mind today. Augustine O'Dea, for example. Tall, in his late fifties, with massive shoulders and the mane of snow-white hair. The very picture of a bishop. He had only one drawback: he was a boob. A view, Desmond Spellacy knew, that was shared by the Cardinal. That big, booming voice always ready to discourse on Saint Patrick and the snakes or the day Babe Ruth said hello to him at Comiskey Park. Two favorite topics. (Desmond Spellacy had once pressed him on the Babe and what the Babe had actually said was, "Hiya, keed.") But. . . . Always the *but*. There was something about Augustine O'Dea that seemed to amuse the Cardinal. With rapt attention, Hugh Danaher listened to the endless monologues about the day little Bernadette met Our Lady at Lourdes or the absence of snakes on the Emerald Isle. Is that right, Augustine? I didn't know that, Augustine. It was as if the vicar general provided the Cardinal with his only relief from the byzantine tedium of running the archdiocese.

It could have been a situation with Augustine O'Dea. Desmond Spellacy was certain of that, but the Cardinal had handled it perfectly. It was a matter of turning a sow's ear into a silk purse. Hugh Danaher was, after all, only an obscure coadjutor archbishop in Boston when he succeeded Daniel Shortell, who had died quietly in his ninety-first year, leaving the archdiocese, in a word, broke. It was easy to get rid of most of the deadwood that had accumulated around Archbishop Shortell, but Augustine O'Dea was vicar general, second in command in the archdiocese, and he had expected to be Daniel Shortell's successor. The simplicity of Hugh Danaher's solution was exquisite: he just took advantage of the vicar general's imposing good looks. If there was a ribbon to be cut or a communion breakfast to attend, there was Augustine O'Dea posing for the photographers, telling of his plan to send a Christmas card to every Catholic in the American League. Because of his long friendship with the Babe, of course. Title after title was piled onto his broad shoulders, each more meaningless than the last. Director of the Apostleship of Prayer. Chairman of the Sodalities of Our Lady. Director of the Priests' Eucharistic Congress. Spiritual Director of the League of the Hard of Hearing.

Vintage Hugh Danaher, Desmond Spellacy thought. He had a gift for turning a liability into an advantage. A complex man. Desmond Spellacy doubted that he would ever really understand the Cardinal. Except for one thing. He would never try to pull a fast one on him. Even now, nearing eighty, in the twelfth year of what had appeared, when he was named archbishop, only a caretaker appointment, the Cardinal could still be ruthless. Desmond Spellacy shivered. He had seen the Cardinal in action too often. That cold stare. Where the seconds seemed like hours. He had seen priests crumble under that stare. John Tracy, sixty-eight years old, who had asked His Eminence why he had never been named a pastor. The stare. Until poor John Tracy wept. The Cardinal never had to give the answer John Tracy had dreaded: because you're a homosexual.

It was that kind of ruthlessness which had helped him pay off the debt of five million dollars left by Daniel Shortell. And create twenty new parishes, eighteen new high schools, sixty-four new parochial schools. Desmond Spellacy knew how the rich laity quaked when Hugh Danaher put on the squeeze. "When Mary O'Brien, a chambermaid, can give seventy-five cents to the Building Fund, I expect Randle J. Toomey, who would like to be a Grand Knight of Malta, to give seventy-five hundred dollars." Not *in camera*. At the annual luncheon of The Holy Name Society. It got the job done. The Pope rewarded Hugh Danaher with a red hat. Spiritual leader of a flock numbering 1,250,000 people. A bookkeeper in ermine was more like it, the Cardinal said. Interest rates and construction costs and real-estate values. These were the problems that filled his days. The application of marriage laws and the businesslike operation of hospitals, orphanages and cemeteries.

Appearances, Desmond Spellacy thought. A sow's ear. A spiritual leader. He wondered if Augustine O'Dea knew about the polyp on the Cardinal's prostate. He thought not. Augustine O'Dea's latest enthusiasm was trying to perfect his Al Smith imitation. Best not to trouble him. Get Chet Hanrahan into the ground. A new chairman of the Building Fund, that was the immediate concern. Not whether Desmond Spellacy was going to succeed Hugh Danaher.

·　·　·

*"Orate fratres . . ."*

In the front pew, Mrs. Chester Hanrahan leaned toward her husband's casket and keened loudly. The organist from Immaculate Conception High School began to play "Lovely Lady Dressed in Blue." It was Chet's favorite "number," according to Mrs. Chester Hanrahan. As Immaculate Conception was his favorite high, because it was there that he had his first fund-raising success, putting the drive for the new gymnasium over the top with six "Put-A-Pool-In-A-Catholic-School" Sunday collections.

The volume of Mrs. Chester Hanrahan's sobbing seemed to embarrass her two children, Brother Bede Hanrahan of the Athanasians and Sister Mary Peter Hanrahan of the Salesian Sisters of Saint John Bosco. What a windfall for the Salesians and the Athanasians, Desmond Spellacy thought. One thing Chet Hanrahan had never figured on was both his children going into the religious. And now the Athanasians and the Salesians would someday be carving up the Hanrahan Development Corporation.

"It's a goddamn shame, Des," Chester Hanrahan had said after his son had entered the Athanasians, "that boy not having more respect for his mother."

If there was one subject Desmond Spellacy had not wished to discuss with Chester Hanrahan, it was his son's vocation. The Athanasians were a mendicant order who devoted their lives to menial service. "He heard the call, Chet," he answered deliberately.

"To clean up the shithouse in some old people's home?" Chester Hanrahan said.

"If he's happy, Chet."

"Up to his elbows in piss, he calls that being happy?" Chester Hanrahan said. "What about his mother? If he had to go in, why didn't he become a priest then, instead of some goddamn brother. At least his mother could watch him say mass then, he was a priest, or give a retreat. She could buy him a car. What is she supposed to do now? Give him a can of Ajax and watch him swab bedpans?"

You work your ass off, Chester Hanrahan had said bitterly. And he had. A pioneer in subdivisions. Del Cerro Heights. Fairway Estates. Rancho Rio. Wishing Well Meadows. Each new tract announced with billboards off every major artery. "Will There Be Underground Utilities in Del Cerro Heights?" " 'YES!' Says Chester Hanrahan." "Will There Be City Water in Fairway Estates?" " 'YES!' Says Chester Hanrahan." "Will There Be Neighborhood Schools in Rancho Rio?" " 'YES!' Says Chester Hanrahan."

It was over the question of neighborhood schools in Rancho Rio, in fact, that Chester Hanrahan had first come officially to the attention of Desmond Spellacy. That day seven years before when he was in the steam room of Knollwood Country Club with Dan T. Campion, the lawyer for the archdiocese.

"I was talking to Chet Hanrahan the other day," Dan T. Campion said. The sweat poured off his bantam-rooster frame. "He's got this grand new development. Rancho Rio, I think it's called. He'd like to give a little piece to His Eminence for a school. Isn't that a grand thing for him to do, Des?"

Desmond Spellacy nodded noncommittally. The little lawyer could sleep behind a corkscrew. He could imagine Dan T. Campion's conversation with Chester Hanrahan. "Let me bounce it off Des Spellacy, Chet. He's just a lad with the dew behind his ears. Hardly thirty, if he's a day. Learned his numbers at the seminary. Where they teach them to count in one-dollar bills." There was a fee in it for Dan T. Campion, along with his retainer from the archdiocese, if he was passing along an offer from Chester Hanrahan. Of that Desmond Spellacy was certain.

"He's having trouble getting rid of his lots then, Dan?"

"My God, you're a suspicious one, Des," Dan T. Campion said.

"It's not selling, Dan," Desmond Spellacy said. "He needs something to make it go. And the city won't put in a school or the county a golf course. On that very same land he offered both of them before his generous offer to us." He'll wonder how I knew that, Desmond Spellacy thought. And he'll figure out its Sonny McDonough. The only Catholic on the board of supervisors. "I hear he's overextended, Chester Hanrahan. The banks want to call in his paper."

"You're a smooth number, Des, that's exactly what I told Chet. No fast ones on Des Spellacy, I said. His Eminence knew his buttons when he made you chancellor. Though there was some that thought the poor man was in his dotage when he made a boy like yourself such a high monkey-monk. Not me, though. 'Never underestimate Des Spellacy,' is what I said. 'A very cool article,' is what I said. 'Looks like a leprechaun, thinks like an Arab.' My very words." The thick frosting of blarney with the brain clicking away under it. "It was Sonny told you, then?"

"A little bird."

"It's still a grand offer, Des," Dan T. Campion said. "What if Chet were to throw in ten thousand dollars for the Building Fund."

"I'd have to catch it on the bounce, is what I hear."

"You have a grand wit, Des," Dan T. Campion said. "Not like most priests, I hate to say. You say hello to some of them fellows and all they got to talk about is how Genial Jimmy Dahill was dancing the jig at his hundredth birthday party in the parish hall. And wasn't it grand the way that Tommy Lawler, the famous bail bondsman, passed away saying the rosary." He wrapped himself tightly in the Turkish towel. "I think I could persuade Chet to let his construction company build the school at cost."

"Which set of books do I get to see, Dan?"

"It's not every father has such a grand head for business, Des," Dan T. Campion said. "You could get blood out of a stone, is what I like about you. And what Chet likes about you, too."

"And let's say you throw your fee from Chet into the Building Fund," Desmond Spellacy said. "Or else it's the receivers for Chester Hanrahan."

Which was how Saint Eugene's got built in Rancho Rio. And Chester Hanrahan got the sash of a Knight of Malta. And accepted the Cardinal's offer to become chairman of the Building Fund. All because of a conversation in the steam room at Knollwood Country Club.

•        •        •

*"Domine, non sum dignus . . ."*

A new chairman of the Building Fund. It was his choice, he knew that. Subject only to the cardinal's veto. "Get the feel of the situation," the Cardinal said the morning after Chester Hanrahan died. "Play a few rounds of tennis, a few sets of golf." The advice nagged. The Cardinal knew the correct terms as well as he did; he wondered why His Eminence had slipped in the needle. Perhaps it was the Cardinal's way of suggesting that there had been complaints about the chancellor from the clergy. Complaints about the amount of time the chancellor spent in country-club locker rooms buttering up the fat cats of the archdiocese. Desmond Spellacy had heard the whispers. And the pastors didn't like the way he nosed around in parish affairs, either. If there was one thing a pastor guarded jealously, it was the freedom to run his parish as he saw fit. The cost of a new boiler was none of the chancery's business. Desmond Spellacy did not operate that way. No, he had said to the new Carrara marble altar at Saint Dominick's. Too expensive. No to the new baseball diamond at Holy Redeemer. Not unless you're thinking of celebrating high mass at third base, Father. Pay off the debt on your church first. And speaking of your church, Father, it smells like a locker room. Tact never had been his long suit. And so the pastors complained.

They criticized him, Desmond Spellacy knew, because they didn't dare criticize the Cardinal. What they didn't know was that the plan to curb their independence had come from the Cardinal himself. Centralization, the Cardinal said—it was the only way to cut costs and melt the deficits. If the pastors didn't like it. . . . That was where he came in. Desmond Spellacy had no illusions about where he fit into the Cardinal's scheme. He was a combination lightning rod, hatchet man and accountant. Someone to fend off the pastors and take the heat off the Cardinal. Young enough not to be infected with old ideas about how to run a parish or to have formed friendships that could not be broken. If necessary. Ruthless enough to sack an old monsignor. If necessary. Tough enough to talk decimal points with a Protestant banker or lean on a contractor. If necessary. In other words, a man to do the dirty work. "A few rounds of tennis, a few sets of golf." Desmond Spellacy knew now what the Cardinal meant: watch your step. One false move and you become an expensive luxury. Off the plank goes Desmond Spellacy.

Not if I can help it, he thought.

•        •        •

*"In principio erat verbum . . ."*

He heard the cough. That one-of-a-kind cough. Desmond Spellacy searched the cathedral. That awful, racking cough meant that Jack Amsterdam was there. He thought, It's only natural. Jack had done business with Chet Hanrahan. And Jack would have a rooting interest in whoever was the new chairman of the Building Fund. Because the new chairman of the Building Fund would have to do business with Jack. Because in the interest of central financing, Desmond Spellacy had let seventeen million dollars in building contracts to Jack Amsterdam. Schools, hospitals, convents, churches, rectories. There was nothing to be alarmed about. The concrete was good. Nothing had fallen down yet.

*Nothing had fallen down yet.* That's a grisly goddamn thought. Desmond Spellacy crossed himself quickly and asked forgiveness for taking the Lord's name in vain.

It was just that there was something about Jack that encouraged thoughts like that. What happened to Ferdinand Coppola when he made the bid on the new Saint Columbkille's Hospital contract was a case in point. The night before the bids were unsealed, two of Ferdie's big rigs were tipped over into the Los Angeles River. "A high Santa Ana wind condition" blew his rigs over, Ferdie said. And withdrew his bid. Six tons each, those rigs were, and they had never taken a dive to a wind before. "It's a rough business, boyo," Dan T. Campion told him. "Stay out of it." And so Jack Amsterdam got the contract to build Saint Columbkille's.

"So Jack's gone legit," Tommy had said when he heard about the contract.

"What's that supposed to mean?" Desmond Spellacy said.

"It means you're doing business with a real sweetheart there," Tom Spellacy said. "Him and His Eminence will get along good. You ever hear his confession, give me a call. That's one I'd like to sit in on. He swears a lot, I bet. And I bet he's missed his Easter Duty."

Desmond Spellacy chose his words carefully. He wanted to know about Jack, but he wasn't sure he wanted to hear it from Tommy.

"You've been checking up, then?"

"There's nothing to check. He's clean."

"So there you are."

"Listen, Des, Mary Magdalene was clean, too. But she used to be a hooker, someone told me once. And the day she signed on with Jay Cee there, some-one pulled her rap sheet."

"That's vivid," Desmond Spellacy said. "And what does this someone tell you about Jack?"

"The ginneys leave him alone is one thing they tell me. They tried to move in on him a few years back, the ginneys. And the story is, Jack took this ginzo from Detroit and dried him out. Dominic. Dominic LoPresti. That was this ginzo's name. Jack took Dominic and stuck him in this dryer in a laundry over to Lincoln Heights there. Shrunk the poor bastard down to twenty-one pounds."

It was Tommy's kind of story. Tommy liked to tell stories about the low-est kind of human behavior. Stories Desmond Spellacy was not likely to hear in confession. This time, however, the story seemed to hold an implicit warn-ing. Desmond Spellacy erased the suggestion.

"You know that for a fact?"

"Des, let me tell you something. I don't know the Holy Ghost for a fact. But you're in the Holy Ghost business. So when you tell me about the Holy Ghost, I believe it."

"Meaning I should believe you."

"Meaning you want to roll around in the shit and think it's clover, then you're not going to believe me, I tell you this is a bad guy to be in the kip with. So let's change the subject. I'm sorry I ever brought it up."

The construction of Saint Columbkille's Hospital was the beginning of a long and profitable relationship between the archdiocese and Jack Amsterdam. None of the other contractors ever bid against him. Perhaps because the cost of cranes was so high. But now there was the story of the asphalt. Chet Hanrahan had mentioned it before he died. Ten tons of asphalt, Jack's invoices said. But the word was nine tons of asphalt and one ton of sand. Which meant that the Cardinal was getting stiffed for a ton of asphalt.

"I don't believe it," Dan T. Campion said. "It's Ferdie Coppola putting out that story, and everyone knows Ferdie's a sorehead."

"Twenty-five grand each those cranes of his cost, is what I hear," Desmond Spellacy said. "Maybe that's why he's such a sorehead."

"The insurance covered it," Dan T. Campion said. "I had Phil Leahy look at the policies for me. Wind damage was one thing Ferdie was specifically cov-ered for."

"I think maybe we better ask Phil Leahy if we've got a policy on someone making a chump out of His Eminence. I keep hearing stories."

"From your brother, the policeman," Dan T. Campion said. "Always think-ing the worst, a policeman. Old stories, Des, never proven. He's getting on, Jack, he wants to make amends."

"For what?" Desmond Spellacy said.

"For any mistakes he might have made," Dan T. Campion said.

"Conscience money is what you mean," Desmond Spellacy said.

"It's all still green, the last time I looked, anyway," Dan T. Campion said. "You've got to take the long view, Des. Anyone who gives $75,000 to the Building Fund, we've got to trust him for a ton of asphalt. Assuming, which I don't, Ferdie's story is true."

"There's a word for that seventy-five," Desmond Spellacy said. "Kickback is the one I had in mind."

"Insurance," Dan T. Campion said. "Insurance is the word I would use. Jesus, Mary and Joseph, Des, it goes with the franchise. He builds a nice hospital, Jack. He builds a nice school, too. But you ask a contractor to be in a state of grace all the time, you'd be saying mass in a wigwam. His Eminence, too. He'd catch cold, I think, an old man like that."

"I'll tell His Eminence that," Desmond Spellacy said. "I'll tell him you're worried about his nose getting all stopped up from saying mass in a tepee. I'll tell you think the best way to get rid of a cold like that is not to sniff around any asphalt. He'll appreciate the diagnosis, His Eminence."

"You do that, Des," Dan T. Campion said. "You take your bathroom scales out to Jack's place there, and you weigh ten tons of asphalt. It's messy is what they tell me, but you do it. Then you tell His Eminence and His Eminence will find you a nice little parish in the middle of Nebraska. It's nice in Nebraska, I hear. You get the change of seasons. A hundred above in the summer, a hundred below in the winter."

"There's one thing I wonder about you, Dan. When was the last time your right hand knew what your left hand was doing?"

"1908," Dan T. Campion said, pronouncing it nineteen ought eight, and punctuating it with the loud laugh, the slap on the back.

•          •          •

*"Et verbum caro factum est . . ."*

There were times, Desmond Spellacy thought, when Dan T. Campion worried him more than Jack Amsterdam. Not that Dan didn't have his uses. The Cardinal sneezed and Dan T. Campion reached for his handkerchief. It was the other noses that he was cleaning that bothered Desmond Spellacy. Give him ten hands and he'd be picking pockets with nine of them and making the sign of the cross with the tenth, Chet Hanrahan had said. And Chet was no altar boy. Which was why the new chairman of the Building Fund was so important. He needed his own man. Someone, to put it bluntly, who belonged to him. Someone to keep tabs on Dan T. Campion. Someone to pass the word to Neddy Flynn and Emmett Flaherty and the other Catholic contractors (were there any non-Catholic contractors, he suddenly wondered) that they should bid against Jack Amsterdam on any new construction projects. There was one thing you could say about Neddy and Emmett. You wouldn't pick up the newspaper in the morning and read that they'd stuck somebody in a dryer. No old stories, never proven. At least no old stories he couldn't live with.

The new chairman. Someone who would help him unload Jack. When the time came.

Who?

Phil Leahy had all he could handle with the diocesan insurance programs. Ed Ginty would have been perfect, if he weren't in the penetentiary for embezzling that ninety-three thousand dollars. Devlin Perkins, but he was a convert and his wife was president of the Guild for Episcopalian Charities. A Protestant prune, Dan T. Campion called Adela Perkins. Take a bite out of her and she'd flush you out like a physic. Putting on airs and calling herself an Episcopalian, Dan said, when she was just another Prod. Fernando Figueroa? Not with Tony Garcia already the lay director of the Welfare Bureau. The rich laity wouldn't like two Mexicans. . . .

Who then. . . .

The vicar general was anointing the casket with incense and reciting the prayers for the dead. Why do people buy caskets like that, Desmond Spellacy wondered. All teak with silver handles. A banquet for the termites and the weevils. A send-off you could be proud of. The superdeluxe McDonough & McCarthy sendoff. . . .

Sonny McDonough.

That was a possibility. A real possibility. Member of the county Board of Supervisors. President of the Planning Commission, too. Which was always useful in condemnation proceedings. Dedicating his life to public service now after making his pile in funeral homes and cemeteries. He was letting Shake Hands McCarthy run the business. John McCarthy, Desmond Spellacy thought. He must remember that. Ever since Shake Hands became a Knight of Saint Gregory, he insisted on being called John.

Desmond Spellacy noted Sonny McDonough's liabilities. Sonny sang *"Tantum Ergo"* in the shower. Or to be specific, Sonny sang *"Tantum Ergo"* in the shower after playing golf with Desmond Spellacy. You couldn't outwait Sonny. You couldn't stay in the locker room until he finished his shower. Not if you minded catching a cold or smelling bad. So into the shower. And there would be Sonny, all lathered up. *"Tantum ergo, Sacramentum, Veneremur cernui; et antiquum documentum . . ."* The memory made Desmond Spellacy flinch. "A grand number, isn't it, Des?" Sonny McDonough would always say. And sing another hymn: "Heads lifted high, Catholic action our cry, And the Cross our only sword." A number made for that voice. When Sonny was feeling like a tenor, he would sing "Lovely Lady Dressed in Blue." Another grand number. "About Our Blessed Virgin," Sonny McDonough had informed him the first time he rendered "Lovely Lady" in the shower.

He was an idiot, Sonny. An idiot who thought there was an advantage in singing hymns in front of a priest in a locker room. But a definite possibility nonetheless. And one way to bring Sonny around to discounting the funeral costs of all the nuns and priests who died each year in the archdiocese. An idea Sonny wasn't too keen on, but if he were chairman, he couldn't very well turn it down. Tommy would be a help. Tommy would know if there were any little colored boy in Sonny McDonough's woodpile. Besides that raffle that was fixed at Our Lady Help of Christians. The memory was painful for Desmond Spellacy. Not one of my finer moments. Although it did get the property condemned. It would be a help knowing that Sonny was shifty going in. The question was, how shifty.

Sonny McDonough . . .

There was a sudden stir at the rear of the sanctuary. And then His Eminence Hugh Cardinal Danaher appeared on the altar. He must have thought better of his flu bug, Desmond Spellacy thought. Put-A-Pool-In-A-Catholic-School. The Cardinal blessed the casket and then stood at the foot of the altar steps until the bustle in the cathedral quieted down.

"It is not the custom in this archdiocese," the Cardinal began, "to deliver a eulogy at the funeral of a layman. But I would be derelict if I did not acknowledge in some way the passing of Chester Hanrahan and pay my respects to his godly wife and his two children, Brother Bede and Sister Mary Peter, whom he gave to his Father Almighty." There was absolute silence in the cathedral. "I remember that day so many years ago, the nation coming from depression into war, when I asked Chester Hanrahan if he would take over the Building Fund. I think you all know what he answered. 'YES!' said Chester Hanrahan. And over the years, everything I ever asked of him, a new boiler for Saint Malachy's, new classrooms for Our Lady of the Assumption, a new hospital for the Sisters of Saint Joseph, you know the answer I always received. 'YES!' said Chester Hanrahan . . ."

# Cyprian

## From: *The Company of Women*

### BY MARY GORDON

◈

I die failed in my vocation. A priest. Thou art a priest for ever. *The priesthood.*
That comes closer to the sense of it, the grand impersonal nature of the
calling, objective as reason or order, a noun majestic as those. Not I, but Christ
in me. *Ex opere operato,* not the worker but the work. So that the state of the
individual soul counts for nothing in the validity of the sacrament. A priest
mad or drunk can make the Body and Blood of Christ. In seminary, we were
told the story of the priest who went mad and consecrated all the bread in a
Chicago bakery. Was it, asked our professor, lawfully consecrated? Each one of
us, even the slowest, knew the answer. It was valid; it was the Body and Blood
of Christ. His brother priests had to consume it on the spot. "Forty loaves, no
fishes," said Father Evangelist. We laughed, imagining the stuffed priests. In
those days, priests had both a sense of humor and a deep sense of the spiritual. Now they have nothing, except a sense of themselves, a sense of what
will get them on television.

It was grandeur I wanted, that I left my family for. I was a child. I see that
now. Perhaps they should have made me wait. A farm boy, ignorant and
smelling of cows, with one good pair of shoes for mass. My family lived what
I thought then a life that lacked in exaltation. Even then I stank of pride. What
I have seen of degradation, of the degradation of the very priests I left my
family for, makes me think I should have stayed there on the farm, working
with my father, with my brothers, achieving my salvation in the blessed way of
the ordinary, the obscure. Perhaps it would have been my glory, and in charity
it was my obligation. Two years after I left, the farm failed. My father died a
bankrupt, delivering mail. An old man walking along the road with aching
muscles. He had been, like all farmers, rheumatic, but there was something to
be won from victorious movement over pain when he was working his own

land. At the end of his life he overcame the pain that stabbed his bones only to give into strange hands the messages of strangers. This is on my head. If I had been his son, as Christ was the son of the carpenter of Nazareth, I might have saved him, he might have died on his land. I could not give my family half the hidden life that Christ gave to Nazareth. At fifteen, drunk on the vision of Father Adolphus in his gold cape holding the prayer book, pronouncing the ancient words, I prayed that I would be delivered of my nature in the priesthood. I would not be the son of my father, the brother of my brothers, bumbling and heavy and uncouth. I would be part of that glorious company, the line of the apostles. I would not be who I was.

The monstrosity of it! I left my home, my family, for a life of poverty and of necessity. I believed all this for years, I thought I had found God in the company of the priests, my brothers.

Two others arrived in my year, John Naylor, given the name Wilfred, and Frank Bass, given the name Augustine. And I, Philip Leonard, renamed Cyprian. We were a small order; we had no schools or parishes. We had to depend for our vocations on the boys our men met in the course of preaching parish missions or retreats. Many of the priests in the house were foreigners, keeping alive the fledgling American community. I was blessed in knowing those men. They had the spiritual life that is so much more natural to those whose language has been for years sacramentalized by the life of the Church. How much harder it is for an Englishman or an American, whose tongue is the tongue of commerce, the language of the marketplace. Our souls are naturally coarsened. There are no great spiritual writers in English, except Newman. And even in Newman, there is no straightforwardness. I hear a gentleman speaking, a man who worried about table manners and the accents of his friends. Nothing in him of the great, rough force of the Spanish mystics, or the plain, imperative Bernard, or the authoritative Bellarmine, who ordered kings. How fortunate I was in learning from those saintly men, the Spanish Father Antonio, the three Italian men, each one a master craftsman as well as a scholar. And the German priest who could not eat our bread and lost, in one year, fifty pounds.

From them I learned the spirit of silence, which must be the true environment for every priest, whatever his ministry. I had been a farm boy, used to the silence of animals, of open land, of winter mornings where the quiet was pierced only by single rays of silver light. I thought I knew silence on the hills when the hushed sun withdrew and I, a boy out with the animals, stood, my heart in my young mouth, covered in beauty. I had known natural silence, but in the monastery I learned the silence shaped by prayer and punctuated by it, the purposeful silence of men gifted with speech and with affection for their brothers, giving God the gift of all the words they could have said and wasted.

The silence that was, in this modern world, a reproach as powerful as the lacerations of the prophets.

Father Celestine, a Frenchman, told me that a priest should have much silence in his life for the sake of his mass. The canon of the mass should emerge from that silence with infinite power and significance. For nine years I studied, learning wisdom from these great old men who had the innocence and the simplicity of children. They were learned, one a great canonist, one a classicist who could not teach me Greek, but they looked on the world with the freshness of the entirely untaught. The charity of God burnt in their hearts; they spent hours hearing the confessions of strangers, for these were not the men who went out to the parishes and built up, as I did, devoted clienteles. These men heard confessions in the monastery church in the middle of Buffalo, the confessions of laborers and drunkards and wives afraid to take the sacrament in their own parishes.

Theirs is the ideal that I have failed, the great ideal whose model is the mass, impersonal, restrained, available, utterly public and yet full of solitude. In the Roman rite there is no room, as there is in the Eastern liturgies, for the gestures that express the personal enthusiasm, the marvel of the celebrant. We understand that we must disappear inside our own office, subsume our personalities in the great honor of our vocations. This I have not done. In this I have failed them, those old, holy men for whom I left my family.

In their great charity, they did not suspect my pride. They referred to it as warmth of heart, my ardor for the souls who came to me. They did not understand that I loved those souls not in God but for themselves, that I wished to talk to them not only for their salvation but for the pleasure of words given and taken, personal gifts. I have not learned the great lesson of these men: the lesson of silence, the lesson of forgetfulness.

For a young priest, many things are easy. Perhaps it is the grace of the sacrament. He walks through the world, the oil of anointment glistening on his temples. He is patient, for the sins of men are new to him. If his advice is ignorant, at least the terrible burden of repetition is not his: he can hide his failures in his loving heart. They are small still, they will not escape and swallow that same heart or eat his entrails with their bitterness. The young priest is a healthy animal; he is blessed with an animal's short memory.

To the eye of the public, which is not the eye of God, I was successful. The lines in front of my confessional were the longest in the church. I slept little; always some soul waited for me. I held back nothing; I involved myself in families, in madness, in the avarice of businessmen, the cunning of politicians. And always I came back to the silence of the monastery, the healing silence, and the great, health-giving liturgy we lived by, the feasts that marked our sleep and waking. The life among the priests, my brothers, gave me back the soul I gave away to other souls. I was perfectly happy. I believed I was doing the work of God.

But I was nothing but a sham. If some of God's work was done, it was through His grace only. I was as full of myself as any of the Irish politicians I accused of graft. The life of the community had become degraded around me, and I was so absorbed in the work I was so full of that I did not see it till it was too late, and I was able to do nothing.

By the time the war came, the old saintly priests had died or gone back to their native monasteries, or to Florida or Utah, where we opened new mother-houses. It is possible to say that the success of our order ruined us. A typically American error. The rejoicing at mere size is a reflex now as automatic for most people as the push buttons they live by. During the war, the fasts were relaxed and we no longer rose at three to sing the matins. The excuse was that we were an active, not a contemplative, order and that we had to keep up our strength for our ministry in the world. Lies, excuses for the weakness of the flesh. There was less sickness in the monastery when we prayed and fasted; afterwards, all you could hear in the choir was the sniffling of the young men, who were always having colds. In their defense, I will say that the war is supposed to have introduced new foreign germs into the country, virulent strains our systems were unused to. A sign of God: we have never, since then, regained our strength, physical, political or moral.

Augustine Bass was made superior in 1946. After that, the monastery could no longer be a place of refreshment for me. There was no more silence, always the sound of activity, of production, the machine that printed mass cards, that washed dishes, that repaired shoes and waxed the floor. And when Augustine turned an old room where vestments were stored into what he called a rec room. All the snot-nosed boys who thought they would be priests played Ping-Pong now and pushed their dimes into the Coke machine Augustine rented from a local gangster.

Then my vocation failed me. The devil pressed me and I could not resist him. The patience I accorded to the most miserable wretches, the pathetic weak souls who came to me in sorrow, I could not accord my brother priests. The monastery soon became a place of torment for me. I raged against them, publicly and privately. Reginald, my confessor, warned me that I was becoming an occasion of sin. Even kneeling before him, in the sacrament of reconciliation, I called up the memory of the great spiritual riches born of silence and discipline, the mysterious consolation springing from adherence to the rule. Even in the confessional, a penitent, I could not bow my head. "They are wrong," I would say, kneeling, my nails pressed into my palms. "They are living the modern error."

"My son," said Reginald, a saint who suffered, I see now, more cruelly than

I the gross corruption of the order, "the source of all error is a failure of charity."

Love left my heart, and that is hell, to be unable to feel the heart, to have the heart a stone, an indigestible hardness in the very center of one's being, so that all movements that sustain life grow full of effort and the dreadful torpor of despair sets in. This is the paralysis the damned are cursed with, and in my paralysis, not yet complete, I struck out with the diseased limbs of my clear rage. I grew impatient with the souls who came before me. Where I once took their suffering into myself was now a stone; the cell where sympathy abode was hardened over with disgust; fellowship turned to boredom. Where I had seen them as wounded, I saw them as corrupt; where I had perceived struggle, I saw pride; where I had seen confusion, I saw only the dull stupidity of vice. This is sin, a blinding, a hardening over. And in my blindness, I did not see myself as standing up for the ideal that I had left my parents for.

It is only now that I, an old man making room for death, forgive them. For years, I carried in my heart the treasure of my grievances, cherishing like a connoisseur the details of my great trove. Over and over I rehearsed the insults of the young priests. They replayed themselves fresh and enchanting twenty years after they had been spoken. I retold in my heart the indignities of Augustine Bass; there I lived, in the cell of my own bitterness, mistaking my own selfishness for holy ardor.

It is only now that I am close to death that I acknowledge the great kindness of my faithful friends. For years, I thought of them as second best. They could not speak to me of the spirit of God; they could not counsel me in my growing bitterness. I could not share with them the great transcendent beauty of a life of consecrated men, receiving from one another's hands the Body of Christ. I saw them as simple and myself as complex. I longed for the refreshment of the monastery; I longed for consolation; I yearned for a brother who could rekindle the heart's flame that burned only in anger now, who could restore to me the blessed peace that fed me in the silence of the monastery.

I saw the affection of these good women as a pitiful travesty of the durable, shining friendship I sought from another man. *O my chevalier,* says Hopkins, the priest-poet, seeing Christ the horseman. When Frank Taylor died, I was inconsolable; I saw myself as left with only womanish affection as a solace, a bulwark against the stinking, petrified disorder of the world. And it would not suffice; it could not solace me.

When the women visited me, I imagined it at first as an intrusion. But my heart lifted at the child Felicitas. Here was a love I saw as clear as the love I had for my brother priests. Each summer when she left, I was bereft. Prayer could not touch the sorrow of my heart. I wanted only her presence, the sound of her sharp, truth-telling voice, her clear, objective gaze when I taught her something, the quickness of her splendid mind. And her uneasy laughter, which I won by imitating, like a night-club comic, the parishioners, the storekeepers, the workers on the street. Each summer when she left, I felt the agony of simple human loss, and I berated myself, for I did not love her with a priestly love, objective and impersonal, concerned for the salvation of her soul. I loved her as a human child, my child, with the terrible possessiveness of parenthood. In the Church's wisdom, priests are denied such love, for it is the most consuming love, the most impartial. A priest must love neutrally, must love evenly, and I knew that to save Felicitas, I would give up the lives and even the salvations of a thousand of my ordinary flock.

When she grew older, grew rebellious, I knew the bitterest of Jesus' sorrows: the agony within the Agony of Gethsemene, when Judas kissed and the three faithful slept. Then my heart closed utterly. I wanted only to die. The physical constriction of my heart was no surprise to me. That I did not die astonished me; it was another punishment.

All the years alone in Arizona, in Canada, the years of moral isolation among men I could not speak to, who despised me and whom I despised, men coarse-grained as animals, all those years of loneliness were nothing to what I felt when Felicita drew back from me, embraced the world and looked on me with scorn or with the ancient, ignoble fear of a bad child. When the news came of her pregnancy, my heart opened to her and I turned to her. But she turned from me, from all of us, into the hard shell of her misery. The birth of Linda brought me back to life. And for the first time, I had faith, the simple faith in God, His loving providence, I had when I left my family. I knew we would be all right. I knew Felicitas would come back to us and we would prosper.

I have had to learn the discipline of prosperous love, I have had to be struck down by age and sickness to feel the great richness of the ardent, the extraordinary love I live among. I have had to learn ordinary happiness, and from ordinary happiness, the first real peace of my life, my life which I had wanted full of splendor. I wanted to live in unapproachable light, the light of the pure spirit. Now every morning is miraculous to me. I wake and see in the thin, early light the faces of my friends.

But I fear that in loving as I do now I betray the priestly love I vowed to live by. There is no way in which my love can be objective or impersonal. I am doomed like the rest of my kind to the terrible ringed accident of human love. I am pulled down by the irresistible gravity of affection and regard. These are the people I love: I choose to be with them above all others. These are the countenances that lift my heart. Sometimes I fear that a priest should never be light-hearted; if he lives his vows, he should be the receptacle for the anonymous, repetitive sorrow of the poor race of humans for whose sanctification he is consecrate.

I wake sometimes in the middle of a dream about the monastery, expecting almost to hear the music of the hours, and I realize that I am on the site of my parent's house, surrounded by the muffling, consoling flesh of women. And I think, They have won me, they have dragged me down to the middling terrain of their conception of the world, half blood instinct, half the impulse of the womb. And I have wanted to rise up in the cold night and close the door of my house forever, to leave behind the comfort, the safety, and to walk out into the cold, searching a cave where I could live, starving for visions like the desert fathers. One night, I did leave the house and walked for hours, wishing to disencumber myself. But my bones failed me and the lights of an all-night diner were irresistible. I entered the steamy, greasy warmth, felt the meat smell cling to my clothing. I sat down at the counter and picked up a matchbox. On it was printed ACE 24-HOUR CAFE—WHERE NICE PEOPLE MEET. And tears came to my eyes for the hopefulness, the sweetness, the enduring promise of plain human love. And I understood the incarnation for, I believe, the first time: Christ took on flesh for love, because the flesh is lovable.

The waitress looked at me, an old man with a night's growth of gray-green beard. My eyes, I knew, were feverish, the mad eyes she must have got used to on the late-night shift. She said, "How about another cup of coffee, dear?" I smiled and thanked her, as Tobias must have thanked the angel. And I thought of them all, of all the women, the terrible vulnerability of sleeping women, alone in their dark houses.

Now they will not be alone; Felicitas will marry. When she and Leo came to tell me, I said, "I suppose you're old enough to know what you're doing." What could I say? I gave them my blessing.

I believe the marriage is a good thing. Leo is a fine boy, simple but, like Felicitas, clean of heart. Like many simple men, he seems to be nearly mute, but I suppose Felicitas requires kindness after her terrible experience with that man, whoever he is, who fathered Linda. No one could be kinder than Leo; I suppose that is what she needs. I never pretended to be a marriage counselor; I can only speak in the name of the Church, which could have no objection to their union.

Whom would I choose for her to marry? I have such small experience of good marriages; priests are allowed details of marriages only when they are at the point of collapse. I always imagined her married to someone like William Buckley, a man of great wit and great probity, so they could spend their days in delightful argument and work together on the proper causes. No, I never meant for her to marry. When she was a child, I saw her as a solitary woman, too objective to stoop to the sort of things men want from a wife. In part, I have always had a small contempt for the women who submit to the degradation that men seem to require in a mate. The men also I condemn, but their fault appears to me more natural. I could never see Felicitas submitting herself to the foolishness that makes what the world calls an attractive woman, and she is not simple enough to make an ordinary good wife, a vocation I hold in the highest esteem. The virtues that state requires are patience and obedience, the qualities Felicitas has lacked since birth.

But I never imagined her a mother. The shock of seeing her in pregnancy, her small child's body so distended, was as much a visual as a moral shock. She was so clearly still a child and her maternity so reluctant. But I have never seen a mother I approved of more; I have never seen a happier child.

I think that the love of Charlotte and the other women has sustained her. They all think Felicitas' marriage will be a good thing. The child needs a father, they say, almost in unison, the *choragi,* the women of Thebes. The words fly into my flesh like arrows. She has me, I want to say. Do not think I am proud of this impulse; it cannot be anything but a failure in a priest. Of course it will be better for the child to go into the world protected by legitimacy. The law was created to shelter the innocent. There is nothing I can do with my life to make a shelter for a child, two children, for Felicitas will always be my child.

It is when these feelings overcome me that I know I have failed in my vocation. When I left my home, my parents and my brothers, I gave up the right to ordinary ties, to loyalties that spring from blood or passion. It is when I face up to this failure that I know it is right that I should die before I do more damage, cause more scandal.

The fifth commandment forbids us to take unnecessary risks with our lives, but it does not require us to take extraordinary precautions to prolong them. I have always taken solace from activity. When I despair, I can look with pleasure at my accomplishments on this land. I have rescued it, brought it from a waste ruined by negligence and circumstance to the cultivated, orderly home of people whose lives are innocent. *Laborare est orare:* to labor is to pray. I fail so badly and so often in my prayer life, at least I have had faith that God accepts the offering of my labor. I cannot sit like an invalid, an old man in carpet slippers, sleeping most of the day, cranky and ridiculously argumentative, to prolong a life which is clearly a great failure, whose only sweetness is derived from the affection of women and children who have nowhere else to go.

And yet sometimes I think that sweetness is worth everything. It is true, I am happier than I have ever been. And when I look out the window and see Linda and Felicitas planting carrots, planting potatoes (Linda prefers root vegetables and flowers that are grown from bulbs), I think it is unbearable that one day I will not see their faces. I fear the moment of death when one longs only for a human face, that beat, that second between death and life eternal when there is nothing, and for a moment one is utterly alone before entering the terrible, beautiful room of judgment.

I do not fear judgment; I do not fear purgatory, where I hope to go; I fear the moment of longing for a human face. And yet I long to be free of this body, only an encumbrance now, to enter into the realm of simple light that is the face of God.

But when I think of the faces of those I love, I am tempted to work to prolong my life. I know they are frightened of my dying, for they will feel alone in spirit, unshepherded. For Muriel it will be the worst, her I have most failed, most wounded. I should have warned her that her love was dangerous, born of fear, the damaged and possessive love that turns on itself. And yet, when I was lonely, I fed off her love. I allowed her to come and live here, for I was afraid, in the solitude that did not serve me, of falling into despair. I did not like her company, but I required her presence. For this I may not be forgiven. This is blasphemy, for I have repented, and the love of God forgives even the sins of our cowardice and of the smallness of our hearts, the terrible temptation to self-hate. Only faith can save us from self-hate. In faith I leave it all behind me, in the hands of God, in the hands of a girl.

Perhaps the greatest grief will be not to see the child grown. I have never understood women who grow bored with their children; they must have no imagination, no interior life. Every question, every observation I find fascinating; her simple physical presence is enchanting. Only a week ago, I interrupted her playing mass. She had memorized some of the Latin, and she copies my gestures perfectly. For a moment I was shocked, a girl child saying the sacred words of God. She asked if I thought she was doing it well. I said she had learned the Latin perfectly.

"I'd like to be a priest when I grow up," she said.

"You can't," I said, "you're female."

"So what?" she said, in the tone she defies her grandmother but not her mother in.

"Girls can't be priests," I said. "Our Lord said so."

"Where?" she asked.

"In the gospel," I said.

"Where?" she insisted.

I told her He didn't say it in so many words, but He chose no women to be apostles, and priests are successors to the apostles. That means they would have to be like the apostles.

"But the apostles were Jewish, and you're not Jewish," she said.

"What's that got to do with it?" I asked her.

"So, you're not like them, and you're a priest." She glowed with successful argument.

I thought of all the foolish, mediocre men who were permitted ordination because of the accident of their sex. And I thought of this child, obviously superior to all others of her age in beauty, grace and wisdom. I told her to pray that the Church would change its mind by the time she grew up.

"You pray, too," she said.

I said I would, but it must be a secret between us. And so each morning, at my mass, I pray for the ordination of women.

Love is terrible. To disentangle oneself from the passions, the affections, to love with a burning heart which demands only itself and never asks for gratitude or kindness. In that I have failed. I have hungered for kindness; I have hungered for gratitude.

But the love of God, untouched by accident and preference and failure, this I long for. *Lumen lumens.* The light giving light.

And yet we are incarnate. I look around me at the faces that I love, at the slant, imperfect sun this evening on the mountains, and I pray neither to live nor to die, but to be empty of desire.

# Hungover

From: *Table Money*

BY JIMMY BRESLIN

⊕

He woke up at dusk. His eyes ran over the wall of his bedroom in the cemetery house. When he picked up his head, he saw the rows of tombstones in the shadows.

Then dusk turned to dawn—or had it been dawn all along?—and he went to work.

When Danny Murphy noticed Dolores walking toward the hog house, he regarded her as the first plane over Diamond Head. He assumed that she was there to collect Owney's paycheck, and this was intolerable, for a man only has one liver and one paycheck. "They're not even here yet," he said.

"My husband isn't here?" Her mouth was open in alarm.

"Oh, he's here. I mean the mahosker isn't here. It don't come until later."

"The what?"

"The checks. The company don't bring them here until after two."

"I'm looking for my husband, not his check."

"He's inside."

"Would you get him, please?"

Murphy hurried inside and then as quickly, embarrassed, Owney came out. He walked past Dolores and made her follow him until they couldn't be seen from the hog house.

"I'm up two straight nights," she said.

He didn't answer.

"I called the police to see if anyone was killed."

He looked at the ground. "How did you get here?"

"I took a cab. For twenty-five dollars. Wasn't that nice?"

He ran a hand over his face.

"I want to ask one question," she said.

"So ask."

"Do you think something is the matter with you?"

"Me?"

"Let me rephrase it. Is there anything the matter with me?"

"You?"

"Can't you please look at me and just say something?"

"What?"

"All I want is for you to hug me and tell me you love me. Everything would be so easy after that."

"I do that."

"In the morning with a hangover. Then all you want to do is screw me and go to work."

"I work. You see me here."

"When you're at a bar, do you ever think of me?"

"Sure."

"Then why do you stay there? How could you still stay there?"

He didn't answer.

"Did you ever think that I could get lonely? I am lonely. Do you realize that I'm a young woman and I'm sitting alone all night? That I can't even go to bed? I'm terrified that you're dead someplace. I certainly didn't have a child so I could live like this."

"I know."

"What did you think of when you married me? What did you think it would be like?"

"I thought I'd get ahead in a hurry and we'd go live someplace nice and be in love with each other."

"Fine. So what's happening?"

"I'm going to get there."

"Like this? Do you ever ask yourself what you're doing?"

"I just keep going."

"Do you think something is the matter with you?"

"No."

"Why didn't you come home last night?"

"I got stewed."

"That's no answer."

"Everybody on this job drinks. What am I going to do at the end of the day, walk out on them?"

"Everybody drinks? Every young guy is a drunk? Should I go inside and ask them?"

"They go for a drink."

"They do?"

"Sure."

"I can't believe that. I can't believe all these people here are drunk. Let me go in there and ask them."

"Come on."

"Or is it that you only know the drunks?"

"I go with my family."

"Well?"

"What did you say about them?"

"That they drink too much. I think your father wants you drunk. He feels like a hero with you next to him. Why aren't you looking at me?"

"I am."

"No, you're not. You're looking at the ground. Are you afraid to talk to me?"

Now his eyes came up and looked right at her. "I'm not afraid of anything on earth."

"Oh, I'm sorry. I think you are."

"Afraid?"

"Yes."

"Me?"

"Yes, you're afraid."

"Of who?"

"You're afraid to face yourself."

He made a face and turned and walked away. After a few steps he spun around and said, "From now on, stay away from this job. This is where I work."

"If they have a mirror inside, why don't you take a look?" she said.

He walked away, and she did not cry until she was outside the gate and back in the cab.

Back in the hog house on the bench next to Owney's locker was a sleeping man who had a face covered with hair and a mouth with no teeth.

The man's eyes opened slightly. "What have you got?" he muttered.

"Hot coffee," Owney said.

The eyes under the hair closed. The derelict's name was Eddie Meagher, and he was there purportedly to shape, but he hadn't worked in weeks and was using the place as a bedroom. But when Owney was dressed, Meagher got up and followed him outside.

"Where are you going?" Owney asked him.

"To work."

Owney walked fast to get away from him. Delaney stood up at the top of the hill, talking to Owney's father.

Meagher, walking with the loosest feet, called out, "You go down one short."

"Be off with you," Delaney said. "The only thing we're short of here is people who can work."

"Hey, Jimmy Morrison. What do you say? The gang's one short. I fuckin' know it," Meagher said.

Owney's father threw a hand at him in the air and walked off toward the equipment shed.

"Bullshit," Meagher said as he approached Delaney. "I counted two gangs going down one short."

"Counted what? What you drank?"

"I counted heads. I'm claimin' one of these fucking jobs."

Owney and Delaney walked slowly and Meagher brushed past them and went up the hill, and as he got closer to the shaft his stride improved and he walked up to the low gate and unhooked a length of wire holding the gates together and the click of this caused the gateman's head to pop out of the shaft. "The lift's not up," he called.

Meagher pushed the gate open and strode in for the lift, which was not there. He was about to step off into the air when he noticed this. He paused on the lip of the elevator shaft, standing on wood that looked like a floor but was actually jutting out over the shaft. He had no balance and he held his hands out to steady himself. The wood under his feet shifted. Meagher's head was turning in alarm when now the wood tilted. Owney, walking up with Delaney, walking quickly now, could see Meagher paw the air as he dropped into the black hole that went deep into the ground.

When they brought the lift up, Meagher's body was covered with a blanket, the indentations of which showed that he was in wet pieces. The lift sat in the shadows and the men stood in the sun and waited for the ambulance to arrive and remove the body.

"Does this mean we take the day off?" one of the blacks asked Delaney.

"Out of respect for him—the man died," Delaney said.

"He never worked here. He just an old drunken *mon.*"

Delaney used a cigarette to disguise his fury. "Eddie Meagher worked here for years."

"I here five years, I never see him do anything but get all drunk up."

"He worked. I say we take the day off just like we would if one of us went down," Delaney said.

"I never walk up to the shaft drunk," another voice said.

Delaney concentrated on his cigarette. Owney, looking around, saw that a few whites, while shaken by the body in pieces in front of them, were thinking through the emotion of the moment and reaching the point on the other side where they could see themselves receiving checks with one day taken out for their honoring of Eddie Meagher, who died a drunk. Then, this instant passed and they all accepted gloom.

Now the crowd parted and an ambulance rocked its way up to the shaft.

Three uniforms jumped out and then became motionless as they saw the blanket over the pieces of body, the blanket, green, now black from the blood beneath it. They brought out black rubber body bags and a wire cage to carry them. The driver got back in behind the wheel, leaving the two medics to pick up the body.

"Let's go, lads, we'll give him a hand. One, two, three."

"They'll do it," the driver said through the window.

"We're just giving them a hand," Delaney said.

"It's their job. Are you trying to take their job from them?"

"I'd never do that. I'm for the workingman."

"Then let them do their job and you do yours."

Delaney called out, "Nobody touch their work. We got our job, they got theirs."

They stood still and waited while the medics shoveled the parts of Meagher's body into the bags and then carried them to the ambulance. When the ambulance backed away, the men stood hesitantly in front of the shaft.

"Do we go down or not?" somebody said.

Delaney seemed confused. "Where the hell is your father?" he said to Owney.

"I'll go down and see what the guys in the hole think," Owney said. "Why doesn't everybody stay here until I find out."

Delaney nodded and Owney stepped onto the lift alone, standing clear of the blood slick atop the mud in the middle of the floor. Owney stared at the sky and then the elevator started down and the sky disappeared and he rode down through the darkness. He wondered if any parts of Meagher's body were still stuck to the sides of the shaft. He tucked his chin inside his slicker, to make the target all the smaller in case one of Meagher's old feet came flying off the side of the shaft.

There was no noise at the bottom of the shaft, as no one was working. A gang was standing along the sullen rock. Before Owney could ask them what they wanted to do, they began walking onto the elevator. At the edge of a puddle, glistening in the light, was a piece of rock that seemed to be a crystal. It was a small piece, and the only one that Owney could name on sight: muscovite. The geologist in the contractor's trailer once had told Owney that the rock was as old as the earth but was named muscovite because in some centuries in the past, the churches in Russia had used this rock for windowpanes.

Owney's thumbnail peeled a wafer off the rock. He held it up so he could see the light coming through. It was stained glass made by the earth a billion years ago. As he looked through it, standing deep under the streets of the city of New York, the glass was first green and then almost pale yellow. He thought about an old woman in Russia someplace staring at the light coming through the window of her church. Russian praying to God. He started to say the Our Father for Eddie Meagher, but then somebody on the elevator called and Owney went over and stepped on and put the rock into his shirt pocket. He forgot to resume the prayer and when the lift brought him back up to the ground, he merely indicated the men around him and Delaney called out, "No work today, lads. We've a man dead."

Passing the picnic table to leave the place, the men took up the bottle of Jim Beam as if they were receiving bus transfers. Some drank from the bottle and left with a hand wiping the mouth; others poured the whiskey into paper cups and walked out gulping. All had a mixture of anguish and excitement and need of a forum in which to stand and make their grief public and at the same time share in the shock and glory, for they, too, work in the place of death.

Now his father was in the hog house, reaching for the bottle. Without looking at Owney, he poured Jim Beam into a paper cup and held it out. Owney took it.

"What was he saying about short gangs?" Owney said.

"Who could listen to the poor bastard?"

"Maybe I could."

"What are you saying?"

"I been down here short twice when I nearly got hurt," Owney said.

His father walked away.

Owney was about to follow him, to begin bringing up everything that he had noticed lately, but then he thought of Dolores and he decided that he had to call her first, to use the excitement of Meagher's death as a reason to talk to her. Of course he couldn't use Meagher as an excuse, and indeed shouldn't even mention his name. There are rules against frightening somebody out of their anger. But he would allow the energy of the moment to recommend something as he talked; he would come up with something good, he knew that.

When she answered, he did not say hello and thus give her the chance to shoot anger at him. He said: "A guy just went right out of my hands into the shaft. I don't know what to do. It brought back the whole freaking Nam to me."

"Oh, Owney. Who?"

"Eddie Meagher. The nicest guy in the world. He just stood in the shaft and the boards fell out from under his feet. I just got my hand on him. Then, poof, he's gone."

"Are you all right?"

"I'm throwing up."

"Come right home."

"If I can. I swear. I was over the shaft myself."

"Just come home. Please don't drink."

"Right away."

He hung up and grabbed for the bottle. He was elated that he was out of trouble with her. As he drank the Jim Beam, he thought of Eddie Meagher. I'm sorry, but I needed you.

She opened the door with wide, worried eyes. He went into his shirt pocket for the piece of muscovite and handed it to her.

"That's beautiful," she said.

"Hold it up."

She murmured as she looked through it.

"That's stone," Owney said.

"It's the same as stained glass."

"That's exactly what they used to do in Moscow. They put it in the church windows. While I was driving here, I was thinking of how you'd look standing in light from a window like that. You'd look beautiful."

"Thank you."

"Standing in church in faint light."

"What was I doing in church?" she asked.

"Praying. You looked beautiful."

"And what was the occasion?"

"You were getting married to me."

When he got out of the shower, she said to him, "Are you all right?"

"Unnerved."

There was something about the way he said the word that caused her eyes to change from open sympathy to inquisitive. She looked at the pouchiness of his eyes. The shower had not taken the weight out of his eyelids.

When he fell asleep, she took the baby over to her mother's.

# Nuptials

From: *At Weddings and Wakes*

BY ALICE MCDERMOTT

Up on the altar, Aunt May and Uncle John raised their chins and closed their eyes, opening their mouths for Communion. Then the priest walked to their mother and the best man. Uncle John suddenly stood—for a moment the children thought he mistakenly believed it was time to go—stepped out of the pew and then stepped back to help Momma out. He followed her to the altar rail, where mother and son knelt side by side, their broad straight backs so similar that everyone in the congregation who knew it considered the fact that he alone of all of them was her full flesh and blood—as if the spinal cord itself were the vehicle of the entire genetic code.

Momma stood again, pushing off from the rail, and as she briefly faced the children as she walked back to her pew, her face seemed as beautiful and severe as they had ever seen it. "From such moments as these," the boy thought, turning the phrase over in his memory, imagining how it would serve him in the future. Uncle John followed his mother, his eyes on his clasped hands.

And then their father was standing in the pew and whispering, Go on, go on, raising the kneeling bench with his instep, and Aunt Agnes behind them was touching the younger girl's shoulder, Go on.

Other people, strangers, were filing out of the pew across from theirs and going to the altar, and as they joined them the children saw how Fred had risen from his kneeling bench and returned to his high-backed chair while Aunt May still knelt, her face in her hands, the clean soles of her new shoes pointing toward them.

They knelt themselves, just as the broad fragrant robes of the priest descended on them, pushing with what seemed a sudden haste the brittle Host onto their tongues. They rose again and, in the confusion of the other wedding guests now standing shoulder to shoulder behind them (Aunt Arlene with her satin-pillow tummy and her two tall children among them), turned this way and that, the two girls nearly walking into each other, before their father held out his arm and showed them the way to go.

It was this confusion and the new energy it inspired, as well as the pale, perfumed breeze set up by the wedding guests as they moved back and forth past their pew, that got the children giggling, poking each other with their elbows as they knelt to place their faces into their palms. Into the blackness of her cupped hands, the older girl let out a single, breathy laugh and received for it as she turned to slide back into her seat a look from Aunt Agnes, shot over her own folded hands as she knelt behind them, that would have melted lead.

Now the remaining wedding guests left the Communion rail and made their way back down the aisle, moving their sealed lips in the mute and unconscious way of Communicants, as if the Host in their mouths had left them struggling with something they could not say. (The boy nudged his sister and then moved his closed lips up and down in imitation of one of them but she felt her aunt's blue eyes on the back of her neck and so only turned away.)

With his hand on his breast and the golden chalice held delicately before him, an altar boy close to his heels, the priest moved swiftly up the bone-pale steps of the altar, where still, still, Aunt May knelt in her post-Communion prayer. Ascending the stair, the priest briefly touched her on the shoulder and she turned her face up to him as she had done to receive Communion. He paused, seemed to pull himself short, and then bent to whisper something to her, Fred all the while sitting alone behind her, his hands on his thighs and his face so sympathetic and confused that, watching him, the best man, unaccountably, felt his heart sink.

She nodded at what the priest said and then briefly bowed her head, blessed herself, and rose into her high-backed chair. In another chair just behind hers their mother quickly leaned forward, flourishing a white tissue. Aunt May took it from her, held it to her eyes and her nose, and then balled it in her hand.

On the altar, the priest was tidying up, finishing off the wine and wiping out the chalice with his sacred cloth. As he began his final prayers the congregation stood, Aunt May and her mailman once more side by side, her arm in its white sleeve brushing his as they all made the sign of the cross beneath the priest's blessing. She turned once more to accept her small bouquet from their mother and then the priest said, in English, "Well, go ahead, man, give her a kiss," and the two leaned toward each other. It was not the soft embrace a bride in a white gown would have received from her young husband but a brief, even hasty meeting of lips, his hands on her elbows, hers on his arms, that a long married couple might exchange on the verge of some unexpected parting.

The notes of the organ seemed to build a staircase in the bleached air above their heads and then to topple it over as Aunt May and Fred walked down the steps, through the altar rail, and out over the white carpet to the door. Their mother followed, looking a little more like herself now, except for the fact that she was on the arm of a stranger.

                *       *       *

In the dark vestibule where racks of white pamphlets offered help in crisis and comfort in sorrow, rules of church order and brief, inspiring narratives of the lives of the saints, Aunt May stood beside her mailman, a married woman now, and greeted her guests. The doors of the church were open but no light reached her where she stood, smiling and nodding and lifting her cheek to be kissed. She touched the children's faces as they filed by but had no words for them, it seemed, although they heard Fred tell someone in the line behind them, "Her sister's kids, she's wild about them," and felt themselves some trepidation that their aunt's careful affection for them had been so boisterously revealed.

Outside, the July sun seemed to cancel even the recollection of the church's cool interior. The heat had descended in the last hour and was rising now in bars of quivering light from asphalt and stone and the roofs of parked cars. Now the brightly dressed wedding guests were milling about, the men squinting into the sun and the women pulling at the fronts of their dresses as if to settle themselves more comfortably into them. Their father passed around a bag of rice. A man beside them shook a handful of it in his fist as if he were about to throw a pair of dice.

Aunt May and her husband stood before the heavy door of the church for a moment as the photographer crouched before them in the sun. Then their mother and the best man were brought in, then the priest, now shed of his white vestments, then Momma and Veronica and Aunt Agnes, who would appear in the photographs to be solemnly preoccupied, looking, it would seem, toward some distant horizon.

Arm in arm, heads bent against the sudden white rain, the wedding party hurried down the steps and through the stone gates and out into the waiting limousine, all the guests trailing behind them, throwing rice, waving and laughing and calling goodbye with such enthusiasm that the younger girl thought for a moment she had somehow misunderstood the protocol and this was, after all, the last of the bride and the groom that would be seen. As their car drove away she brushed the grains of rice that had stuck to her damp palm and then saw how all the others were doing the same, brushing at palms or suit skirts, shaking caught rice from their hair, quieted now and somehow desolate. There was a crumpled paper tissue in the gutter.

But then Aunt Agnes began giving orders—Johnny, help Momma into the car. Arlene, you'll come with us. Bob, Mr. Doran here will follow you. Who else needs directions?—and the children found themselves rushing after their father over the gray, erupting sidewalk, their two new cousins in tow.

It was their father who started the horn-blowing, leaning playfully on his steering wheel as he maneuvered the car into the street and getting the man behind him to do the same. They pulled up in back of the limo that carried Uncle John and his wife as well as Momma and Veronica and Agnes, and even the limo driver, glancing into his rearview mirror, tapped his horn a few times. And then the other guests, pulling out of parking spaces on other streets, began to do the same and the children, excited by the wild cacophony, by the mad hunch of their father's shoulders as he pounded the horn, put their hands to their ears and shouted loud, nonsensical objections, amazed at the volume they and the cars had attained, at the sheer bravura, in this hot sun and after the wedding ceremony's cool solemnity, of the noise they were making, a noise that seemed to defy not only the heat and the lingering holiness but that encroaching sense of desolation as well. Laughing, their hands to their ears, they hoped that Aunt May could hear them from whatever street she was now on.

Their cousins—Rosemary and Patrick were their names—sat beside their father in the front seat, and when the horns finally died down he began to shout questions at them, as if he had been directed by Aunt Agnes herself to keep this morning's silence at bay. The cousins answered that she was a freshman at Notre Dame Academy, he an eighth-grader at Saint Stanislaus. She played basketball and he liked bowling. They had an uncle who lived in Brooklyn but they weren't sure where, they'd only visited him once or twice. It wasn't around here, though. She had once been to Girl Scout camp on Long Island. She'd loved everything about it but the jellyfish—a remark that seemed to delight their father, although the two girls in the back seat noted that he'd never found it so delightful when each summer they said much the same.

Looking out the car windows, the children saw that the heat had succeeded in changing the day into something ordinary. The shops they passed were busy with people, people who seemed to move in clumps, brushing their thick, bared arms together and scuffing their feet against one another's heels. Bins of towels and fruit and racks of clothing had oozed out of the stores toward the street and the sun was blasting the sidewalks and sending steam through the manholes. Even a fire hydrant had burst under its weight. A thin park sat perfectly still in the heat, the sunlight through its weak trees scattered across the ground like debris. They drove on. "Where's Mom?" the younger girl asked and their father answered that she was off with Fred and Aunt May and Mr. Sheehy the best man, getting her picture taken. "For posterity," he said. "So years from now we can look at them all and see how we've aged."

They drove across a series of shaded streets and then once more pulled up behind the limousine, this time in front of a small brick restaurant with a long maroon awning that stretched to the curb. Momma and Veronica, Arlene and John were already under it, and their father turned to say the children should follow them while he parked.

Inside, it was cool and dark, a hushed, wood-paneled place flanked by two dim dining rooms set for lunch and lit, like a library or a pulpit, with thin, shaded tubes of light. Only Aunt Agnes was there, speaking quietly to a tall man in a dark suit who had his head lowered, his ear to her mouth like a priest in a confessional. "Very good," the children heard him whisper, nodding, his hands clasped before him. "Very good." And then he quickly stood erect—they would not have been surprised to see him genuflect—elegantly raised one hand toward a white-jacketed waiter in one corner of the dark room and stepped back to let Aunt Agnes proceed. She turned briefly—until that moment the children had not known for certain that she knew they were there—and said, "Come along." The tall maître d' smiling kindly at them, nodding still, as they filed past.

The restaurant seemed to grow both cooler and darker as they proceeded, as if they were descending into a catacomb. They passed the two dining rooms, went down a narrow corridor and across a carpeted anteroom and then through a set of double doors where they suddenly found daylight again, pouring from four plain rectangular windows across one wall of a wide but cozy room, reflecting just as brightly from the semicircle of polished parquet floor at its center and making a black silhouette of the five-tiered wedding cake in the middle of the room.

Aunt Agnes paused, all of them halted behind her. There was one long table at the head of the dance floor and then, on the carpet that surrounded it, a number of others covered in long white cloths and topped with baby's breath and roses. There was a bar to the far right, a portable thing about the size of an upright piano and manned already by another man in a short white jacket. There was a real piano to the far left, a small baby grand, a set of drums, and a folding chair that held a trumpet case. The three men who were to play moved toward their instruments when they saw her, themselves made shadowy by the bright sun.

Agnes raised a gloved hand to her brow, squinted, and then began to speak without turning toward anyone. The maître d' quickly stepped forward, bending, nodding, and then once more raised his hand. Suddenly two pale opaque curtains moved across the windowed wall and in just the moment before they met the children realized that the blue they'd been seeing was not merely sky but water: that the place was on the river or the sea.

The light from the chandelier grew brighter and then softer (directed, they saw, by Aunt Agnes's gloved hand) and then—how restful it seemed—just right, confounding somehow both the season and the time of day and giving the impression that neither season nor time of day had ever touched the place. The piano began to play, light, happy notes, and then, as if they had only been waiting for the sound, bright voices began to come from the room behind them. Aunt Agnes turned toward the door, smiling, pulling off her gloves, and the tall maître d' slipped away.

Now the wedding guests were filing into the room, laughing and lighting cigarettes and stirring their drinks with black swizzle sticks, settling into the celebration as if it had not just begun but was continuing, as if for each of them such parties were always going on somewhere—underground, at the edge of the water—and they only had to find the right opportunity to rejoin them. Women in face powder and perfume patted the girls' hair and touched the two boys' cheeks, men smiled at them, passing by with their elbows raised and three or four glasses woven among their fingers. Their father appeared as one of these, a cigarette in his mouth and a trinity of Cokes held high before him. He handed them to the three girls and, with the cigarette held in the V of his fingers, told the two boys to saunter up to the bar and order something for themselves. "None of the hard stuff, though," he said, laughing, and the two sisters saw with some envy how their brother glanced up at his taller cousin and with an easy, silent gesture that said, "Wanna go?" walked off casually with him, a couple of swells.

Their father plunged again into the crowd, pumping hands and touching forearms, leaning to kiss women the girls didn't know. Rosemary, their cousin, tucked a thin hand under her elbow and looked out over their heads as she sipped her drink. She was tall and skinny with dark hair and a small face, no chin to speak of, but with large, heavy-lidded eyes that seemed so familiar to the two sisters that they wondered if they had met before, perhaps during that same shadowy time of their early childhoods when Aunt May had appeared wrapped in a heavy habit, stocked with gifts.

"I like your dress," the older girl told her, sincerely, although she suspected that Aunt Agnes would have found it inappropriate, too dressy for daytime or too sophisticated for a fifteen-year-old girl. It was teal blue, sleeveless, with a scooped neck and a skirt like an inverted tulip. The material had a dull shine and was studded here and there with what looked like white nailheads.

"Thank you," the girl said and then added over the rim of her glass, "I didn't have anything else."

Waiters were circulating now, silver plates balanced on their white-gloved fingers. One dipped a platter into the center of the three girls and asked, "Caviar?" but their cousin turned up her lip and said, "Fish eggs," so that the girls, despite their curiosity, pulled back their hands. "No?" said the waiter. "God, no," Rosemary said, suddenly speaking for them all.

Out of the music and the murmur of the crowd they could hear Aunt Arlene's sweet "Yeah? Oh yeah. *Yeah!*" and their father's laughter and someone else saying they had known Fred in his "dancing days." Smoke rose with the talk and the laughter and Rosemary leaned to the two sisters to say, "Get a load of that dress, is that tacky?" although neither sister knew for sure just which dress she meant.

Aunt Agnes approached and said, "Come, girls," and led them to one of the nearer tables, where Momma was seated primly beside two old women who by contrast seemed merely plopped. They were heavy, somewhat slovenly-looking old women with gray hair and gray dresses and a squat, battered look about their square heads. Each held an identical tumbler of some identical liquid in her wide lap.

"Johnny's girl, Rosemary," Aunt Agnes was saying, lightly touching the girl's shoulder. "And Lucy's two, Margaret and Maryanne." The younger girl felt her aunt's hand like a pistol at the small of her back, urging her to step forward as the other two had, put out a hand and say "How do you do?" "These are the Miss McGowans," Aunt Agnes added. "Our cousins."

The two women grinned—one had a blackened tooth—and said how much the children resembled each other. One of them pointed at the older girl. "And there's Annie's face at that age, as clear as if I'm remembering her," she said. The other nodded. "Lord, yes, God love her. There she is."

They were the nieces of Momma's stepfather, who had been so good to her when she first arrived here and a shanty Irish thorn in her side ever since. ("No blood of mine," she would declare later that week when they had all gathered again. "Thank God for that.") "Quite a dynasty," one of them told Momma when Agnes called the two boys over to be introduced as well. "And all handsome, God bless them." The Miss McGowans had never married. They had come over together in their teens and had not spent a single night of their lives since with any other creature but the other. They'd lived in Harlem, done factory work and office cleaning and so missed the refinement that life as a domestic might have lent them. They were generous, bighearted, bitter. They had been angels of mercy for Momma in the months that followed her sister's death, cooking and cleaning, caring for the girls and holding her in their big arms when that was what she had needed. Propriety and convenience aside, they had not seen the need for her marriage to Annie's husband. They had drawn in their breath and pulled their white lips over their mouths when she turned up pregnant and did not speak to her again until Jack's wake, where they whispered to the other mourners, "It's a judgment, no doubt."

"Five," said one of them now. "Imagine that, five lovely grandchildren."

She was stroking the younger girl's bare arm. "And I bet you're all smart, too, aren't you? Top of the class in school."

"Oh, sure," the other answered for them. "Your grandfather was a brilliant man." She shook her head. "God rest his soul, a genius."

The children stood grinning but Momma turned to Agnes, straighter than they'd ever seen her, and said in a voice that seemed suddenly to have shed its brogue, "Would you get me some soda water, dear?" ("Dear?" the children thought) and then to the children themselves, "Yes, that's fine now but run off and enjoy yourselves," freeing them, they saw, not only from the lumpish, grinning pair but from all the stories they might tell, tales that seemed to swell the various parts of them in their gray shapeless clothes, tales that had, until this moment, been Momma's alone. *Annie's face, at that age.*

Back among the crowd the boy shoved his glass under his older sister's nose. "Taste this," he said. Patrick was grinning behind him.

She pulled back her head. "What is it?" she asked.

"Just taste it." She took it from him and put it to her lips just as Patrick said, "It's bourbon." She pulled it away, taking only a sip of the Coke, which had, perhaps, another aftertaste.

"The bartender made a mistake," their brother said, his voice straining to keep both low and free of squeakiness. "We saw him. He gave us bourbon and Coke."

"Both of us," Patrick said. He had his mother's pale skin but with freckles across his nose, and his father's dark wavy hair. "Double shots even."

The girls saw their brother hesitate before he said, "Yeah," and so were certain that this part, anyway, was a lie.

Rosemary took the glass from her brother's hand and sniffed it. It was nearly empty. "You're dreaming," she said. She took a sip. "It's just soda."

"It's bourbon, I'm telling you," he said. "I'm already getting a buzz."

Their brother looked cautiously at the two girls—he was never very good at mischief—and then grinned and took another sip of his own. Rosemary rolled her eyes. "That's just what this family needs," she said, her eyelids dropping with disdain. "Another alcoholic."

She turned on her heels and without a thought the two girls quickly followed her over to a small table in the corner where rows of pale place cards were lined up like dominoes. Rosemary plucked her name from among them, Miss Rosemary Towne, in Aunt Agnes's fine hand, and then the two girls, delighted, found their own.

"We're all at the same table," their cousin told them. "The kids' table I guess."

But there were adults settling there as well. A Mrs. Hynes and her husband, who said she'd grown up with their mother and her sisters—"I'm sure they've

mentioned me, Margy Delahey"—transforming the impish child from their
mother's stories into a permed and perfumed grown woman. A youngish couple with dark skin and heavy accents, neighbors of Fred's. A single man with a
round bald head, Fred's second cousin, he told them, joining, the children
thought, the endless number of cousins who had filled the room. The table
before them was set with a wealth of silverware and crystal and at the head of
each gold-rimmed plate there was a pretty net bag filled with pastel almonds
and tied with a white ribbon. Other guests had begun to find their seats.
"They're here," Fred's cousin whispered to the table as all across the room the
noise and the laughter began to quiet down. All three musicians began to play
now as their mother and Mr. Sheehy appeared at the double doors. There was
a round of applause as they crossed the dance floor together and took their
seats at the head table, where Momma and Uncle John, their father and the
priest who had said the Mass already sat. And then Aunt May and Fred
appeared and everyone in the room stood to cheer, as if, it seemed to the children, they had all gotten word that something fabulous had occurred to the pair
of them in the hour of their absence.

Aunt May's face was bright red as she crossed the dance floor but Fred
grinned and waved and, just as they reached the head table, turned his bride
around and took her into his arms. Surprisingly for the children, the man with
the trumpet began to sing in a soft and foggy voice.

> *You are the promised kiss of springtime*
> *That makes the lonely winter seem long . . .*

Fred was a dancer, a natural, even the children saw it. He was light-footed,
elegant in all his movements, and although Aunt May was not—they could see
that, too—by the song's second verse she was gliding rather smoothly, carefully
following his lead but shed, too, of her initial self-consciousness. It seemed a
revelation: that two such subdued and cautious people could transform themselves in this way, could hold each other so closely and yet move with such
grace, hand to waist, hand to shoulder, the other two hands held high. Fred did
not clasp Aunt May's hand in his as the children had seen other dancers do. No,
he kept his fingers out, his palm open, and she draped her own thin hand
between his thumb and forefinger, as if they needed only the gentlest touch to
hold them fast.

> *The dearest things I know, are what you are.*

Mrs. Hynes at their table, their mother's childhood friend, sighed heavily
and wiped a tear from her eye, but no one else in the room made a sound. On

the dance floor, May and Fred gracefully parted, their hands still joined, took a few steps side by side and then moved into each other's arms again.

*Someday, my happy arms will hold you, and someday . . .*

His pants leg touched her pale skirt. His cheek touched her forehead. May closed her eyes and it was clear to the children, at least, that something indeed had happened in that hour since they'd left the church together. A consummation of sorts that had made them clearly husband and wife, made them so firmly husband and wife that it seemed for the moment that they could no longer be aunt, sister, stepdaughter, stranger, mailman, as well. They had shed, in the past hour, or perhaps only in the time since they entered this perfectly lit, hourless, seasonless place, everything about themselves but one another.

There was another round of applause as the song ended (Fred turning her once, twice, and then finishing the dance with a delicate, debonair dip) and the two of them kissed and went to their places at the table. Now the waiters who had paused to watch the dance scurried through to pour champagne, putting just a mouthful into each child's glass, which was enough anyway to make Patrick roll his eyes as if to say this was just what he needed.

At the head table the best man stood and waved a rectangular magazine clipping in his hand to quiet the guests once more. He raised his champagne glass, turned to the bride and groom, and was just about to speak when the glass disappeared. There was a tiny, tinkling crash. Fred pulled back his chair, Aunt May put her hand to her breast, and the best man looked with astonishment at his empty hand. Patrick said, "Oops" and across the dance floor the two Miss McGowans made the sign of the cross over their gray dresses.

"Sorry, folks," the best man said as the waiters rushed forward. "Must be nerves." And everyone laughed consolingly, someone among them shouting, "It's good luck—like the Jews do." "Yes," Mrs. Hynes said to everyone at their table, "They always break a glass, don't they?" And the Cuban couple, Mr. and Mrs. Castro themselves, nodded vigorously, yes, yes.

Another glass was brought and filled and the man said, "Let's try that again." Once more the guests quieted. "Fred and May," he said and then looked at the clipping in his trembling hand. "May the road rise up to meet you," he read, squinting a little, moving the paper closer and then farther away, "May the road rise up to meet you, may the wind always be at your back, and the sunshine warm on your face. And may you be in heaven ten minutes before the devil knows you're dead."

This drew a great laugh from the wedding guests, many of whom nodded to indicate that they had heard it before.

"That's an old Irish blessing," the best man explained, slipping the paper into his suit pocket. Mrs. Hynes said to the table, "Oh, sure," although the children could see by the disdainful look on Momma's face that given the chance she would deny it: say, as she said of most such things, "I never heard of it until I got over here," as if all such claims to Irish wit or lyricism were mere American hoax. "Which seemed appropriate to use today," the best man went on, "since Fred and I are a couple of old Irishmen." Another good laugh from the crowd and Momma clearly thinking, "Half Swede," as the children had already heard her say from her chair in the dining room. "But now here's a new one, too," he continued, growing comfortable in his role, "from all of us, to you." He raised the glass, gripping it carefully. "Fred and May, your best days are all ahead of you. God bless you in them. Good luck." And all the wedding guests touched glasses and called good luck and drank their champagne, which struck the two girls as bitter, although their cousin Patrick drank his down in one gulp and then smacked his lips as if it had been peach nectar, their brother laughing delightedly at this, enchanted.

Mrs. Hynes suddenly picked up her fork and began pinging her water glass. Slowly, the other guests followed. "It means they're supposed to kiss," Rosemary explained to the two girls above the din, which seemed a milder, more subdued version of the car horns. Fred and May leaned together, there was more cheering, and then the waiters began to distribute the fruit cup.

# Sources and Permissions